SCHOLASTIC

GO MATHS

Ruchi Mehta

Course Book

Level 8

Published by Scholastic India Pvt. Ltd.
A subsidiary of Scholastic Inc., New York, 10012 (USA)

Publishers since 1920, with international operations in Canada, Australia, New Zealand, the United Kingdom, India, and Hong Kong.

For information regarding permission, write to:
Scholastic India Pvt. Ltd.
A-27, Ground Floor, Bharti Sigma Centre
Infocity-1, Sector 34, Gurgaon (Haryana) - 122001
Email: education@scholastic.co.in

Typeset by: Access to Solutions

Series editor: Sonia Kapoor

First edition: 2010
Reprinted: 2011 (twice), 2012 (twice), 2013, 2014 (fourth time), 2015, 2016 (thrice), 2017 (twice), 2018 (twice), 2019 (twice), 2021, 2022, 2023, 2024, 2025,2026

ISBN-13 978-81-8477-496-2

Contents

Introduction

Go Maths is a graded series of middle school mathematics course books that have been authored by a highly respected and experienced mathematics educator. The series conforms to the NCERT syllabus and the books are provided with tools for Continuous and Comprehensive Evaluation (CCE). The objective of these books is to move away from the rote method of learning and associate the knowledge gained with everyday life experiences.

These books are designed to help students learn a wide range of mathematical concepts including the number system, algebra, geometry, mensuration, data handling and much more. Each topic has a set of challenging and imaginative activities.

The *Go Maths* series is comprehensive and rigorous. It has been created based on the following beliefs:

Learning through involvement

Students learn through involvement and substantive communication between teachers and students, as well as between students and students. This helps students internalise and acquire new skills

Learning through interaction

Students build their mathematical understanding by interacting with the world around them through a range of engaging learning experiences using real-life contexts to explore mathematical ideas. Quality teaching and learning is required for students to develop a rich conceptual understanding of mathematical ideas.

Learning through thinking critically

Learning should be as much 'minds on' as it is 'hands on'. Students should be encouraged to think critically.

Learning through practice

Skills should be practiced after they have developed from deep conceptual understanding.

Some of the unique features of this series are:

- Mathematical concepts introduced in a simple and concise manner and aid in developing sharp calculation skills and clear concepts.
- Summary **Highlights** at the end of each chapter and **Rewind** after every two chapters to recapitulate and reinforce concepts and formulae.
- Several practice exercises, **Test Yourself** and a **Model question paper** to assess mathematical proficiency with a focus on confidence, speed and accuracy.
- Enrichment material and **HOTS** questions for curious minds and fast finishers.
- **Maths Lab Activity** to strengthen basic mathematical concepts.
- **Alert**, a section emphasising the important points and brainteasers/jokes in every chapter.

The *Go Maths* series provides an innovative and interactive approach to learning mathematics. The emphasis on critical thinking ensures that students learn concepts and basic operations with great thoroughness and clarity.

Ruchi Mehta is a post graduate in mathematics with thirty-five years of teaching experience. She started her career at St Joseph's College, Allahabad and has taught at Mount Saint Mary's, New Delhi, for thirty-one years. Post retirement, she is a visiting faculty member at DPSSL, Gurgaon.

Rational Numbers

CHAPTER 1

A rational number can be expressed in the form $\frac{p}{q}$, where p and q are integers and q is not equal to 0.

The four basic or fundamental operations that can be performed on rational numbers are: addition, subtraction, multiplication and division.

All integers are rational numbers; every integer can be expressed as $\frac{x}{1}$, where x is an integer.

Zero is also a rational number since it can be written as $\frac{0}{1}, \frac{0}{2}, \frac{0}{3}$ … etc. These rational numbers are equal to zero.

Every fraction is a rational number, but every rational number is not a fraction. A rational number may be positive, negative or 0. Any rational number that has the same sign in the numerator as well as the denominator (either both positive or both negative), is positive.

Any rational number that has opposite signs (one positive and the other negative) in the numerator and the denominator is negative.

Alert!

1. Every natural number is a whole number.
2. Every natural number is an integer.
3. Every fraction is a rational number.
4. Every integer is a rational number.

Properties of Rational Numbers

The properties of rational numbers for the four fundamental operations—addition, subtraction, multiplication and division—are as follows.

Properties of Addition of Rational Numbers

Closure Property

The sum of two rational numbers always results in a rational number. Thus, rational numbers are closed under addition.

If $\frac{p}{q}$ and $\frac{r}{s}$ are two rational numbers, then $\left(\frac{p}{q} + \frac{r}{s}\right)$ is always a rational number.

$\frac{p}{q} + \frac{r}{s} = \frac{ps + rq}{qs}$, that is, a rational number, where q and s are not equal to 0.

Example 1: $\frac{2}{3} + \frac{1}{9} = \frac{6 + 1}{9} = \frac{7}{9}$

Example 2: $\left(-\frac{4}{5}\right) + \frac{16}{25} = \frac{(-20) + 16}{25} = \left(-\frac{4}{25}\right)$

Example 3: $\left(-\frac{3}{5}\right) + \left(-\frac{4}{7}\right) = \frac{(-21) + (-20)}{35} = \left(-\frac{41}{35}\right)$

Commutative Property

The sum of two rational numbers gives the same answer even if the order of the addends is interchanged. Thus, addition is commutative for rational numbers.

If $\frac{p}{q}$ and $\frac{r}{s}$ are two rational numbers, then $\frac{p}{q} + \frac{r}{s} = \frac{r}{s} + \frac{p}{q}$, where q and s are not equal to 0.

Example 1: $\frac{2}{3} + \frac{3}{5} = \frac{3}{5} + \frac{2}{3}$

$$= \frac{5 \times 2 + 3 \times 3}{15} \qquad = \frac{3 \times 3 + 2 \times 5}{15}$$

$$= \frac{10 + 9}{15} \qquad = \frac{9 + 10}{15}$$

$$= \frac{19}{15} \qquad = \frac{19}{15}$$

Example 2: $\left(-\frac{1}{2}\right) + \frac{3}{4} = \frac{3}{4} + \left(-\frac{1}{2}\right)$

$$= \frac{(-2) + 3}{4} \qquad = \frac{3 + (-2)}{4}$$

$$= \frac{1}{4} \qquad = \frac{1}{4}$$

Example 3: $\left(-\frac{1}{2}\right) + \left(-\frac{2}{3}\right) = \left(-\frac{2}{3}\right) + \left(-\frac{1}{2}\right)$

$$= \frac{(-3) + (-4)}{6} \qquad = \frac{(-4) + (-3)}{6}$$

$$= \left(-\frac{7}{6}\right) \qquad = \left(-\frac{7}{6}\right)$$

Associative Property

The sum of three rational numbers remains the same even if the grouping of the addends is changed. Thus, associative property exists for the addition of rational numbers. If $\frac{p}{q}$, $\frac{r}{s}$ and $\frac{t}{u}$ are three rational numbers, then $\left(\frac{p}{q} + \frac{r}{s}\right) + \frac{t}{u} = \frac{p}{q} + \left(\frac{r}{s} + \frac{t}{u}\right)$.

Example 1: $\left(\frac{1}{2} + \frac{2}{3}\right) + \frac{3}{4} = \frac{1}{2} + \left(\frac{2}{3} + \frac{3}{4}\right)$

$$= \left(\frac{3 + 4}{6}\right) + \frac{3}{4} = \frac{1}{2} + \left(\frac{8 + 9}{12}\right)$$

$$= \frac{7}{6} + \frac{3}{4} = \frac{1}{2} + \frac{17}{12}$$

$$= \frac{14 + 9}{12} \qquad = \frac{6 + 17}{12}$$

$$= \frac{23}{12} \qquad = \frac{23}{12}$$

Example 2: $\left[\frac{(-4)}{5} + \frac{3}{5}\right] + \frac{2}{5} = \frac{(-4)}{5} + \left[\frac{3}{5} + \frac{2}{5}\right]$

$$= \left[\frac{(-4) + 3}{5}\right] + \frac{2}{5} = \left(-\frac{4}{5}\right) + \left[\frac{3 + 2}{5}\right]$$

$$= \frac{(-1)}{5} + \frac{2}{5} = \left(-\frac{4}{5}\right) + \frac{5}{5}$$

$$= \frac{(-1) + 2}{5} \qquad = \frac{(-4) + 5}{5}$$

$$= \frac{1}{5} \qquad = \frac{1}{5}$$

Example 3: $\left[\frac{(-1)}{5}+\frac{3}{4}\right]+\frac{(-1)}{3} \quad = \quad \frac{(-1)}{5}+\left[\frac{3}{4}+\frac{(-1)}{3}\right]$

$= \left[\frac{(-4)+15}{20}\right]+\left(-\frac{1}{3}\right) \quad = \quad \left(-\frac{1}{5}\right)+\left[\frac{9+(-4)}{12}\right]$

$= \left(\frac{11}{20}\right)+\left(-\frac{1}{3}\right) \quad = \quad \frac{(-1)}{5}+\frac{5}{12}$

$= \frac{33+(-20)}{60} \quad = \quad \frac{(-12)+25}{60}$

$= \frac{13}{60} \quad = \quad \frac{13}{60}$

Additive Identity

The addition of 0 to any rational number is the rational number itself. Thus, 0 is the additive identity for rational numbers.

If $\frac{p}{q}$ is a rational number, then $\frac{p}{q}+0$ is equal to $0+\frac{p}{q}=\frac{p}{q}$.

Example 1: $\frac{3}{7}+0 \quad = \quad 0+\frac{3}{7}$

$= \frac{3}{7}+\frac{0}{1} \quad = \quad \frac{0}{1}+\frac{3}{7}$

$= \frac{3+0}{7} \quad = \quad \frac{0+3}{7}$

$= \frac{3}{7} \quad = \quad \frac{3}{7}$

Example 2: $\frac{(-2)}{5}+0 \quad = \quad 0+\left(\frac{-2}{5}\right)$

$\frac{(-2)}{5}+\frac{0}{1} \quad = \quad \frac{0}{1}+\left(\frac{-2}{5}\right)$

$\frac{(-2)+0}{5} \quad = \quad \frac{0+(-2)}{5}$

$-\frac{2}{5} \quad = \quad -\frac{2}{5}$

Additive Inverse

If $\frac{p}{q}$ is a rational number, then $\frac{p}{q}+\left(-\frac{p}{q}\right)=0$.

The rational number $\left(-\frac{p}{q}\right)$ is the additive inverse of $\frac{p}{q}$. Similarly, if $\left(-\frac{p}{q}\right)$ is the number, then its additive inverse is $\frac{p}{q}$.

Example 1: $\frac{3}{7}+\left(-\frac{3}{7}\right) \quad = \quad \frac{3+(-3)}{7}=\frac{0}{7}=0$

Thus, $-\frac{3}{7}$ is the additive inverse of $\frac{3}{7}$.

Example 2: $\frac{(-4)}{5}+\left(\frac{4}{5}\right) \quad = \quad \frac{(-4)+4}{5}=\frac{0}{5}=0$

Thus $\frac{4}{5}$ is the additive inverse of $\frac{(-4)}{5}$.

Alert!

A rational number plus its additive inverse is equal to the additive identity.

Properties of Subtraction of Rational Numbers

Closure Property

The difference between two rational numbers is always a rational number. Thus, rational numbers are closed under subtraction.

If $\frac{p}{q}$ and $\frac{r}{s}$ are two rational numbers, then $\frac{p}{q} - \frac{r}{s}$ is always a rational number.

$$\frac{p}{q} - \frac{r}{s} = \frac{ps - rq}{qs}, \text{ where q and s are not equal to 0.}$$

$\frac{ps - rq}{qs}$ is a rational number.

Example 1: $\frac{2}{3} - \frac{1}{9} = \frac{6-1}{9} = \frac{5}{9}$

Example 2: $\left(-\frac{4}{5}\right) - \frac{16}{25} = \frac{-20-16}{25} = \left(-\frac{36}{25}\right)$

Example 3: $\left(-\frac{3}{5}\right) - \left(-\frac{4}{7}\right) = \frac{(-21)-(-20)}{35} = \frac{(-21)+20}{35} = \left(-\frac{1}{35}\right)$

Commutative Property

The difference of two rational numbers is not the same if the position of the numbers is interchanged. Thus, subtraction is not commutative for rational numbers.

If $\frac{p}{q}$ and $\frac{r}{s}$ are two rational numbers, then $\frac{p}{q} - \frac{r}{s} \neq \frac{r}{s} - \frac{p}{q}$ where q and s are not equal to 0.

Example 1: $\frac{2}{3} - \frac{3}{5}$ is not equal to ($\neq$) $\frac{3}{5} - \frac{2}{3}$

$$= \frac{10-9}{15} \neq = \frac{9-10}{15}$$

$$\frac{1}{15} \neq \left(-\frac{1}{15}\right)$$

Example 2: $\left(-\frac{4}{9}\right) - \left(-\frac{3}{9}\right) \neq \left(-\frac{3}{9}\right) - \left(-\frac{4}{9}\right)$

$$= \frac{(-4)+3}{9} \neq = \frac{(-3)+4}{9}$$

$$\left(-\frac{1}{9}\right) \neq \frac{1}{9}$$

Associative Property

The difference of three rational numbers does not remain the same if the grouping of the numbers is changed. Thus, the associative property does not exist for subtraction of rational numbers.

If $\frac{p}{q}$, $\frac{r}{s}$ and $\frac{t}{u}$ are three rational numbers, then $\left(\frac{p}{q} - \frac{r}{s}\right) - \frac{t}{u}$ is not equal to $\frac{p}{q} - \left(\frac{r}{s} - \frac{t}{u}\right)$

Example 1:

$$\left(\frac{(-1)}{2}-\frac{2}{3}\right)-\frac{5}{6} \qquad \frac{(-1)}{2}-\left(\frac{2}{3}-\frac{5}{6}\right)$$
$$=\left(\frac{(-3)-4}{6}\right)-\frac{5}{6} \qquad =\frac{(-1)}{2}-\left(\frac{4-5}{6}\right)$$
$$=\left(-\frac{7}{6}\right)-\frac{5}{6} \qquad =\frac{(-1)}{2}-\left(\frac{-1}{6}\right)$$
$$=\frac{(-7)-5}{6} \qquad =\frac{(-3)-(-1)}{6}$$
$$=\left(-\frac{12}{6}\right) \qquad =\frac{-3+1}{6}$$
$$\left(-\frac{12}{6}\right) \neq \left(-\frac{2}{6}\right)$$

Example 2:

$$\left(\frac{2}{5}-\frac{6}{5}\right)-\frac{1}{10} \qquad \frac{2}{5}-\left(\frac{6}{5}-\frac{1}{10}\right)$$
$$=\left(\frac{2-6}{5}\right)-\frac{1}{10} \qquad =\frac{2}{5}-\left(\frac{12-1}{10}\right)$$
$$=\frac{(-4)}{5}-\frac{1}{10} \qquad =\frac{2}{5}-\frac{11}{10}$$
$$=\frac{(-8)-1}{10} \qquad =\frac{4-11}{10}$$
$$=\left(-\frac{9}{10}\right) \qquad =\left(-\frac{7}{10}\right)$$
$$\therefore \left(-\frac{9}{10}\right) \neq \left(-\frac{7}{10}\right)$$

Example 3:

$$\left(\frac{7}{8}-\frac{1}{3}\right)-\frac{1}{6} \qquad \frac{7}{8}-\left(\frac{1}{3}-\frac{1}{6}\right)$$
$$=\left(\frac{21-8}{24}\right)-\frac{1}{6} \qquad =\frac{7}{8}-\left(\frac{2-1}{6}\right)$$
$$=\frac{13}{24}-\frac{1}{6} \qquad =\frac{7}{8}-\frac{1}{6}$$
$$=\frac{13-4}{24} \qquad =\frac{21-4}{24}$$
$$=\frac{9}{24} \qquad =\frac{17}{24}$$
$$\therefore \frac{9}{24} \neq \frac{17}{24}$$

Identity Element

The identity element for subtraction does not exist. When we subtract 0 from any rational number, we have the number itself. Consider a rational number $\frac{p}{q}$.

Here $\frac{p}{q}-0$ is equal to $\frac{p}{q}$.

Thus, $0-\frac{p}{q}=\left(-\frac{p}{q}\right)$. However, when we subtract any rational number from 0, we do not get the number itself.

Hence, $\frac{p}{q}$ is not equal to $\left(-\frac{p}{q}\right)$.

Practice Exercise 1.1

1. List the properties of addition that are satisfied by the following statements.

   a. $\frac{1}{3} + \frac{5}{9} = \frac{5}{9} + \frac{1}{3}$

   b. $\frac{2}{3} + 0 = 0 + \frac{2}{3} = \frac{2}{3}$

   c. $\left(\frac{7}{8} + \frac{3}{8}\right) + \frac{5}{8} = \frac{7}{8} + \left(\frac{3}{8} + \frac{5}{8}\right)$

   d. $\left(\frac{-2}{3}\right) + \frac{2}{3} = 0 = \frac{2}{3} + \left(\frac{-2}{3}\right)$

   e. $\frac{7}{9} + \frac{3}{4}$ is a rational number

2. Verify that a + b = b + a, using the values of a and b given below.

   a. $a = \frac{2}{3}$ $b = \left(-\frac{3}{5}\right)$

   b. $a = \left(-\frac{7}{8}\right)$ $b = \frac{9}{16}$

   c. $a = \left(-\frac{1}{3}\right)$ $b = \left(-\frac{3}{4}\right)$

   d. $a = \frac{5}{16}$ $b = \frac{3}{4}$

   e. $a = \left(-\frac{1}{8}\right)$ $b = \frac{4}{5}$

3. What is the additive inverse of each of the following numbers?

   a. $-\frac{7}{12}$ b. $\frac{4}{5}$ c. $-\frac{2}{3}$ d. $\frac{13}{(-15)}$ e. $\frac{6}{7}$

4. Verify the associative property of addition—(a + b) + c = a + (b + c)—using the values of a, b and c given below.

   a. $a = \frac{5}{12}$ $b = \frac{1}{2}$ $c = \frac{7}{12}$

   b. $a = \left(-\frac{2}{3}\right)$ $b = \frac{4}{9}$ $c = \frac{5}{9}$

   c. $a = \left(-\frac{7}{8}\right)$ $b = \frac{3}{4}$ $c = \frac{3}{8}$

5. Solve the following problems.

   a. $\frac{21}{4} - \frac{5}{4}$ b. $\frac{16}{7} - \frac{6}{7}$ c. $\frac{1}{3} - \frac{3}{9}$ d. $\frac{22}{7} - \frac{7}{22}$ e. $\frac{2}{3} - \frac{3}{7}$

6. Subtract the following.

   a. $\frac{5}{12}$ from $-\frac{7}{12}$ b. $-\frac{5}{12}$ from 0 c. $\frac{5}{9}$ from $\frac{7}{9}$

   d. $\frac{4}{13}$ from $-\frac{9}{13}$ e. $-\frac{11}{20}$ from $\frac{1}{4}$

7. Using the values of a and b given below, show that $a - b \neq b - a$ in the following cases.

   a. $a = \frac{7}{10}$ $b = \left(-\frac{3}{5}\right)$

   b. $a = \frac{4}{13}$ $b = \left(-\frac{9}{13}\right)$

   c. $a = \left(-\frac{1}{2}\right)$ $b = \frac{4}{9}$

   d. $a = \frac{11}{20}$ $b = \frac{1}{4}$

   e. $a = \left(-\frac{1}{3}\right)$ $b = \left(-\frac{2}{3}\right)$

8. Solve the following problems and compare the two answers.

a. $\left(\frac{9}{11}-\frac{4}{11}\right)-\frac{6}{9}$ and $\frac{9}{11}-\left(\frac{4}{11}-\frac{6}{9}\right)$

b. $\left(\frac{7}{12}-0\right)-\frac{4}{9}$ and $\frac{7}{12}-\left(0-\frac{4}{9}\right)$

c. $\left(\frac{2}{3}-\frac{6}{9}\right)-\frac{6}{12}$ and $\frac{2}{3}-\left(\frac{6}{9}-\frac{6}{12}\right)$

9. Simplify the following expressions.

a. $\left(-\frac{2}{5}\right)-\left(-\frac{3}{10}\right)-\left(-\frac{4}{15}\right)$ b. $\frac{5}{3}-\frac{7}{6}+\left(-\frac{2}{3}\right)$ c. $\left(-\frac{3}{2}\right)+\left(\frac{5}{4}-\frac{7}{4}\right)$

d. $\frac{5}{4}-\frac{7}{6}-\left(-\frac{2}{3}\right)$ e. $\frac{6}{17}-\frac{4}{5}+\frac{11}{17}$

10. Indicate whether the following statements are true (T) or false (F).

a. $\frac{(-2)}{(-5)}$ is the additive inverse of $\frac{2}{5}$.

b. $\frac{1}{2}$ added to $\frac{2}{3}$ results in a rational number.

c. 0 is the additive inverse of a rational number 'a'.

d. 0 is the additive inverse of itself.

e. $-\frac{5}{7}$ added to $\frac{5}{(-7)}$ is equal to 0.

f. $-\frac{3}{7}$ is the additive inverse of $\frac{3}{7}$.

g. The negative of a negative rational number is also a negative number.

h. $-\frac{5}{7}+0=0$.

i. The identity element of addition is 1.

j. The identity element of addition is 0.

Properties of Multiplication of Rational Numbers

Closure Property

The product of two rational numbers always results in a rational number. Thus, rational numbers are closed under multiplication or follow the closure property.

If $\frac{p}{q}$ and $\frac{r}{s}$ are two rational numbers, then $\frac{p}{q}$ multiplied by $\frac{r}{s}$ is equals to $\frac{pr}{qs}$.

Example 1: $\frac{2}{3}\times\frac{4}{5}=\frac{2\times4}{3\times5}=\frac{8}{15}$

Example 2: $\left(-\frac{4}{7}\right)\times\frac{2}{3}=\frac{(-4)\times2}{7\times3}=\left(-\frac{8}{21}\right)$

Example 3: $\left(-\frac{5}{6}\right)\times\left(-\frac{7}{9}\right)=\frac{(-5)\times(-7)}{6\times9}=\frac{35}{54}$

Commutative Property

The product of two rational numbers remains the same even if the order of the numbers is changed. Thus, multiplication is commutative for rational numbers.

If $\frac{p}{q}$ and $\frac{r}{s}$ are two rational numbers, then $\frac{p}{q}\times\frac{r}{s}$ is equal to $\frac{r}{s}\times\frac{p}{q}$.

Example 1: $\frac{4}{7} \times \frac{3}{5} = \frac{3}{5} \times \frac{4}{7}$

$\frac{12}{35} = \frac{12}{35}$

Example 2: $\left(-\frac{7}{8}\right) \times \frac{1}{3} = \frac{1}{3} \times \left(-\frac{7}{8}\right)$

$\left(-\frac{7}{24}\right) = \left(-\frac{7}{24}\right)$

Example 3: $\left(-\frac{3}{8}\right) \times \left(-\frac{4}{7}\right) = \left(-\frac{4}{7}\right) \times \left(-\frac{3}{8}\right)$

$\frac{(-3) \times (-4)}{8 \times 7} = \frac{(-4) \times (-3)}{7 \times 8}$

$\frac{12}{56} = \frac{12}{56}$

Associative Property

The product of three rational numbers remains the same even if their grouping is changed. Thus, the associative property exists for multiplication of rational numbers.

If $\frac{p}{q}$, $\frac{r}{s}$ and $\frac{t}{u}$ are three rational numbers, then $\left(\frac{p}{q} \times \frac{r}{s}\right) \times \frac{t}{u}$ is equal to $\frac{p}{q} \times \left(\frac{r}{s} \times \frac{t}{u}\right)$.

Example 1: $\left(\frac{4}{7} \times \frac{2}{3}\right) \times \frac{1}{5} = \frac{4}{7} \times \left(\frac{2}{3} \times \frac{1}{5}\right)$

$\left(\frac{8}{21}\right) \times \frac{1}{5} = \frac{4}{7} \times \left(\frac{2}{15}\right)$

$\frac{8}{105} = \frac{8}{105}$

Example 2: $\left(-\frac{2}{3} \times \frac{4}{9}\right) \times \frac{1}{5} = \left(-\frac{2}{3}\right) \times \left(\frac{4}{9} \times \frac{1}{5}\right)$

$\left(-\frac{8}{27}\right) \times \frac{1}{5} = \left(-\frac{2}{3}\right) \times \left(\frac{4}{45}\right)$

$\left(-\frac{8}{135}\right) = \left(-\frac{8}{135}\right)$

Example 3: $\left(-\frac{3}{5} \times \frac{6}{(-7)}\right) \times \frac{1}{2} = \left(-\frac{3}{5}\right) \times \left(\frac{6}{(-7)} \times \frac{1}{2}\right)$

$\left(\frac{(-3)}{(+5)} \times \frac{6}{(-7)}\right) \times \frac{1}{2} = \left(-\frac{3}{5}\right) \times \left(\frac{6}{(-7)} \times \frac{1}{2}\right)$

$\left(\frac{(-18)}{(-35)}\right) \times \frac{1}{2} = \left(-\frac{3}{5}\right) \times \left(\frac{6}{(-14)}\right)$

$\frac{18}{70} = \frac{18}{70}$

Multiplicative Identity

The multiplication of the rational number 1 will always result in the rational number itself. Hence '1' is called the multiplicative identity for rational numbers.

If $\frac{p}{q}$ is a rational number, then $\frac{p}{q} \times 1$ and $1 \times \frac{p}{q}$ is equal to $\frac{p}{q}$.

Example 1: $\frac{3}{4} \times 1 = \frac{3}{4} = 1 \times \frac{3}{4}$ Example 2: $\left(-\frac{5}{7}\right) \times 1 = \left(-\frac{5}{7}\right) = 1 \times \left(-\frac{5}{7}\right)$

Multiplicative Inverse

If $\frac{p}{q}$ is a rational number that is not equal to 0, then $\frac{p}{q} \times \frac{q}{p} = 1 = \frac{q}{p} \times \frac{p}{q}$, such that $\frac{p}{q} \times \frac{q}{p} = 1$. $\frac{q}{p}$ is the multiplicative inverse of $\frac{p}{q}$. The multiplicative inverse is also called the reciprocal of the rational number, where p and q are integers and are not equal to 0.

Example 1: $\frac{3}{7} \times \frac{7}{3} = 1$ **Example 2:** $\left(-\frac{4}{7}\right) \times \frac{7}{(-4)} = 1$

Alert!

1. Zero has no reciprocal.
2. The reciprocal of 1 is 1.
3. The reciprocal of (-1) is (-1).
4. The product of a rational number and its multiplicative inverse (or its reciprocal) is equal to 1.

Zero Property

The product of a rational number and 0 is always equal to 0. Zero is the multiplicative identity for rational numbers.

If $\frac{p}{q}$ is a rational number, then $\frac{p}{q} \times 0$ is equal to 0.

Example 1: $\frac{4}{9} \times 0 = 0 = 0 \times \frac{4}{9}$ **Example 2:** $\left(-\frac{3}{8}\right) \times 0 = 0 = 0 \times \left(-\frac{3}{8}\right)$

Distributive property

The distributive property of multiplication over addition exists for rational numbers. If $\frac{p}{q}$, $\frac{r}{s}$ and $\frac{t}{u}$ are rational numbers, then $\frac{p}{q} \times \left(\frac{r}{s} + \frac{t}{u}\right) = \frac{p}{q} \times \frac{r}{s} + \frac{p}{q} \times \frac{t}{u}$.

The distributive property of multiplication over subtraction exists for rational numbers. If $\frac{p}{q}$, $\frac{r}{s}$ and $\frac{t}{u}$ are rational numbers, then $\frac{p}{q} \times \left(\frac{r}{s} - \frac{t}{u}\right) = \frac{p}{q} \times \frac{r}{s} - \frac{p}{q} \times \frac{t}{u}$.

Example:

$$\frac{2}{5} \times \left[\frac{5}{7} + \frac{6}{7}\right] = \frac{2}{5} \times \frac{5}{7} + \frac{2}{5} \times \frac{6}{7}$$

$$\frac{2}{5} \times \left[\frac{5+6}{7}\right] = \frac{10}{35} + \frac{12}{35}$$

$$\frac{2}{5} \times \frac{11}{7} = \frac{10+12}{35}$$

$$\frac{22}{35} = \frac{22}{35}$$

Properties of Division of Rational Numbers

If $\frac{p}{q}$ and $\frac{r}{s}$ are two rational numbers, then $\frac{p}{q} \div \frac{r}{s}$ is equal to $\frac{p}{q} \times \frac{s}{r}$.

To perform division, the dividend is multiplied by the multiplicative inverse of the divisor to obtain the answer.

If $\frac{p}{q}$ is divided by $\frac{r}{s}$, then $\frac{p}{q}$ is called the **dividend**, $\frac{r}{s}$ is called the **divisor** and the resultant, $\frac{ps}{qr}$ is called the **quotient**.

Alert!

The division of a rational number by 0 is not defined.

Closure Property

When a rational number is divided by another rational number, the quotient is always a rational number. If $\frac{p}{q}$ and $\frac{r}{s}$ are two rational numbers, then $\frac{p}{q} \div \frac{r}{s}$ is equal to $\frac{p}{q} \times \frac{s}{r}$, which is equal to $\frac{ps}{qr}$, where q, r and s are non-zero integers.

Example 1: $\frac{2}{3} \div \frac{3}{5} = \frac{2}{3} \times \frac{5}{3} = \frac{10}{9}$

Example 2: $\left(-\frac{4}{5}\right) \div \frac{6}{7} = \left(-\frac{4}{5}\right) \times \frac{7}{6} = \left(-\frac{28}{30}\right)$

Example 3: $\left(-\frac{4}{7}\right) \div \left(-\frac{3}{5}\right) = \left(-\frac{4}{7}\right) \times \left(-\frac{5}{3}\right) = \left(-\frac{20}{21}\right)$

However, $\frac{6}{9} \div 0 = \frac{6}{9} \times \frac{1}{0}$, which is not defined.

Thus, rational numbers are not closed under division.

Commutative Property

The commutative property does not hold true for rational numbers in division or division is not commutative for rational numbers. If $\frac{p}{q}$ and $\frac{r}{s}$ are two rational numbers, then $\frac{p}{q} \div \frac{r}{s}$ is not equal to $\frac{r}{s} \div \frac{p}{q}$.

To prove this, consider the following steps:

$\frac{p}{q} \div \frac{r}{s}$ is $\frac{p}{q} \times \frac{s}{r}$, which is equal to $\frac{ps}{qr}$

$\frac{r}{s} \div \frac{p}{q}$ is $\frac{r}{s} \times \frac{q}{p}$, which is equal to $\frac{rq}{sp}$

Both the answers obtained are different.

Example:

$\frac{2}{3} \div \frac{4}{5}$		$\frac{4}{5} \div \frac{2}{3}$
$\frac{2}{3} \times \frac{5}{4}$		$\frac{4}{5} \times \frac{3}{2}$
$\frac{10}{12}$	$\neq$	$\frac{12}{10}$
$\therefore \frac{2}{3} \div \frac{4}{5}$	$\neq$	$\frac{4}{5} \div \frac{2}{3}$

Associative Property

The associative property does not exist for division of rational numbers.

If $\frac{p}{q}$, $\frac{r}{s}$ and $\frac{t}{u}$ are three rational numbers and p, q, r, s, t and n are non-zero integers, then $\left(\frac{p}{q} \div \frac{r}{s}\right) \div \frac{t}{u}$ is not equal to $\frac{p}{q} \div \left(\frac{r}{s} \div \frac{t}{u}\right)$.

$\left(\frac{p}{q} \div \frac{r}{s}\right) \div \frac{t}{u}$		$\frac{p}{q} \div \left(\frac{r}{s} \div \frac{t}{u}\right)$
$\left(\frac{p}{q} \times \frac{s}{r}\right) \div \frac{t}{u}$		$\frac{p}{q} \div \left(\frac{r}{s} \times \frac{u}{t}\right)$
$\left(\frac{ps}{qr}\right) \div \frac{t}{u}$		$\frac{p}{q} \div \left(\frac{ru}{st}\right)$
$\frac{ps}{qr} \times \frac{u}{t}$		$\frac{p}{q} \times \frac{st}{ru}$
$\frac{psu}{qrt}$	$\neq$	$\frac{pst}{qru}$

Example: Consider the three rational numbers, $\frac{3}{4}, \frac{4}{5}$ and $\frac{5}{6}$.

$\left(\frac{3}{4} \div \frac{4}{5}\right) \div \frac{5}{6}$	$\frac{3}{4} \div \left(\frac{4}{5} \div \frac{5}{6}\right)$
$\left(\frac{3}{4} \times \frac{5}{4}\right) \div \frac{5}{6}$	$\frac{3}{4} \div \left(\frac{4}{5} \times \frac{6}{5}\right)$
$\frac{15}{16} \div \frac{5}{6}$	$\frac{3}{4} \div \frac{24}{25}$
$\frac{15}{16} \times \frac{6}{5}$	$\frac{3}{4} \times \frac{25}{24}$
$\frac{90}{80}$ $\neq$	$\frac{75}{96}$

Alert!

The difference between the additive inverse and the multiplicative inverse is tabulated below.

Rational Number	Additive Inverse	Multiplicative Inverse
$\frac{p}{q}$	$-\frac{p}{q}$ The number remains the same, only the sign changes.	$\frac{q}{p}$ The sign remains the same while the numerator and the denominator are interchanged.

The properties of rational numbers for the four operations are tabulated below.

Properties	Addition	Subtraction	Multiplication	Division
Closure	Yes	Yes	Yes	No
Commutative	Yes	No	Yes	No
Associative	Yes	No	Yes	No
Identity	0	No	1	No
Inverse	$\frac{p}{q}, \left(-\frac{p}{q}\right)$	No	$\frac{p}{q}, \frac{q}{p}$	No

Practice Exercise 1.2

1. Multiply the following rational numbers.

   a. $\frac{3}{7}$ and $\frac{5}{8}$ b. $-\frac{3}{5}$ and $\frac{7}{10}$ c. $\frac{6}{7}$ and $-\frac{9}{8}$

   d. $-\frac{5}{2}$ and $\frac{17}{-3}$ e. $-\frac{3}{5}$ and $-\frac{25}{12}$

2. Using each of the following values of p and q, verify p $\times$ q is equal to q $\times$ p.
   Which property are you verifying?

a. $p = \frac{1}{2}$ $q = \frac{3}{7}$ b. $p = \left(-\frac{4}{7}\right)$ $q = \frac{3}{5}$ c. $p = \left(-\frac{3}{4}\right)$ $q = \left(-\frac{6}{7}\right)$

d. $p = \frac{21}{25}$ $q = \frac{50}{63}$ e. $p = \frac{4}{9}$ $q = \left(-\frac{5}{12}\right)$

3. Using each of the following values of p, q and r, verify $(p \times q) \times r$ is equal to $p \times (q \times r)$.

   Which property are you verifying?

   a. $p = \frac{3}{4}$ $q = \left(-\frac{4}{9}\right)$ $r = \frac{3}{5}$ b. $p = \frac{4}{11}$ $q = \left(-\frac{11}{17}\right)$ $r = \left(-\frac{34}{55}\right)$

   c. $p = \left(-\frac{7}{10}\right)$ $q = \left(-\frac{10}{11}\right)$ $r = \left(-\frac{11}{33}\right)$

4. Using each of the following values of a, b and c, verify $a \times (b + c)$ is equal to $a \times b + a \times c$.

   Which property are you verifying?

   a. $a = \frac{2}{3}$ $b = \left(-\frac{4}{5}\right)$ $c = \frac{5}{8}$ b. $a = \left(-\frac{2}{3}\right)$ $b = \left(-\frac{7}{8}\right)$ $c = \frac{6}{7}$

   c. $a = \frac{4}{11}$ $b = \frac{22}{25}$ $c = \frac{5}{11}$

5. Solve each of the following expressions and verify if they are equal.

   a. $\frac{2}{3} \times \left(-\frac{6}{13}\right) = \left(-\frac{6}{13}\right) \times \frac{2}{3}$ b. $\frac{1}{2} \times \left(\frac{2}{3} + \frac{3}{4}\right) = \frac{1}{2} \times \frac{2}{3} + \frac{1}{2} \times \frac{3}{4}$

   c. $\frac{1}{2} \times \left(\frac{2}{(-6)} \times \frac{15}{16}\right) = \left(\frac{1}{2} \times \left(-\frac{2}{6}\right)\right) \times \frac{15}{16}$ d. $\frac{2}{3} \times \left(\frac{1}{2} - \frac{3}{4}\right) = \frac{2}{3} \times \frac{1}{2} - \frac{2}{3} \times \frac{3}{4}$

   e. $\frac{3}{4} \times \frac{4}{3} = \frac{4}{3} \times \frac{3}{4} = 1$

6. Write the reciprocal rational numbers of each of the following.

   a. $\frac{2}{3}$ b. $-\frac{1}{3}$ c. $\frac{5}{(-11)}$ d. $-\frac{4}{19}$ e. 0

7. Divide the following rational numbers.

   a. $\frac{8}{3}$ by $\frac{2}{9}$ b. $-\frac{5}{8}$ by $\frac{15}{6}$ c. $-\frac{7}{8}$ by $-\frac{14}{9}$ d. $\frac{2}{5}$ by $-\frac{15}{8}$ e. $\frac{61}{12}$ by $\frac{12}{5}$

8. If $x = \frac{2}{3}$, $y = \frac{4}{5}$ and $z = \frac{5}{6}$, prove the following.

   a. $x \div y \neq y \div x$ b. $y \div z \neq z \div y$

   c. $x \div (y \div z) \neq (x \div y) \div z$ d. $x \div (y + z) \neq (x \div y) + x \div z$

   e. $x \div (y - z) \neq (x \div y) - x \div z$

9. Divide the sum of $\left(-\frac{8}{7}\right)$ and $\frac{3}{14}$ by their difference.

10. Divide the sum of $2\frac{1}{4}$ and $5\frac{1}{5}$ by the product of $2\frac{1}{4}$ and $5\frac{1}{5}$.

Representation of Rational Numbers on the Number Line

Natural numbers, whole numbers and integers can be represented on the number line as shown below.

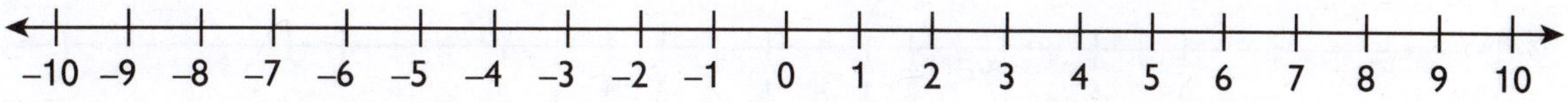

The natural numbers (N) begin from 1 and extend on the right side.

We can count the natural numbers between any two given numbers on the number line.

The natural numbers between 1 and 7 are 2, 3, 4, 5 and 6.

The whole numbers (W) begin from 0 and extend on the right side.

We can count the whole numbers between any two given numbers on the number line.

The whole numbers between 0 and 5 are 1, 2, 3 and 4.

The integers (Z) extend on either side of 0. The positive integers are on the right side of 0 and the negative integers are on the left side of 0.

We can count the integers between any two given numbers on the number line.

The integers between -5 and 5 are -4, -3, -2, -1, 0, 1, 2, 3 and 4.

Let us study the representation of rational numbers (Q) on the number line.

To represent (-3) and 3 on the number line, we draw a line and mark a point O in the middle and extend it on the right for positive numbers and on the left for negative numbers.

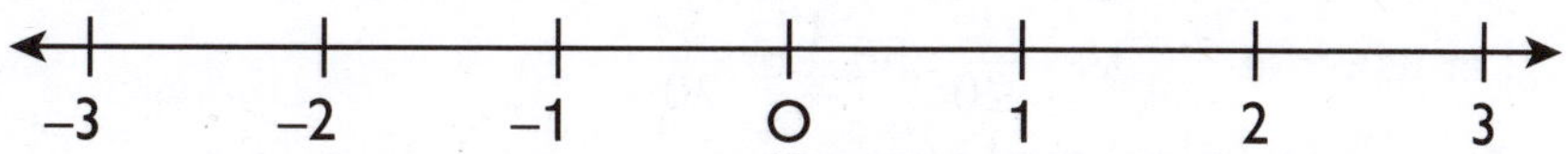

To represent $\left(-\frac{1}{2}\right)$ and $\frac{1}{2}$, we divide the portion between 0 and -1 as well as 0 and 1 into two equal parts each.

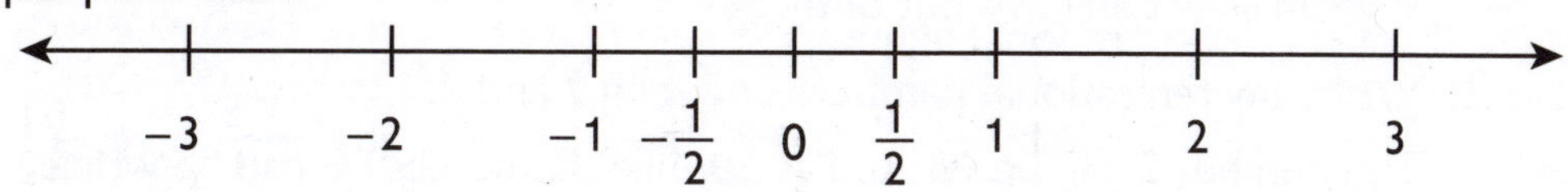

When the denominator is '2', we divide the portion between 0 and 1 as well as 0 and (-1) into two equal parts.

When we have to represent $\left(-\frac{2}{3}\right)$ and $\frac{2}{3}$ on the number line, we divide the portion between 0 and 1 as well as 0 and (-1) into three equal parts.

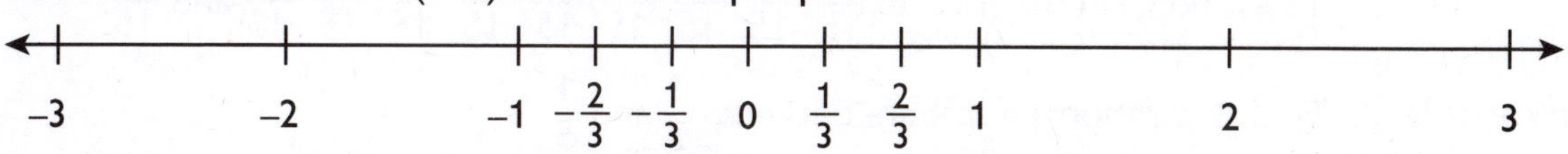

When the denominator is '3', we divide the portion between 0 and 1 as well as 0 and -1 into three equal parts.

To represent $-\frac{6}{5}$ and $\frac{7}{5}$ on the number line, we convert them into mixed fractions that are $-1\frac{1}{5}$ and $1\frac{2}{5}$, respectively. Then we divide the portion between -1 and -2 into five equal parts, since $-1\frac{1}{5}$ lies between -1 and -2. Similarly, $1\frac{2}{5}$ lies between 1 and 2 and since the denominator is 5, we divide the line between 1 and 2 into five equal parts.

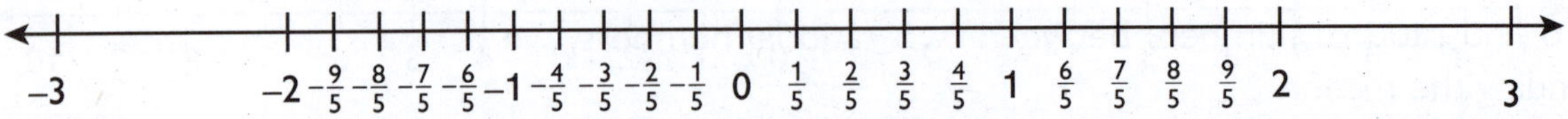

Rational Numbers Between Two Rational Numbers

We can count the numbers between two natural numbers, two whole numbers and two integers, since they are fixed.

The rational numbers between $\frac{1}{4}$ and $\frac{7}{4}$ are $\frac{2}{4}, \frac{3}{4}, \frac{4}{4}, \frac{5}{4}$ and $\frac{6}{4}$. So, there are five rational numbers between $\frac{1}{4}$ and $\frac{7}{4}$.

However, $\frac{1}{4}$ and $\frac{7}{4}$ can also be written as $\frac{5}{20}$ and $\frac{35}{20}$. The rational numbers between $\frac{5}{20}$ and $\frac{35}{20}$ will be $\frac{6}{20}, \frac{7}{20}, \frac{8}{20}, \frac{9}{20}$ and $\frac{10}{20}$. So, there are twenty-nine rational numbers between $\frac{5}{20}$ and $\frac{35}{20}$.

Similarly, $\frac{1}{4}$ and $\frac{7}{4}$ can also be written as $\frac{100}{400}$ and $\frac{700}{400}$ that will have 699 rational numbers in between. This process can continue several times indefinitely. Thus, there are an indefinite number of rational numbers between any two rational numbers.

Example 1: Find any five rational numbers between $-\frac{1}{4}$ and $\frac{1}{4}$.

Let us write $-\frac{1}{4}$ as $-\frac{5}{20}$ and $\frac{1}{4}$ as $\frac{5}{20}$.

The rational numbers between

$-\frac{5}{20}$ and $\frac{5}{20}$ are: $-\frac{4}{20}, -\frac{3}{20}, -\frac{2}{20}, -\frac{1}{20}, \frac{0}{20}, \frac{1}{20}, \frac{2}{20}, \frac{3}{20}$ and $\frac{4}{20}$.

We can select any five out of these.

Example 2: Write any ten rational numbers between 2 and 3.

The number 2 can be written as $\frac{2}{1}$ while the number 3 can be written as $\frac{3}{1}$.

Let us write $\frac{2}{1}$ as $\frac{30}{15}$ and $\frac{3}{1}$ as $\frac{45}{15}$.

There are fourteen rational numbers between $\frac{30}{15}$ and $\frac{45}{15}$. We can select any ten out of these.

The rational numbers are: $\frac{31}{15}, \frac{32}{15}, \frac{33}{15}, \frac{34}{15}, \frac{35}{15}, \frac{36}{15}, \frac{37}{15}, \frac{38}{15}, \frac{39}{15}$ and $\frac{40}{15}$.

Example 3: Find two rational numbers between $\frac{1}{3}$ and $\frac{1}{5}$.

We convert $\frac{1}{3}$ and $\frac{1}{5}$ into like fractions and hence $\frac{1}{3}$ is equal to $\frac{5}{15}$ and $\frac{1}{5}$ is equal to $\frac{3}{15}$.

Now, find two rational numbers between $\frac{3}{15}$ and $\frac{5}{15}$.

We can write $\frac{3}{15}$ as $\frac{6}{30}$ and $\frac{5}{15}$ as $\frac{10}{30}$.

The rational numbers between $\frac{6}{30}$ and $\frac{10}{30}$ are $\frac{7}{30}, \frac{8}{30}, \frac{9}{30}$.

We can select any two rational numbers from them.

To find rational numbers between two rational numbers, we can also use the method of finding the mean.

If a and b are two rational numbers such that a is less than b, then $\frac{a+b}{2}$ will lie between a and b.

Hence, $a < \frac{a+b}{2} < b$

Thus, $\frac{a+b}{2}$ is a rational number between two rational numbers.

Next we can find a rational number between a and $\frac{a+b}{2}$ by finding the mean again. We can also find a number between $\frac{a+b}{2}$ and b by finding the mean again. This process can continue indefinitely.

Example 1: Find one rational number between 5 and 6.

The mean of 5 and 6 is $\frac{5+6}{2}$ that is equal to $\frac{11}{2}$, which lies between 5 and 6.

Example 2: Find two rational numbers between 5 and 6.

First find the mean of 5 and 6, which is $\frac{5+6}{2} = \frac{11}{2}$.

Then we find the mean of 5 and $\frac{11}{2}$, which is $\left(\frac{5}{1} + \frac{11}{2}\right) \div 2$.

$\left(\frac{10+11}{2}\right) \div 2 = \frac{21}{2} \times \frac{1}{2} = \frac{21}{4}$

Hence, the two rational numbers between 5 and 6 are $\frac{11}{2}$ and $\frac{21}{4}$.

Example 3: Find three rational numbers between $\frac{1}{2}$ and $\frac{1}{3}$.

The first rational number will be $\left(\frac{1}{2} + \frac{1}{3}\right) \div 2$

$= \left(\frac{3+2}{6}\right) \div 2 = \frac{5}{6} \div 2 = \frac{5}{6} \times \frac{1}{2} = \frac{5}{12}$.

The second rational number will be

$\left(\frac{1}{2} + \frac{5}{12}\right) \div 2 = \left(\frac{6+5}{12}\right) \div 2 = \frac{11}{12} \div 2$

$= \frac{11}{12} \times \frac{1}{2} = \frac{11}{24}$.

The third rational number will be

$\left(\frac{5}{12} + \frac{1}{3}\right) \div 2 = \left(\frac{5+4}{12}\right) \div 2 = \frac{9}{12} \div 2$

$\frac{9}{12} \times \frac{1}{2} = \frac{9}{24}$.

Thus, the three rational numbers are $\frac{5}{12}, \frac{11}{24}$ and $\frac{9}{24}$.

Practice Exercise 1.3

1. a. Write the rational numbers corresponding to the points M, N, P, Q and R on the number line.

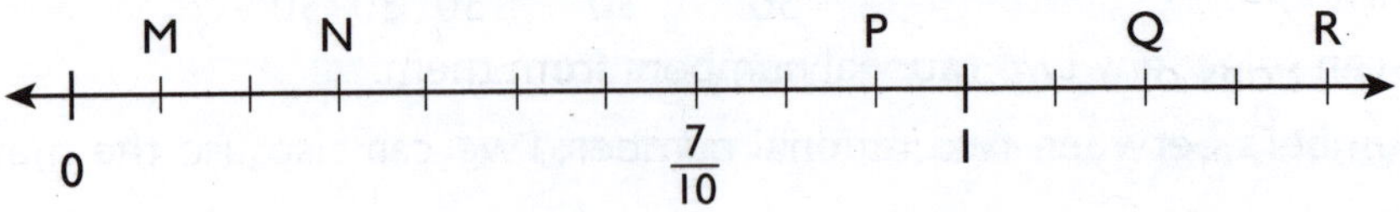

b. Write the rational numbers corresponding to the points A, B and C on the number line.

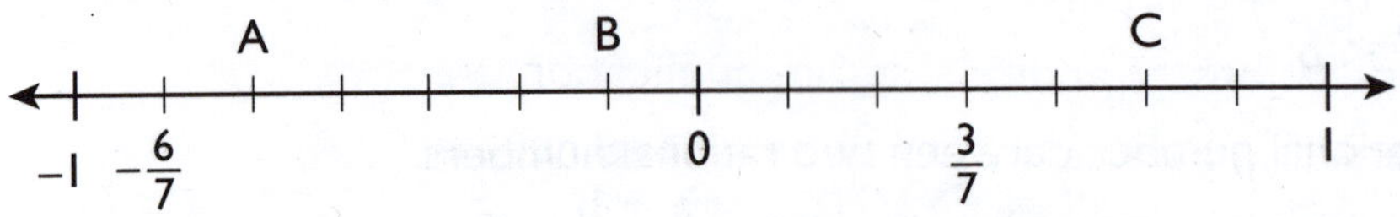

c. Write the rational numbers corresponding to the points X, Y and Z on the number line.

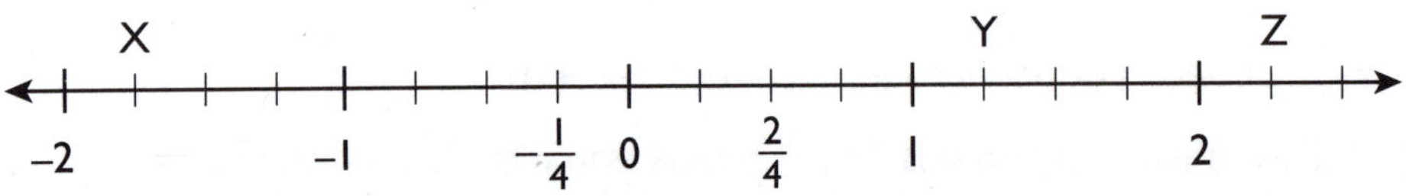

2. Draw a number line and represent the following rational numbers on it.
   a. $-\frac{5}{8}$ b. $\frac{14}{10}$ c. $-\frac{11}{6}$ d. $\frac{9}{5}$ e. $\frac{9}{7}$
3. Represent the following rational numbers on a number line.
   a. $\frac{1}{2}$ b. $\frac{1}{3}$ c. $\frac{7}{6}$ d. $\frac{11}{6}$ e. $-\frac{1}{6}$
4. Identify any five rational numbers between $\frac{1}{6}$ and $\frac{1}{5}$ using a number line.
5. Identify any nine rational numbers between 0 and $\frac{1}{9}$ using a number line.
6. Identify any ten rational numbers between $\frac{1}{9}$ and $\frac{1}{4}$ using a number line.
7. Use the method of mean to find three rational numbers between -1 and 0.
8. Use the method of mean to find three rational numbers between 4 and 5.
9. Use the method of mean to find three rational numbers between -2 and -3.
10. Write any ten rational numbers that are greater than $-\frac{7}{9}$ and ten rational numbers that are less than $-\frac{7}{9}$.

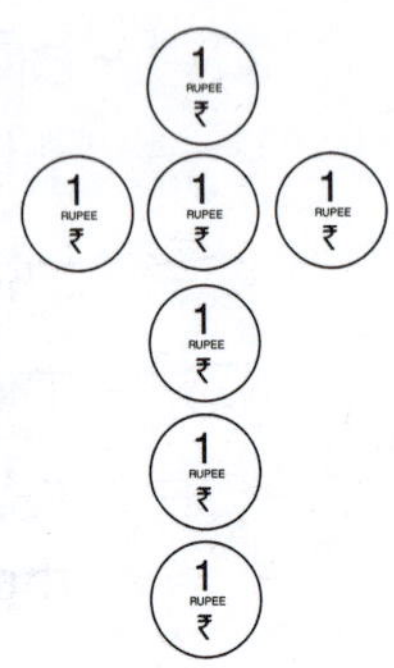

Coin trick

Arrange 7 coins on a table in the form of a cross as shown in the figure. Place 5 coins vertically and 3 coins horizontally. The middle coin will be common to both the row and the column. Change the position of any 2 coins so that the vertical and horizontal arms have an equal number of coins.

Answer for Brainteaser on page 22

Highlights

- Rational numbers follow the closure property for addition, subtraction and multiplication.
- The operations of addition and multiplication are commutative in rational numbers. If $\frac{p}{q}$ and $\frac{r}{s}$ are two rational numbers, then

$$\frac{p}{q} + \frac{r}{s} = \frac{r}{s} + \frac{p}{q} \qquad \text{where q and s} \neq 0$$

$$\frac{p}{q} \times \frac{r}{s} = \frac{r}{s} \times \frac{p}{q} \qquad \text{where q and s} \neq 0$$

- The operations of addition and multiplication are associative for rational numbers. If $\frac{p}{q}$, $\frac{r}{s}$ and $\frac{t}{u}$ are any three rational numbers, then

$$\left(\frac{p}{q} + \frac{r}{s}\right) + \frac{t}{u} = \frac{p}{q} + \left(\frac{r}{s} + \frac{t}{u}\right) \qquad \text{where q, s and u} \neq 0$$

$$\left(\frac{p}{q} \times \frac{r}{s}\right) \times \frac{t}{u} = \frac{p}{q} \times \left(\frac{r}{s} \times \frac{t}{u}\right) \qquad \text{where q, s and u} \neq 0$$

- The additive identity of rational numbers is 0.
- The multiplicative identity of rational numbers is 1.
- The additive inverse of a rational number $\frac{p}{q}$ is $\left(-\frac{p}{q}\right)$ and vice versa where $q \neq 0$.
- The multiplicative inverse or reciprocal of a rational number $\frac{p}{q}$ is $\frac{q}{p}$, where p and q are non-zero integers.
- For rational numbers, the distributive property of multiplication exists over addition and subtraction. If $\frac{p}{q}$, $\frac{r}{s}$ and $\frac{t}{u}$ are any three rational numbers, then

$$\frac{p}{q} \times \left(\frac{r}{s} + \frac{t}{u}\right) = \frac{p}{q} \times \frac{r}{s} + \frac{p}{q} \times \frac{t}{u} \text{ and}$$

$$\frac{p}{q} \times \left(\frac{r}{s} - \frac{t}{u}\right) = \frac{p}{q} \times \frac{r}{s} - \frac{p}{q} \times \frac{t}{u} \text{ where q, s and u} \neq 0.$$

- Rational numbers can be represented on a number line.
- Between any two rational numbers, there are an indefinite number of rational numbers.
- The method of finding the mean can be used to find rational numbers between any two rational numbers. If $\frac{p}{q}$ and $\frac{r}{s}$ are two rational numbers, such that $\frac{p}{q}$ is less than $\frac{r}{s}$, then one of the rational numbers between them is $\left(\frac{p}{q} + \frac{r}{s}\right) \div 2$.
- Division of any number by 0 is undefined.
- The integer 0 has no reciprocal.
- The reciprocal of the number 1 is 1.
- The reciprocal of the number -1 is -1.
- For any rational number a, that is not equal to 0, and m is any positive integer, then a^{-m} denotes the reciprocal of a^m.

Maths Lab Activity

Objective: To study the commutative property.

Material required: a pen

Procedure: Each student will have to fill in the name of the property followed in each of the following activities.

Activity	Property
1. Wear a shirt; wear a tie	____________
2. Wear the right shoe; wear the left shoe	____________
3. Wear the socks; wear the shoe	____________
4. Apply butter on a toast; eat the toast	____________
5. Wash clothes; dry them	____________
6. Switch off the light; sleep	____________
7. Hold your bag; go to school	____________
8. Lock the house; come out of the house	____________
9. Write on the blackboard; erase it	____________
10. Bake a cake; eat it	____________

Higher Order Thinking Skills

HOTS

1. The multiplicative inverse of a negative rational number is:
   a. a positive rational number
   b. a negative rational number
   c. can either be a positive or negative rational number
   d. non existent.

2. Which out of these is the greatest rational number: $-\frac{11}{28}, -\frac{5}{7}, \frac{9}{(-14)}$ and $\frac{22}{(-42)}$?

3. The cost of $8\frac{1}{2}$ m of cloth is ₹157 $\frac{1}{4}$. What is the cost of 1 m of cloth?

Answer for Brainteaser from page 20

Take 2 coins from the bottom of the vertical arm and place them 'on' the middle coin.

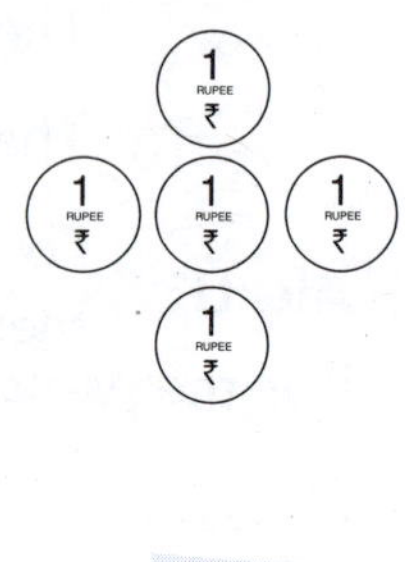

Squares

A number obtained by multiplying the number by itself is called a square. Thus,

$2 \times 2 = 4$ (4 is the square of 2)

$3 \times 3 = 9$ (9 is the square of 3)

$4 \times 4 = 16$ (16 is the square of 4)

$5 \times 5 = 25$ (25 is the square of 5)

We can also depict squares with the help of diagrams. They represent the area of a square of the given side.

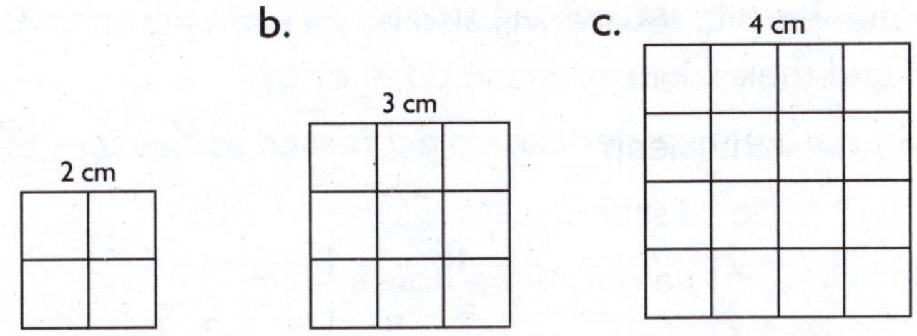

$2 \times 2 = 4\ cm^2$ $3 \times 3 = 9\ cm^2$ $4 \times 4 = 16\ cm^2$

Perfect Squares

A perfect square or a square number 'm' is a natural number that is the square of another natural number 'n', such that $n^2 = m$.

In order to find whether a given number is a perfect square or not, we write the number as a product of its prime factors. If it forms pairs of identical factors and no factor is left without a pair, the number is a perfect square.

Table 2.1 Squares of the first twenty natural numbers

Number (n)	$n^2 = n \times n = m$	Number (n)	$n^2 = n \times n = m$
1	$1 \times 1 = 1$	11	$11 \times 11 = 121$
2	$2 \times 2 = 4$	12	$12 \times 12 = 144$
3	$3 \times 3 = 9$	13	$13 \times 13 = 169$
4	$4 \times 4 = 16$	14	$14 \times 14 = 196$
5	$5 \times 5 = 25$	15	$15 \times 15 = 225$
6	$6 \times 6 = 36$	16	$16 \times 16 = 256$
7	$7 \times 7 = 49$	17	$17 \times 17 = 289$
8	$8 \times 8 = 64$	18	$18 \times 18 = 324$
9	$9 \times 9 = 81$	19	$19 \times 19 = 361$
10	$10 \times 10 = 100$	20	$20 \times 20 = 400$

Alert!

If all the prime factors of a natural number can be paired, it is a perfect square.

Properties of Squares

1. If a natural number ends in 2, 3, 7 or 8, it is not a perfect square. In Table 2.1, none of the values end in the digits 2, 3, 7 or 8.
2. If a number ends in an odd number of zeros, it is not a perfect square. Thus, 110 and 1,14,000 are not perfect squares. To be a perfect square, a number should end in an even number of zeros.

   However, it is not true that all numbers ending in an even number of zeroes are always perfect squares.

   The squares of 10, 20 and 30 are 100, 400 and 900, respectively. The squares of 100, 200 and 300, are 10,000, 40,000 and 90,000, respectively.
3. Squares of odd numbers are always odd.
4. Squares of even numbers are always even. If we check Table 2.1, we see that if we have an even number, its square will also be an even number. Even numbers end in 0, 2, 4, 6 or 8 and their squares end in 00, 4 or 6.
5. The square of a natural number can be expressed as the sum of consecutive odd numbers.

Examples:

$2^2 = 4 \quad 1 + 3$

$3^2 = 9 \quad 1 + 3 + 5$

$4^2 = 16 \quad 1 + 3 + 5 + 7$

$5^2 = 25 \quad 1 + 3 + 5 + 7 + 9$

$6^2 = 36 \quad 1 + 3 + 5 + 7 + 9 + 11$

Here, we can observe that the square of 2 is 4, which is the sum of the first two consecutive odd numbers. The square of 3 is 9, which is the sum of the first three consecutive odd numbers. The square of 4 is 16, which is the sum of the first four consecutive odd numbers.

Hence, we can derive the formula n^2 = sum of the first 'n' odd numbers where n is any natural number.

6. The difference between the squares of two consecutive natural numbers is equal to the sum of the two numbers.

Examples:

$2^2 - 1^2 = 4 - 1 = 3 = 2 + 1$

$3^2 - 2^2 = 9 - 4 = 5 = 3 + 2$

$7^2 - 6^2 = 49 - 36 = 13 = 7 + 6$

$11^2 - 10^2 = 121 - 100 = 21 = 11 + 10$

$101^2 - 100^2 = 10201 - 10000 = 201 = 101 + 100$

7. The square of an odd number is expressed as the sum of two consecutive natural numbers.

Examples:

$3^2 = 9 = 4 + 5$

$5^2 = 25 = 12 + 13$

$7^2 = 49 = 24 + 25$

$21^2 = 441 = 220 + 221$

$101^2 = 10201 = 5100 + 5101$

Hence, if 'a' is an odd natural number, then

$$a^2 = \left(\frac{a^2 + 1}{2}\right) + \left(\frac{a^2 - 1}{2}\right).$$

8. The square of the product of two numbers is equal to the product of the squares of the two numbers.

   Example 1: $(2 \times 3)^2 = 6^2 = 36$ and $2^2 \times 3^2 = 4 \times 9 = 36$

   Example 2: $(5 \times 6)^2 = 30^2 = 900$ and $5^2 \times 6^2 = 25 \times 36 = 900$

   Example 3: $(8 \times 9)^2 = 72^2 = 5184$ and $8^2 \times 9^2 = 64 \times 81 = 5184$

   If 'a' and 'b' are two numbers, then $(a \times b)^2 = a^2 \times b^2$.

9. The square of the ratio of two numbers or rational numbers is equal to the ratio of their squares.

   Example 1: $\left(\frac{1}{3}\right)^2 = \frac{1}{3} \times \frac{1}{3} = \frac{1}{9}$ and $\frac{1^2}{3^2} = \frac{1 \times 1}{3 \times 3} = \frac{1}{9}$

   Example 2: $\left(\frac{4}{5}\right)^2 = \frac{4}{5} \times \frac{4}{5} = \frac{16}{25}$ and $\frac{4^2}{5^2} = \frac{4 \times 4}{5 \times 5} = \frac{16}{25}$

   Example 3: $\left(\frac{11}{13}\right)^2 = \frac{11}{13} \times \frac{11}{13} = \frac{121}{169}$ and $\frac{11^2}{13^2} = \frac{11 \times 11}{13 \times 13} = \frac{121}{169}$

   If 'a' and 'b' are two numbers, then $\left(\frac{a}{b}\right)^2 = \frac{a^2}{b^2}$, where $b \neq 0$.

10. The square of a negative integer is always positive.

    Examples:

    $(-1)^2 = (-1) \times (-1) = 1$
    $(-5)^2 = (-5) \times (-5) = 25$
    $(-8)^2 = (-8) \times (-8) = 64$

Alert!

If the last digit of any number is 1, then the square of that number will always end in 1. If the last digit of a number is 2, then the square of that number will always end in 4.

Patterns of Squares

1. Perfect squares can be represented geometrically by dots that form squares.

   Example 1: $1 \times 1 = (1)$

   •

   Example 2: $2 \times 2 = (4)$

   • •
   • •

   Example 3: $3 \times 3 = (9)$

   • • •
   • • •
   • • •

Example 4: $4 \times 4 = (16)$

Example 5: $5 \times 5 = (25)$

2. The squares of natural numbers with digits '1' follow an interesting pattern.

Examples:

$(1)^2$	=	1
$(11)^2$	=	1 2 1
$(111)^2$	=	$1\,2\,\underline{3}\,2\,1$
$(1111)^2$	=	$1\,2\,3\,\underline{4}\,3\,2\,1$
$(11111)^2$	=	$1\,2\,3\,4\,\underline{5}\,4\,3\,2\,1$
$(111111)^2$	=	$1\,2\,3\,4\,5\,\underline{6}\,5\,4\,3\,2\,1$
$(1111111)^2$	=	$1\,2\,3\,4\,5\,6\,\underline{7}\,6\,5\,4\,3\,2\,1$
$(11111111)^2$	=	$1\,2\,3\,4\,5\,6\,7\,\underline{8}\,7\,6\,5\,4\,3\,2\,1$
$(111111111)^2$	=	$1\,2\,3\,4\,5\,6\,7\,8\,\underline{9}\,8\,7\,6\,5\,4\,3\,2\,1$

The digit in the centre of the number on the right hand side that is underlined is the same as the number of 1's on the left hand side. For example $(1111)^2$ has four ones, and the answer is 1234321, that has 4, as the centre digit.

3. If we add 1 to the product of two consecutive odd numbers, we get the square of the even number that is between the two odd numbers.

Examples:

$1 \times 3 + 1 = 4 = 2^2$

$3 \times 5 + 1 = 16 = 4^2$

$5 \times 7 + 1 = 36 = 6^2$

$13 \times 15 + 1 = 196 = 14^2$

$21 \times 23 + 1 = 484 = 22^2$

4. If there exist three numbers a, b and c such that $a^2 + b^2 = c^2$, then these are known as Pythagorean triplets.

Examples:

$3^2 + 4^2 = 5^2$ (3, 4 and 5 are Pythagorean triplets.)

$6^2 + 8^2 = 10^2$ (6, 8 and 10 are Pythagorean triplets.)

$9^2 + 12^2 = 15^2$ (9, 12 and 15 are Pythagorean triplets.)

Thus, for any natural number where n is greater than 1, we get the Pythagorean triplets using the formulae: $2n$, $n^2 - 1$, $n^2 + 1$. Let us verify this using an example. Let us assume 'n' = 17. Using the formula, we can get the Pythagorean triplets.

a. $2n = 2 \times 17 = 34$

b. $n^2 - 1 = (17)^2 - 1 = 289 - 1 = 288$

c. $n^2 + 1 = (17)^2 + 1 = 289 + 1 = 290$

Hence, $(34)^2 + (288)^2 = (290)^2$

$1{,}156 + 82{,}944 = 84{,}100$

Alert!

We use the formulae, $2n$, $n^2 - 1$, $n^2 + 1$ as a method to find Pythagorean triplets. Here, $2n$ will be the smallest and $n^2 + 1$ will be the largest number.

Practice Exercise 2.1

1. Identify the numbers that are not perfect squares in the following list.
   a. 12 b. 36 c. 6,250 d. 462 e. 625
   f. 1,118 g. 5,476 h. 5,613 i. 6,688 j. 8,866
2. Which of the following numbers are squares of odd numbers?
   a. 196 b. 1,521 c. 1,024 d. 15,129 e. 37
   f. 2,128 g. 1,225 h. 2,209 i. 12,321 j. 3,236
3. Which of the following numbers are squares of even numbers?
   a. 9,371 b. 256 c. 441 d. 729 e. 1,296
   f. 7,744 g. 7,938 h. 9,216 i. 2,378 j. 6,400
4. Without finding the squares, find the difference of the two numbers in each of the following.
   a. $68^2 - 67^2$ b. $75^2 - 74^2$ c. $88^2 - 87^2$ d. $99^2 - 98^2$
   e. $121^2 - 120^2$ f. $110^2 - 109^2$ g. $221^2 - 220^2$ h. $334^2 - 333^2$
   i. $555^2 - 554^2$ j. $1000^2 - 999^2$
5. Express each of the following squares of odd numbers as a sum of two consecutive natural numbers.
   a. 3^2 b. 5^2 c. 7^2 d. 9^2 e. 19^2
   f. 17^2 g. 15^2 h. 13^2 i. 11^2 j. 21^2
6. Which of the following sets are Pythagorean triplets? Give reasons for your answers.
   a. 11, 22, 33 b. 30, 40, 50 c. 9, 40, 41
   d. 29, 31, 33 e. 50, 624, 626.
7. Find the Pythagorean triplets, where one member of the triplets is given.
   a. 4 b. 10 c. 16 d. 36 e. 50

8. Without adding the numbers, find the sum of the numbers.
   a. $1 + 3 + 5 + 7$
   b. $1 + 3 + 5 + 7 + 9 + 11$
   c. $1 + 3 + 5 + 7 + 9 + 11 + 13 + 15$
   d. $1 + 3 + 5 + 7 + 9$
   e. $1 + 3 + 5 + 7 + 9 + 11 + 13 + 15 + 17 + 19 + 21$

9. Fill in the blanks.
   a. $(5 \times 6)^2 =$ _______^{2}
   b. $(11 \times 5)^2 =$ _______^{2}
   c. $(48)^2 = 3^2 \times$ _______^{2}
   d. $(96)^2 = 4^2 \times$ _______^{2}
   e. $(80 \times 1)^2 =$ _______^{2}
   f. $(101)^2 = (100 \times$ _______$)^2$
   g. $(25 \times 4)^2 =$ _______^{2}
   h. $(6 \times 8)^2 =$ _______^{2}
   i. $(121)^2 = 11^2 \times$ _______^{2}
   j. $(40 \times 4)^2 =$ _______^{2}

10. Perform the following actions:
   a. Express 64 as the sum of eight odd numbers.
   b. Express 121 as the sum of eleven odd numbers.
   c. Express 49 as the sum of seven odd numbers.
   d. Express 100 as the sum of ten odd numbers.
   e. Express 144 as the sum of twelve odd numbers.

Square Roots

The square root of a number 'n' is that number which when multiplied by itself gives n. The square root of 'n' is denoted as $\sqrt{n}$.

The symbol of square root is $\sqrt{}$.

We know that 9, 25 and 64 are perfect squares and can be expressed as follows:

$$9 = 3 \times 3 = 3^2$$
$$25 = 5 \times 5 = 5^2$$
$$64 = 8 \times 8 = 8^2$$

Example 1: The square root of 9 is 3 and the square of 3 is 9. This is represented as:

$$\sqrt{9} = 3;\ 3^2 = 9$$

Example 2: The square root of 25 is 5 and the square of 5 is 25. This is represented as:

$$\sqrt{25} = 5;\ 5^2 = 25$$

We can find the square root of a number by different methods. We shall learn two methods in this chapter.

1. By prime factorisation
2. By the long division method

Square Root of a Perfect Square by Prime Factorisation

A number that occurs twice in the prime factorisation of a square will occur only once in the square root. To find the square root of a perfect square by prime factorisation, we follow the following steps.

Step 1 Find the prime factors of the given number.

Step 2 Group the factors into pairs of same numbers.

Step 3 Select one factor from each pair.

Step 4 Find the product of the factors selected in step 3.

The product thus obtained is the square root of the given number.

Example 1: Find the square root of the following numbers:

a. 324

2	324
2	162
3	81
3	27
3	9
3	3
	1

Step 1 We find the prime factors of the number.

Factors are written in pairs.

Step 2 $2 \times 2 \times 3 \times 3 \times 3 \times 3$

Step 3 $2 \quad 3 \quad 3$

Step 4 $2 \times 3 \times 3 = 18$. The square root of 324 is 18.

b. 489

2	484
2	242
11	121
11	11
	1

Step 1 $2 \times 2 \times 11 \times 11$

Step 2 2×11

Step 3 $\sqrt{484} = 2 \times 11 = 22$. The square root of 484 is 22.

Example 2: By what number should we multiply 882 to get a perfect square? Find the square root of the number obtained.

2	882
3	441
3	147
7	49
7	7
	1

$2 \times \underline{3 \times 3} \times \underline{7 \times 7}$

Here, we see that 2 does not have a pair. Hence, if we multiply the number by 2, we will have a perfect square.

Thus, $882 \times 2 = 1,764$, which is a perfect square.

$\sqrt{1764} = 2 \times 3 \times 7 = 42$

Example 3: By what number should we divide 8,820 to get a perfect square. Find the square root of the number obtained.

2	8820
2	4410
5	2205
3	441
3	147
7	49
7	7
	1

$\underline{2 \times 2} \times 5 \times \underline{3 \times 3} \times \underline{7 \times 7}$

Here, we see that 5 does not have a pair. Hence, if we divide 8820 by 5 we will get a perfect square.

Thus, $8820 \div 5 = 1764$, which is a perfect square.

$1764 = \underline{2 \times 2} \times \underline{3 \times 3} \times \underline{7 \times 7}$

$2 \quad 3 \quad 7$

$\sqrt{1764} = 2 \times 3 \times 7 = 42$

Square Root of Rational Numbers

Consider a rational number $\frac{a}{b}$, where $b \neq 0$. We know that $\left(\frac{a}{b}\right)^2 = \frac{a^2}{b^2}$. Thus, the square root of $\sqrt{\frac{a}{b}} = \frac{\sqrt{a}}{\sqrt{b}}$.

Examples:

Find the square roots of the following.

a. $\sqrt{\frac{49}{625}} = \frac{\sqrt{49}}{\sqrt{625}} = \frac{\sqrt{7 \times 7}}{\sqrt{5 \times 5 \times 5 \times 5}} = \frac{7}{25}$

b. $\sqrt{\frac{289}{361}} = \frac{\sqrt{289}}{\sqrt{361}} = \frac{\sqrt{17 \times 17}}{\sqrt{19 \times 19}} = \frac{17}{19}$

c. $\sqrt{\frac{169}{289}} = \frac{\sqrt{169}}{\sqrt{289}} = \frac{\sqrt{13 \times 13}}{\sqrt{17 \times 17}} = \frac{13}{17}$

Square Root of Decimals

While finding the square root of a decimal number, we convert it into a fraction and then find the square root of the number.

Examples: Find the square roots of the following numbers.

a. $1.44 = \frac{144}{100}$

$\sqrt{1.44} = \sqrt{\frac{144}{100}} = \frac{\sqrt{144}}{\sqrt{100}} = \frac{\sqrt{12 \times 12}}{\sqrt{10 \times 10}} = \frac{12}{10} = 1.2$

b. $2.56 = \frac{256}{100}$

$\sqrt{2.56} = \sqrt{\frac{256}{100}} = \frac{\sqrt{256}}{\sqrt{100}} = \frac{\sqrt{16 \times 16}}{\sqrt{10 \times 10}} = \frac{16}{10} = 1.6$

c. $0.0324 = \frac{324}{10000}$

$\sqrt{0.0324} = \sqrt{\frac{324}{10,000}} = \frac{\sqrt{324}}{\sqrt{10,000}} = \frac{\sqrt{18 \times 18}}{\sqrt{100 \times 100}} = \frac{18}{100} = 0.18$

Alert!

The square root of a square natural number 'n' can never be greater than 'n'. However, if a number is less than 1, then its square root is always greater than the number.

1. $\sqrt{25} = 5$ where $5 < 25$
2. $\sqrt{\frac{1}{25}} = \frac{1}{5}$ where $\frac{1}{5} > \frac{1}{25}$

Practice Exercise 2.2

1. Find the square root of the following numbers by the prime factorisation method.

a. 441	b. 625	c. 1764	d. 3136	e. 2401
f. 3600	g. 4761	h. 5625	i. 6084	j. 9801

2. What is the smallest number that can be multiplied to each of the following numbers to make them perfect squares? Find the square root of the perfect squares.
   a. 2,100 b. 3,388 c. 7,203 d. 8,820 e. 9,680
3. What is the smallest number that can be used to divide each of the following numbers to make them perfect squares? Find the square root of the perfect squares.
   a. 3,388 b. 7,623 c. 7,938 d. 9,075 e. 7,605
4. Find the square root of the following fractions.
   a. $\frac{324}{441}$ b. $\frac{361}{729}$ c. $\frac{625}{1296}$ d. $\frac{4225}{6400}$ e. $\frac{1936}{2601}$
5. Find the square root of the following fractions.
   a. $38\frac{11}{25}$ b. $23\frac{26}{121}$ c. $10\frac{74}{169}$ d. $7\frac{393}{529}$ e. $41\frac{25}{144}$.
6. Find the square root of the following decimals.
   a. 6.25 b. 7.29 c. 0.09 d. 0.0081 e. 0.0121
7. The area of a square field is 784 m^2. Find the length of its side.
8. In an orchard, there are as many apple trees as there are rows of them. How many rows of trees are there if there are 5,929 apple trees?
9. The cost of ploughing a square field at the rate of ₹10 per m^2 is ₹1,23,210. Find the cost of fencing the field at ₹7 per m.
10. Find the smallest square number that can be completely divided by 9, 15 and 20.

Finding the Square Root of a Perfect Square by the Long Division Method

We have learnt how to find the square root of a number by prime factorisation. However, it is a time-consuming process and becomes cumbersome when we have to find factors of large numbers. The long-division method is also useful in finding the approximate value of square roots of numbers that are not perfect squares. Let us observe the pattern that can be seen in the number of digits a square number has and the number of digits in its square root.

Table 2.2 Number of digits in the square and the square root of a number

Number	Square	Digits	Square root	Digit
2	4	1	2	1
9	81	2	9	1
10	100	3	10	2
100	10000	5	100	3

If the number of digits in the square of a number are 1or 2, the square root will have 1 digit, if the number of digits in the square of a number are 3 or 4, the square root will have 2 digits, if the number of digits in the square of a number are 5 or 6, the square root will have 3 digits and so on. We can derive the following formulae when we consider the number of digits in a square to be 'n'.

1. $\frac{n}{2}$ digits if 'n' is even.
2. $\frac{n+1}{2}$ digits if 'n' is odd.

Let us study the long division method of finding the square root of a number step by step with the help of examples.

Example 1: Find the square root of 1,296.

Step 1 Form pairs of numbers starting from the digits in the the unit's place and place a bar over every pair. The number will be $\overline{12}\,\overline{96}$. The number of bars indicate the number of digits in the square root.

Step 2 Now we begin with the long division by taking the number under the bar on the extreme left to be the dividend. Find the largest number whose square is less than or equal to the dividend. Here, the number will be 3, since its square (9) is less than 12. We divide the dividend by 3 and get 3 as the quotient. In this case, the remainder is also 3.

$$\begin{array}{r|l} & 3 \\ \hline 3 & \overline{12}\,\overline{96} \\ & -9 \\ \hline & 3 \end{array}$$

Step 3 Now we add the quotient and the divisor, which is $3 + 3 = 6$ and place this number in the divisor column. Bring down the next pair, that is, 96 in this case. The new dividend will be 396.

$$\begin{array}{r|l} & 3 \\ \hline 3 & \overline{12}\,\overline{96} \\ +\underline{3} & -9 \;\downarrow \\ \hline 6 & 3\,96 \end{array}$$

Step 4 Now find the largest possible number which will be written next to 6 and by which we multiply the new divisor so that the product is less than or equal to the new dividend 396. This number will be 6.

Step 5 Write 6 next to 6 in the divisor column to get a new divisor 66 and also in the quotient such that $66 \times 6 = 396$ and the remainder is 0.

$$\begin{array}{r|r} & 3\,6 \\ \hline 3 & \overline{12}\,\overline{96} \\ +\underline{3} & -9 \;\downarrow \\ \hline 6\,6 & 3\,96 \\ & -3\,96 \\ \hline & 0 \end{array}$$

Step 6 Since the remainder is 0 and no more digits are left in the given number, the solution concludes here.

Hence, $\sqrt{1296} = 36$.

Example 2: Find the square root of 9,62,361.

Step 1 Place a bar on every pair of digits beginning from the digit in the unit's place, that is, $\overline{96}\,\overline{23}\,\overline{61}$.

Step 2 Now we start with the division. The pair on the extreme left is the dividend, that is, 96. Find the largest number whose square is less than or equal to 96. Here, the number is 9 since its square is 81, which is less than 96. Thus, we divide the dividend by 9. The quotient is 9 and the remainder is 15.

$$\begin{array}{r|l} & 9 \\ \hline 9 & \overline{96}\,\overline{23}\,\overline{61} \\ & -81 \\ \cline{2-2} & 15 \end{array}$$

Step 3 Now we add the quotient and the divisor, which is $9 + 9 = 18$ and bring down the next pair, that is, 23. The new dividend is 1,523.

$$\begin{array}{r|l} & 9 \\ \hline 9 & \overline{96}\,\overline{23}\,61 \\ +\underline{9} & -\underline{81}\downarrow \\ \hline 18 & 1523 \end{array}$$

Step 4 Now find the largest possible number which will be written alongside 18 and then multiply the divisor with this number so that the product is less than 1,523.

Step 5 The number is 8 since $188 \times 8 = 1{,}504$, which is less than 1,523.

$$\begin{array}{r|l} & 9\,8 \\ \hline 9 & \overline{96}\,\overline{23}\,\overline{61} \\ +\underline{9} & -81\downarrow \\ \hline 188 & 15\,23 \\ & -15\,04 \\ \cline{2-2} & 19 \end{array}$$

Step 6 Now bring down the next pair 61, so the new dividend is 1,961.

Step 7 Now adding 8, which is the quotient of the previous step to 188, we get196.

$$\begin{array}{r|l} & 9\;\;8\;\;1 \\ \hline 9 & \overline{96}\,\overline{23}\,\overline{61} \\ +\underline{9} & -81\downarrow \\ \hline 188 & 15\,23 \\ +\underline{8} & -15\,04\downarrow \\ \hline 1961 & 19\,61 \\ & -19\,61 \\ \cline{2-2} & 0 \end{array}$$

Step 8 We write 1 along 196 and the new divisor is 1,961. We also write 1 in the quotient and multiply 1,961 by 1. The product is 1,961.

Step 9 We write 1,961 below 1,961 and the remainder is 0.

Thus, $\sqrt{962361} = 981$.

Example 1: Find the square root of 15,625.

```
          1 2 5
      ___________
   1  | 1 56 25
  +1  | −1
  ----|------
  22  |   56
  +2  |  −44
  ----|------
 245  |   12 25
      |  −12 25
      |------
      |       0
```

So, the square root of 15,625 is 125.

Example 2: Find the smallest number that must be subtracted from 3,94,484 to make it a perfect square. Find the square root of the perfect square.

```
          6 2 8
      ___________
   6  | 39 44 84
  +6  | −36
  ----|---------
 122  |    344
  +2  |   −244
  ----|---------
1248  |    100 84
      |    −99 84
      |---------
      |       100
```

In the example, there are no pairs left to proceed with the division and we have 100 as the remainder.

We can conclude that if 100 is subtracted from the given number, it will become a perfect square.

Example 3: Find the smallest number that must be added to 7,600 to make it a perfect square. Find the square root of the perfect square.

We apply the long division method to find the square root.

```
         8 7
      ________
   8  | 76 00
  +8  | −64
  ----|-------
 167  |  12 00
      | −11 69
      |-------
      |     31
```

We have 87 as the quotient and 31 as the remainder.

The number 7,600 is greater than the square of the number 87 by 31. The next perfect square for 88 is 7,744. Hence, we need to add a number to 7,600 that will make it 7,744. This number is: 7744 − 7600 = 144.

Thus, if we add 144 to 7,600 we get a perfect square, the square root of which is 88.

Alert!

1. To find the smallest number that is to be subtracted to get a perfect square, the remainder after the long division method is to be subtracted from the perfect square.
2. To find the smallest number that is to be added to get a perfect square, we find the next square from the quotient derived by the long division method. Then the difference between this square and the number given is added to get the perfect square.

Square Roots of Decimals by the Long Division Method

The method is similar to what we have learnt earlier. The only difference is in the pairing of the digits and placing the bars. In a decimal number, the pairs are made keeping the decimal point as the centre. In the digits on the right side of the decimal point, the bars are placed on every two numbers starting from the decimal point and continuing on the right. Similarly, for the digits on the left side of the decimal point, the bars are placed on every two numbers starting from the decimal point and continuing on the left.

Examples: $\overleftarrow{67} \cdot \overrightarrow{25}$

$\overline{1}\,\overleftarrow{42} \cdot \overrightarrow{62}\,\overline{5}$

We know that the decimal number 4.265 can be written as 4.2650 and both are equal. Hence, if a given number has odd number of digits after the decimal point, we can add a 0 in the end to get even places and then place the bar on the two digits.

Examples: Find the square roots of the following.

a. 42.25

We continue with the long division method as explained earlier but place the bars as explained above.

	6 · 5
6	$\overline{42} \cdot \overline{25}$
+6	−36 ↓
125	6 25
	−6 25

Place the decimal point in the quotient as soon as the digits in the decimal place are brought down.

Hence $\sqrt{42.25} = 6.5$

b. 23.04

	4 . 8
4	$\overline{23} . \overline{04}$
+4	16 ↓
88	7 04
	−7 04
	0

Place the decimal point in the quotient as soon as the digits in the decimal place are brought down.

Hence, $\sqrt{23.04} = 4.8$

c. 449.44

	2 1 . 2
2	$\overline{4}\ \overline{49}.\overline{44}$
+2	−4
41	49
+1	41
422	8 44
	−8 44
	0

Hence, $\sqrt{449.44} = 21.2$

Approximate Value of a Square Root

When a number is not a perfect square, we find the square root to an approximate value using the long division method. If we have to find the value of the square root of a number upto two places of the decimal, we find the square root upto three places of the decimal and then round it off.

Example 1: Find the square root of 20.592 upto two places of the decimal.

We find the square root by the long division method upto three places of the decimal and then round it off. We add zeros where required, place the bars and then start the division.

	4 · 5 3 7
4	$\overline{20}\cdot\overline{59}\ \overline{20}\ \overline{00}$
+4	−16
8 5	4 59
+5	− 4 25
903	34 20
+3	−27 09
9067	7 11 00
	−63 4 69
	7 6 31

The square root is 4.537. Since 7 is greater than 5, we round off to 4.54.

The square root of 20.59 upto two places, of the decimal is 4.54.

Example 2: Find the square root of 0.3745 upto three places of the decimal.

	0 · 6 1 1 9
0	0 · 37 45 00 00
+0	
06	37
+6	−36
121	1 45
+1	−1 21
1221	24 00
+1	−12 21
12229	11 79 00
	−11 00 61
	7 8 39

The square root is 0.6119. Since 9 is greater than 5, we round off as 0.612.

The square root of 0.3745 upto three places of the decimal is 0.612.

Example 3: Find the square root of 5 upto two places of the decimal.

	2 · 2 3 6
2	5 . 00 00 00
+2	−4
42	1 00
+2	84
443	16 00
+3	13 29
4466	27100
	−26796
	304

The square root is 2.236. Since 6 is greater than 5, we round off to 2.24.

The square root of 5 upto two places of the decimal is 2.24.

Estimating the Square Root

We know that the square root of 100 is 10 and the square root of 400 is 20.

If we have to find the square root of 300, which is not a perfect square, it will be between 10 and 20. We estimate the square root of 300.

Here, $17^2 = 289$ and $18^2 = 324$.

Since 300 is between 324 and 289, the $\sqrt{300}$ will be between $\sqrt{324}$ and $\sqrt{289}$.

Since, $300 - 289 = 11$ and $324 - 300 = 24$, we can say that 300 is closer to 289 than to 324. In this case, the estimation of $\sqrt{300}$ will be 17. We can confirm this by the long division method.

Examples: Estimate the square root of the following.

a. 150

To estimate the square root of 150, we find a number that is closest to it.

We know that $12^2 = 144$ and $13^2 = 169$.

The square root of 150 lies between $\sqrt{144}$ and $\sqrt{169}$.

Now, $150 - 144 = 6$ and $169 - 150 = 19$.

The square root of 150 will be closer to 12.

The approximate value of $\sqrt{150} = 12$.

b. 227

We know that $15^2 = 225$ and $16^2 = 256$.

Hence, the square root of 225 is equal to 15 and the square root of 256 is equal to 16.

Thus, $\sqrt{227}$ will lie between 15 and 16.

By subtracting, $227 - 225 = 2$ and $256 - 227 = 29$.

Since, 227 is closer to 225 than 256, the approximate value of $\sqrt{227}$ is 15.

Practice Exercise 2.3

1. Find the square root of the following numbers using the long division method.

   a. 3,481 b. 9,216 c. 9,409 d. 10,201 e. 11,881
   f. 60,025 g. 99,856 h. 1,10,889 i. 3,90,625 j. 1,68,100

2. Find the smallest number that should be subtracted from the following numbers to get a perfect square. Find the square root of the perfect square.

   a. 2,509 b. 7,581 c. 6,252 d. 12,330 e. 45,156

3. Find the smallest number that should be added to the following numbers to get a perfect square. Find the square root of the perfect square.

   a. 6,203 b. 8,400 c. 10,460 d. 15,185 e. 44,841

4. Find the square root of the following decimal numbers.

   a. 73.96 b. 132.25 c. 249.64 d. 26.2144 e. 412.4961

5. Find the approximate value of the square root of the following numbers upto three places of the decimal.

   a. 1.45 b. 0.052 c. 4.3025 d. 0.3745 e. 84.8241

6. Estimate the square root of the following numbers.

   a. 90 b. 250 c. 375 d. 889 e. 650

7. Find the length of the side of a square whose area is 104.6529 m^2.
8. Find the length of each side of a square whose area is equal to the area of a rectangle of length 13.6 m and breadth 3.4 m.
9. Find the greatest five-digit number that is a perfect square.

10. A battalion of 3,100 jawans had to stand in rows and columns for an 'Army Day' function. The number of rows and columns were the same. Some of the jawans who were being honoured stood in a special squad. Find the number of jawans who stood in a special squad. How many rows in all were there for the rest of the jawans?

Cubes

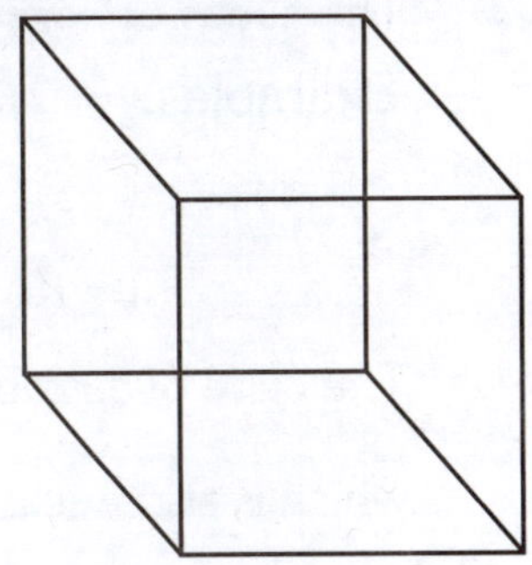

All objects in the world are three-dimensional. They have length, breadth and height. Three-dimensional figures are called solid figures. A cube is a solid figure that has all sides equal in measurement.

A cube has six faces, twelve edges and eight vertices. If a cube has an edge of 2 cm, it has length, breadth and height of 2 cm each and its volume will be equal to $2 \times 2 \times 2$ cm^3 = 8 cm^3.

If we multiply a number by itself twice, we get the cube of a number. Examples are, $3 \times 3 \times 3 = 3^3$ or $10 \times 10 \times 10 = 10^3$.
If 'n' is a natural number, then $n \times n \times n = n^3$. The numbers are read as three cube, ten cube and 'n' cube, respectively.

While a square represents area, a cube represents volume.

In the first nine natural numbers, there are only two numbers whose cubes are single-digit numbers, there are only two numbers whose cubes are two-digit numbers there are five numbers whose cubes are three-digit numbers.

Perfect Cubes

A number 'y' is said to be a perfect cube if there is an integer x such that $y = x \times x \times x$.

In order to check whether a given number is a perfect cube or not, we express the given number in the form of prime factors. We then group the factors in triplets so that all three factors of the triplets are the same. If some factor is left ungrouped or does not form a triplet, the given number is not a perfect cube. If no factor is left ungrouped, we choose factors from each triplet and multiply them. The resultant number is the cube of the given number. The following table gives the cubes of the first twenty natural numbers.

Table 2.3 Cubes of the first twenty natural numbers

Number	Cube	Number	Cube
1	1	11	1331
2	8	12	1728
3	27	13	2197
4	64	14	2744
5	125	15	3375
6	216	16	4096
7	343	17	4913
8	512	18	5832
9	729	19	6859
10	1000	20	8000

Properties of Cubes

1. The cubes of even natural numbers are always even.

   Examples: $8^3 = 512$; $14^3 = 2,744$; $16^3 = 4,096$.

2. The cubes of odd natural numbers are always odd.

   Examples: $5^3 = 125$; $11^3 = 1,331$; $15^3 = 3,375$.

3. The cubes of negative integers are always negative.

   Examples: $(-2)^3 = (-2) \times (-2) \times (-2) = (-8)$

   $(-5)^3 = (-5) \times (-5) \times (-5) = (-125)$

   $(-10)^3 = (-10) \times (-10) \times (-10) = (-1,000)$

4. The cube of a rational number $\frac{a}{b}$ is $\frac{a^3}{b^3}$. The number can also be written as $\left(\frac{a}{b}\right)^3$, which is also equal to $\frac{a^3}{b^3}$.

   Example 1: $\left(\frac{2}{3}\right)^3 = \frac{2^3}{3^3} = \frac{8}{27}$

   Example 2: $\left(-\frac{4}{5}\right)^3 = \frac{(-4)^3}{5^3} = \left(-\frac{64}{125}\right)$

   Example 3: $\left(\frac{10}{-11}\right)^3 = \frac{10^3}{(-11)^3} = \frac{1000}{(-1331)} = \frac{(-1000)}{1331}$

5. The cube of the product of numbers is equal to the product of their cubes. Consider two number a and b.

   Here, $(a \times b)^3 = a^3 \times b^3.$

   Example 1: $(2 \times 3)^3 = 2^3 \times 3^3 = 8 \times 27 = 216$ or $(2 \times 3)^3 = 6^3 = 216$

   Example 2: $(4 \times 5)^3 = 4^3 \times 5^3 = 64 \times 125 = 8,000$ or $(4 \times 5)^3 = 20^3 = 8,000$

   Example 3: $[(-2) \times 4]^3 = (-2)^3 \times 4^3 = (-8) \times 64 = -512$ or $[(-2) \times 4]^3 = (-8)^3 = (-512)$

Alert!

The square of a negative integer is positive but the cube of a negative integer is negative.

6. The cube of any multiple of 2 is divisible by 8.

   Examples: $4^3 = 64$

   $6^3 = 216$

   $14^3 = 2744$

   Thus, $(2n)^3 = 2n \times 2n \times 2n$

   $= 2 \times n \times 2 \times n \times 2 \times n$

   $= 8 \times n^3$

   The cube of any multiple of 3 is divisible by 27.

Examples: $3^3 = 27$

$6^3 = 216$

$9^3 = 729$

Thus, $(3n)^3 = 3n \times 3n \times 3n$

$= 3 \times n \times 3 \times n \times 3 \times n$

$= 27 \times n^3$

Digits in the One's Place of Numbers and their Cubes

1. If the digit in the one's place of a number is either 0, 1, 4, 5, 6 or 9, then the digit in the one's place of the cube of the number will also be the same.

Examples:

Digits	Cubes	Cubes	Cubes
0	$10^3 = 1000$;	$20^3 = 8000$;	$30^3 = 27000$
1	$11^3 = 1331$;	$21^3 = 9261$;	$31^3 = 29791$
4	$14^3 = 2744$;	$24^3 = 13824$;	$34^3 = 39304$
5	$15^3 = 3375$;	$25^3 = 15625$;	$35^3 = 42875$
6	$16^3 = 4096$;	$26^3 = 17576$;	$36^3 = 46656$
9	$19^3 = 6859$;	$29^3 = 24389$;	$39^3 = 59319$

2. If the digit in the one's place of a number is 2, then the digit in the one's place of its cube is 8 and vice versa.

Examples:

Digits	Cubes	Cubes	Cubes
2	$12^3 = 1728$;	$22^3 = 10648$;	$32^3 = 32768$
8	$18^3 = 5832$;	$28^3 = 21952$;	$38^3 = 54872$

3. If the digit in the one's place is 3, then the digit in the one's place of its cube is 7 and vice versa.

Examples:

Digits	Cubes	Cubes	Cubes
3	$13^3 = 2197$;	$23^3 = 12167$;	$33^3 = 35937$
7	$17^3 =4913$;	$27^3 = 19683$;	$37^3 = 50653$

Alert!

The digit in the one's place of a number and the digit in the one's place of the cube of the number are tabulated below.

Digits in the one's place	0	1	2	3	4	5	6	7	8	9
Digits in the one's place of their cubes	0	1	8	7	4	5	6	3	2	9

Example 1: Find the cubes of the following numbers.

a. $\frac{2}{3}$ $\left(\frac{2}{3}\right)^3 = \frac{2^3}{3^3} = \frac{2 \times 2 \times 2}{3 \times 3 \times 3} = \frac{8}{27}$

b. 0.8 $(0.8)^3 = \left(\frac{8}{10}\right)^3 = \frac{8^3}{10^3} = \frac{512}{1000} = 0.512$

c. $5\frac{1}{2}$ $\left(5\frac{1}{2}\right)^3 = \left(\frac{11}{2}\right)^3 = \frac{11^3}{2^3} = \frac{1331}{8}$

d. $\left(\frac{-1}{7}\right)$ $\left(\frac{-1}{7}\right)^3 = \frac{(-1)^3}{(7)^3} = \frac{(-1)}{343}$

e. (-1.4) $(-1.4)^3 = \left(\frac{-14}{10}\right)^3 = \frac{(-14)^3}{(10)^3} = \frac{(-2744)}{1000} = (-2.744)$

Example 2: Find the volume of a cube having an edge of 3.2 cm.

Volume $= (\text{Edge})^3 = (3.2 \text{ cm})^3$

$(3.2 \text{ cm})^3 = \left(\frac{32}{10} \text{ cm}\right)^3 = \frac{32^3}{10^3} \text{ cm}^3 = \frac{32768}{1000} \text{ cm}^3 = 32.768 \text{ cm}^3$

The volume of the cube is 32.768 cm^3.

Example 3: Write the digit in the one's place of the cubes of the following numbers using the rules discussed earlier. Find the cubes of the numbers and verify your answers.

a. 72 b. 49 c. 33 d. 40 e. 57

f. 56 g. 81 h. 64 i. 75 j. 28

	Number	Unit's digit in cube	Cube		Number	Unit's digit in cube	Cube
a.	72	8	3,73,248	f.	56	6	1,75,616
b.	49	9	1,17,649	g.	81	1	5,31,441
c.	33	7	35,937	h.	64	4	2,62,144
d.	40	0	64,000	i.	75	5	4,21,875
e.	57	3	1,85,193	j.	28	2	21,952

Alert!

If a number has one place of decimal, its square will have two places of decimal and its cube will have three places of decimal.

Practice Exercise 2.4

1. Find the cubes of the following rational numbers.

   a. $\frac{7}{11}$ b. $\left(-\frac{4}{5}\right)$ c. $\left(-\frac{6}{13}\right)$ d. $3\frac{1}{4}$ e. $2\frac{3}{8}$

2. Find the cubes of the following decimal numbers.

   a. 0.5 b. (−0.06) c. (−3.2) d. 4.1 e. 2.5

3. Find the digit in the one's place of the cubes of the following numbers using the rules discussed earlier. Verify by finding the cubes.

a. 65	b. 89	c. 77	d. 90	e. 32
f. 51	g. 63	h. 84	i. 36	j. 58

4. Find the volume of a cube using the following measures of the edge.

   a. 1.5 cm b. 2.4 cm c. 3.6 cm d. 2.13 cm e. 0.7 cm

5. Indicate whether the following statements are true (T) or false (F).
   a. Perfect cubes of odd numbers are even.
   b. The cube of a negative number is positive.
   c. Perfect cubes may end in an even number of zeroes.
   d. For a number to be a perfect cube, it must have prime factors that are in pairs.
   e. The number 6,400 is a perfect cube.

Cube Roots

The cube root of a natural number is that number whose cube is equal to the natural number. If n is a natural number such that $n^3 = x$, then n is said to be the cube root of x.

The symbol for cube root is $\sqrt[3]{\ }$. As the cube of 3 is 27, 3 is the cube root of 27.

Finding the Cube Root of a Perfect Cube by the Factorisation Method

To find the cube root of a perfect cube, we follow the steps given below:

Step 1 Write the given number as a product of prime factors.

Step 2 Make sets of three similar factors.

Step 3 Take one factor from each triplet and write their product.

Step 4 The product obtained is the required cube root.

Example 1: Find the cube root of 216.

Find the prime factors of 216.

2	216
2	108
2	54
3	27
3	9
3	3
	1

The prime factors of 216 are $\underbrace{2 \times 2 \times 2}_{2} \times \underbrace{3 \times 3 \times 3}_{3}$.

We select one factor from each set, that is 2 and 3.

Thus, the cube root of 216 = 2 × 3 = 6.

Example 2: Find the cube root of (-4096).

The cube root of a negative number is negative.

Find the prime factors of $(-4{,}096)$.

2	4096
2	2048
2	1024
2	512
2	256
2	128
2	64
2	32
2	16
2	8
2	4
2	2
	1

The prime factors of 4,096

$$= \underbrace{2 \times 2 \times 2}_{2} \times \underbrace{2 \times 2 \times 2}_{2} \times \underbrace{2 \times 2 \times 2}_{2} \times \underbrace{2 \times 2 \times 2}_{2}$$

Multiplying one factor from each set: $2 \times 2 \times 2 \times 2$.

Thus the cube root of $(-4096) = -(2 \times 2 \times 2 \times 2)$
$= (-16)$ or

$\sqrt[3]{-4096} = (-16)$.

Example 3: By which smallest number should 8,232 be multiplied to make it a perfect cube? Find the cube root of the perfect cube.

Find the prime factors of 8,232.

2	8232
2	4116
2	2058
3	1029
7	343
7	49
7	7
	1

The prime factors are $\underbrace{2 \times 2 \times 2} \times 3 \times \underbrace{7 \times 7 \times 7}$.

Here, we have two sets of three numbers each, namely, 2 and 7. However, the last set comprises only one number, namely, 3. To make it a set of three numbers, we need to multiply it by 3×3. Hence, to make 8,232 a perfect cube, we need to multiply it by 3×3.

Thus, the smallest number that we need to multiply 8,232 with to make it a perfect cube is 9.

The perfect cube will be $8{,}232 \times 9 = 74{,}088$. The cube root is $2 \times 3 \times 7 = 42$.

Example 4: By which smallest number should 6,655 be divided to make it a perfect cube? Find the cube root of the perfect cube.

Find the prime factors of 6,655.

5	6655
11	1331
11	121
11	11
	1

The prime factors of 6,655 are $5 \times \underbrace{11 \times 11 \times 11}$. Here, 5 is a factor which does not form a triplet. Hence, we divide 6,655 by 5 and get 1,331. Thus, the cube root of 1,331 is 11.

Estimating the Cube Root

We know the perfect cubes of the first twenty natural numbers from Table 2.3 of cubes. Here, the $\sqrt[3]{343}$ is 7 and the $\sqrt[3]{1000}$ is 10, but we do not know the $\sqrt[3]{500}$ since it is not a perfect cube. However, it is possible to estimate the cube root of a number between two perfect cubes. For example, the cube of 7 is 343, and the $\sqrt[3]{343}$ is 7. The cube of 8 is 512 and the $\sqrt[3]{512}$ is 8. If we have to find the cube root of 400, we know that it will be between $\sqrt[3]{343}$ and $\sqrt[3]{512}$ since 400 lies between 343 and 512. As $\sqrt[3]{343}$ is 7 and $\sqrt[3]{512}$ is 8, the cube root of 400 will lie between 7 and 8.

To represent this, $343 < 400 < 512$

$$\sqrt[3]{343} < \sqrt[3]{400} < \sqrt[3]{512}$$

$$7 < \sqrt[3]{400} < 8$$

However, $400 - 343 = 57$ and $512 - 400 = 112$.

The difference between 400 and 343 is less than the difference between 512 and 400, thus the approximate value of $\sqrt[3]{400} = 7$.

Practice Exercise 2.5

1. Find the cube root of the following numbers.

   a. (−125) b. (−2,197) c. 3,375 d. 27,000 e. 42,875

   f. 35,937 g. 74,088 h. (−59,319) i. 91,125 j. (−46,656)

2. Find the cube root of the following numbers.

   a. $2\frac{93}{125}$ b. $1\frac{91}{125}$ c. 0.001 d. 0.064 e. (−0.125)

   f. $\left(-2\frac{10}{27}\right)$ g. $1\frac{271}{729}$ h. 0.343 i. (−0.729) j. 0.001331

3. Find the cube root of the following numbers.

   a. 4.096 b. 9.261 c. 42.875 d. 74.088 e. 110.592

4. By which smallest number should we multiply the following numbers to make them perfect cubes? Find the cube root of the perfect cube.

   a. 6,655 b. 31,944 c. 2,00,704 d. 64,827 e. 1,63,840

5. By which smallest number should we divide the following numbers to make them perfect cubes? Find the cube root of the perfect cube.

   a. 30,375 b. 43,200 c. 16,384 d. 24,000 e. 1,45,800

6. Estimate the cube root of the following numbers.

   a. 200 b. 800 c. 1,500 d. 2,500 e. 5,000

7. Verify the following equations.

a. $\sqrt[3]{27} \times \sqrt[3]{64} = \sqrt[3]{27 \times 64}$

b. $\sqrt[3]{216} \div \sqrt[3]{8} = \sqrt[3]{\dfrac{216}{8}}$

c. $\sqrt[3]{125} \times \sqrt[3]{1000} = \sqrt[3]{125 \times 1000}$

d. $\sqrt[3]{1000} \div \sqrt[3]{125} = \sqrt[3]{\dfrac{1000}{125}}$

e. $\sqrt[3]{1331} \times \sqrt[3]{8} = \sqrt[3]{1331 \times 8}$

8. The volume of a cube is 17.576 cm^3. Find the length of an edge of the cube.

9. The volume of a cube is 0.125 cm^3. Find the length of its edge. If the length of the edge is increased three times, by how many times will the volume increase?

10. The volume of a cube is double the volume of a cuboid. If the volume of the cuboid is 6.912 cm^3, find the length of an edge of the cube.

Higher Order Thinking Skills

HOTS

1. Two towers AB and CD are 20 m and 25 m high, respectively. The base of the towers is 12 m apart. What is the distance between their tops?

2. Find the sum of the cubes of the first five natural numbers. Verify your answer using the formula $\left[\dfrac{n(n+1)}{2}\right]^2$, where n is a natural number.

   Also find the sum of the cubes of the first ten natural numbers.

3. Sonia drove 15 km north to a shopping mall and then 8 km east to her friend's house. While returning home from her friend's house, she took the diagonal path. What distance did she cover on her journey back home?

Spot the odd one out.

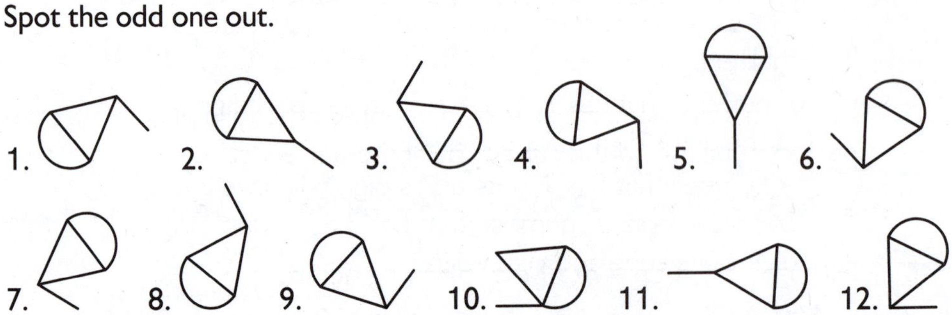

Answer for Brainteaser on page 50

Highlights

- A natural number 'm' is a perfect square if there exists another natural number 'n' such that $n^2 = m$.
- All perfect squares end in 0, 1, 4, 5, 6 or 9.
- If a number ends in 2,3,7,8 or an odd number of zero, it is not a perfect square.
- The squares of even numbers are always even and the squares of odd numbers are always odd.
- The squares of negative integers are always positive.
- The difference of the squares of two consecutive numbers is equal to their sum.
- The sum of the first odd natural number 'n' is n^2.
- The square of any natural number 'n' can be expressed as the sum of the first 'n' odd numbers.
- A triplet of three natural numbers a, b and c is called a Pythagorean triplet, if $a^2 + b^2 = c^2$, where c is the largest number.
- The square root of a number x is that number which when multiplied by itself gives x as the product, that is, $y \times y = x$ or $y = \sqrt{x}$.
- The symbol for square root is $\sqrt{\ }$.
- The square root of a perfect square number can be found by the method of prime factorisation.
- There are two integral square roots of a square number: $\sqrt{x}$ and $-\sqrt{x}$.
- The long division method can be used to find the square root of any number.
- For any two positive numbers a and b, we have
  1. $\sqrt{ab} = \sqrt{a} \times \sqrt{b}$ and 2. $\sqrt{\frac{a}{b}} = \frac{\sqrt{a}}{\sqrt{b}}$
- A number x is a perfect cube if $x = n^3$, where n is any natural number.
- A natural number n is the cube root of x, if $n = \sqrt[3]{x}$.
- The cube of an even natural number is always even.
- The cube of an odd natural number is always odd.
- The cube of a negative integer is always negative.
- If a and b are two integers, then $(a \times b)^3 = a^3 \times b^3$ and $\left(\frac{a}{b}\right)^3 = \frac{a^3}{b^3}$, where a and $b \neq 0$.
- If a and b are two integers, then $\sqrt[3]{a} \times \sqrt[3]{b} = \sqrt[3]{a \times b}$ and $\frac{\sqrt[3]{a}}{\sqrt[3]{b}} = \sqrt[3]{\frac{a}{b}}$, where a and $b \neq 0$.
- The cube root of perfect cubes can be found by the prime factorisation method.
- A number that has 1, 4, 5, 6 or 9 in its unit's digit will have the same numbers in the unit's digit of its cube.
- A number that has 2 in its unit's digit will have 8 in the unit's digit of its cube and vice versa. A number that has 3 in its unit's digit will have 7 in the unit's digit of its cube and vice versa.

Maths Lab Activity

Numbering a Line

Aim: To identify and write appropriate numbers on the number line.

Material required: a pen

Method: Fill in the missing numbers on each number line given below.

1. 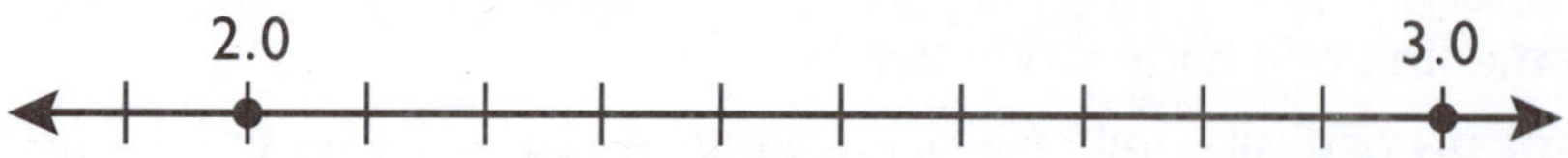

2. 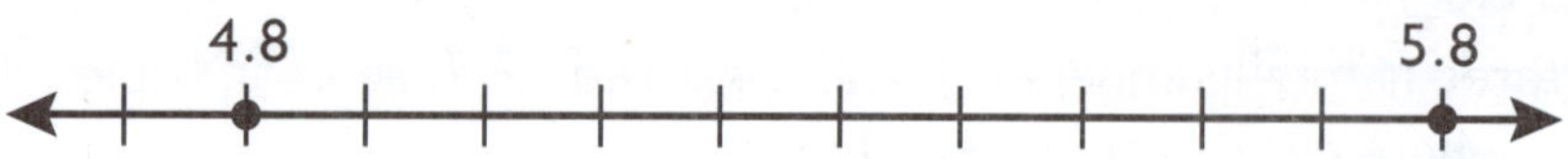

3. 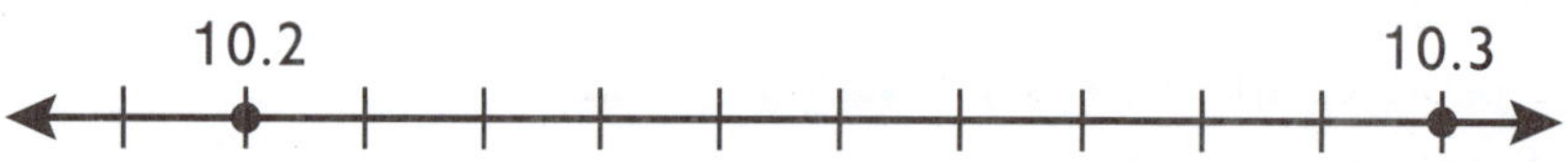

4. 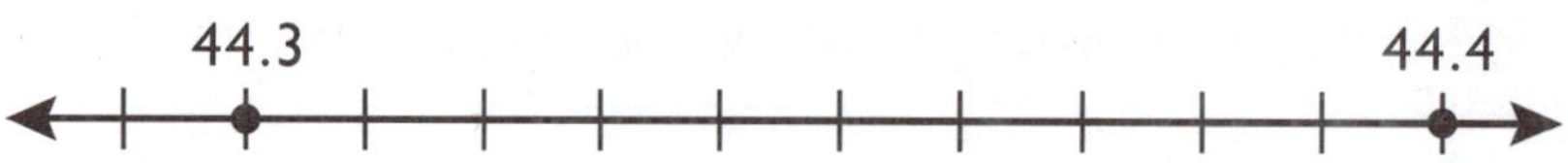

5. 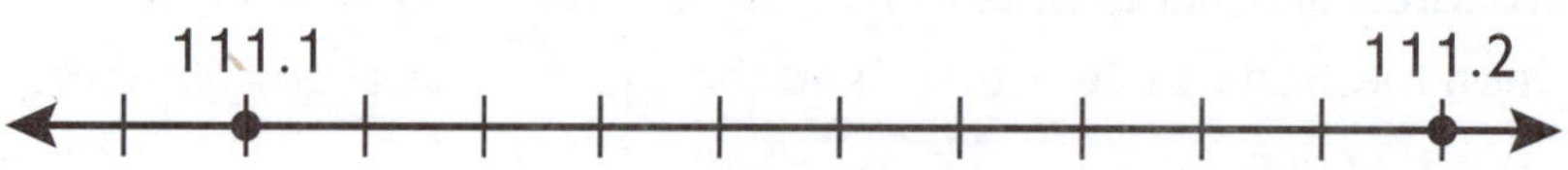

Write the number that is halfway between the two numbers in each case.

1. Between 2 and 10

2. Between 3 and 9

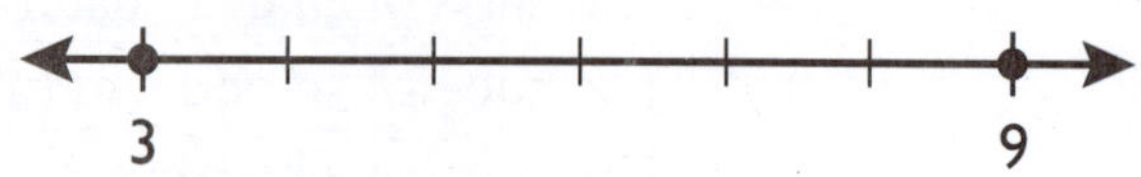

3. Between 1 and 7

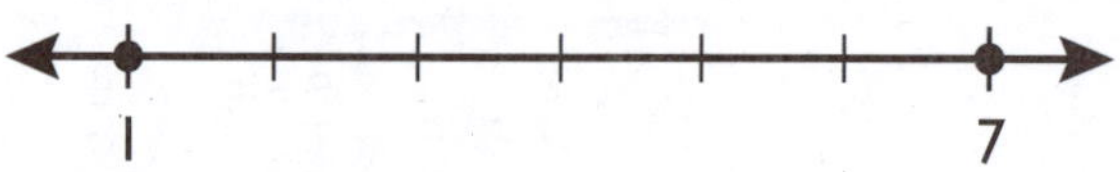

4. Between 10 and 18

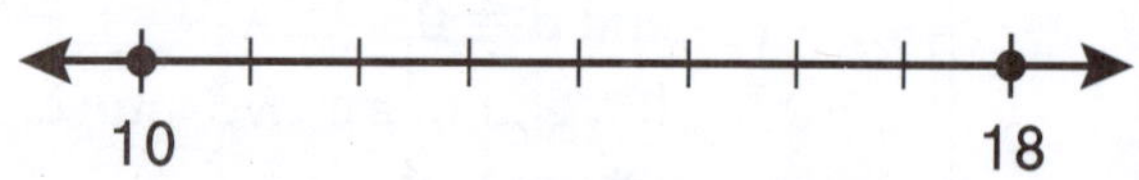

5. Between 80 and 84

6. Between 120 and 126

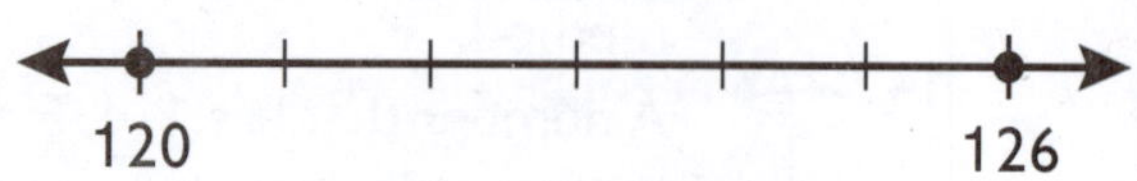

7. Between 552 and 558

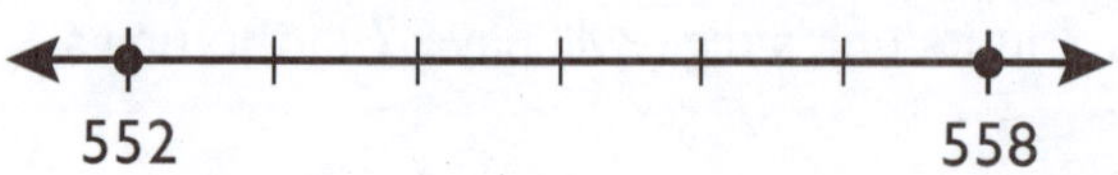

8. Between 1234 and 1242

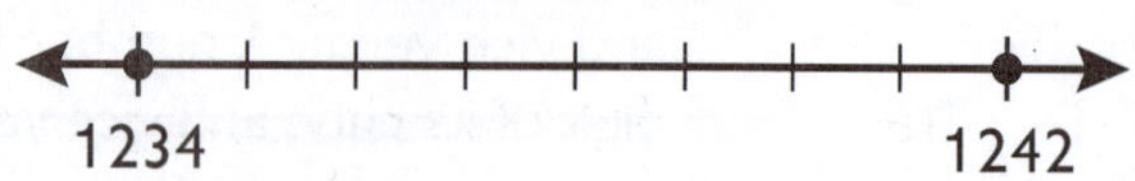

Rewind

CHAPTERS 1–2

1. Find the sum of the rational numbers $\frac{(-5)}{16}$ and $\frac{7}{12}$.

2. Find the value of $\frac{(-9)}{16} \times \frac{8}{15}$.

3. Sujata bought $2\frac{1}{2}$ kg of onions at ₹$18\frac{1}{2}$ per kg and $3\frac{3}{4}$ kg of potatoes at ₹$12\frac{1}{2}$ per kg. How much did she pay the shopkeeper?

4. Find the value of $\left(\frac{2}{5}\right)^{(-3)}$.

5. Simplify $\left\{\left(\frac{1}{3}\right)^{(-3)} - \left(\frac{1}{2}\right)^{(-3)}\right\} \div \left(\frac{1}{4}\right)^{(-3)}$.

6. Find the value of x if $\left(\frac{7}{12}\right)^{(-4)} \times \left(\frac{7}{12}\right)^{3x} = \left(\frac{7}{12}\right)^{5}$.

7. Which of the following rational numbers is in the standard form?

   a. $\frac{(-12)}{26}$ b. $\frac{(-49)}{91}$ c. $\frac{(-9)}{16}$ d. $\frac{28}{(-105)}$

8. The product of two rational numbers is $\frac{(-16)}{9}$. If one of the numbers is $\frac{(-4)}{3}$, find the other.

9. How many square metres of glass will be required for a window which has six panes, each pane measuring 25 cm by 14 cm?

10. Express the following rational numbers as exponents.

    a. $\frac{1}{27}$ b. $\left(-\frac{1}{243}\right)$ c. $\left(-\frac{1}{64}\right)$

    d. $\left(-\frac{1}{1000}\right)$ e. $\left(-\frac{243}{3125}\right)$

11. Simplify the following.

    a. $\left(\frac{3}{4}\right)^{3} \times \left(\frac{4}{9}\right)^{3}$ b. $\left(\frac{5}{11}\right)^{6} \div \left(\frac{10}{11}\right)^{6}$ c. $\left(\frac{1}{4}\right)^{2} \times \left(\frac{1}{2}\right)^{4} \div \left(\frac{1}{4}\right)^{3}$

    d. $\left(\frac{2}{3}\right)^{5} \times \left(\frac{4}{9}\right)^{2} \div \left(\frac{2}{3}\right)^{9}$ e. $\left(\frac{1}{5}\right)^{4} \div \left(\frac{2}{5}\right)^{4} \times (2)^{4}$

12. From an 11 m wire, two pieces of lengths $2\frac{2}{3}$ m, and $3\frac{3}{10}$ m are cut off. What is the length of the remaining wire?

13. Find the perimeter of a rectangular park that is $36\frac{3}{5}$ m long and $16\frac{2}{3}$ m broad.

14. An aeroplane covers 1,020 km in an hour. How much distance will it cover in $4\frac{1}{6}$ hours?

15. If $\frac{3}{5}$th of a number exceeds its $\frac{2}{7}$th by 44, find the number.

16. Find three rational numbers between $\frac{1}{4}$ and $\frac{1}{3}$.

17. Divide the sum of $\frac{65}{12}$ and $\frac{8}{3}$ by their difference.

18. Verify the following and name the property used.

a. $\frac{3}{7} \times \left(\frac{5}{6} + \frac{12}{13}\right) = \left(\frac{3}{7} \times \frac{5}{6}\right) + \left(\frac{3}{7} \times \frac{12}{13}\right)$

b. $\left(\frac{(-8)}{3} + \frac{(-13)}{12}\right) \times \frac{5}{6} = \left(\frac{(-8)}{3} \times \frac{5}{6}\right) + \left(\frac{(-13)}{12} \times \frac{5}{6}\right)$

c. $\frac{(-16)}{7} \times \left(\frac{(-8)}{9} + \frac{(-7)}{6}\right) = \left(\frac{(-16)}{7} \times \frac{(-8)}{9}\right) + \left(\frac{(-16)}{7} \times \frac{(-7)}{6}\right)$

19. Fill in the boxes with the correct symbol (>, = or <).

a. $\frac{(-3)}{7}$ ☐ $\frac{6}{(-13)}$ b. $\frac{5}{(-13)}$ ☐ $\frac{(-35)}{91}$

c. (-2) ☐ $\frac{(-13)}{5}$ d. $\frac{(-2)}{3}$ ☐ $\frac{(-5)}{8}$

d. 0 ☐ $\frac{(-3)}{(-5)}$

20. Write the following numbers in their scientific notation.

a. 276000000000 b. 0.000000000076 c. 0.0000000000001

Answer for Brainteaser from page 46

10.

Exponents

CHAPTER 3

We have learnt about squares and cubes. When 3 is multiplied by itself we get $3 \times 3 = 3^2$ and we read it as 3 square or 3 to the power of 2. If 4 is multiplied by itself three times we get $4 \times 4 \times 4 = 4^3$ and we read it as 4 cube or 4 to the power of 3. Taking this further, if we write $4 \times 4 \times 4 \times 4 \times 4$, it means the number 4 is multiplied by itself 5 times and we write it as 4^5. A number multiplied by itself many times is written in the power relation or the exponential notation.

In 3^2, 3 is the base and 2 is the power or the exponent.

In 4^3, 4 is the base and 3 is the power or the exponent.

In 4^5, 4 is the base and 5 is the power or the exponent.

If a is a rational number, then n times the product of a with itself be represented by a^n.

$$a^n = \underbrace{a \times a \times a \times \ldots \times a}_{n \text{ times}}$$

Here a is called the base and n is the power or the exponent of a.

1. If a is positive, the value of a^n is always positive.
2. If a is negative, the value of a^n will depend on the value of n:
   a. If n is an even number, then a^n will be positive.
   b. If n is an odd number, then a^n will be negative.

   Here, a and b are non-zero integers, such that $\frac{a}{b}$ is any rational number and n is any positive number.

If a and b are non-zero integers such that $\frac{a}{b}$ is any rational number and n is any positive integer then

$$\left(\frac{a}{b}\right)^n = \frac{a^n}{b^n} \quad \text{and} \quad \left(-\frac{a}{b}\right)^n = (-1)^n \quad \frac{a^n}{b^n}$$

Reciprocals or Negative Exponents

The reciprocal of a rational number x is denoted by $x^{(-1)}$ and is written as $x^{(-1)} = \frac{1}{x}$.

In general, for a non-zero integer a we have $a^{(-m)} = \frac{1}{a^m}$.

We say that $a^{(-m)}$ is the reciprocal or multiplicative inverse of a^m and vice versa.

Example 1: $5^{(-2)} = \frac{1}{5^2} = \frac{1}{5 \times 5} = \frac{1}{25}$

Example 2: $2^{(-6)} = \frac{1}{2^6} = \frac{1}{2 \times 2 \times 2 \times 2 \times 2 \times 2}$

In these two examples we see that $5^2 = 25$ and $2^6 = 64$.

If we multiply 5^2 by $5^{(-2)}$, we get $25 \times \frac{1}{25} = 1$. Similarly, when we multiply 2^6 by $2^{(-6)}$ we get $64 \times \frac{1}{64} = 1$.

Thus, $a^m \times a^{(-m)} = 1$, where a^m and $a^{(-m)}$ are called the reciprocals or multiplicative inverses of each other, since their product is equal to 1.

Also the reciprocal of $\left(\frac{a}{b}\right)$, where a and b are non-zero integers, is given by $\left(\frac{b}{a}\right)$ or

$$\left(\frac{a}{b}\right)^{(-1)} = \frac{1}{\left(\frac{a}{b}\right)} = \frac{b}{a}$$

We can derive a general formula: $\left(\frac{a}{b}\right)^{(-m)} = \frac{1}{\left(\frac{a}{b}\right)^m} = \left(\frac{b}{a}\right)^m$

Also $x^{(-m)} = \frac{1}{x^m}$ and $\frac{1}{x^{(-m)}} = x^m$

Example 1: Express each of the following products in the power notation (exponential notation). Identify the respective bases and exponents.

a. $3 \times 3 \times 3 \times 3 \times 3$

$= 3^5$

The base is 3 and the exponent or power is 5.

b. $(-7) \times (-7) \times (-7) \times (-7)$

$= (-7)^4$

The base is (-7) and the exponent or power is 4.

c. $\frac{1}{2} \times \frac{1}{2} \times \frac{1}{2} \times \frac{1}{2} \times \frac{1}{2} \times \frac{1}{2}$

$= \left(\frac{1}{2}\right)^6$

The base is $\frac{1}{2}$ and the exponent or power is 6.

Example 2: Find the values of the following.

a. $(5)^3$

$= 5 \times 5 \times 5 = 125$

b. $(-4)^5$

$= (-4) \times (-4) \times (-4) \times (-4) \times (-4) = (-1024)$

c. $\left(\frac{1}{3}\right)^4$

$= \frac{1}{3} \times \frac{1}{3} \times \frac{1}{3} \times \frac{1}{3} = \frac{1}{81}$

Example 3: Verify each of the following.

a. $\left(\frac{2}{5}\right)^4 = \frac{2^4}{5^4}$

Solving LHS: $\left(\frac{2}{5}\right)^4 = \frac{2}{5} \times \frac{2}{5} \times \frac{2}{5} \times \frac{2}{5} = \frac{16}{625}$

$\frac{16}{625} = \frac{2^4}{5^4}$

Solving RHS: $\frac{2^4}{5^4} = \frac{2 \times 2 \times 2 \times 2}{5 \times 5 \times 5 \times 5} = \frac{16}{625}$

LHS = RHS

$\therefore \left(\frac{2}{5}\right)^4 = \frac{2^4}{5^4}$

b. $\left(\frac{-3}{7}\right)^3 = \frac{(-3)^3}{(7)^3}$

Solving LHS: $\left(\frac{-3}{7}\right)^3 = \frac{(-3)}{7} \times \frac{(-3)}{7} \times \frac{(-3)}{7} = \frac{(-27)}{343}$

Solving RHS: $\frac{(-3)^3}{(7)^3} = \frac{(-3) \times (-3) \times (-3)}{7 \times 7 \times 7} = \frac{(-27)}{343}$

$\therefore \left(\frac{-3}{7}\right)^3 = \frac{(-3)^3}{7^3} = \frac{(-27)}{343}$

c. $(2 \times 3)^5 = 2^5 \times 3^5$

Solving LHS: $(2 \times 3)^5 = 6 \times 6 \times 6 \times 6 \times 6 = 7{,}776$

Solving RHS: $2^5 \times 3^5 = 2 \times 2 \times 2 \times 2 \times 2 \times 3 \times 3 \times 3 \times 3 \times 3$

$= 32 \times 243 = 7{,}776$

$\therefore (2 \times 3)^5 = 2^5 \times 3^5$

d. $(-3 \times 4)^4 = (-3)^4 \times 4^4$

Solving LHS: $(-3 \times 4)^4 = (-12)^4 = (-12) \times (-12) \times (-12) \times (-12)$

$= 144 \times 144 = 20{,}736$

Solving RHS: $(-3)^4 \times 4^4 = (-3) \times (-3) \times (-3) \times (-3) \times 4 \times 4 \times 4 \times 4$

$= 81 \times 256 = 20{,}736$

$\therefore (-3 \times 4)^4 = (-3)^4 \times 4^4$

e. $\left(\frac{-1}{3}\right)^4 = \frac{(-1)^4}{(3)^4}$

Solving LHS: $\left(\frac{-1}{3}\right)^4 = \left(\frac{-1}{3}\right) \times \left(\frac{-1}{3}\right) \times \left(\frac{-1}{3}\right) \times \left(\frac{-1}{3}\right) = \frac{1}{81}$

Solving RHS: $\frac{(-1)^4}{(3)^4} = \frac{(-1) \times (-1) \times (-1) \times (-1)}{3 \times 3 \times 3 \times 3} = \frac{1}{81}$

$\therefore \left(\frac{-1}{3}\right)^4 = \frac{(-1)^4}{(3)^4}$

Example 4: Express the following in the exponential forms.

a. $\frac{27}{125}$

$= \frac{3 \times 3 \times 3}{5 \times 5 \times 5} = \left(\frac{3}{5}\right)^3$

b. $\frac{(-64)}{343}$

$= \frac{(-4) \times (-4) \times (-4)}{7 \times 7 \times 7}$

$= \frac{(-4)}{7} \times \frac{(-4)}{7} \times \frac{(-4)}{7}$

$= \left(\frac{-4}{7}\right)^3$

c. $\frac{27}{1000}$

$= \frac{3 \times 3 \times 3}{10 \times 10 \times 10} = \left(\frac{3}{10}\right)^3$

d. $\frac{(-8)}{27}$

$= \left(-\frac{2 \times 2 \times 2}{3 \times 3 \times 3}\right)$

$= \frac{(-2) \times (-2) \times (-2)}{3 \times 3 \times 3}$

$= \left(\frac{-2}{3}\right) \times \left(\frac{-2}{3}\right) \times \left(\frac{-2}{3}\right) = \left(\frac{-2}{3}\right)^3$

e. $\frac{256}{625}$

$= \frac{4 \times 4 \times 4 \times 4}{5 \times 5 \times 5 \times 5} = \frac{4}{5} \times \frac{4}{5} \times \frac{4}{5} \times \frac{4}{5} = \left(\frac{4}{5}\right)^4$

Example 5: Express the following with the positive exponents.

a. $5^{(-2)}$ $= \frac{1}{5^2}$

b. $7^{(-3)}$ $= \frac{1}{7^3}$

c. $13^{(-8)}$ $= \frac{1}{13^8}$

d. $(-2)^{(-4)}$ $= \frac{1}{(-2)^4}$

e. $\left(\frac{1}{2}\right)^{(-7)}$ $= \left(\frac{2}{1}\right)^7 = 2^7$

Example 6: Write the reciprocals of the following.

a. $7^{(-3)}$

The reciprocal of 7 is $\frac{1}{7}$, thus the reciprocal of $(7)^{(-3)}$ is $\left(\frac{1}{7}\right)^{(-3)} = 7^3$.

b. $100^{(-2)}$

The reciprocal is 100^2.

c. 17^6

The reciprocal is $17^{(-6)}$.

d. $\left(\frac{7}{8}\right)^{(-2)}$

The reciprocal is $\left(\frac{7}{8}\right)^2$.

e. $\left(\frac{2}{3}\right)^{(-4)}$

The reciprocal is $\left(\frac{2}{3}\right)^4$.

Practice Exercise 3.1

1. Indicate the base and the exponent for each of the following.

a. $(2)^7$ b. $(-7)^4$ c. $\left(\frac{4}{5}\right)^6$ d. $\left(\frac{-3}{8}\right)^5$ e. $\left(\frac{-9}{13}\right)^2$

2. Express each of the following products in their exponential notation.

a. $(-3) \times (-3) \times (-3) \times (-3) \times (-3)$

b. $9 \times 9 \times 9 \times 9$

c. $\frac{2}{5} \times \frac{2}{5} \times \frac{2}{5} \times \frac{2}{5} \times \frac{2}{5}$

d. $\frac{(-1)}{10} \times \frac{(-1)}{10} \times \frac{(-1)}{10} \times \frac{(-1)}{10}$

e. $\frac{5}{12} \times \frac{5}{12} \times \frac{5}{12}$

3. Express the following as rational numbers.

a. $\left(\frac{2}{7}\right)^3$ b. $\left(-\frac{3}{7}\right)^4$ c. $\left(\frac{1}{3}\right)^6$ d. $\left(-\frac{2}{11}\right)^4$ e. $\left(-\frac{2}{5}\right)^5$

4. Express the following in the power notation.

a. $\left(-\frac{1}{27}\right)$ b. $\frac{1}{243}$ c. $\left(-\frac{1}{1000}\right)$ d. $\frac{243}{3125}$ e. $\frac{64}{15625}$

5. Write the following with positive exponents.

a. $5^{(-3)}$ b. $7^{(-2)}$ c. $11^{(-8)}$ d. $13^{(-5)}$ e. $(-12)^{(-2)}$

f. $\left(\frac{1}{3}\right)^{(-7)}$ g. $\left(\frac{-4}{5}\right)^{(-8)}$ h. $\left(\frac{5}{8}\right)^{(-9)}$ i. $\left(-\frac{13}{5}\right)^{(-4)}$ j. $(-1)^{(-10)}$

6. Find the values of the following.

a. $6^{(-2)}$ b. $4^{(-3)}$ c. $2^{(-5)}$ d. $8^{(-1)}$ e. $\left(\frac{1}{3}\right)^{(-5)}$

f. $(-10)^{(-4)}$ g. $(10)^{(-3)}$ h. $\left(\frac{9}{11}\right)^{(-2)}$ i. $\left(\frac{-1}{4}\right)^{(-3)}$ j. $\left(\frac{-7}{8}\right)^{-1}$

7. Write the reciprocals of the following.

a. $\left(\frac{7}{8}\right)^{(-3)}$ b. $\left(\frac{14}{19}\right)^{(-4)}$ c. $\left(\frac{11}{17}\right)^{3}$ d. $\left(\frac{1}{8}\right)^{(-6)}$ e. $\left(\frac{2}{3}\right)^{(-5)}$

f. $\left(\frac{5}{-7}\right)^{(-3)}$ g. $\left(\frac{-3}{-11}\right)^{4}$ h. $\left(\frac{7}{13}\right)^{(-5)}$ i. $\left(\frac{-3}{4}\right)^{11}$ j. $\left(\frac{1}{8}\right)^{(-4)}$

8. Find the values of the following.

a. $2^2 \times 3^2$ b. $2^3 \times 3^3$ c. $2^4 \times 10^4$

d. $\left(\frac{1}{2}\right)^3 \times \left(\frac{3}{2}\right)^2$ e. $\left(\frac{3}{5}\right)^3 \times \left(\frac{5}{9}\right)^2$

9. Verify the following expressions.

a. $\left(\frac{1}{4}\right)^3 = \frac{1^3}{4^3}$ b. $\left(\frac{-2}{3}\right)^5 = \frac{(-2)^5}{3^5}$ c. $\left(\frac{-3}{5}\right)^2 = \frac{(-3)^2}{5^2}$

d. $\left(\frac{-7}{-8}\right)^3 = \frac{(-7)^3}{(-8)^3}$ e. $\left(\frac{9}{11}\right)^3 = \frac{9^3}{11^3}$

10. Simplify the following and express the results as rational numbers.

a. $\left(\frac{2}{3}\right)^4 \times \left(\frac{3}{4}\right)^5$ b. $\left(\frac{2}{3}\right)^3 \times \left(\frac{-3}{4}\right)^4$ c. $\left(\frac{-2}{3}\right)^3 \times \left(\frac{-3}{4}\right)^3$

d. $\left(\frac{5}{7}\right)^3 \times \left(\frac{-7}{10}\right)^4$ e. $\left(\frac{2}{7}\right)^3 \times \left(\frac{7}{8}\right)^2$ f. $\left(\frac{-1}{2}\right)^3 \times 2^2 \div \left(\frac{4}{3}\right)^2$

g. $\left(\frac{-1}{2}\right)^2 \times \left(\frac{-1}{3}\right)^3$ h. $\left(\frac{1}{2}\right)^3 \times \left(\frac{3}{4}\right)^3 \div \left(\frac{3}{5}\right)^3$

i. $\left(\frac{1}{2}\right)^2 \times \left(\frac{2}{3}\right)^3 \div \left(\frac{4}{5}\right)^3$ j. $\left(\frac{-3}{4}\right)^3 \times \left(\frac{-4}{3}\right)^3 \div \left(\frac{3}{4}\right)^2$

Laws of Exponents

The numbers that are expressed in the exponential notation form are governed by certain laws that are discussed below.

Law 1: If x is a rational number and m and n are positive integers, then $x^m \times x^n = x^{m+n}$.

Example: If x = 2, m = (−3) and n = (−2),

$x^m \times x^n = 2^{(-3)} \times 2^{(-2)}$

$2^{(-3)} = \frac{1}{2^3}$ and $2^{(-2)} = \frac{1}{2^2}$

Therefore, $x^m \times x^n = 2^{(-3)} \times 2^{(-2)} = \frac{1}{2^3} \times \frac{1}{2^2}$

$= \frac{1}{2^3 \times 2^2} = \frac{1}{2^{3+2}} = \frac{1}{2^5}$

Hence, $2^{(-3)} \times 2^{(-2)} = 2^{(-3)+(-2)} = 2^{(-5)}$

Therefore, the first law is true for negative exponents or integral exponents.

Also, if $x = \frac{2}{3}$, m = (−2) and n = (−3), $x^m \times x^n = \left(\frac{2}{3}\right)^{(-2)} \times \left(\frac{2}{3}\right)^{(-3)}$

$\left(\frac{2}{3}\right)^{(-2)} = \frac{1}{\left(\frac{2}{3}\right)^2} = \left(\frac{3}{2}\right)^2$ and $\left(\frac{2}{3}\right)^{(-3)} = \frac{1}{\left(\frac{2}{3}\right)^3} = \left(\frac{3}{2}\right)^3$

Hence, $\left(\frac{2}{3}\right)^{(-2)} \times \left(\frac{2}{3}\right)^{(-3)} = \left(\frac{3}{2}\right)^2 \times \left(\frac{3}{2}\right)^3$

$= \frac{3 \times 3}{2 \times 2} \times \frac{3 \times 3 \times 3}{2 \times 2 \times 2}$

$= \frac{3^5}{2^5} = \left(\frac{3}{2}\right)^5 = \left(\frac{2}{3}\right)^{(-5)}$

Thus, $\left(\frac{2}{3}\right)^{(-2)} \times \left(\frac{2}{3}\right)^{(-3)} = \left(\frac{2}{3}\right)^{(-2)+(-3)}$

$= \left(\frac{2}{3}\right)^{(-5)}$

Hence, the first law of exponents is true for all rational numbers.

Law 2: $x^m \div x^n = x^{m-n}$

Example 1: Consider x = 3, m = (−5) and n = (−2), then

$x^m \div x^n = 3^{(-5)} \div 3^{(-2)}$

Now, $3^{(-5)} = \frac{1}{3^5}$ and $3^{(-2)} = \frac{1}{3^2}$

Hence, $x^m \div x^n = \frac{1}{3^5} \div \frac{1}{3^2}$

$= \frac{1}{3 \times 3 \times 3 \times 3 \times 3} \div \frac{1}{3 \times 3}$

$= \frac{1}{3 \times 3 \times 3 \times 3 \times 3} \times \frac{3 \times 3}{1} = \frac{3 \times 3}{3 \times 3 \times 3 \times 3 \times 3} = \frac{1}{3^3}$

Thus, $3^{(-5)} \div 3^{(-2)} = \frac{3^{(-5)}}{3^{(-2)}} = 3^{(-5)-(-2)}$

$= 3^{(-5)+2} = 3^{(-3)}$

Example 2: Consider $x = \frac{3}{4}$, m= (−4) and n = (−7), then

$$x^m \div x^n = \left(\frac{3}{4}\right)^{(-4)} \div \left(\frac{3}{4}\right)^{(-7)}$$

$$\left(\frac{3}{4}\right)^{(-4)} = \frac{1}{\left(\frac{3}{4}\right)^4} = \left(\frac{4}{3}\right)^4 \text{ and } \left(\frac{3}{4}\right)^{(-7)} = \frac{1}{\left(\frac{3}{4}\right)^7} = \left(\frac{4}{3}\right)^7$$

$$\text{Hence, } \left(\frac{3}{4}\right)^{(-4)} \div \left(\frac{3}{4}\right)^{(-7)} = \left(\frac{4}{3}\right)^4 \div \left(\frac{4}{3}\right)^7$$

$$= \left(\frac{4}{3}\right)^4 \times \left(\frac{3}{4}\right)^7$$

$$= \frac{4}{3} \times \frac{4}{3} \times \frac{4}{3} \times \frac{4}{3} \times \frac{3}{4} \times \frac{3}{4} \times \frac{3}{4} \times \frac{3}{4} \times \frac{3}{4} \times \frac{3}{4} \times \frac{3}{4}$$

$$= \frac{3 \times 3 \times 3}{4 \times 4 \times 4}$$

$$= \frac{3^3}{4^3} = \left(\frac{3}{4}\right)^3$$

$$\left(\frac{3}{4}\right)^{(-4)} \div \left(\frac{3}{4}\right)^{(-7)} = \frac{\left(\frac{3}{4}\right)^{-4}}{\left(\frac{3}{4}\right)^{-7}} = \left(\frac{3}{4}\right)^{(-4)-(-7)}$$

$$= \left(\frac{3}{4}\right)^{(-4)+7} = \left(\frac{3}{4}\right)^3$$

Law 3: $(x^m)^n = x^{mn}$

Example 1: Consider x = 2, m= (−3), n = (−1), we have

$$(x^m)^n = [(2)^{(-3)}]^{(-1)}$$

$$(2)^{(-3)} = \frac{1}{2^3} \text{ and } \left(\frac{1}{2^3}\right)^{(-1)} = 2^3$$

$$(2^{(-3)})^{(-1)} = 2^{(-3) \times (-1)} = 2^3$$

Example 2: Consider $x = \frac{3}{4}$, m = (−2) and n = (−1), we have

$$(x^m)^n = \left[\left(\frac{3}{4}\right)^{(-2)}\right]^{(-1)}$$

$$\left(\frac{3}{4}\right)^{(-2)} = \frac{1}{\left(\frac{3}{4}\right)^2} = \left(\frac{4}{3}\right)^2 \text{ and } \left[\left(\frac{4}{3}\right)^2\right]^{(-1)} = \frac{1}{\left(\frac{4}{3}\right)^2} = \left(\frac{3}{4}\right)^2$$

$$\text{Hence, } \left(\frac{3}{4}\right)^{(-2)(-1)} = \left(\frac{3}{4}\right)^{(-2) \times (-1)} = \left(\frac{3}{4}\right)^2$$

Law 4: $x^m \times y^m = (xy)^m$

Example 1: Consider x = 2, y = 5 and m = (−3), then

$$x^m \times y^m = 2^{(-3)} \times 5^{(-3)} = \frac{1}{2^3} \times \frac{1}{5^3} = \frac{1}{2^3 \times 5^3} = \frac{1}{(2 \times 5)^3}$$

$$= (2 \times 5)^{(-3)}$$

Example 2: Consider $x = \frac{2}{3}$, $y = \frac{3}{4}$ and $m = (-2)$, then

$$x^m \times y^m = \left(\frac{2}{3}\right)^{(-2)} \times \left(\frac{3}{4}\right)^{(-2)} = \frac{1}{\left(\frac{2}{3}\right)^2} \times \frac{1}{\left(\frac{3}{4}\right)^2} = \frac{1}{\left(\frac{2}{3}\right)^2 \times \left(\frac{3}{4}\right)^2} = \frac{1}{\left(\frac{2}{3} \times \frac{3}{4}\right)^2}$$

$$= \left(\frac{2}{3} \times \frac{3}{4}\right)^{(-2)}$$

Law 5: $\frac{x^m}{y^m} = \left(\frac{x}{y}\right)^m$

Example 1: Consider $x = 2$, $y = 3$ and $m = (-5)$, then

$$\frac{x^m}{y^m} = \frac{2^{(-5)}}{3^{(-5)}} = \frac{3^5}{2^5} = \left(\frac{3}{2}\right)^5 = \left(\frac{2}{3}\right)^{(-5)}$$

Example 2: If $x = \frac{3}{4}$, $y = \frac{2}{7}$ and $m = (-2)$, then

$$\frac{x^m}{y^m} = \frac{\left(\frac{3}{4}\right)^{(-2)}}{\left(\frac{2}{7}\right)^{(-2)}} = \frac{\left(\frac{2}{7}\right)^2}{\left(\frac{3}{4}\right)^2} = \left(\frac{\frac{2}{7}}{\frac{3}{4}}\right)^2 = \left(\frac{2}{7} \times \frac{4}{3}\right)^2$$

Zero as the Exponent

If x is a rational number and $x \neq 0$, then $x^0 = 1$. We can verify this using the first law of exponents, namely, $x^m \times x^n = x^{m+n}$. For example, $6^5 \times 6^{(-5)} = 6^{5+(-5)} = 6^0$

$6^{-5} = \frac{1}{6^5}$, hence $6^5 \times \frac{1}{6^5} = 1$

Thus, $6^0 = 1$

Example 1: Use the laws of exponents and simplify the following.

a. $(-5)^{(-3)} \times (-5)^{(-4)}$

$= (-5)^{(-3)+(-4)}$ (By the first law of exponents)

$= (-5)^{(-3-4)}$

$= (-5)^{(-7)} = \frac{1}{(-5)^7}$

b. $(9)^{(-5)} \div (9)^{(-4)}$

$= (9)^{(-5)-(-4)}$ (By the second law of exponents)

$= (9)^{(-5)+4}$

$= (9)^{-1} = \frac{1}{9}$

c. $\left(\frac{1}{81}\right) \times (2)^{(-4)}$

$= \frac{1}{3^4} \times 2^{(-4)} = 3^{(-4)} \times 2^{(-4)}$

$= (3 \times 2)^{(-4)}$ (By the fourth law of exponents)

$= (6)^{(-4)} = \frac{1}{6^4}$

d. $(2^{(-3)})^{(-5)} = 2^{(-3) \times (-5)}$

$= 2^{15}$ (By the third law of exponents)

e. $\frac{1}{27} \div 2^{(-3)}$

$= \frac{1}{3^3} \div 2^{(-3)}$

$= 3^{(-3)} \div 2^{(-3)} = 3^{(-3)} \times \frac{1}{2^{(-3)}}$

$= \frac{3^{(-3)}}{2^{(-3)}} = \left(\frac{3}{2}\right)^{(-3)} = \frac{1}{\left(\frac{3}{2}\right)^3} = \left(\frac{2}{3}\right)^3$ (By the fifth law of Exponents)

Example 2: Simplify and write the answers in the positive exponential form.

a. $(2^3 \div 2^4)^5 \times 2^{(-6)}$

$= \left(\frac{2^3}{2^4}\right)^5 \times 2^{(-6)}$

$= (2^{3-4})^5 \times 2^{(-6)}$

$= (2^{-1})^5 \times 2^{(-6)}$

$= 2^{(-5)} \times 2^{(-6)} = 2^{(-5)+(-6)} = 2^{(-11)} = \frac{1}{2^{11}}$

b. $3^{(-5)} \times 3^{(-2)} \times 3^{(-6)}$

$= 3^{(-5)+(-2)} \times 3^{-6}$

$= (3^{-5-2}) \times 3^{(-6)}$

$= 3^{(-7)} \times 3^{(-6)}$

$= 3^{(-7)+(-6)}$

$= 3^{(-7-6)}$

$= 3^{(-13)} = \frac{1}{3^{13}}$

c. $(7^{-3})^{(-2)} \div 7^{(-6)}$

$= 7^{(-3) \times (-2)} \div 7^{(-6)}$

$= 7^6 \div 7^{(-6)}$

$= 7^6 \times \frac{1}{7^{(-6)}}$

$= 7^6 \times 7^6 = 7^{6+6} = 7^{12}$

d. $(4^{(-3)} \times 4^{(-2)}) \div 4^{(-4)}$

$= (4^{-3+(-2)}) \div 4^{-4}$

$= (4^{(-3-2)}) \div 4^{(-4)}$

$= (4^{-5}) \div 4^{(-4)}$

$= (4^{-5}) \times \frac{1}{4^{(-4)}} = (4^{-5}) \times 4^4$

$= 4^{(-5)+4} = 4^{(-1)} = \frac{1}{4}$

e. $2^{(-3)} \times 5^{(-3)} = (2 \times 5)^{(-3)} = 10^{(-3)} = \frac{1}{10^3}$

3. Find the value of a in the following.

a. $5^3 \times 5^{a-2} = 5^{(-2)}$

LHS $= 5^3 \times 5^{a-2} = 5^{3+a-2} = 5^{a+1}$; RHS $= 5^{(-2)}$

But, we know that LHS = RHS or $5^{(a+1)} = 5^{(-2)}$

Since the base is the same, we equate the powers. Thus, $a + 1 = (-2)$.

$a = (-3)$.

b. $\left(\frac{6}{7}\right)^a \times \left(\frac{6}{7}\right)^{(-4)} = \left(\frac{6}{7}\right)^4$

LHS $= \left(\frac{6}{7}\right)^a \times \left(\frac{6}{7}\right)^{(-4)} = \left(\frac{6}{7}\right)^{a-4}$; RHS $= \left(\frac{6}{7}\right)^4$

But LHS = RHS. Since the base is the same, we equate the powers. Thus $a - 4 = 4$.

$a = 4 + 4 = 8$

c. $9^{(-7)} \div 9^a = 9^{(-3)}$

LHS $= 9^{(-7)} \div 9^a = \frac{9^{(-7)}}{9^a} = 9^{(-7-a)}$; RHS $= 9^{(-3)}$

Since the base is the same, we equate the powers. Thus, $-7 - a = (-3)$.

$(-a) = 7 - 3 = 4$ or $a = (-4)$

d. $\left(\frac{1}{4}\right)^{2a} \div \left(\frac{1}{4}\right)^3 = \left(\frac{1}{4}\right)^3 \times \left(\frac{1}{4}\right)^a$

LHS $= \left(\frac{1}{4}\right)^{2a} \div \left(\frac{1}{4}\right)^3 = \frac{\left(\frac{1}{4}\right)^{2a}}{\left(\frac{1}{4}\right)^3} = \left(\frac{1}{4}\right)^{(2a-3)}$; RHS $\left(\frac{1}{4}\right)^3 \div \left(\frac{1}{4}\right)^a = \frac{\left(\frac{1}{4}\right)^3}{\left(\frac{1}{4}\right)^a} = \left(\frac{1}{4}\right)^{(3-a)}$

Since the base is the same, we equate the powers. Thus $2a - 3 = 3 - a$.

$2a + a = 3 + 3$

$3a = 6$; $a = \frac{6}{3} = 2$

e. $\left(\left(\frac{1}{10}\right)^3\right)^a = \left(\frac{1}{10}\right)^6$

LHS $= \left(\left(\frac{1}{10}\right)^3\right)^a = \left(\frac{1}{10}\right)^{3a}$; RHS $= \left(\frac{1}{10}\right)^6$

$\left(\left(\frac{1}{10}\right)^3\right)^a = \left(\frac{1}{10}\right)^6$

Since the base is the same, we equate the powers. Thus, $3a = 6$.

$a = \frac{6}{3} = 2$

Practice Exercise 3.2

1. Solve the following.

a. $\left(\frac{2}{3}\right)^2 \times \left(\frac{2}{3}\right)^3$ b. $\left(\frac{2}{5}\right) \times \left(\frac{2}{5}\right)^2$ c. $\left(-\frac{5}{6}\right)^2 \times \left(-\frac{5}{6}\right)^3$

d. $\left(-\frac{1}{2}\right)^2 \times \left(-\frac{1}{2}\right)^4$ e. $\left(\frac{2}{9}\right)^0 \times \left(\frac{2}{9}\right)^2$

2. Solve the following.

a. $\left(\frac{2}{7}\right)^5 \div \left(\frac{2}{7}\right)^3$ b. $6^7 \div 6^5$ c. $(-8)^4 \div (-8)^2$

d. $\left(-\frac{3}{5}\right)^{10} \div \left(-\frac{3}{5}\right)^6$ e. $\left(-\frac{2}{5}\right)^{10} \div \left(-\frac{2}{5}\right)^9$

3. Simplify and write in the exponential form.

a. $9^2 \times 9^3 \times 9^4$ b. $(-8)^2 \times (-8)^4 \times (-8)^5$ c. $\left(\frac{3}{7}\right)^{11} \div \left(\frac{3}{7}\right)^4$

d. $7^{(-15)} \div 7^{(-8)}$ e. $\left[\left(\frac{4}{7}\right)^3\right]^2$ f. $[(-7)^6]^{(-2)}$

g. $5^{(-6)} \times 9^{(-6)}$ h. $\left(\frac{7}{8}\right)^{(-3)} \times \left(\frac{4}{7}\right)^{(-3)}$ i. $5^7 \div 9^7$

j. $\left(-\frac{3}{4}\right)^{10} \div \left(-\frac{4}{3}\right)^{10}$

4. Find the value of p in the following.

a. $(-5)^3 \times (-5)^p = (-5)^7$ b. $(-8)^{2p} \div (-8)^3 = (-8)^5$

c. $\left(\frac{11}{15}\right)^p \div \left(\frac{11}{15}\right)^{(-4)} = \left(\frac{11}{15}\right)^7$ d. $\left[\left(\frac{1}{6}\right)^4\right]^p = \left(\frac{1}{6}\right)^4 \times \left(\frac{1}{6}\right)^8$

e. $\left(\frac{3}{5}\right)^p = \left[\left(\frac{3}{5}\right)^2\right]^4$

5. Solve the following.

a. $3^0 \times 3^0 \times 3^0$ b. $3^0 + 4^0 + 5^0$ c. $3^0 \div 5^0$ d. $5^0 - 4^0$ e. $[(3)^5]^0$

6. Find the value of x in each of the following.

a. $\left(\frac{5}{3}\right)^{(-4)} \times \left(\frac{5}{3}\right)^{(-5)} = \left(\frac{5}{3}\right)^{3x}$ b. $\left(\frac{4}{7}\right)^4 \times \left(\frac{4}{7}\right)^{(-7)} = \left(\frac{4}{7}\right)^{2x-1}$

c. $5^{2x+1} \div 25 = 125$ d. $\left(\frac{7}{9}\right)^{(-4)} \times \left(\frac{7}{9}\right)^{3x} = \left(\frac{7}{9}\right)^5$

e. $[(-5)^8 \times (-5)^x] \div (-5)^3 = (-5)^6$

7. Express each of the following exponential expressions as a rational number.

a. $(8)^{(-2)}$ b. $\left(\frac{2}{5}\right)^{(-3)}$ c. $\left(\frac{2}{3}\right)^{(-1)} + \left(\frac{3}{2}\right)^{(-2)}$

d. $\left(\frac{1}{2}\right)^{(-1)} + \left(\frac{2}{3}\right)^{(-2)} - \left(\frac{3}{4}\right)^{(-3)}$ e. $\left(\frac{4}{5}\right)^{10} \times \left[\left(\frac{4}{5}\right)^2\right]^3 \div \left[\left(\frac{4}{5}\right)^4\right]^4$

8. Simplify the following.

a. $3^3 \times 2^5$ b. $\left(\frac{3}{4}\right)^3 \times \left(\frac{4}{9}\right)^3$ c. $\left(\frac{5}{11}\right)^6 \div \left(\frac{10}{11}\right)^6$

d. $\left(\frac{2}{3}\right)^5 \times \left(\frac{4}{9}\right)^2 \div \left(\frac{2}{3}\right)^9$ e. $\left(\frac{1}{5}\right)^4 \div \left(\frac{2}{5}\right)^4 \times 2^4$

9. Evaluate and solve the following equations.

a. $\left[\left(\frac{1}{3}\right)^{(-3)} - \left(\frac{1}{2}\right)^{(-3)}\right] \div \left(\frac{1}{4}\right)^{(-3)}$ b. $\left[\left(\frac{4}{3}\right)^{(-1)} - \left(\frac{1}{4}\right)^{(-1)}\right]^{(-1)}$

c. $[(5^{(-1)} \times 3^{(-1)})^{(-1)} \div 6^{(-1)}]$ d. $\left[\left[\left(\frac{-1}{5}\right)^{2}\right]^{(-2)}\right]^{(-1)}$ e. $\left[\left(\frac{3}{2}\right)^{(-2)}\right]^{2}$

10. Place the correct symbol (+, −, × or ÷) in each of the boxes below.

a. 5^2 ☐ $5^{(-5)} = 5^{(-3)}$ b. $\left(\frac{2}{11}\right)^7$ ☐ $\left(\frac{2}{11}\right)^3 = \left(\frac{2}{11}\right)^4$

c. 9^0 ☐ $10^0 = 0$ d. $\left(\frac{5}{8}\right)^{(-4)}$ ☐ $\left(\frac{5}{8}\right)^4 = 1$

e. 2^0 ☐ $5^0 = 2$

Expressing Small Numbers in the Standard Form or Scientific Notation

In the previous class, we have studied the standard form or the scientific notation used for expressing very large numbers.

Example: The number 1,03,90,00,00,000 is written as 1.039×10^{11} and the number 5,73,00,00,00,00,00,00,000 is written as 5.73×10^{17} in scientific notation.

Very small numbers can also be expressed in the standard form or in scientific notation.

Example: The number 0.000000000048 can be written as a fraction

$$\frac{48}{10,00,00,00,00,000} = \frac{48}{10^{12}} = 48 \times 10^{(-12)} = (4.8 \times 10^1) \times 10^{(-12)}$$

$$= 4.8 \times 10^{(-11)}$$

Hence, 0.000000000048 can be expressed in scientific notation as $4.8 \times 10^{(-11)}$.

Let us consider another example.

$$0.00000000000000000000267 = \frac{267}{10,00,00,00,00,00,00,00,00,00,00,000} = \frac{267}{10^{23}} = 267 \times 10^{(-23)}$$

$$= 2.67 \times 10^2 \times 10^{(-23)} = 2.67 \times 10^{(-21)}$$

Thus, we conclude that a number is said to be in the standard form when written as $K \times 10^n$ where $1 \times K \times 10$ (K lies between 1 and 10) and n is an integer.

Comparison of Big and Small Numbers

We can compare very big and very small numbers using the standard form. The two numbers to be compared are written in the form of a ratio.

Alert!

Before adding or subtracting numbers in the standard form, we must convert them into numbers having the same exponents.

Example 1: Compare the two numbers 2.56×10^{17} and 1.28×10^{16}.

Let us find the ratio of the two given numbers.

$$\frac{2.56 \times 10^{17}}{1.28 \times 10^{16}} = \frac{2.56 \times 10^{17} \times 10^{(-16)}}{1.28} = \frac{2.56 \times 10}{1.28}$$

$$= \frac{256 \times 10 \times 10}{128 \times 10} = 20$$

The first number is 20 times the second.

Example 2: Compare the two numbers $1.6 \times 10^{(-3)}$ and $5 \times 10^{(-3)}$.

Let us write the two numbers in the form of a ratio.

$$\frac{1.6 \times 10^3}{5 \times 10^{(-3)}} = \frac{1.6 \times 10^{(-3)} \times 10^3}{5} = \frac{1.6}{5} = 0.32$$

The first number is 0.32 times the second number.

Example 3: The mass of the earth is 5.97×10^{24} kg and the mass of the moon is 7.35×10^{22} kg. What would be the total mass of the two put together?

Total mass = Mass of the earth + Mass of the moon

The total mass $= 5.97 \times 10^{24} + 7.35 \times 10^{22}$

$= 5.97 \times 10^2 \times 10^{22} + 7.35 \times 10^{22}$

$= 597 \times 10^{22} + 7.35 \times 10^{22}$

$=(597 + 7.35) \times 10^{22}$ kg

$= 604.35 \times 10^{22}$ kg

The total mass of the earth and the moon put together is 604.35×10^{22} kg.

Practice Exercise 3.3

1. Write the following numbers in the standard form.

   a. 576 000000000 b. 369 00000000000 c. 134 00000000

   d. 129 0000000000 e. 250000000000000

2. Write the following numbers in the standard form.

   a. 0.0000000000048 b. 0.000000000000005 c. 0.00000000000000025

   d. 0.000000000000000000267 e. 0.0000000000000000000000261

3. Write the following in the non-exponential form.

   a. 7.2×10^6 b. 2.48×10^4 c. 9.21×10^8

   d. 2.569×10^5 e. 7.777×10^7

4. Write the following in the non-exponential form.

   a. $4.8 \times 10^{(-6)}$ b. $3.7 \times 10^{(-5)}$ c. $6.72 \times 10^{(-7)}$

   d. $9.8 \times 10^{(-10)}$ e. $4.31 \times 10^{(-9)}$

5. The mass of four steel girders used for the construction of a building are $1.5 \times 10^{(-3)}$ kg, 2.6×10^2 kg, 3.4×10^3 kg and 4.8×10^2 kg. Find the total weight of the steel girders.

Highlights

- For any number x, where $(x \neq 0)$, $x^{(-m)} = \frac{1}{x^m}$.
- The reciprocal of $x^{(-m)}$ is x^m.
- The reciprocal of $\left(\frac{a}{b}\right)^{(-m)}$ is $\left(\frac{a}{b}\right)^m$.
- For a rational number $\frac{a}{b}$, $\left(\frac{a}{b}\right)^{(-m)} = \left(\frac{b}{a}\right)^m$.
- Decimal numbers can be written in the expanded form with powers of 10.
  Thus, 27.65 can be expressed as: $2 \times 10^1 + 7 \times 10^0 + 6 \times 10^{-1} + 5 \times 10^{(-2)}$.
- The laws of exponents for all numbers with integral exponents (including negative integers) are as follows:
  Law 1: $x^m \times x^n = x^{m+n}$
  Law 2: $x^m \div x^n = x^{m-n}$
  Law 3: $(x^m)^n = x^{mn}$
  Law 4: $x^m \times y^m = (xy)^m$
  Law 5: $x^m \div y^m = \left(\frac{x}{y}\right)^m$
  where x and y are non-zero integers.
- Any number with 0 as the exponent is equal to 1, that is, $x^0 = 1$.
- Very large and very small numbers can be expressed in the standard form or in scientific notation. Here, $K \times 10^n$, where K lies between 1 and 10 and n is any integer.

Higher Order Thinking Skills

HOTS

1. Find the value of $\left(\frac{-3}{8}\right)^{-3} \times \left(\frac{4}{9}\right)^{-2}$.
2. Find the value of $(3^{(-1)} + 4^{(-1)})^{(-1)} \div 5^{(-1)}$.
3. The size of a bacterium is $5.1 \times 10^{(-6)}$ m and the size of a plant cell is $1.26 \times 10^{(-5)}$ m. Compare the two sizes and find out which is larger.

Place appropriate mathematical operations in the shaded boxes to get the answer. All calculations are to be performed from left to right.

a.

4		6		8		10	=	22

b.

6		3		6		7	=	84

c.

8		2		9		4	=	9

d.

3		5		2		9	=	21

Answer for Brainteaser on page 65

Comparing Numbers

Aim: To compare two numbers in the exponential form.

Material required: a pen

Method: Given below is a set of numbers. Write the correct symbol in the box in order to indicate which of the two numbers is greater or smaller.

Use $>$, $<$ or $=$ signs.

23^3	☐	27^3	5^1	☐	27^4	4^3	☐	25^4
18^4	☐	20^5	7^3	☐	6^1	29^5	☐	3^1
9^3	☐	15^2	11^4	☐	18^3	26^5	☐	17^3
12^1	☐	27^3	29^2	☐	8^5	24^2	☐	9^2
14^5	☐	20^2	11^2	☐	6^5	18^4	☐	19^3

Answer for Brainteaser from page 64

a.	4	×	6	+	8	−	10	=	22
b.	6	÷	3	×	6	×	7	=	84
c.	8	÷	2	+	9	−	4	=	9
d.	3	×	5	×	2	−	9	=	21

CHAPTER 4

Playing with Numbers

In the earlier classes we have learnt about natural numbers (N), whole numbers (W), integers (Z) and rational numbers (Q).

We have also learnt to perform the four basic or fundamental operations of addition (+), subtraction (−), multiplication (×) and division (÷) on these numbers. We have also learnt about the various tests of divisibility of numbers. We shall study divisibility in detail.

Generalised Form of Numbers

Each digit in a number has a place value that depends upon its position. Consider a two-digit number, 92. The digit in the unit's place is 2 and the digit in the ten's place is 9. Hence, the place value of 2 is 2×1 and the place value of 9 is 9×10.

Consider a three-digit number, 267. The place value of 7 is 7×1, the place value of 6 is 6×10 and the place value of 2 is 2×100.

In general, if the digits in a three-digit number are, a, b and c, where a is in the hundred's place b is in the ten's place and c is in the unit's place, the number will be represented as $100a + 10b + 1c$.

Similarly, if abcd is a four-digit number, it implies that the number is $1000a + 100b + 10c + 1d$.

Alert!

If we have a two-digit number, then 0 cannot be in the ten's place. If we have a three-digit number, then 0 cannot be in the hundred's place. If we have a four-digit number, then 0 cannot be in the thousand's place.

Divisibility of Numbers

Consider a three-digit number, abc. Let us study its divisibility by 2, 3, 5, 9 and 10.

Divisibility by 2

We know that abc is equal to $100a + 10b + c$.

It is clear that 2 will divide 100a and 10b, completely because 100a and 10b are multiplies of 100 and 10, respectively. We then check for c. If c is divisible by 2, the number abc will be divisible by 2.

If the unit's digit is either 0, 2, 4, 6 or 8, then the unit's digit will be divisible by 2. A number is divisible by 2 if its unit's digit is divisible by 2.

Divisibility by 3

Let us consider a three-digit number, abc.

The number abc is equal to $100a + 10b + c$

This can be written as $(33 \times 3 + 1)\,a + (3 \times 3 + 1)b + c$.

$$= (33 \times 3)a + a + (3 \times 3)b + b + c$$
$$= 3 \times (33a + 3b) + (a + b + c)$$

However, $3(33a + 3b)$ is divisible by 3 since 3 is one of the factors. The number 3 should also be a factor of $a + b + c$ for it to be divisible. Hence, a three-digit number will be divisible by 3 if $a + b + c$ is divisible by 3.

A number is divisible by 3 if the sum of its digits is divisible by 3.

Divisibility by 5

A three-digit number, abc is equal to $100 \times a + 10 \times b + c$. The numbers 100a and 10b are divisible by 5. If c is divisible by 5, then the complete number abc will be divisible by 5.

A number is divisible by 5 if the unit's digit is divisible by 5.

The unit's digit will be divisible by 5 if the digit is 0 or 5.

Divisibility by 9

A three-digit number, abc is equal to $100 \times a + 10 \times b + c$.

$= (99 + 1)a + (9 + 1)b + c$

$= 99a + 9b + (a + b + c)$

Here, 99a is divisible by 9 and 9b is divisible by 9. If $(a + b + c)$ is divisible by 9, then abc will be divisible by 9.

A number is divisible by 9 if the sum of its digits is divisible by 9.

Divisibility by 10

If abc is a three-digit number, then $abc = 100 \times a + 10 \times b + c$.

Here, $100 \times a$ and $10 \times b$ are divisible by 10. The number c will be divisible by 10 if the digit in the unit's place is 0.

A number is divisible by 10 if the digit in the unit's place is 0.

Alert!

The tests of divisibility by 2, 3, 5, 9 and 10 are also true for numbers that have more than three digits.

Example 1: Which of the following numbers are divisible by 2?

a. 212 b. 315 c. 406 d. 840 e. 947

f. 420 g. 728 h. 644 i. 529 j. 672

If the unit's digit in a given number is either 0, 2, 4, 6 or 8, the number is divisible by 2. Thus, the numbers that are divisible by 2 are: 21<u>2</u>, 40<u>6</u>, 84<u>0</u>, 42<u>0</u>, 72<u>8</u>, 64<u>4</u> and 67<u>2</u>.

Example 2: Check if the following numbers are divisible by 3.

a. 432 b. 999 c. 136 d. 235 e. 267

We know that a number is divisible by 3 if the sum of its digits is divisible by 3. Let us verify the same.

a. Adding the digits of 432, we get $4 + 3 + 2 = 9$.

The sum of the digits is 9, which is divisible by 3. Hence, 432 is divisible by 3.

b. 999

The sum of the digits is: $9 + 9 + 9 = 27$

The sum of the digits is 27, which is divisible by 3. Hence, 999 is divisible by 3.

c. 136

The sum of the digits is: $1 + 3 + 6 = 10$

The sum of the digits is 10, which is not divisible by 3. Hence, 136 is not divisible by 3.

d. 235

The sum of the digits is: $2 + 3 + 5 = 10$

The sum of the digits is 10, which is not divisible by 3. Hence, 235 is not divisible by 3.

e. 267

The sum of the digits is: $2 + 6 + 7 = 15$

The sum of the digits is 15, which is divisible by 3. Hence, 267 is divisible by 3.

Example 3: Identify the numbers that are divisible by 5 in the following list.

a. 235	b. 465	c. 551	d. 400	e. 625
f. 254	g. 250	h. 715	i. 578	j. 900

We know that for a number to be divisible by 5, it should have either 5 or 0 in the unit's place.

The numbers that are divisible by 5 in the above list are: 235, 465, 400, 625, 250, 715 and 900.

Example 4: Without dividing, write the remainder when the following numbers are divided by 9.

a. 876	b. 397	c. 735	d. 246	e. 990

We know that a number is divisible by 9 if the sum of their digits is divisible by 9.

a. 875

The sum of the digits is: $8 + 7 + 5 = 20$

The sum of the digits is 20, which is not divisible by 9. We know that $9 \times 2 = 18$, which is exactly divisible by 9. Hence, when 875 is divided by 9, the remainder is $20 - 18 = 2$.

b. 387

The sum of the digits is: $3 + 8 + 7 = 18$

The sum of the digits is 18, which is exactly divisible by 9, hence the remainder is 0.

c. 735

The sum of the digits is: $7 + 3 + 5 = 15$

The sum of the digits is 15, which is not divisible by 9. We know that $9 \times 1 = 9$, which is exactly divisible by 9.

Hence, when 735 is divided by 9, the remainder will be $15 - 9 = 6$.

d. 246

The sum of the digits is: $2 + 4 + 6 = 12$

The sum of the digits is 12, which is not divisible by 9. We know that $9 \times 1 = 9$, which is exactly divisible by 9. Hence, when 246 is divided by 9, the remainder will be $12 - 9 = 3$.

e. 990

The sum of the digits is: $9 + 9 + 0 = 18$

The sum of the digits is 18, which is exactly divisible by 9. Hence, when 990 is divided by 9, the remainder will be 0.

Example 5: Identify the numbers that are divisible by 10.

a. 645	b. 700	c. 60	d. 929	e. 500
f. 335	g. 80	h. 205	i. 900	j. 750

We know that a number is divisible by 10 if it has 0 in its unit's place.

Thus, the numbers that are divisible by 10 are 700, 60, 500, 80, 900 and 750.

Example 6: Consider the three digits, 5, 4 and 0.

a. How many numbers can be formed using these digits without repeating any of them? Write the numbers formed.

The numbers that can be formed are either one-digit, two-digit or three-digit numbers. They are:

one-digit numbers: 0, 4, 5; two-digit numbers: 40, 50, 45, 54; and three-digit numbers: 405, 450, 504, 540.

b. List the numbers formed using the digits 5, 4 and 0 that are divisible by 2, 3, 5, 9 and 10.

The numbers that are divisible by 2 are 0, 4, 40, 50, 54, 450, 504 and 540.

The numbers that are divisible by 3 are 0, 45, 54, 405, 450, 504 and 540.

The numbers that are divisible by 5 are 0, 5, 40, 50, 45, 405, 450 and 540.

The numbers that are divisible by 9 are 0, 45, 54, 405, 450, 504 and 540.

The numbers that are divisible by 10 are 0, 40, 50, 450 and 540.

Representation of Digits by Letters

To find the missing numerals, which we represent as letters, involving any of the four fundamental operations, we follow two rules.

Rule 1. Each letter must represent only one digit in a particular problem.

Rule 2. A number cannot begin with a 0. For example, 65 cannot be written as 065 or 0065.

Let us use these rules in the following examples to clarify their meaning.

Example 1: Find the values of a, b and c in the following addition problems.

a. If 4a2 +28a = 715, find the value of a.

```
  4a2
 +28a
 ----
  715
 ----
```

Here, a occurs in two places, however, it will have the same value according to Rule 1.

If we consider the unit's place we see, 2 + a = 5.

Hence, a should be equal to 3.

If a = 3 then 8 + 3 = 11, which gives 1 in the sum and 1 is carried over to give 1 + 4 + 2 = 7. Replacing the value of a in the sum, we arrive at the correct answer.

b. If 6a3 + 22b = bb1, find the values of a and b.

```
  6a3
 +22b
 ----
  bb1
 ----
```

If we look at the unit's place, we see 3 + b = 1. Thus, b has to be 8, so that 3 + 8 = 11. Replacing the value of b in the answer, we arrive at the value for a that is 5.

c. If 2ab + c78 = 713, find the value of a, b and c.

$$\begin{array}{r} 2ab \\ +c78 \\ \hline 713 \\ \hline \end{array}$$

In the unit's place, b + 8 = 3, so the value of b should be 5 since 5 + 8 = 13. The number 3 is written in the answer and 1 is carried over. In the ten's place, 1 + a + 7 = 1. If a has a value of 3, we get 11. We write 1 in the answer and carry over 1. In the hundred's place, 1 + 2 + c = 7, so c should be equal to 4.

Example 2: Find the values of a, b and c in the following subtraction problems.

a. If 4a2 − 21a = 219, find the value of a.

$$\begin{array}{r} 4a2 \\ -21a \\ \hline 219 \\ \hline \end{array}$$

In the unit's place 2 − a = 9, hence 2 should be 12 so that a number can be subtracted from it. Thus, 12 − a = 9 a will have a value of 3. In the ten's place, a has to be the same. Now if a is 3 and we borrow 1 for the unit's place, it becomes 2 and 2 − 1 = 1.

b. If 64a − 3b5 = a97, find the values of a and b.

$$\begin{array}{r} 64a \\ -3b5 \\ \hline a97 \\ \hline \end{array}$$

In the unit's place, a − 5 = 7, hence a should be 2 since 12 − 5 = 7. In the ten's place, 4 becomes 3 since the unit's place has borrowed a number from here. Now 13 − b = 9, thus b = 4. Replacing the values in the sum, we arrive at the answer.

c. If 53a −1b5 = c96, find the values of a, b and c.

$$\begin{array}{r} 53a \\ -1b5 \\ \hline c96 \\ \hline \end{array}$$

In the unit's place, we have a − 5 = 6. We know that 11 − 5 = 6, thus a should have a value of 1. In the ten's place 1 has been borrowed from 3, which becomes 2 and 2 − b = 9. Now, 12 − b = 9, hence, b should be 3. To get 12, we borrowed 1 from the hundred's place which has become 4, thus 4 − 1 = 3, hence c has a value of 3.

Example 3: Find the values of a, b and c in the following problems.

a. If 3b × a = 252, find the values of a and b.

$$\begin{array}{r} 3b \\ \times\ a \\ \hline 252 \\ \hline \end{array}$$

In the unit's place b × a = 2, so the possible combinations could be 1 × 2 or 2 × 1; 2 × 6 or 6 × 2; 3 × 4 or 4 × 3; 4 × 8 or 8 × 4; 6 × 7 or 7 × 6 and 8 × 9 or 9 × 8.

By substituting each possible number, we realise that when a = 7 and b = 6, we get the correct answer.

b. If ab × 5 = cab, find the values of a, b and c.

$$\begin{array}{r} ab \\ \times\ 5 \\ \hline cab \\ \hline \end{array}$$

Now b × 5 gives the digit b hence b is either 0 or 5. Since a × 5 gives the same digit a in the ten's place, there should be no carry over from 5 × b. Hence, b has a value of 0. Since a × 5 gives a in the ten's place, a has to be either 0 or 5. It cannot be 0 since ab cannot be 0, thus the value of a has to be 5 and the value of c will be 2.

c. If b3 × ca = 1035, find the values of a, b and c.

$$\begin{array}{r} b3 \\ \times\ ca \\ \hline 115 \\ +\ 920 \\ \hline 1035 \\ \hline \end{array}$$

Since, a × 3 gives the one's digit as 5, a should be 5. On multiplying 5 × 3 we get 15 where 1 is carried over to the ten's place. Now, 5 × b + 1 = 11 hence b should be 2. Finally, 3 × c = 2, hence c should be 4 since 4 × 3 = 12.

By replacing the values of a, b and c in the sum, we get the correct answer.

Example 4: Find the values of a, b and c for the following division sums.

a.

$$\begin{array}{r|l} & \ \ \ 6 \\ \hline 16 & 116 \\ & -11b \\ \hline & \ \ \ 4 \end{array}$$

Find the value of b.

Since 6 − b = 4, the value of b should be 2. Replacing the value in the sum, gives the correct answer.

b.

$$\begin{array}{r|l} & \ \ 3b \\ \hline 11 & 3ac \\ & -33 \\ \hline & \ \ 6c \\ & -55 \\ \hline & \ \ \ 7 \end{array}$$

Find the values of a, b and c.

In the first step, 11 × 3 = 33 and the remainder is 6, hence a should have a value of 9. In the next step, 11 × b = 55, hence b = 5. By subtracting 6c − 55 we get 7, thus c, should be equal to 2 (since 12 − 5 = 7).

c.
$$\begin{array}{r|r} & 7 \\ \hline b & 3a \\ & -3c \\ \cline{2-2} & 2 \end{array}$$

Find the value of a, b and c.

In the first step, b $\times$ 7 = 3c. If 7 is multiplied by 5, we get 35 which is the only number with 3 in the ten's place when any number is multiplied with 7. Hence, b has to have a value of 5 and then c will be 5. Now, a − 5 = 2, hence a will have a value of 7.

Practice Exercise 4.1

1. Answer the following questions.
   a. How many digits can be placed in the blank box of a three-digit number that begins with 67 ☐ ?
   b. Write all numbers between 60 and 70 that are divisible by 2.
2. The following numbers are divisible by 3. Give the smallest possible value of a in the numbers.

   a. 23a   b. a54   c. 6a7   d. a83   e. 9a1
   f. 39a   g. 9a2   h. 40a   i. 33a   j. 7a7
3. Write the smallest possible value of c so that the given numbers are exactly divisible by 9.

   a. 85c   b. 9c7   c. c67   d. 4c3   e. 90c
   f. 85c6   g. 983c   h. c472   i. 3c65   j. 19c4
4. Write down nine consecutive numbers between 20 and 70 that are exactly divisible by 5.
5. Without dividing write the remainder if the following numbers are divided by 5.

   a. 643   b. 419   c. 845   d. 969   e. 324
   f. 567   g. 627   h. 726   i. 192   j. 958
6. If the unit's digit of a number is 7, state the remainder in each case when the number is divided by 2, 5 and 10.
7. Find the values of a, b and c in the following problems.

$$\text{a.}\ \begin{array}{r} 5ab \\ +c12 \\ \hline 999 \\ \hline \end{array} \qquad \text{b.}\ \begin{array}{r} 4b5 \\ +\ c7a \\ \hline 804 \\ \hline \end{array} \qquad \text{c.}\ \begin{array}{r} 25a \\ +186 \\ \hline aa0 \\ \hline \end{array} \qquad \text{d.}\ \begin{array}{r} 4a2 \\ +\ 96 \\ \hline b7a \\ \hline \end{array} \qquad \text{e.}\ \begin{array}{r} 3c2 \\ +245 \\ \hline c0b \\ \hline \end{array}$$

8. Find the values of a, b and c in the following problems.

$$\text{a.}\ \begin{array}{r} 32a \\ -\ 1b9 \\ \hline c82 \\ \hline \end{array} \qquad \text{b.}\ \begin{array}{r} 5b7 \\ -c9a \\ \hline 128 \\ \hline \end{array} \qquad \text{c.}\ \begin{array}{r} 6b4 \\ -23a \\ \hline cab \\ \hline \end{array} \qquad \text{d.}\ \begin{array}{r} b9a \\ -a67 \\ \hline c89 \\ \hline \end{array} \qquad \text{e.}\ \begin{array}{r} 8a4 \\ -a03 \\ \hline 6a1 \\ \hline \end{array}$$

9. Find the values of a, b and c in the following problems.

a. $\begin{array}{r} b3b \\ \times \quad 6 \\ \hline 139b \\ \hline \end{array}$
b. $\begin{array}{r} a5b \\ \times \quad b \\ \hline 273b \\ \hline \end{array}$
c. $\begin{array}{r} 4c5 \\ \times \quad 7 \\ \hline c975 \\ \hline \end{array}$
d. $\begin{array}{r} a1 \\ \times \ cb \\ \hline 306 \\ +\ 357x \\ \hline 3876 \\ \hline \end{array}$
e. $\begin{array}{r} ba \\ \times \ c9 \\ \hline 189 \\ +\ 63x \\ \hline 819 \\ \hline \end{array}$

10. Write down all possible three-digit numbers using the digits 0, 1, 3 and 6 that are divisible by

a. 3
b. 9
c. 10

Number Games and Puzzles

We have already learnt about replacing numbers by letters and performing the four fundamental operations. Now we will try to solve puzzles with the help of magical squares and magical triangles and also explore different sequences in numbers.

Magical Square

A magical square could have $3 \times 3 = 9$ or $4 \times 4 = 16$ numbers. In magical squares, the sum of the horizontal rows, the vertical columns and the diagonals add up to the same number.

Example 1: A magical square has 3×3 numbers. Complete the square so that the sum of the numbers in each row, column and diagonal is equal to 15. Find the values of a, b, c, d, e and f.

6	1	a
f	5	b
e	d	c

We begin with the first row since two numbers are known. The value of a will be 8. Next proceed to the diagonal where again two numbers are known. The value of c will be 4. Now we can find the value of b since two values in the column are known. The value of b is 3. Now in the next column that has d, the value of d is 9. The value of e will be 2 and the value of f will be 7.

Example 2: A magical square has 4×4 numbers. The sum of the numbers in each row, column and diagonal adds up to 54.

21	7	8	18
10	16	15	13
14	12	11	17
9	19	20	6

A Magical Triangle

In the triangle, the numbers from 1 to 6 have been used (without repeating any number) so that each side of the magical triangle adds up to 12.

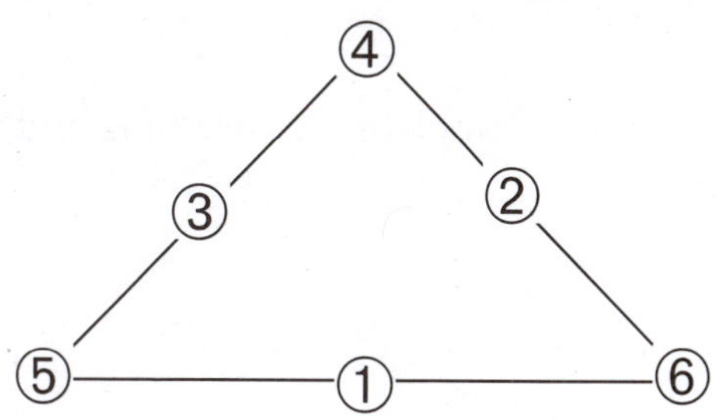

Number Sequences

Here, we shall learn about two number sequences.

Arithmetic Sequences

When the terms of a sequence are determined by **adding** a certain fixed number to the previous term, it is called an arithmetic sequence.

Example 1: 1, 6, 11, 16, 21, 26 …
Here, we add 5 to the previous term and get the next term.

Example 2: 3, 7, 11, 15, 19, 23, 27 …
Here, we add 4 to the previous term and get the next term.

Example 3: 7, 15, 23, 31, 39, 47 …
Here, we begin with 7 and then add to the previous term to get the next term.

Geometric Sequences

When the terms of a sequence are determined by **multiplying** the previous term by a certain fixed number, the sequence is said to be geometric.

Example 1: 2, 4, 8, 16, 32 … Each preceeding term is multiplied by 2.

Example 2: 5, 25, 125, 625 … Each preceeding term is multiplied by 5.

Example 3: 6, 18, 54, 162, 486 … Each preceeding term is multiplied by 3.

Fibonacci Numbers

Fibonacci numbers are a set of numbers where the first two terms are 0 and 1 and the following terms are the sum of the two previous terms. For example, 0, 1, 1, 2, 3, 5, 8, 13, 21, 34, 55, 89, 144 … is a Fibonacci sequence.

Practice Exercise 4.2

1. a. Complete the following grid so that the rows, columns and diagonals add upto 27.

6		
	9	5
8		

b. Complete the following grid so that the rows, columns and diagonals add upto 33.

	15	
	11	
9		17

c. Complete the following grid so that the rows, columns and diagonals add upto 60.

5		25
	20	
	10	

2. a. Complete the following grid so that the rows, columns and diagonals add upto 42.

18			15
	13	12	10
	9		
6		17	3

b. Complete the following grid so that the rows, columns and diagonals add upto 60.

30			
	20	18	
16	12	10	
6			

c. Complete the following grid so that the rows, columns and diagonals add upto 30.

	14		0
8	6		11
4			5
	2	1	12

3. Find the pattern in the following sequences and write the next three terms.

a. 2, 7, 12, 17, 22 … b. 6, 16, 26, 36 … c. 1, 2, 4, 8, 16, 32 …

d. 1, 4, 16, 64, 256 … e. 1, 4, 9, 16, 25, 36 …

4. Find the values of a, b, c and d to complete the number triangle given below.

2

2 2

2 4 2

2 [a] 6 2

2 8 [b] 8 2

2 [c] 20 [d] 10 2

5. In the 4 × 5 grid given below, place the numbers 1 to 20 without repeating any number, so that a chain of numbers is obtained. You can move to the adjacent cell either to the left or right or up or down but not diagonally to get your answers. The position of the numbers that already exist are fixed.

	7	10		
	2			17

Highlights

- A three-digit number that has a in the hundred's place, b in the ten's place and c in the unit's place is represented by $100a + 10b + c$.
- A number is divisible by:
  - 2 if the unit's digit of the number is 0, 2, 4, 6 or 8.
  - 3 if the sum of the digits is divisible by 3.
  - 5 if the unit's digit is 0 or 5.
  - 9 if the sum of the digits is divisible by 9.
  - 10 if the unit's digit is 0.
- Number sequences follow a set pattern.
- Sometimes letters can be used instead of digits to make interesting puzzles.
- Magical squares consist of numbers arranged such that the sum of digits in each row, column and diagonal adds upto the same number.

Higher Order Thinking Skills

HOTS

1. Insert the symbols $+$, $-$, $\times$, $\div$ and parenthesis in the following sequence of numbers so that the expression equals 100.

   1 2 3 4 5 6 7 8 9

2. Find the pattern in each of the following sequences and write the next three terms.

   a. 5, 9, 13, 17, ___, ___, ___

   b. 1, 3, 9, 27, ___, ___, ___

   c. 71, 62, 53, 44, ___, ___, ___

3. Complete the magical square so that the sum of the digits in each row, column and diagonal is equal to 15.

6	1	
	5	

Playing with Numbers

Objective: To use the concept of magical squares to solve multiple grids within a grid.

Material required: pencil and eraser

Method: Fill in the grid so that every horizontal row, every vertical column and every 3×3 box contains the digits 1–9. without repeating the numbers in the same row, column or box.

The numbers given below are fixed.

			2	3	5			
		9				7		1
		4						6
	1		8				4	
7	5		1		6		9	3
	6				2		7	
3		1				5		
8		7				9		
			4	7	1			

How many squares are there in the following figure?

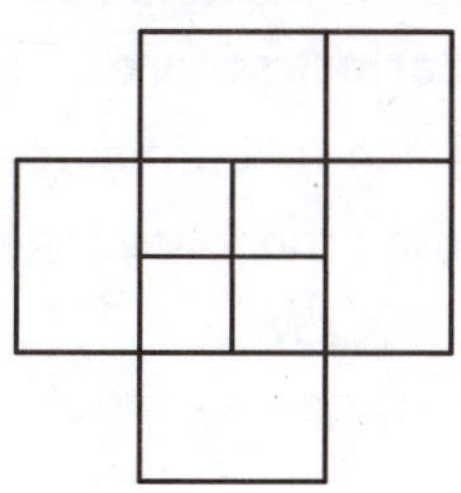

Answer for Brainteaser on page 80

CHAPTERS 3–4 Rewind

1. A perfect square number can never have the digit ______ in the unit's place

   a. 1 b. 4 c. 8 d. 9
2. Which is the smallest number that can be multiplied with 12,288 so that the product becomes a square number? Find the square root of the perfect square.
3. Find the square root of $4\frac{57}{196}$.
4. Which of the following numbers is not a perfect cube?

   a. 2,197 b. 512 c. 2,916 d. 343
5. Find the cube root of $\left(-\frac{1728}{2744}\right)$.
6. Which of the following numbers are divisible by either 3, 6 or 9? Which of the numbers are divisible by 3, 6 and 9?

   12, 71, 93, 48, 86, 127, 455, 671, 994 and 548
7. Find the smallest number by which 3,675 should be divided to make it a perfect square. Also find the square root of the perfect square.
8. A rectangular field where the length is twice the breadth has an area of 11,858 m^2. Find the length and breadth of the field.
9. Find the square root of 0.012321.
10. Find the smallest four-digit number that is a perfect square. Find the square root of the perfect square.
11. If a number is tripled show that the cube is 27 times the cube of the given number.
12. What should be the values of x, y and z so that the following subtraction problems are true?

    a. $\begin{array}{r} 3\,2\,x \\ -1\,y\,9 \\ \hline z\,8\,2 \\ \hline \end{array}$ b. $\begin{array}{r} 5\,y\,7 \\ -z\,9\,x \\ \hline 1\,2\,8 \\ \hline \end{array}$ c. $\begin{array}{r} 6\,y\,4 \\ -2\,3\,x \\ \hline z\,8\,9 \\ \hline \end{array}$
13. Write down ten three-digit numbers that are exactly divisible by 2 using the digits 1, 3, 6 and 0 only once.
14. A cubical box of volume 2,197 cc is put in a large cubical box of side 39 cm. How many such boxes can be put in the large box?
15. Find the smallest number that should be subtracted from 99,230 to get a perfect square. Find the square root of the perfect square.
16. Find the smallest square number that can be completely divided by 9, 15 and 20.
17. Without dividing find the remainder when the following numbers are divided by 9.

    a. 8,883 b. 6,652 c. 7,296
18. Find the cube of the following.

    a. 0.8 b. (−1.2) c. $3\frac{1}{2}$
19. By which smallest number should we multiply 16,384 to make it a perfect cube. Find the cube root of the perfect cube.
20. The volume of a cube is double the volume of the cuboid having volume 6.912 cm^3. Find the length of an edge of the cube.

Test Yourself

Unit I

1. Write any ten rational numbers between $\frac{(-7)}{9}$ and $\frac{2}{9}$.

2. Verify the equation $(a + b) + c = a + (b + c)$ where $a = \frac{1}{7}$, $b = \frac{(-2)}{7}$ and $c = \frac{5}{7}$. Name the property used in the verification process.

3. Simplify the following.

   a. $\left(-\frac{2}{5}\right) - \left(\frac{3}{10}\right) - \left(-\frac{4}{10}\right)$ b. $\left(-\frac{3}{2}\right) + \left(\frac{5}{4} - \frac{7}{4}\right)$ c. $\frac{5}{4} + \frac{7}{6} - \left(-\frac{2}{3}\right)$

4. If $x = \frac{3}{4}$, $y = \frac{4}{5}$ and $z = \frac{2}{3}$, verify that $x \times (y + z) = x \times y + y \times z$. Name the property used. Write the reciprocals of x, y and z.

5. Divide the difference of $\frac{12}{7}$ and $\frac{13}{4}$ by the product of $\frac{4}{5}$ and $\frac{25}{2}$.

6. Express the following in the exponential form.

   a. $\frac{25}{36}$ b. $\frac{1}{625}$ c. $\left(-\frac{8}{125}\right)$ d. $\frac{81}{256}$ e. $\left(-\frac{1}{8000}\right)$

7. Simplify the following.

   a. $x^0 \times x^4$ b. $x^5 \div x^3$ c. $(x^5)^3$ d. $(2^{-3})^{-2}$ e. $(5^2)^0$

8. Find the smallest number by which each of the following should be multiplied to make them perfect squares. Find the square root of the perfect square in each case.

   a. 6,480 b. 847 c. 3,168

9. Find the smallest number by which each of the following should be divided to make them perfect squares. Find the square root of the perfect square in each case.

   a. 243 b. 512 c. 3,675

10. For a mass drill at a school function, 2,401 students are standing in rows such that the number of rows is equal to the number of students in each row. Find the number of students in each row.

11. Find the square root of the following decimal numbers.

    a. 57.1536 b. 538.24 c. 1814.76

12. Find the smallest number by which 3,456 must be divided so that the quotient becomes a perfect cube. Find the cube root of the quotient.

13. The volume of a cube is 17.576 cm^3. Find the length of the edge of the cube. If the length of the edge of the cube is doubled, how many times will the volume increase?

14. Write down seven consecutive numbers after 90 that are exactly divisible by 5.

15. Write the smallest value of 'm' for each of the following three-digit numbers, all of which are divisible by 3.

    a. 23m b. m47 c. 5m2 d. m83 e. 8m5

16. Write the smallest value of 'p' for each of the following numbers, all of which are divisible by 6.

    a. 81p4 b. 106p c. 87p8 d. 5p30 e. 85p6

17. Write the value of 'a' for each of the following numbers, all of which are divisible by 9.

    a. 85a6 b. 983a c. 4a72 d. 47a2 e. 3a65

18. Without dividing, write the remainder when the following numbers are divided by 5.

    a. 2,468 b. 3,491 c. 7,493 d. 9,547 e. 9,999

19. Without dividing, write the remainder when the following numbers are divided by 9.

    a. 823 b. 7,419 c. 8,462 d. 9,231 e. 6,239

20. Complete the grid so that each row, column and diagonal adds upto the same number.

	14		0
8		6	11
4			7
	2	1	12

Answer for Brainteaser from page 77

There are 11 squares in the figure.

Algebraic Expressions

CHAPTER 5

In the previous class, we have learnt about like terms and unlike terms. The concepts of monomial (single term), binomial (two terms), trinomial (three terms) and polynomial (many terms) have also been introduced. In this chapter, we shall study multiplication and division of algebraic expressions.

Let us recall the addition and subtraction of algebraic expressions.

Addition and Subtraction of Algebraic Expressions

While adding an algebraic expression, we collect the like terms and add them. The sum of several like terms is the sum of the coefficients of the like terms. While subtracting, we write the given algebraic expressions in two rows in such a way that the like terms occur one below the other. The expression from which we have to subtract is in the first row and the expression which is to be subtracted is in the second row.
An algebraic expression is a combination of numerals, literal numbers (letters) and the symbols of the fundamental operations.

Example 1: Add the following algebraic expressions.

a. $5x^2y, -4x^2y, 3x^2y$

b. $m^2 - 3mn, m^2 + mn, mn + n^2$

c. $6a + 8b - 5c, 2b + c - 4a, a - 3b - 2c$

a. $5x^2y$, $-4x^2y$ and $3x^2y$

$5x^2y + (-4x^2y) + 3x^2y$ (monomials)

$= 5x^2y - 4x^2y + 3x^2y$

$= (5 - 4 + 3)\,x^2y$ (by collecting the coefficients of the like terms)

$= 4x^2y$

b. $m^2 - 3mn$, $m^2 + mn$ and $mn + n^2$

$= (m^2 + m^2) + (-3mn + mn + mn) + n^2$ (by collecting like terms)

$= 2m^2 - mn + n^2$

c. $6a + 8b - 5c$, $2b + c - 4a$ and $a - 3b - 2c$

To solve this expression, we shall use the vertical method and write the like terms in columns.

$$\begin{array}{r} 6a + 8b - 5c \\ -4a + 2b + c \\ + a - 3b - 2c \\ \hline 3a + 7b - 6c \\ \hline \end{array} \quad \text{(trinomials)}$$

$= 3a + 7b - 6c$

Example 2: Subtract the following algebraic expressions.

a. $7x^2 y^2$ from $-11x^2 y^2$

$(-11x^2 y^2) - (7x^2 y^2)$ (monomials)

$= -11x^2 y^2 - 7x^2 y^2$

$= -18 x^2 y^2$

b. $11 ab^2 + ab$ from $16 ab^2 - 3ab$

$= (16 ab^2 - 3ab) - (11ab^2 + ab)$ (binomials)

$= 16ab^2 - 11ab^2 - 3ab - ab$

$= (16ab^2 - 11ab^2) + (-3ab - ab)$

$= 5ab^2 - 4ab$

c. $4a + 5b - 3c$ from $6a - 3b + c$

We shall use the vertical method to solve this algebraic expression. We will write like terms below each other and change the signs of the terms to be subtracted.

$6a - 3b + c$	(trinomials)	$6a - 3b + c$
$-(4a + 5b - 3c)$	(by changing the signs)	$-(4a + 5b - 3c)$
		$2a - 8b + 4c$

$= 2a - 8b + 4c$

Example 3: From the sum of $5a + 6b - 7c$ and $9a - 16b - 2c$ subtract $7a - 10b + 9c$.

Adding the two expressions we get,

$$\begin{array}{r} 5a + 6b - 7c \\ +9a - 16b - 2c \\ \hline 14a - 10b - 9c \\ \hline \end{array}$$

Now, by subtracting $7a - 10b + 9c$ from the above sum we get,

$14a - 10b - 9c$	or	$14a - 10b - 9c$
$-(7a - 10b + 9c)$		$-7a + 10b - 9c$
		$7a + 0 - 18c$

$= 7a - 18c$

Practice Exercise 5.1

1. Add the following algebraic expressions.

a. $8xy, -5xy, 3xy, -xy$ b. $7b, -3b, 5b, -b, -2b$ c. $6x^2, -3x^2, 4x^2$

d. $mn, -8mn, 7mn, 6mn$ e. $11ab^2, -12ab^2, ab^2$

2. Add the following algebraic expressions.

a. $3mn - 4m^2, 5mn - 7m^2$

b. $9abc - 3p, 10abc + 4p, -7abc - p$

c. $8x^2 - y^2, 11x^2 + 3y^2, -9x^2 + 2y^2$

d. $a^2 + b^2, -7a^2 - b^2, 8a^2 + 5b^2$

e. $6pq + 7qr, -13\,pq - 13qr, 4pq + 8qr$

3. Subtract the following.

a. $3a^2b$ from $-5a^2b$

b. $(-8pq)$ from $6pq$

c. $(-10\,p)$ from $10p$

d. $(-2abc)$ from $(-8abc)$

e. $11mn$ from $-16mn$

4. Subtract the following.

a. $8a^2 - b^2$ form $11a^2 + 3b^2$

b. $7pq - 6qr$ from $8pq + 9qr$

c. $10xy - 4\,yz$ from $7yz + 10\,xy$

d. $81\,mn - 21m$ from $11m - 18mn$

e. $11a^2b - 14ab^2$ from $17a^2b - 9ab^2$

5. Find the sum of the following.

a. $3a - 4b + 4c, 2a + 3b - 8c$ and $a - 16b + c$

b. $5x - 8y + 2z, 3x - 2y - 3z$ and $6x - y - z$

c. $6ax - 2by + 3cz, 6by - 11ax - cz$ and $10cz - 2ax - 3by$

d. $6p + 4q - r, 2r - 4p - 6q$ and $2q - 3r + 4p$

e. $4x^2 - 7xy + 4y^2, x^2 - 8xy + 6y^2$ and $2x^2 - 2xy - 5y^2$

6. Subtract the following.

a. $2a - 5b + 2c$ from $3a - 4b - c$

b. $-6p + q + 3r$ from $p - 2q - 5r$

c. $x^3 + 3x^2 - 5x$ from $3x^3 - x^2 + 2x$

d. $4p^2 + 5q^2 - 6r^2$ from $-5r^2 - 4\,q^2 + 3p^2$

e. $9m^2n^2 - 8mn - n^2$ from $7n^2 - 9mn + 8m^2n^2$

7. Add the sum of $3m^2n + 4mn - n^2$ and $6n^2 - mn$ to $11m^2n - 7n^2 + 12mn$.

8. Subtract $16a^2 - 4b^2 + c^2$ from the sum of $5a^2 + 6b^2$ and $9c^2 - 16a^2 - 2b^2$.

9. What should be added to the sum of $x^2 - 5y^2 + xy$ and $6y^2 - 10xy + x^2$ to get $5y^2 + 15xy$?

10. The perimeter of a triangle is $6p^2 - 4p + 9$ and its two sides are $p^2 - 2p + 1$ and $3p^2 - 5p + 3$. Find the third side of the triangle.

Multiplication of Algebraic Expressions

The multiplication of algebraic expressions involves several possible combinations such as the multiplication of a monomial with a monomial, a monomial with a polynomial, a polynomial with a polynomial, etc.

We can perform multiplication either by the horizontal or the vertical method. We shall study each case with the help of examples.

Multiplication of a Monomial by a Monomial

Example 1: Multiply $3x^2$ by $-2y^2$

$3x^2 \times (-2y^2) = 3 \times x \times x \times (-2) \times y \times y$

$= 3 \times (-2) \times x \times x \times y \times y$

$= (-6) \times x^2 \times y^2$

$= -6x^2y^2$

Example 2: Multiply 7xy by $-3x^2y^3$

$7xy \times (-3x^2y^3) = 7 \times x \times y \times (-3) \times x \times x \times y \times y \times y$

$= 7 \times (-3) \times x \times x \times x \times y \times y \times y \times y$

$= (-21) \times x \times x \times x \times y \times y \times y \times y$

$= (-21) \times x^3 \times y^4$

$= -21x^3y^4$

Example 3: Multiply 7ab by $4bc \times -3ca$

$7ab \times 4bc \times (-3)ca = 7 \times a \times b \times 4 \times b \times c \times (-3) \times c \times a$

$= 7 \times 4 \times (-3) \times a \times a \times b \times b \times c \times c$

$= (-84) \times a^2 \times b^2 \times c^2$

$= -84a^2b^2c^2$

When two monomials are multiplied together, the product of the coefficients is determined and then the product of the literal factors.

Alert

1. The powers or exponents of the variables follow the laws of exponents when two algebraic expressions are multiplied.
2. When two or more monomials are multiplied together, the product is also a monomial.

Multiplication of a Binomial by a Monomial

When we multiply a binomial by a monomial, we use the distributive property. Each term of the binomial is multiplied by the monomial. The multiplication of a binominal by a monomial results in a binomial product.

Example 1: Multiply $4x + 7y$ by $-3xy$

$(4x + 7y) \times (-3xy)$

$= 4x \times (-3xy) + 7yx(-3xy)$

$= -12x^2y - 21xy^2$

Example 2: Multiply $5x + 2y$ by $-5x^2$

$(5x + 2y) \times - 5x^2$

$= 5x \times (-5x^2) + 2y \times (-5x^2)$

$= -25x^3 - 10x^2y$

$= -25x^3 - 10x^2y$

Example 3: Multiply $2x^2 + 3y^2$ by $10xy$

$(2x^2 + 3y^2) \times 10xy$

$= 2x^2 \times 10xy + 3y^2 \times 10xy$

$= 20x^3y + 30xy^3$

Multiplication of a Trinomial by a Monomial

To multiply a trinomial by a monomial, we use the distributive property and each term of the trinomial is multiplied by the monomial. The product of a trinomial and a monomial is a trinomial.

Example: Multiply $(x^2 + 4x + 3)$ by $7y$

$= (x^2 + 4x + 3) \times 7y$

$= x^2 \times 7y + 4x \times 7y + 3 \times 7y$

$= 7x^2y + 28xy + 21y$

Multiplication of a Polynomial by a Monomial

In the multiplication of a polynomial by a monomial, each term of the polynomial is multiplied by the monomial.

Example: Multiply $x^3 + 3x^2y + 3xy^2 + y^3$ by $8xy$

$= (x^3 + 3x^2y + 3xy^2 + y3) \times 8xy$

$= x^3 \times 8xy + 3x^2y \times 8xy + 3xy^2 \times 8xy + y^3 \times 8xy$

$= 8x^4y + 24x^3y^2 + 24x^2y^3 + 8xy^4$

Multiplication of a Binomial by a Binomial

The multiplication of a binomial by a binomial can be done either by horizontal or vertical method. In the horizontal method, we use the distributive property of multiplication over addition.

Example: Multiply $3x + 5y$ by $2x - 7y$ using the horizontal method.

$(3x + 5y)(2x - 7y)$

Each term of the first binomial is to be multiplied by each term of the second binomial. Thus, we have,

$3x(2x) + 3x(-7y) + 5y(2x) + 5y(-7y)$

$= 6x^2 \underbrace{- 21xy + 10xy} - 35y^2$

By adding the like terms we get,

$6x^2 - 11xy - 35y^2$

Multiply $3x + 5y$ by $2x - 7y$ using the vertical method.

We first multiply 3x + 5y by (−7y) and then by 2x and write the like terms below each other as follows.

$$\begin{array}{r} 3x + 5y \\ \times \quad 2x - 7y \\ \hline -21xy - 35y^2 \\ 6x^2 + 10xy \qquad \\ \hline 6x^2 - 11xy - 35y^2 \\ \hline \end{array}$$

Multiplication of a Trinomial by a Binomial

To multiply a trinomial by a binomial, we follow the same method as that used for multiplying a binomial with a binomial.

Example: Multiply $x^2 + 2x + 1$ by $x - 4$ using the vertical method.

$$\begin{array}{r} x^2 + 2x + 1 \\ \times \qquad x - 4 \\ \hline -4x^2 - 8x - 4 \\ x^3 + 2x^2 + x \qquad \\ \hline x^3 - 2x^2 - 7x - 4 \\ \hline \end{array}$$

We first multiply by (−4) and then by x and write the like terms below each other.

The product of $x^2 + 2x + 1$ and $x - 4$ is $x^3 - 2x^2 - 7x - 4$.

Multiplication of a Polynomial by a Binomial

This is an extension of the multiplication of a trinomial by a binomial. Since a trinomial is also a polynomial with three terms, the multiplication process is the same in both the cases.

Multiplication of a Trinomial by a Trinomial

To multiply a trinomial by another trinomial, first we multiply each term of the trinomial with each term of the second trinomial.

Example: Multiply $p^2 + 2p + 2$ by $p^2 - p - 5$ using the vertical method.

$$\begin{array}{r} p^2 + 2p + 2 \\ \times \qquad p^2 - p - 5 \\ \hline -5p^2 - 10p - 10 \\ -p^3 - 2p^2 - 2p \qquad \\ p^4 + 2p^3 + 2p^2 \qquad\qquad \\ \hline p^4 + p^3 - 5p^2 - 12p - 10 \\ \hline \end{array}$$

The product of $p^2 + 2p + 2$ and $p^2 - p - 5$ is $p^4 + p^3 - 5p^2 - 12p - 10$.

We first multiply by (-5), followed $(-p)$ and p^2. Each term of the first trinomial is multiplied by each term of the second trinomial. Then we write the like terms below each other and after adding, arrive at the answer.

Multiplication of a Polynomial by a Trinomial

To multiply a polynomial with a trinomial, we multiply each term of the polynomial with each term of the trinomial.

Example: Multiply $x^2 - 5x + 2$ by $5x^2 + 2x - 2$.

By the vertical method:

$$\begin{array}{rrrrr} & & x^2 & -5x & +2 \\ & \times & 5x^2 & +2x & -2 \\ \hline & & -2x^2 & +10x & -4 \\ & 2x^3 & -10x^2 & +4x & \\ 5x^4 & -25x^3 & +10x^2 & & \\ \hline 5x^4 & -23x^3 & -2x^2 & +14x & -4 \\ \hline \end{array}$$

The product is $5x^4 - 23x^3 - 2x^2 + 14x - 4$.

Multiplication of a Polynomial by a Polynomial

To multiply a polynomial with a polynomial, we multiply each term of the first polynomial with each term of the second polynomial.

Example: Multiply $x^3 + 3x^2 + 3x + 1$ by $2x^3 - x^2 - 3x + 2$

By the vertical method:

$$\begin{array}{rrrrrrr} & & & x^3 & +3x^2 & +3x & +1 \\ & & \times & 2x^3 & -x^2 & -3x & +2 \\ \hline & & & 2x^3 & +6x^2 & +6x & +2 \\ & & -3x^4 & -9x^3 & -9x^2 & -3x & \\ & -x^5 & -3x^4 & -3x^3 & -x^2 & & \\ 2x^6 & +6x^5 & +6x^4 & +2x^3 & & & \\ \hline 2x^6 & +5x^5 & +0 & -8x^3 & -4x^2 & +3x & +2 \\ \hline \end{array}$$

The product is $2x^6 + 5x^5 - 8x^3 - 4x^2 + 3x + 2$.

Alert

1. A trinomial is a polynomial with *three* terms. It can also be referred to as a polynomial.
2. When using the vertical method, start multiplying from the extreme right, taking one term at a time and multiplying each term of the top row.
3. Always write the like terms one below the other in one column and then add.
4. When we add, the coefficients are added but the literal terms remain the same.
5. When we multiply, the numerical coefficients are multiplied and the literal terms follow the Laws of Exponents.

Practice Exercise 5.2

1. Find the products of the following monomials.

   a. $(-6)x^2 \times 7xy$ b. $2ab \times (-6)ab$ c. $7x^2 \times 2xy^2$
   d. $(-4x^2y^2) \times 3x^2y^2$ e. $9xyz \times 2z^3$

2. Multiply the following.

   a. $(2xy - 3yz)$ by $4z$ b. $3mn - 7m^2$ by $6m$ c. $5ab$ by $(2a - 3b)$
   d. $(2y^2 + xy)$ by $(-3xy)$ e. $(a^3 - a^2)$ by $7a$

3. Solve the following expressions.

   a. $x(x - y - z) - y(x - y - z)$
   b. $ab(ab + bc + cd) + bc(bc + cd + ab)$
   c. $a(a + b + c) - b(a - b + c) + c(a + b - c)$
   d. Multiply $(x^2y^2 - xy - 1)$ by $(-3x^2)$.
   e. Multiply $\left(\frac{1}{4}x^2y - \frac{2}{3}x^2y^2 - \frac{1}{6}xy^2\right)$ by $-12x^2y^2$.

4. Find the products of the following.

   a. $(x + y) \times (x - y)$ b. $(a + 2b) \times (a + 3b)$ c. $(7x - 1) \times (8 - x)$
   d. $(mn + 3) \times (mn - 4)$ e. $(7p - 6q) \times (2p + 9q)$

5. Find the products of the following.

   a. $(2x + 3y + 4) \times (2x + 3)$ b. $(a + b + 3c) \times (2a - 3b)$
   c. $(2a - 3b - 4c) \times (3a - 4b)$ d. $(2x - 6y + 7z) \times (x - 9y)$
   e. $(6a + 5b + 2c) \times (a - 7b)$

6. Multiply the following.

   a. $(x + 1 - y) \times (y + 1 - x)$ b. $(a + b - c) \times (a - b - c)$
   c. $(m + 2n - 1) \times (2m + n - 4)$ d. $(x^2 + 2xy + y^2) \times (x - y - 1)$
   e. $(m^2 + n^2 - p^2) \times (m - n + p)$

7. Add $3x^2 + 4x - 2$ to the product of $(3x - 4)$ and $(x + 5)$.

8. From the product of $(xy + y + 1)$ and $(y - 6)$ subtract $4xy^2 + 9y^2$.

9. Add the sum of $(6m^2 - n^2 + 1)$ and $(4m^2 - n^2)$ to the product of $(6m + n)$ and $(2m - 3n)$.

10. Add the product of $(4ab + b)$ and $(b - 7)$ to the product of $(-3ab + 1)$ and $(b + 2)$.

Division of Algebraic Expressions

We shall now study simple division of algebraic expressions for the following cases:

1. Division of a monomial by a monomial.
2. Division of a polynomial by a monomial.
3. Division of a polynomial by a polynomial.

Division of a Monomial by a Monomial

When we divide a monomial by a monomial, we divide the numerals in the numerator by the numerals in the denominator followed by the literals. Each like literal in the numerator is divided by the the literal in the denominator. We can also use the Laws of Exponents to perform the division.

Example 1: $12x^5 \div 3x^2$

$$\frac{12x^5}{3x^2} = \frac{12 \times x \times x \times x \times x \times x}{3 \times x \times x} = 4x^3$$

$$\text{or } \frac{12}{3} x^{5-2} = 4x^3$$

Example 2: $-130x^6 \div 10x^3$

$$\frac{-130x^6}{10x^3} = -13x^{6-3} = -13x^3$$

Example 3: $6x^3y^2 \div 3x^2y$

$$\frac{6x^3y^2}{3x^2y} = 2x^{3-2}y^{2-1} = 2xy$$

Division of a Polynomial by a Monomial

When we divide a polynomial by a monomial, we divide each term of the polynomial by the monomial.

Example 1: $(8x^2y - 9xy^2 + 7xy) \div xy$

$$= \frac{8x^2y - 9xy^2 + 7xy}{xy}$$

$$= \frac{8x^2y}{xy} - \frac{9xy^2}{xy} + \frac{7xy}{xy}$$

$$= 8x - 9y + 7$$

Example 2: $(12a^4 - 16a^3 + 20a^2 - 8a) \div 4a$

$$= \frac{12a^4 - 16a^3 + 20a^2 - 8a}{4a}$$

$$= \frac{12a^4}{4a} - \frac{16a^3}{4a} + \frac{20a^2}{4a} - \frac{8a}{4a}$$

$$= 3a^3 - 4a^2 + 5a - 2$$

Example 3: $(25y^5 + 20y^3 - 15y) \div 5y$

$$= \frac{25y^5 + 20y^3 - 15y}{5y}$$

$$= \frac{25y^5}{5y} + \frac{20y^3}{5y} - \frac{15y}{5y}$$

$$= 5y^4 + 4y^2 - 3$$

Dividing a Polynomial by a Polynomial

To divide a polynomial by a polynomial, we use the long-division method. We have a divisor and a dividend and on division we get the quotient and the remainder. If the remainder is 0, the divisor is a factor of the dividend.

We proceed with long division following the steps given below.

Step 1 Write the dividend and the divisor in the descending order of their degrees, which is the standard form.

Step 2 Divide the first term of the dividend by the first term of the divisor to get the first term of the quotient.

Step 3 Multiply all terms of the divisor by the quotient and subtract from the dividend.

Step 4 Now this is the new dividend. Again, divide the first term of this dividend by the first term of the divisor and continue in the same manner.

Step 5 The division continues till the remainder is 0 or a polynomial that has a degree less than that of the divisor.

Example 1: Divide $6a^3 - 10a^2 - 8a + 8$ by $a - 2$.

Step 1 Multiply $a - 2$ by $6a^2$

Step 2 Subtract

Step 3 Multiply $a - 2$ by $2a$

Step 4 Subtract

Step 5 Multiply $a - 2$ by -4

Step 6 Subtract to get a reminder of 0

$$
\begin{array}{r|l}
 & 6a^2 + 2a - 4 \\
\hline
a-2 & 6a^3 - 10a^2 - 8a + 8 \\
 & -(6a^3 - 12a^2) \\
\hline
 & 2a^2 - 8a - 8 \\
 & -(2a^2 - 4a) \\
\hline
 & -4a + 8 \\
 & -(-4a + 8) \\
\hline
 & 0
\end{array}
$$

The quotient is $6a^2 + 2a - 4$ and the reminder is 0.

Check:

$$
\begin{aligned}
\text{Dividend} &= \text{Divisor} \times \text{Quotient} + \text{Remainder} \\
&= (a - 2)(6a^2 + 2a - 4) + 0 \\
&= a(6a^2 + 2a - 4) - 2(6a^2 + 2a - 4) \\
&= 6a^3 + 2a^2 - 4a - 12a^2 - 4a + 8 \\
&= 6a^3 - 10a^2 - 8a + 8
\end{aligned}
$$

Example 2: Divide $x^3 + 7x^2 + 16x + 12$ by $x + 3$.

Step 1 Multiply $x + 3$ by x^2

Step 2 Subtract

Step 3 Multiply $x + 3$ by $4x$

Step 4 Subtract

Step 5 Multiply $x + 3$ by 4

Step 6 Subtract to get a remainder of 0

$$
\begin{array}{r|l}
 & x^2 + 4x + 4 \\
\hline
x+3 & x^3 + 7x^2 + 16x + 12 \\
 & -(x^3 + 3x^2) \\
\hline
 & 4x^2 + 16x - 12 \\
 & -(4x^2 + 12x) \\
\hline
 & 4x + 12 \\
 & -(4x + 12) \\
\hline
 & 0
\end{array}
$$

The quotient is $x^2 + 4x + 4$ and the reminder is 0.

Check:

Dividend $= \text{Divisor} \times \text{Quotient} + \text{Remainder}$

$= (x + 3)(x^2 + 4x + 4) + 0$

$= x(x^2 + 4x + 4) + 3(x^2 + 4x + 4)$

$= x^3 + 4x^2 + 4x + 3x^2 + 12x + 12$

$= x^3 + 7x^2 + 16x + 12$

Example 3: Find the quotient and remainder when $7 + 15x - 13x^2 + 5x^3$ is divided by $4 - 3x + x^2$.

Arranging the terms of dividend and divisor in descending order and then dividing we get,

Step 1 Multiply $x^2 - 3x + 4$ by $5x$

Step 2 Subtract

Step 3 Multiply $x^2 - 3x + 4$ by 2

Step 4 Subtract

$$\begin{array}{r|l} & 5x + 2 \\ \hline x^2 - 3x + 4 & 5x^3 - 13x^2 + 15x + 7 \\ & -(5x^3 - 15x^2 + 20x) \\ \hline & 2x^2 - 5x + 7 \\ & -(2x^2 - 6x + 8) \\ \hline & x - 1 \\ \hline \end{array}$$

The quotient is $5x + 2$ and the reminder is $x - 1$.

Check:

Dividend $= \text{Divisor} \times \text{Quotient} + \text{Remainder}$

$= (x^2 - 3x + 4) \times (5x + 2) + x - 1$

$= x^2(5x + 2) - 3x(5x + 2) + 4(5x + 2) + x - 1$

$= 5x^3 + 2x^2 - 15x^2 - 6x + 20x + 8 + x - 1$

$= 5x^3 - 13x^2 + 15x + 7$

Practice Exercise 5.3

1. Divide the following.

   a. $24x^2y^3$ by $3xy$
   b. $(-64m^4n^3)$ by $4m^2n$
   c. $343m^3n^3$ by $(-7mn^2)$
   d. $75x^3y^2z$ by $15xyz$
   e. $(-81a^5b^3c^2)$ by $(-9a^2bc)$

2. Divide the following.

   a. $16y^3 - 14y^2$ by $2y^2$
   b. $16m^4 - 4m^3 - 8m^2$ by $(-2m^2)$
   c. $7y^3 - 6y^2 + 2y$ by $(-y)$
   d. $77x^4 - 66x^3 + 55x^2 - 44x$ by $(-11x)$
   e. $8x^2y^2 - 6xy^2 + 10x^2y$ by $(-2xy)$

3. Divide the following using the long-division method and verify the formula:
   Dividend = Divisor × Quotient + Remainder

   a. $x^2 - 4x + 4$ by $x - 2$
   b. $15x^2 + 3x - 4$ by $3x + 2$
   c. $2x^3 + x^2 - 5x + 4$ by $2x + 3$
   d. $x^3 - 6x^2 + 11x - 6$ by $x^2 - 5x + 6$
   e. $8x^4 + 10x^3 - 5x^2 - 4x + 1$ by $2x^2 + x - 1$

4. Using the long-division method, find the quotient and remainder for the following algebraic expressions.

   a. $3x^3 + 4x^2 + 5x + 18 \div x + 2$
   b. $3a^4 - 3a^3 - 4a^2 - 4a \div (a^2 - 2a)$

c. $y^4 - 2y^3 + 2y^2 + y + 4 \div y^2 + y + 1$
d. $2p^3 - 5p^2 + 8p - 5 \div 2p^2 - 3p + 5$
e. $5m^3 - 12m^2 + 12m + 13 \div m^2 - 3m + 4$

5. Show that the divisors in each case are the factors of the corresponding dividends.
   a. $2p^2 - 9p - 18 \div p - 6$
   b. $6x^2 - 3y^2 + 7xy - 21x + 7y \div 3x - y$
   c. $x^3 + 7x^2 + 16x + 12 \div x + 3$
   d. $6x^5 + 15x^4 + 16x^3 + 4x^2 + 10x - 35 \div 3x^2 + 5$
   e. $18y^3 - 9y^2 - 17y + 10 \div 6y - 5$
6. What should be subtracted from $14a^2 + 13a - 15$ to make it divisible by $7a - 4$?
7. What should be subtracted from $8x + 7 + 4x^3 + 8x^2$ to make it divisible by $2x^2 - x + 1$?
8. Show that $x^2 + x + 1$ is not a factor of the expression $x^4 - 4x^3 + x^2 - 5x + 6$.
9. Add $6a^2 - 6a + 10$ to the quotient of $3a^3 + 13a^2 + 2a - 8$ divided by $a + 4$.
10. The expression $2x^4 - x^3 - 3x^2 + 5x - 2$ should be divided by which expression to get $x^2 + x - 1$ as the quotient?

Algebraic Identities

We have studied about simple or linear equations in the previous class. The solution or root of an equation is the value which makes the equation true. For every given equation, a particular value is its solution.

For example: $2x + 3 = 15$

$$2x = 15 - 3$$

$$2x = 12, x = \frac{12}{2}$$

$$\therefore x = 6$$

Here we will say that $x = 6$ is the root or the solution of the equation. No other value of x will balance the equation. Thus, $x = 6$ is *a unique* solution of the equation.

Another type of equality that holds true for all values of the variables it contains is called an algebraic identity.

Consider the equation $(x + 6)(x + 7) = x^2 + 13x + 42$.

Now let us replace 'x' with different values and see if the left hand side (LHS) and right hand side (RHS) are balanced.

If $x = 2$, $(2 + 6)(2 + 7) = 2^2 + 13 \times 2 + 42$

LHS: $(2 + 6)(2 + 7) = 2 \times 2 + 2 \times 7 + 6 \times 2 + 6 \times 7$

$$= 4 + 14 + 12 + 42$$

$$= 72$$

RHS: $2^2 + 13x2 + 42 = 2 \times 2 + 13 \times 2 + 42$

$= 4 + 26 + 42$

$= 72$

If $x = 3$, $(-3 + 6)(-3 + 7) = (-3)^2 + 13 \times (-3) + 42$

LHS: $(-3 + 6)(-3 + 7) = (-3) \times (-3) + (-3) \times 7 + 6 \times (-3) + 6 \times 7$

$= 9 - 21 - 18 + 42$

$= 12$

RHS: $(-3)^2 + 13 \times (-3) + 42 = (-3) \times (-3) + 13 \times (-3) + 42$

$= 9 - 39 + 42$

$= 12$

Important Identities

The four identities mentioned below are very important. They help solve several algebraic problems with ease.

Identity 1: $(a + b)^2 = a^2 + 2ab + b^2$

Let us prove this,

Using horizontal method:

$$\begin{aligned}(a + b)^2 &= (a + b)(a + b)\\ &= a(a + b) + b(a + b)\\ &= a^2 + ab + ba + b^2\\ &= a^2 + 2ab + b^2\end{aligned}$$

Using vertical method:

$$\begin{array}{r} a + b \\ \times \quad a + b \\ \hline ab + b^2 \\ a^2 + ab \quad\quad \\ \hline a^2 + 2ab + b^2 \\ \hline \end{array}$$

Identity 2: $(a - b)^2 = a^2 - 2ab + b^2$

Let us prove this.

Using horizontal method:

$$\begin{aligned}(a - b)^2 &= (a - b)(a - b)\\ &= a(a - b) - b(a - b)\\ &= a^2 - ab - ba + b^2\\ &= a^2 - 2ab + b^2\end{aligned}$$

Using vertical method:

$$\begin{array}{r} a - b \\ \times \quad a - b \\ \hline -ab - b^2 \\ a^2 - ab \quad\quad \\ \hline a^2 - 2ab - b^2 \\ \hline \end{array}$$

Identity 3: $(a + b)(a - b) = a^2 - b^2$

Let us prove this.

Using horizontal method:

$$\begin{aligned}(a + b)(a - b) &= a(a - b) + b(a - b)\\ &= a^2 - ab + ab - b^2\\ &= a^2 - ab + ab - b^2\\ &= a^2 - b^2\end{aligned}$$

Using vertical method:

$$\begin{array}{r} a + b \\ \times \quad a + b \\ \hline -ab - b^2 \\ a^2 + ab \quad\quad \\ \hline a^2 - b^2 \quad\quad \\ \hline \end{array}$$

Identity 4: $(x + a)(x + b) = x^2 + (a + b)x + ab$

Let us prove this.

Using horizontal method:

$$(x + a)(x + b) = x(x + b) + a(x + b)$$
$$= x^2 + xb + ax + ab$$
$$= x^2 + bx + ax + ab$$
$$= x^2 + (b + a)x + ab$$
$$= x^2 + (a + b)x + ab$$

Using vertical method:

$$\begin{array}{r} x + a \\ \times \quad x + b \\ \hline +xb + ab \\ x^2 + xa \quad\quad \\ \hline x^2 + ax + bx + ab \\ \hline x^2 + x(a + b) + ab \\ \hline \end{array}$$

Alert!

It is easy to memorise the four identities mentioned above if we concentrate on the pattern.

Applications of Identities

Let us apply the identities in different examples and see how problems can be solved with ease.

Example 1: Use the identity $(a + b)^2 = a^2 + 2ab + b^2$ to find the value, of the following.

a. $(108)^2$

$(108)^2 = (100 + 8)^2$

We apply the identity $(a + b)^2 = a^2 + 2ab + b^2$

Here, $a = 100$ and $b = 8$

$$(100 + 8)^2 = (100)^2 + 2 \times 100 \times 8 + (8)^2$$
$$= 10,000 + 1600 + 64$$
$$= 11,664$$

Hence, $(108)^2 = 11,664$

b. $(2x + 7)^2$

In $(2x + 7)^2$, $a = 2x$ and $b = 7$

$$(2x + 7)^2 = (2x)^2 + 2(2x)(7) + 7^2$$
$$= 4x^2 + 28x + 49$$

Hence, $(2x + 7)^2 = 4x^2 + 28x + 49$

c. $(6x + 7y)^2$

In $(6x + 7y)^2$, $a = 6x$ and $b = 7y$

$$(6x + 7y)^2 = (6x)^2 + 2 \times 6x \times 7y + (7y)^2$$
$$(6x + 7y)^2 = 36x^2 + 84xy + 49y^2$$

Example 2: Use the identity $(a - b)^2 = a^2 - 2ab + b^2$ to find the value of the following.

a. $(97)^2$ can also be written as $(100 - 3)^2$

We apply $(a - b)^2 = a^2 - 2ab + b^2$

Here, $a = 100$ and $b = 3$

$(100 - 3)^2 = (100)^2 - 2(100)(3) + (3)^2$

$= 10000 - 600 + 9$

$= 9{,}409$

Hence, $(97)^2 = 9{,}409$

b. $(3x - 2)^2$

In $(3x - 2)^2$, $a = 3x$ and $b = 2$

$(3x - 2)^2 = (3x)^2 - 2(3x)(2) + (2)^2$

$(3x - 2)^2 = 9x^2 - 12x + 4$

Hence, $(3x - 2)^2 = 9x^2 - 12x + 4$

c. $(7x - 6y)^2$

In $(7x - 6y)^2$, $a = 7x$, $b = 6y$

$(7x - 6y)^2 = (7x)^2 - 2(7x)(6y) + (6y)^2$

$(7x - 6y)^2 = 49x^2 - 84xy + 36y^2$

Hence, $(7x - 6y)^2 = 49x^2 - 84xy + 36y^2$

Example 3: Use the identity $(a + b)(a - b) = a^2 - b^2$ to find the values of the following.

a. $(128)^2 - (72)^2$

In $(128)^2 - (72)^2$, $a = 128$ and $b = 72$

$a^2 - b^2 = (a + b)(a - b)$

$(128)^2 - (72)^2 = (128 + 72)(128 - 72)$

$= (200)(56)$

$= 11{,}200$

Hence, $(128)^2 - (72)^2 = 11{,}200$

b. $(2x + 7)(2x - 7)$

In $(2x + 7)(2x - 7)$, $a = 2x$ and $b = 7$

$(2x + 7)(2x - 7) = (2x)^2 - (7)^2$

$= 4x^2 - 49$

Hence, $(2x + 7)(2x - 7) = 4x^2 - 49$

c. $(6a + 2b)(6a - 2b)$

In $(6a + 2b)(6a - 2b)$, $a = 6a$ and $b = 2b$

$(6a + 2b)(6a - 2b) = (6a)^2 - (2b)^2$

$= 36a^2 - 4b^2$

Hence, $(6a + 2b)(6a - 2b) = 36a^2 - 4b^2$

Example 4: Use the identity $(x + a)(x + b) = x^2 + (a + b)x + ab$ to find the values of the following.

a. $(2m + 7)(2m + 6)$

In $(2m + 7)(2m + 6)$, $x = 2m$, $a = 7$ and $b = 6$

Since, $(x + a)(x + b) = x^2 + (a + b) x + ab$

$$\begin{aligned}(2m + 7)(2m + 6) &= (2m)^2 + (7 + 6)2m + (7 \times 6)\\ &= 4m^2 + (13)(2m) + 42\\ &= 4m^2 + 26m + 42\end{aligned}$$

Hence, $(2m + 7)(2m + 6) = 4m^2 + 26m + 42$

b. $(4x + 3)(4x + 7)$

In $(4x + 3)(4x + 7)$, $x = 4x$, $a = 3$ and $b = 7$

$$\begin{aligned}(4x + 3)(4x + 7) &= 4x^2 + (3 + 7)4x + 3 \times 7\\ &= 16x^2 + 10(4x) + 21\\ &= 16x^2 + 40x + 21\end{aligned}$$

Hence, $(4x + 3)(4x + 7) = 16x^2 + 40x + 21$

c. $(3p + 1)(3p + 2)$

In $(3p + 1)(3p + 2)$, $x = 3p$, $a = 1$ and $b = 2$

$$\begin{aligned}(3p + 1)(3p + 2) &= (3p)^2 + (1 + 2)3p + (1 \times 2)\\ &= 9p^2 + (3 \times 3)p + 2\\ &= 9p^2 + 9p + 2\end{aligned}$$

Hence, $(3p + 1)(3p + 2) = 9p^2 + 9p + 2$

Example 5: If $a + b = 15$ and $ab = 30$, find the value of $a^2 + b^2$.

We know that $(a + b)^2 = a^2 + 2ab + b^2$. By substituting the given values, we have:

$$\begin{aligned}(15)^2 &= a^2 + 2(30) + b^2\\ 225 &= a^2 + 60 + b^2\\ 225 - 60 &= a^2 + b^2\\ 165 &= a^2 + b^2\end{aligned}$$

Thus, $a^2 + b^2 = 165$.

Example 6: If $a^2 + b^2 = 49$ and $ab = 20$, find the value of $a - b$.

We know that $(a - b)^2 = a^2 - 2ab + b^2$.

By substituting the given values we have:

$$\begin{aligned}(a - b)^2 &= a^2 - 2ab + b^2\\ &= a^2 + b^2 - 2ab\\ &= 49 - (2 \times 20)\\ &= 49 - 40\end{aligned}$$

$$(a - b)^2 = 9$$

$$(a - b) = \pm\sqrt{9} = \pm 3$$

Example 7: Find the value of 95×105 by using the formula for identities.

We use the identity $a^2 - b^2 = (a + b)(a - b)$, to solve this problem.

$95 \times 105 = (100 - 5)(100 + 5)$

Here, $a = 100$ and $b = 5$.

So, $(100 - 5)(100 + 5) = (100)^2 - (5)^2$

$= 10,000 - 25$

$= 9,975$

Hence, $95 \times 105 = 9,975$.

Example 8: Find the value of 105×102 by using the formula for identities.

We use the identity $(x^2 + a)(x + b) = x^2 + (a + b)x + ab$, to solve this problem.

$105 \times 102 = (100 + 5)(100 + 2)$

Here, $x = 100$, $a = 5$ and $b = 2$.

$(100 + 5)(100 + 2) = (100)^2 + (5 + 2)100 + 5 \times 2$

$= 10,000 + 7 \times 100 + 10$

$= 10,000 + 700 + 10$

$= 10,710$

Hence, $105 \times 102 = 10,710$

Example 9: Find the product of $(x - 3)(x + 3)(x^2 + 9)$.

$(x - 3)(x + 3) = x^2 - 9$

Using the identity $(a - b)(a + b) = a^2 - b^2$ we get,

$(x^2 - 9)(x^2 + 9) = x^4 - 81$

Here, $a = x^2$ and $b = 9$.

$\therefore (x - 3)(x + 3)(x^2 + 9) = x^4 - 81$

The product of $(x - 3)(x + 3)(x^2 + 9)$ is $x^4 - 81$.

Example 10: If $m = 3$, find the value of $25m^2 + 10m + 1$.

Using the identity 1 $(a + b)^2 = a^2 + 2ab + b^2$ we get,

$(25m^2 + 10m + 1) = (5m)^2 + 2(5m)1 + 1^2$

$= (5m + 1)^2$

$\therefore (5m + 1)^2 = (5 \times 3 + 1)^2 = (15 + 1)^2 = (16)^2 = 256$

The value of $25m^2 + 10m + 1$ is 256.

Alert!

Equations are true for certain values of the contained variables, but identities are true for all values of the contained variables.

Practice Exercise 5.4

1. Find the product of the following using the identity $(a + b)^2 = a^2 + 2ab + b^2$.

a. $(2x + 7)(2x + 7)$ b. $(5y + 3)(5y + 3)$ c. $(7 + 2p)(7 + 2p)$

d. $(1.5 + x)(1.5 + x)$ e. $\left(\frac{3}{4}a + 2\right)\left(\frac{3}{4}a + 2\right)$

2. Find the product of the following using the identity $(a - b)^2 = a^2 - 2ab + b^2$.

a. $(x - 7)(x - 7)$ b. $(2y - 6)(2y - 6)$ c. $(m - 8)(m - 8)$

d. $(1.2a - 1)(1.2a - 1)$ e. $\left(\frac{1}{2}x - 10\right)\left(\frac{1}{2}x - 10\right)$

3. Find the product of the following using the identity $(a + b)(a - b) = a^2 - b^2$.

a. $(x + 7)(x - 7)$ b. $(2y - 7)(2y + 7)$ c. $(7x + 6y)(7x - 6y)$

d. $(4m - 1)(4m + 1)$ e. $\left(\frac{p}{q} + r\right)\left(\frac{p}{q} - r\right)$

4. Find the products of the following using the identity $(x + a)(x + b) = x^2 + ax + bx + ab$.

a. $(2m + 6)(2m + 7)$ b. $(5a + 7)(5a + 3)$ c. $(4r + 1)(4r + 9)$

d. $\left(\frac{1}{2}p + 3\right)\left(\frac{1}{2}p + 8\right)$ e. $(7 + 2a)(11 + 2a)$

5. Using suitable identities, evaluate the following.

a. $(103)^2$ b. $(96)^2$ c. $(68)^2$ d. $(999)^2$ e. $(205)^2$

6. Evaluate the following using the identity $(a + b)(a - b) = a^2 - b^2$.

a. $(90)^2 - 10^2$ b. $(65)^2 - (15)^2$ c. $(99)^2 - (11)^2$

d. $(502) \times 498$ e. 103×97

7. Using suitable identities, evaluate the following.

a. $(5a - 7b)(5a - 7b)$ b. $(5x - 2y)(5x + 2y)$

c. $(5x + 3)(5x + 3)$ d. $(2k + 3)(2k + 7)$

e. $\left(\frac{2}{5}x - \frac{7}{6}y\right)\left(\frac{2}{5}x + \frac{7}{6}y\right)$ f. $\left(\frac{5}{2}x - \frac{4}{3}y\right)\left(\frac{5}{2}x - \frac{4}{3}y\right)$

g. $\left(\frac{11}{3}x + \frac{13}{19}y\right)\left(\frac{11}{3}x + \frac{13}{19}y\right)$ h. $\left(4a - \frac{1}{4}a\right)\left(4a + \frac{1}{4}a\right)$

i. $(z + 7)(z + 6)$ j. $(8y + 4)(8y + 3)$

8. Find the value of 'x' in each of the following cases.

a. $4x = (42)^2 - (38)^2$ b. $7x = (42)^2 - (28)^2$ c. $5x = (60)^2 - (40)^2$

d. $6x = (50)^2 - (14)^2$ e. $2x = (98)^2 - (2)^2$

9. If $2a + 7b = 11$ and $ab = 2$, find the value of $4a^2 + 49b^2$.

10. If $7x - 6y = 30$ and $xy = 5$, find the value of $49x^2 + 36y^2$.

Higher Order Thinking Skills

HOTS

1. a. If $a - \frac{1}{a} = 5$, find the value of $a^2 + \frac{1}{a^2}$.

b. If $b + \frac{1}{b} = 7$, find the value of $b^2 + \frac{1}{b^2}$.

2. Using suitable identities, find the value of the following.

a. $(105)^2$ b. $(48)^2$ c. $\frac{(6.8)^2 - (3.2)^2}{6.8 - 3.2}$

3. Solve the expression $25x^2 + 9y^2 + 30xy$ given that $x = 4$ and $y = 5$.

Highlights

- Expressions that contain one, two or three terms are called monomials, binomials and trinomials, respectively. In general, any expression with three or more terms can be called a polynomial.
- Terms with same literal factors are called like terms. If the literal factors are not the same, they are called unlike terms.
- Only like terms can be added or subtracted.
- When a monomial is multiplied by another monomial, the product is a monomial.
- While multiplying a polynomial by a monomial, every term in the polynomial is to be multiplied by the monomial.
- While multiplying two polynomials, every term in one polynomial is to be multiplied by every term in the other polynomial.
- While dividing a polynomial by a monomial, every term of the polynomial is to be divided by the monomial.
- To divide a polynomial by a polynomial, the long division method is used.
- On performing long division, we arrange the dividend and the divisor in the standard form, that is, arrange them in descending order of the divisor.
- On performing long division, if the remainder is 0, the divisor is a factor of the dividend.
- The degree of the remainder has to be less than the degree of the divisor.
- An identity is an equation which is true for all values of the variables that it contains.
- The important and useful identities are:

  Identity 1: $(a + b)^2 = a^2 + 2ab + b^2$

  Identity 2: $(a - b)^2 = a^2 - 2ab + b^2$

  Identity 3: $(a + b)(a - b) = a^2 - b^2$ (It is called the difference of two squares.)

  Identity 4: $(x + a)(x + b) = x^2 + (a + b)x + ab$

Move 3 matchsticks to make 2 squares.

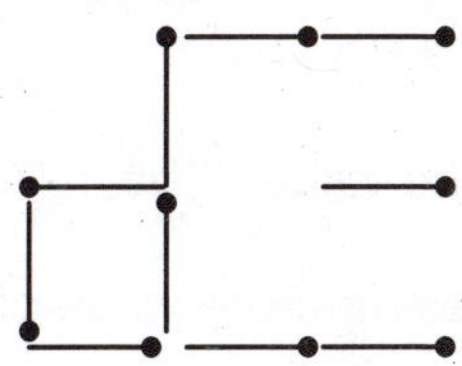

Answer for Brainteaser on page 100

Proving Identities

Objective: To visualise and reinforce the concept of identities.

Material required: chart paper/graph paper and coloured sketch pens

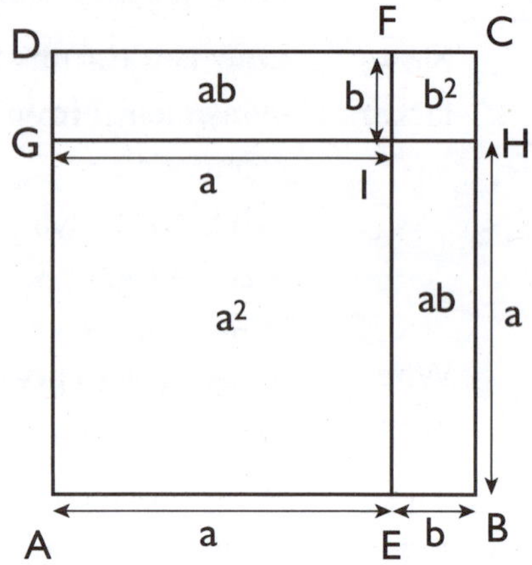

Method:

To prove $(a + b)^2 = a^2 + 2ab + b^2$ using a diagram, proceed with the following steps:

Step 1 Draw a square ABCD and divide it into two squares and two rectangles as shown in the figure using a black sketch pen.

Step 2 Let AE denote 'a' units and EB denote 'b' units. Since AB = AE + EB, we have AB = (a + b) units.

Step 3 Shade the two squares in one colour and the two rectangles in another colour to distinguish between squares and rectangles

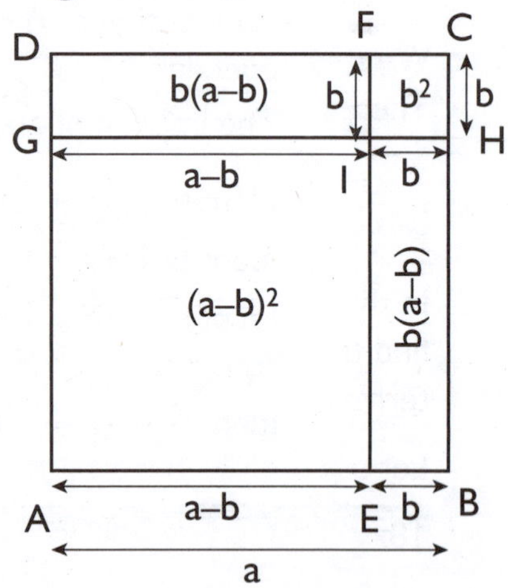

Area of square ABCD = Area of square AEIG + Area of square FCHI + Area of rectangle IHBE + Area of rectangle DGIF.

$\therefore (a + b)^2 = a^2 + b^2 + ab + ab$

$(a + b)^2 = a^2 + b^2 + 2ab$

We can take any numerical value of a and b and verify the equation. For example, use a = 6 and b = 2 and verify the equation.

Answer for Brainteaser from page 99

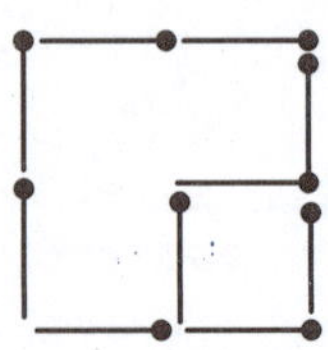

Factorisation

CHAPTER 6

We have learnt earlier about 'factors' of natural numbers. We also know what are 'prime factors'. The process of finding the factors of a given number is called *factorisation*. The factors of 30 are 6×5 or 10×3. The prime factors of 30 are $2 \times 3 \times 5$.

One is a factor of every number. It is a unique number and is *not* a prime number.

Now, we shall consider the factors of algebraic expressions. We are already familiar with the factors of *monomials*. Now, we will study how to find the factors of *polynomials*.

Factorisation of Algebraic Expressions

When an algebraic is expression is written as the product of two or more expressions, then each of these expressions is called a factor of the given expression.

The process of finding two or more expressions whose product is the given expression is called factorisation.

Factorisation is the reverse process of multiplication.

Alert!

The factors of the monomial, $15x^3y^2$, can be written as $3 \times 5 \times x \times x \times x \times y \times y$.

We shall study various methods that can be used to find the factors of algebraic expressions. These are discussed next.

Factorisation Using Common Factors

In this method, we find the factors of each term in the given algebraic expression and then find the common factors. In other words, we find the highest common factor (HCF) of the terms.

Let us consider the monomials $10xy^2$ and $15x^2y$. The factors of the monomials are

$10xy^2 = 2 \times \textcircled{5} \times \textcircled{x} \times \textcircled{y} \times y$

$15x^2y = 3 \times \textcircled{5} \times \textcircled{x} \times x \times \textcircled{y}$

The common factors are encircled. They are 5xy. Hence, 5xy is the HCF of the two monomials. Let us divide each term by the HCF (5xy). We get 2y and 3x, respectively, which do not have any common factor.

Example 1: Factorise $7x + 14xy$.

$7x = 7 \times x$

$14xy = 7 \times 2 \times x \times y$

The common factors are 7 and x. If we take 7x to be common from the given expression, we get $7x(1 + 2y)$.

These factors cannot be reduced further.

Hence, $7x + 14xy$ can be factorised into $7x(1 + 2y)$.

$7x$ and $(1 + 2y)$ are called the factors of the expression $7x + 14xy$. When we multiply $7x$ and $(1 + 2y)$ we get the product $7x + 14xy$.

Example 2: Factorise $2n^2 + 3n$.

$2n^2 + 3n = 2 \times n \times n + 3 \times n$

Here, we see that 'n' is the only common factor. So, we can write the factors of $2n^2 + 3n$ as $n(2n + 3)$.

Example 3: Factorise $4x^3y^3 - 12x^4y^5 + 16x^6y^6$.

Let us take each term separately and find the HCF.

$4x^3y^3 = \textcircled{2} \times \textcircled{2} \times \textcircled{x} \times \textcircled{x} \times \textcircled{x} \times \textcircled{y} \times \textcircled{y} \times \textcircled{y}$

$12x^4y^5 = \textcircled{2} \times \textcircled{2} \times 3 \times \textcircled{x} \times \textcircled{x} \times \textcircled{x} \times x \times \textcircled{y} \times \textcircled{y} \times \textcircled{y} \times y \times y$

$16x^6y^6 = \textcircled{2} \times \textcircled{2} \times 2 \times 2 \times \textcircled{x} \times \textcircled{x} \times \textcircled{x} \times x \times x \times x \times \textcircled{y} \times \textcircled{y} \times \textcircled{y} \times y \times y \times y$

The common factors are encircled. Hence, the HCF is $2 \times 2 \times x \times x \times x \times y \times y \times y = 4x^3y^3$.

Taking $4x^3y^3$, which is common from the given expression, we get, $4x^3y^3 (1 - 3xy^2 + 4x^3y^3)$.

$= 4x^3y^3 (1 - 3xy^2 + 4x^3y^3)$

Factorisation by Regrouping the Terms

In a given expression, all the terms may not have a common factor, but, if rearranged, some terms may have one common factor and the other terms may have another common factor. By the suitable arrangement of terms in groups, such that each group has a common factor, we can factorise the given expression. Let us look at the expression $5ab + 5b + 7a + 7$. Here, there is no common factor for all the four terms. However, if we consider the first two terms, 5b is a common factor and if we consider the next two terms, then 7 is a common factor. Let us group the terms as $5ab + 5b$ in one group and $7a + 7$ in the second group.

Now, $5ab + 5b = 5b(a + 1)$ and $7a + 7 = 7(a + 1)$.

Hence, $(5ab + 5b) + (7a + 7)$ can be written as $5b(a + 1) + 7(a + 1)$.

Now, $(a + 1)$ is a common factor, so if we take $(a + 1)$ as common, we get $(a + 1)(5b + 7)$.

These are the factors of the given expression.

Let us study a few more examples to get a clear understanding of the concept.

Example 1: Factorise $a^2 + bc + ab + ac$.

By suitable grouping, we can factorise the given expression. Let us rearrange the terms and rewrite them as:

$$\underbrace{a^2 + ab} + \underbrace{bc + ac}$$

In $a^2 + ab$, we can see that 'a' is a common factor and in $bc + ac$, 'c' is a common factor.

So, we have $a(\underline{a + b}) + c(\underline{b + a})$.

Addition is commutative, so $a + b$ and $b + a$ are the same. Taking $a + b$ common, we have $(a + b)(a + c)$.

The factors of the given expression are $(a + b)(a + c)$.

Example 2: Factorise $ax^2 + by^2 + bx^2 + ay^2$.

Let us regroup the terms and write them as: $\underbrace{ax^2 + bx^2} + \underbrace{ay^2 + by^2}$.

In the first group, we can take x^2 to be the common factor and in the second group, y^2 is the common factor. So we get $x^2(\underline{a + b}) + y^2(\underline{a + b})$.

Now $a + b$ is a common factor. Hence, we get $(a + b)(x^2 + y^2)$.

Thus, the factors of the given expression are $(a + b)(x^2 + y^2)$.

We can factorise the given expression by grouping them in another way. We can write the expression as: $ax^2 + ay^2 + bx^2 + by^2$.

Now a is the common factor in the first group and b is the common factor in the second group. So we have: $a(x^2 + y^2) + b(x^2 + y^2)$.

Now $(x^2 + y^2)$ is a common factor and we get $(x^2 + y^2)(a + b)$.

However, the answer in both the cases is the same, that is, $(x^2 + y^2)(a + b)$ or $(a + b)(x^2 + y^2)$.

Example 3: Factorise $xy - pq + qy - px$.

By rearranging the terms and grouping them, we get,

$$xy - px + qy - pq$$
$$= x(\underline{y - p}) + q(\underline{y - p})$$
$$= (y - p)(x + q)$$

The factors of the given expression are $(x + q)(y - p)$.

Practice Exercise 6.1

1. Find the greatest common factor or HCF in the given groups of monomials.

a. $8x^3y^2, 16x^2y^3$
b. $18x^2yz, 6xy^2z$
c. $-8x^3, 4x^2y, 16xy$
d. $11a^3b^2, 22a^2b, 33ab^3$
e. $15pq, 5p^2q, 20pq^2$
f. $10m^2n^2, 40m^3n^2, 20mn$
g. $19pqr, 95p^2q^2r^2, 57p^2$
h. $9xy, -27x^2y^2, 36x^3y^3$
i. $-3a^3, -6b^3, -9c^3$
j. $-7s^2, 28s^2t^3, 14s^3t^3$

2. Find the HCF in each of the following cases.

a. $7x^2 - 14xy$
b. $11x^3y^2 - 10x^2y$
c. $15mn - 30m^2n^3$
d. $60x^3 - 20x^2$
e. $56a^4b^2 - 14a^2b^4 + 7ab$
f. $9lm + 99mn + 999lmn$
g. $16a^2b - 8ab^2 + 4ab$
h. $42xyz + 35x^2y^2z^2 + 63x^3y^3z^3$
i. $25a^3 - 50b^3 + 15c^3 + 100d^3$
j. $7abc + 14bca + 21cab$

3. Factorise the following expressions.

a. $6x^2 - 18x^3$
b. $5xy - 5xy^2$
c. $24x^3 + 18x^4$
d. $10x^2 + 10y^2$
e. $17xy + 51x^2y^2$
f. $-54a^4 - 27a^3$
g. $25mn^2 + 50m^2n$
h. $36x^3y - 60x^2y^3z$
i. $24x^3 - 36x^2y$
j. $6ab - 9bc$

4. Factorise the following expressions.

a. $y^4 - 4y^3 + 2y^2$
b. $12x^2y + 16xy^2 - 8x^2y^2$
c. $15a^2b^2 + 25ab + 30$
d. $m^5 - m^4 + m^2$
e. $30x^3 - 60x^2 + 90x$
f. $12x^3y^2 - 14x^2y^3 + 28xy^4$
g. $21a^2 - 14a^2b^2 + 35a^4$
h. $9x^3 - 6x^2 + 12x$
i. $8x^2 - 72xy + 12x$
j. $-5 - 10p + 20p^2$

5. Factorise the following.

a. $x^2y + 3x + xy + 3$
b. $ab + bc + ad + cd$
c. $a^2 - 2a + ab - 2b$
d. $x^2 - ax - bx + ab$
e. $ab^2 - bc^2 - ab + c^2$
f. $x^2 - xz + xy - yz$
g. $a(x + 5) - b(x + 5)$
h. $11(m + n) - 5(m + n)$
i. $7x^2 + 2xy + 63x + 18y$
j. $2y^2 + 3x + xy + 6y$

Factorisation by Using Identities

We have studied important identities in the previous chapter. We shall now learn to use the identities for the factorisation of algebraic expressions. Let us recall the identities.

Identity 1: $(a + b)^2 = a^2 + 2ab + b^2$

Identity 2: $(a - b)^2 = a^2 - 2ab + b^2$

Identity 3: $(a + b)(a - b) = a^2 - b^2$

The first two identities are used for the factorisation of algebraic expressions that are *perfect squares*. The third identity is applicable when a binomial is the *difference* of two squares.

The following examples will illustrate the application of the identities.

Example 1: Factorise $x^2 + 10x + 25$.

Since the entire algebraic expression has positive signs, we can use the identity, $(a + b)^2 = a^2 + 2ab + b^2$ to factorise.

We can write $x^2 + 10x + 25$ as $(x)^2 + 2 \times x \times 5 + (5)^2$.

Comparing it to $a^2 + 2ab + b^2 = (a + b)^2$, we have

$(x^2) + 2 \times x \times 5 + 5^2 = (x + 5)^2$ or

$x^2 + 10x + 25 = (x + 5)^2 = (x + 5)(x + 5)$

Factors of $x^2 + 10x + 25$ are $(x + 5)(x + 5)$.

Example 2: Factorise $4x^2 + 12xy + 9y^2$.

Since the entire algebraic expression has positive signs, we can use the identity $(a + b)^2 = a^2 + 2ab + b^2$ to factorise.

We can write $4x^2 + 12xy + 9y^2$ as $(2x)^2 + 2 \times (2x) \times (3y) + (3y)^2$

where $a = 2x$ and $b = 3y$.

$a^2 = (2x)^2 = 4x^2$

$b^2 = (3y)^2 = 9y^2$

$2ab = 2 \times (2x) \times (3y) = 12xy$

Therefore, $(2x)^2 + 2 \times (2x) \times (3y) + (3y)^2 = (2x + 3y)^2$

$4x^2 + 12xy + 9y^2 = (2x + 3y)^2$

$= (2x + 3y)(2x + 3y)$

Factors of $4x^2 + 12xy + 9y^2$ are $(2x + 3y)(2x + 3y)$.

Alert!

When all the signs are positive in the algebraic expression, we use the identity $(a + b)^2 = a^2 + 2ab + b^2$. The two extreme terms have to be perfect squares and the middle term should be twice the product of the square root of the extremes.

Example 3: Factorise $x^2 - 6x + 9$.

Here, we use the identity $(a - b)^2 = a^2 - 2ab + b^2$ to factorise the expression. The two extreme terms are perfect squares and the middle term is negative. Hence, we can write

$x^2 - 6x + 9$ as $(x)^2 - 2 \times x \times 3 + (3)^2$.

Comparing it to $a^2 - 2ab + b^2 = (a - b)^2$, we have

$$x^2 - 6x + 9 = (x)^2 - 2 \times x \times 3 + (3)^2$$
$$= (x - 3)^2$$
$$x^2 - 6x + 9 = (x - 3)^2 = (x - 3)(x - 3)$$

The factors of $x^2 - 6x + 9$ are $(x - 3)(x - 3)$.

Example 4: Factorise $9x^2 - 12xy + 4y^2$.

Here again we see that the extreme terms are perfect squares with a positive sign and the middle term is negative. Hence, we can write

$9x^2 - 12xy + 4y^2$ as

$$(3x)^2 - 2 \times 3x \times 2y + (2y)^2 = (3x - 2y)^2$$
$$9x^2 - 12xy + 4y^2 = (3x)^2 - 2 \times 3x \times 2y + (2y)^2$$
$$= (3x - 2y)^2$$
$$9x^2 - 12xy + 4y^2 = (3x - 2y)^2$$
$$= (3x - 2y)(3x - 2y)$$

The factors of $9x^2 - 12xy + 4y^2$ are $(3x - 2y)(3x - 2y)$.

Alert!

In a trinomial expression, the square terms will be positive, the middle terms will be positive or negative. If the middle term is positive, use the identity $(a + b)^2 = a^2 + 2ab + b^2$ and if the middle term is negative, use the identity $(a - b)^2 = a^2 - 2ab + b^2$.

Example 5: Factorise $x^2 - 225$.

Here, we use the identity $(a + b)(a - b) = a^2 - b^2$ to factorise the expression since it is a binomial and a difference of two squares.

We know that $a^2 - b^2 = (a + b)(a - b)$, thus

$$x^2 - 225 = (x + 15)(x - 15)$$

The factors of $x^2 - 225$ are $(x + 15)(x - 15)$.

Example 6: Factorise $49m^2 - 81n^2$.

The given binomial expression is the difference of two squares, hence, we apply the identity $(a + b)(a - b) = a^2 - b^2$.

We can write $49m^2 - 81n^2$ as $(7m)^2 - (9n)^2$.

$(7m)^2 - (9n)^2 = (7m + 9n)(7m - 9n)$ or

$49m^2 - 81n^2 = (7m + 9n)(7m - 9n)$

The factors of $49m^2 - 81n^2$ are $(7m + 9n)(7m - 9n)$.

Example 7: Factorise $x^2 + 4x - 8y + 4y^2 - 4xy$.

Here, there are five terms in the expression. We identify the trinomial that can be factorised by the identity $(a + b)^2 = a^2 + 2ab + b^2$ and the identity $(a - b)^2 = a^2 - 2ab + b^2$ and then group it.

The expression $x^2 - 4xy + 4y^2$ can be factorised by the identity $(a - b)^2 = a^2 - 2ab + b^2$. The first and the third terms are perfect squares and the middle term is the product of x and y and has a negative sign, so we apply Identity 2.

$\underbrace{x^2 - 4xy} + 4y^2 + 4x - 8y$

$= x^2 - 2 \times x \times (2y) + (2y)^2 + 4x - 8y$

$= (x - 2y)^2 + 4x - 8y.$

In $4x - 8y$, we see that the common factor is 4, so we have

$= (x - 2y)^2 + 4(x - 2y)$

$= \underline{(x - 2y)}\ \underline{(x - 2y)} + 4\underline{(x - 2y)}$

Now $(x - 2y)$ is a common factor, so we can write it as

$(x - 2y)(x - 2y + 4).$

$x^2 + 4x - 8y + 4y^2 - 4xy = (x - 2y)(x - 2y + 4)$

The factors of $x^2 + 4x - 8y + 4y^2 - 4xy$ are $(x - 2y)(x - 2y + 4)$.

Example 8: Factorise $x^2 - y^2 - z^2 + 2yz$.

Here y and z are perfect squares and yz is the product term, so the given expression can be written as

$x^2 - (y^2 + z^2 - 2yz)$

$= x^2 - (y^2 - 2yz + z^2)$

Now we can apply Identity 2 in $y^2 - 2yz + z^2$ and get $x^2 - (y - z)^2$.

We see two square terms with a negative sign in between, hence, we can use the identity $(a + b)(a - b) = a^2 - b^2$ and get, $x^2 - (y - z)^2 = [x + (y - z)][x - (y - z)]$

$(x + y - z)\ (x - y + z)$

The factors of $x^2 - y^2 - z^2 + 2yz$ are $(x + y - z)\ (x - y + z)$.

Example 9: Factorise: $m^2 + 4n^2 + 4mn - 64$.

Here there are four terms, where the first three terms form a trinomial with two square terms and one product term with a positive sign. Hence, for the first three terms we can use the identity $(a + b)^2 = a^2 + 2ab + b^2$.

$m^2 + 4mn + 4n^2 - 64$

$m^2 + 2 \times m \times 2n + (2n)^2 - 64$

$(m + 2n)^2 - (8)^2$

Now we have a binomial expression with two squared terms and a negative sign. Hence, we can apply Identity 3.

The factors of $m^2 + 4n^2 + 4mn - 64$ are $(m + 2n + 8)(m + 2n - 8)$.

Example 10: Factorise the numerator and find the quotient.

$$\frac{4m^2 + 12mn + 9n^2}{2m + 3n}$$

Here, the numerator is a trinomial that can be factorised using Identity 1.

$$\begin{aligned} \text{Numerator} &= 4m^2 + 12mn + 9n^2 \\ &= (2m)^2 + 2 \times 2m \times 3n + (3n)^2 \\ &= (2m + 3n)^2 \end{aligned}$$

Now we have, $\dfrac{(2m + 3n)^2}{(2m + 3n)} = \dfrac{(2m + 3n)(2m + 3n)}{(2m + 3n)} = 2m + 3n$

Alert!

1. We can have expressions where only one identity is used for factorisation.
2. We also have expressions where grouping is done and then different identities are applied.
3. Sometimes the numerator as well as the denominator are factorised and then we cancel the common terms.

Practice Exercise 6.2

1. Factorise the following.

a. $4x^2 + 4x + 1$ b. $9y^2 + 12yz + 4z^2$ c. $16p^2 + 40p + 25$
d. $9m^2 + 24m + 16$ e. $4t^2 + 20t + 25$ f. $a^2 + 8a + 16$
g. $b^2 + 14b + 49$ h. $36n^2 + 36n + 9$ i. $1 + 18k + 81k^2$
j. $36x^2 + 6x + \frac{1}{4}$

2. Factorise the following.

a. $x^2 - 6x + 9$ b. $a^2 - 10a + 25$ c. $9p^2 - 12p + 4$
d. $16d^2 - 24d + 9$ e. $1 - 2m + m^2$ f. $81y^2 - 36y + 4$
g. $121b^2 - 22b + 1$ h. $36 - 12k + k^2$ i. $\frac{1}{4} - 3n + 9n^2$
j. $p^2q^2 - 2pq + 1$

3. Factorise the following.

a. $4x^2 - y^2$ b. $81 - 25b^2$ c. $121p^2 - 49q^2$

d. $36a^2b^2 - 100$ e. $\frac{1}{49}m^2 - \frac{1}{25}n^2$ f. $0.49a^2 - 0.36b^2$

g. $(2a + 3b)^2 - 16c^2$ h. $9 - (a + b)^2$ i. $(4x + y)^2 - (x + 3y)^2$

j. $(45a)^2 - (5a)^2$

4. Factorise the following.

a. $a^2 + b^2 + 2ab - 4c^2$ b. $81x^2 - 4y^2 - z^2 + 4yz$

c. $4m^2 + 9p^2 + 12mp - 64n^2$ d. $a^2 + b^2 + 2ab - 121$

e. $100c^2 - 20c + 1 - 100$ f. $36y^2 + 84xy + 49x^2 - 49$

g. $t^2 + 24st + 144s^2 - 144$ h. $25 - a^2 - b^2 - 2ab$

i. $9x^2 - y^2 + 4y - 4$ j. $m^2 - n^2 - 2n - 1$

5. Factorise the numerator and find the quotient.

a. $\frac{am + bm + an + bn}{a + b}$ b. $\frac{x^2 - ax - bx + ab}{x - a}$

c. $\frac{6ab - b^2 + 12ac - 2bc}{b + 2c}$ d. $\frac{121 - 4x^2}{2x + 11}$

e. $\frac{x^2 + 2xy + y^2 - 4z^2}{(x + y - 2z)}$ f. $\frac{225t^2 - 100s^2}{(15t + 10s)}$

g. $\frac{4q^2 - p^2 - 2pr - r^2}{p + r + 2q}$ h. $\frac{y^2 + 24xy + 144x^2}{12x + y}$

i. $\frac{4m^2 + m + \frac{1}{16}}{\frac{1}{4} + 2m}$ j. $\frac{25m^2 - 110m + 121}{5m - 11}$

Factorisation by Splitting the Middle Term

This is the most frequently used factorisation in any quadratic trinomial. In this case, we use Identity 4 for factorisation. According to Identity 4

$$(x + a)(x + b) = x^2 + (a + b)x + ab.$$

So, the coefficient of x is the *sum* of a and b. The constant term is the product of a and b Hence, we observe the product term and find its factors. The coefficient of x is the *sum* of these factors.

Let us understand this method of factorisation with the help of the following examples.

Example 1: Factorise $x^2 + 9x + 20$.

Find the factors of the constant term, that is, 20. The factors are 1×20, 20×1, 10×2, 5×4, 4×5. Out of these, we select those factors whose sum is the coefficient of x. The coefficient of x is $4 + 5 = 9$ and the constant term is $4 \times 5 = 20$.

Therefore, $x^2 + 9x + 20$

$= x^2 + 5x + 4x + 20$

By grouping the terms, we get

$(x^2 + 5x) + (4x + 20)$

$= x(\underline{x + 5}) + 4(\underline{x + 5})$

$= (x + 5)(x + 4)$

Thus, the factors of $x^2 + 9x + 20$ are $(x + 5)(x + 4)$.

Another way to find the factors is by applying the Identity $(x + a)(x + b) = x^2 + (a + b)x + ab$, directly.

$x^2 + 9x + 20 = x^2 + 4x + 5x + 20$

$= x^2 + (4 + 5)x + 4 \times 5$

$= (x + 4)(x + 5)$

Example 2: Factorise: $x^2 + 10x + 24$.

The factors of 24 are 1×24, 24×1, 2×12, 12×2, 6×4, 4×6, 3×8 and 8×3.

Select the factors that give a sum of 10.

$4 + 6 = 10$ and $4 \times 6 = 24$

We have $x^2 + 10x + 24$

$= x^2 + 4x + 6x + 24$

$= x^2 + (4 + 6)x + 4 \times 6$

$= (x + 4)(x + 6)$ (using Identity 4)

where $a = 4$, $b = 6$, $a + b = 10$, $a \times b = 24$.

Another method of factorisation is by grouping the terms.

$x^2 + 10x + 24$

$= x^2 + 4x + 6x + 24$

By grouping the terms we have,

$= \underbrace{x^2 + 4x} + \underbrace{6x + 24}$

$= x(\underline{x + 4}) + 6(\underline{x + 4})$

$= (x + 4)(x + 6)$

The factors of $x^2 + 10x + 24$ are $(x + 4)(x + 6)$.

Example 3: Factorise: $x^2 - 7x + 12$.

The factors of 12 are 1×12, 12×1, 2×6, 6×2, 3×4 and 4×3.

If we want the sum as 7, we have to choose the factors 3 and 4.

$x^2 - 7x + 12$

$= x^2 - 3x - 4x + 12$

$= x(x - 3) - 4(x - 3)$

$=(x - 3)(x - 4)$

Using the identity method we have,

$x^2 - 7x + 12$

$= x^2 - 3x - 4x + 12$

$= x^2 - (3 + 4)x + 3 \times 4$

$= (x - 3)(x - 4)$

The factors of $x^2 - 7x + 12$ are $(x - 3)(x - 4)$.

Example 4: Factorise: $x^2 - 4x - 77$.

The product of the two numbers is (-77).

Thus, the factors will be 1×77 and 7×11. Here, one number will be positive and the other will be negative. Since the sum is (-4), the greater number will be negative, that is, 11 will be negative and 7 will be positive. Thus, $a = (-11)$ and $b = 7$.

$a + b = (-11) + 7 = (-4)$ and $a \times b = (-11) \times 7 = (-77)$

$x^2 - 4x - 77$

$= x^2 - 11x + 7x + (-11) \times 7$

$= x^2 - (11 + 7)x + (-11) \times 7$

$= (x - 11)(x + 7)$ (using Identity 4)

or

$x^2 - 4x - 77$

$x^2 - 11x + 7x - 77$

$= x(x - 11) + 7(x - 11)$

$= (x - 11)(x + 7)$

The factors of $x^2 - 4x - 77$ are $(x - 11)(x + 7)$.

Example 5: Factorise: $3x^2 + 17x + 20$.

Here, the coefficient of x^2 is not 1 as in the previous examples. In this case, the product of the constant term and the coefficient of x^2 has to be taken, which is $3 \times 20 = 60$. Now, this product has to be split to obtain the middle term for which we will find out the factors. The factors of 60 are 1×60, 2×30, 3×20, 4×15, 5×12 and 6×10.

To obtain the middle term, we choose 5×12 since the sum will be $5 + 12 = 17$.

$5 + 12 = 17$ and $5 \times 12 = 60$

$3x^2 + 17x + 20$

$= 3x^2 + 5x + 12x + 20$

$= x(3x + 5) + 4(3x + 5)$

$= (3x + 5)(x + 4)$

The factors of $3x^2 + 17x + 20$ are $(3x + 5)(x + 4)$.

Example 6: Factorise $8x^2 - 18x + 9$.

The product of the constant term and the coefficient of x^2 is $9 \times 8 = 72$. The factors of 72 are 1×72, 2×36, 3×24, 4×18, 6×12 and 8×9.

To obtain 18 as the middle term, we use the factors 6 and 12. The sum of 6 and 12 will give us 18. However, since 18 is negative, we use -6 and -12.

$8x^2 - 18x + 9$

$= 8x^2 - 6x - 12x + 9$

$= 2x(4x - 3) - 3(4x - 3)$

$= (4x - 3)(2x - 3)$

The factors of $8x^2 - 18x + 9$ are $(4x - 3)(2x - 3)$.

Alert!

1. In the factorisation of quadratic trinomials, we write the expression in the descending order as $x^2 + bx + c$ or $ax^2 + bx + c$.
2. We find the product of the coefficient of x^2 and the constant term and then find the factors of this term. From these the factors that give the sum of the middle term are chosen.
3. If the product is negative and the middle term is also negative, then the sum will have one positive factor.
4. If the product is positive and the middle term is negative, then both the factors will be negative.
5. The table below shows a summary of the positive and negative signs to be used.

Product of the Extremes	Middle Terms	Factors	
+	+	+	+
+	−	−	−
−	−	+	−
−	+	+	−

Practice Exercise 6.3

1. Factorise the following expressions.

a. $x^2 + 14x + 45$ b. $x^2 + 12x + 36$

c. $x^2 + 15x + 56$ d. $x^2 + 19x + 60$

e. $x^2 + 13x + 40$ f. $3x^2 + 10x + 8$

g. $3x^2 + 48x + 117$ h. $3x^2 + 14x + 8$

i. $2x^2 + 13x + 20$ j. $3x^2 + 11x + 6$

2. Factorise the following expressions.

a. $m^2 - 33m + 90$ b. $m^2 - 9m + 14$

c. $m^2 - 36m + 99$ d. $m^2 - 23m + 42$

e. $m^2 - 22m + 117$ f. $2m^2 - 22m + 48$

g. $3m^2 - 10m + 8$ h. $5m^2 - 45m + 70$

i. $2m^2 - 24m + 70$ j. $3m^2 - 15m + 18$

3. Factorise the following expressions.

a. $a^2 - 5a - 24$ b. $a^2 - 13a - 30$

c. $a^2 - 3a - 54$ d. $a^2 - 8a - 48$

e. $a^2 + 19a - 150$ f. $6a^2 + 11a - 10$

g. $7a^2 + 7a - 42$ h. $4a^2 - 20a - 24$

i. $2a^2 - 17a - 30$ j. $4a^2 + 52a - 56$

4. Factorise the numerator and simplify.

a. $\dfrac{x^2 + 9x + 20}{x + 5}$ b. $\dfrac{x^2 + 10x - 24}{x + 12}$

c. $\dfrac{y^2 + 8y + 7}{y + 7}$ d. $\dfrac{y^2 - y - 42}{y + 6}$

e. $\dfrac{a^2 - 10a - 11}{a - 11}$ f. $\dfrac{a^2 - 6a - 40}{a - 10}$

g. $\dfrac{m^2 + 5m - 14}{m - 2}$ h. $\dfrac{m^2 + 11m + 24}{m + 8}$

i. $\dfrac{2a^2 + 11a + 12}{2a + 3}$ j. $\dfrac{3m^2 + 13m - 10}{3m - 2}$

5. Factorise the following trinomials.

a. $x^2 + 6x + 5$ b. $x^2 - 2x - 15$

c. $x^2 - 4x + 3$ d. $x^2 - 18x + 65$

e. $x^2 - 6x - 7$ f. $4x^2 + 8x + 3$

g. $4x^2 - 4x - 15$ h. $4x^2 - 16x + 15$

i. $6x^2 - 19x + 15$ j. $2x^2 + 3x - 5$

Highlights

- Factorisation of an algebraic expression is the procedure to find the factors and write the expression as a product of its factors, that cannot be reduced or simplified further.
- The factors could be constants, variables or algebraic expressions.
- Factorisation can be done by:
  - selecting common factors after finding their HCF.
  - regrouping terms and selecting the common terms.
  - using the identities directly in case of perfect squares.
  - splitting the middle term in a quadratic trinomial.
- The four identities used for factorisation are:

  Identity 1: $(a + b)^2 = a^2 + 2ab + b^2$

  Identity 2: $(a - b)^2 = a^2 - 2ab + b^2$

  Identity 3: $(a + b)(a - b) = a^2 - b^2$

  Identity 4: $(x + a)(x + b) = x^2 + (a + b)x + ab$

Higher Order Thinking Skills

HOTS

1. Factorise the following.

   a. $pq - mn + pn - mq$

   b. $pq^2 + q(p - 1) - 1$

   c. $y^2 - xy(1 - x) - x^3$

2. Find the binomial which is a common factor in the following cases.

   a. $a^2 - 4b^2$ and $a^2 - 4ab + 4b^2$

   b. $\frac{4}{9} - 16x^2$ and $16x^2 + \frac{16x}{3} + \frac{4}{9}$

   c. $4p^2 - 9$ and $2p^2 + 11p - 21$

3. Factorise $4x^2 - y^2 + 6y - 9$.

Solving Equations

Aim: To write a word problem in the form of an equation and then factorise it.

Material required: a pen

Method: Write the equations and their fractions.

Problem	Equation	Factors
1. A number square plus eight times the same number minus three is equal to 38.		
2. Forty divided by a number plus seven times the number is equal to 10.		
3. A number plus its cube plus seven times the number added to 21 is 1.		
4. Twenty divided by a number minus the cube of another number plus 87 is seven.		
5. Thirty-nine times the square of a number is equal to three times the number plus 12.		

What is the number that is 5 more than the number that is one-fifth of one-fifth of one-half of 1,050?

Answer for Brainteaser on page 117

Rewind

1. Add $3a - 4b + 4c$, $2a - 3b - 8c$ and $a - 6b + c$.

2. Find the sum of $2x^3 - 9x^2 + 8$, $3x^2 - 6x - 5$, $7x^3 - 10x + 1$ and $3 + 2x - 5x^2 - 4x^3$.

3. Subtract $x^3 + 3x^2 - 5x + 4$ from $3x^3 - x^2 + 2x - 4$.

4. What must be subtracted from $3p^2 - 6pq - 3q^2 - 1$ to get $4p^2 - 7pq - 4q^2 + 1$?

5. Find the products of the following.

   a. $(2x + 5) \times (4x - 3)$ b. $(9x + 5y) \times (4x + 3y)$ c. $(x^2 - y^2) \times (x + 2y)$

6. Write the quotient and remainder for each of the following.

   a. $(x^2 - 4x + 4) \div (x - 2)$ b. $(15x^2 + x - 6) \div (3x + 2)$
   c. $(2x^3 + x^2 - 5x - 2) \div (2x + 3)$

7. Expand the following using suitable identities.

   a. $(8a + 3b)^2$ b. $(7x + 2y)^2$ c. $(5x + 11)^2$

8. Evaluate the following using suitable identities.

   a. $(63)^2 - (17)^2$ b. (10.3×9.7) c. 502×498

9. If $3a + 5b = 11$ and $ab = 2$, find the value of $9a^2 + 25b^2$.

10. If $x = 2$, find the value of $4x^2 + 12x + 9$.

11. Factorise the following.

    a. $36x^3y - 60x^2y^3z$ b. $5x(x - 4) - 7(x - 4)$
    c. $9a(3a - 5b) - 12a^2(3a - 5b)$

12. Factorise the following.

    a. $81 - 49m^2$ b. $9a^2b^2 - 25$ c. $1 - (b - c)^2$

13. Factorise the following.

    a. $1 + 2x + x^2$ b. $4x^2 + 20x + 25$ c. $x^2 + x + \frac{1}{4}$

14. Factorise the following.

    a. $x^2 + 12x + 27$ b. $x^2 + 13x + 40$ c. $x^2 - 17x + 16$

15. Factorise the numerator and find the quotient.

a. $\dfrac{121 - 4x^2}{2x + 11}$ b. $\dfrac{0.25a^2 + ab + b^2}{0.5a + b}$

c. $\dfrac{4p^2 - m^2 + 2mn - n^2}{2p + m - n}$

16. Factorise the numerator and simplify the expression.

a. $\dfrac{4m^2 + 17m + 15}{(m + 3)}$ b. $\dfrac{8x^2 - 22xy + 15y^2}{(4x - 5y)}$

c. $\dfrac{2a^2 - 35a - 18}{(a - 18)}$

17. Multiply $(x^3 + 3x^2 - 4x + 1)$ by $(x^2 - 3x - 2)$ and write the answer in order of descending powers of x.

18. Divide $5m^4 - 3m^3 + 5m^2 - 9m + 6$ by $5m^2 - 4$.

19. Simplify using suitable identities.

a. $\dfrac{729 \times 729 - 271 \times 271}{729 - 271}$ b. $\dfrac{629 \times 629 - 371 \times 371}{629 - 371}$

c. $\dfrac{631 \times 631 - 369 \times 369}{631 - 369}$

20. A train travels $(2x^2 + 13x + 15)$ km in $(x + 5)$ hours. What is the average speed of the train?

If $x = 20$, find the speed of the train using the formula, Speed $= \dfrac{\text{Distance}}{\text{Time}}$.

Answer for Brainteaser from page 115

Let the number be x

$\frac{1}{5} \times \frac{1}{5} \times \frac{1}{2} \times 1050 + 5 = 26.$

CHAPTER 7

Linear Equations

An equation is a statement that equates two algebraic expressions that may contain one or more than one unknown variable.

A linear equation is an equation where the power of the variable is one. We shall recall the rules for solving a linear equation that we have learnt earlier.

An equation is like a balance which has a left hand side and a right hand side. Only when both the sides are equal, we say that the equation is balanced.

An operation done on one side of an equation has to be done on the other side as well to maintain the balance.

Basic Rules for Solving a Linear Equation

1. The same number or variable can be added on both sides of the equation without changing the value of the equation.
2. The same number or variable can be subtracted from both sides of the equation without changing the value of the equation.
3. The same number or variable can be multiplied on both sides of the equation without changing the value of the equation.
4. The same number or variable can be divided on both sides of the equation without changing the value of the equation.

Using the above rules, let us solve the examples.

Example 1: Solve $2x + 3 = 15$.

If we subtract 3 from both sides, we get

$$2x + 3 - 3 = 15 - 3$$

$$2x = 12$$

If we divide both sides by 2, we get

$$\frac{2x}{2} = \frac{12}{2}$$

$$x = 6$$

Thus, the unknown number is 6.

Example 2: Solve $5x - 7 = 23$.

By adding 7 on both sides of the equation, we get:

$$5x - 7 + 7 = 23 + 7$$

$$5x = 30$$

If we divide both sides by 5, we get

$$\frac{5x}{5} = \frac{30}{5}$$

$$x = 6$$

Thus, the unknown number is 6.

Example 3: Solve $\frac{4x - 5}{9} = 7$.

By multiplying both sides of the equation by 9, we get

$$\frac{(4x - 5) \times \cancel{9}}{\cancel{9}} = 7 \times 9$$

$$4x - 5 = 63$$

If we add 5 on both the sides of the equation, we get

$$4x - 5 + 5 = 63 + 5$$

$$4x = 68$$

Now, if we divide by 4 on both the sides of the equation, we get

$$\frac{4x}{4} = \frac{68}{4}$$

$$x = 17$$

Thus, the unkown number is 17.

The above examples show the application of the basic rules in solving a linear equation.

A linear equation can also be solved by the method of transposition.

Transposition

In this method, any term of an equation may be moved from one side of the equation to the other, that is from the LHS to the RHS or vice versa by following certain rules.

When a term moves from one side of the equation to the other side, its operation changes. Thus, addition (+) becomes subtraction (−), subtraction (−) becomes addition (+), multiplication (×) becomes division (÷) and division (÷) becomes multiplication (×).

Example 1: Solve $3x - 7 = 11$.

$3x - 7 = 11$

When we transpose (-7) to the RHS, it becomes $(+7)$.

$3x = 11 + 7$ or $3x = 18$

When we transpose 3 to the RHS, multiplication will change to division.

Thus, $x = \frac{18}{3} = 6$

Thus, the unkown variable is 6.

Example 2: Solve $11x + 3 = 47$.

When we transpose $(+3)$ to the RHS, it becomes (-3).

$11x = 47 - 3$

$11x = 44$

We transpose 11 to the RHS, multiplication will change to division.

$x = \frac{44}{11} = 4$

Thus, the unkown variable is 4.

Example 3: Solve $\frac{y + 6}{5} = 3$.

In this case, y + 6 is divided by 5, hence when we take 5 on the other side, we multiply by 5.

Thus, $y + 6 = 3 \times 5$

$y + 6 = 15$

When we transpose (+6) on the other side, it becomes (−6).

$y = 15 - 6$

$y = 9$

Thus, the unknown variable is 9.

Practice Exercise 7.1

1. Solve the following equations.

a. $8x + 3 = 27$	b. $2a + 5 = 11$
c. $7x - 5 = 16$	d. $3a - 10 = 8$
e. $\frac{3x + 1}{2} = 5$	f. $\frac{4m - 3}{7} = 11$
g. $\frac{3x}{4} + 3 = 18$	h. $\frac{a}{4} - 1 = 5$
i. $\frac{2x}{3} - 15 = 5$	j. $\frac{3a}{8} + 1 = 22$
k. $0.5x + 7.5 = 11.5$	l. $4a - 3.8 = 8.2$
m. $\frac{10x + 0.5}{7} = 1.5$	n. $\frac{x}{1.5} + 2.7 = 7.7$
o. $\frac{2}{3}x + 1 = \frac{7}{3}$	p. $\frac{x}{4} - 7 = 2$
q. $7 + \frac{3x}{4} = -2$	r. $3(x - 2) = 15w$
s. $\frac{x - 5}{2} + \frac{x - 3}{2} = 4$	t. $\frac{4x + 1}{3} - \frac{x - 2}{3} = 9$

To find the value of the variable in an equation or to solve an equation, the variable has to be on one side of the equation. But sometimes we see that the variable is on both sides of the equation. In such a case, we transpose the variables to one side of the equation and then solve it. Transposition of the variable from one side to the other is done in the same manner as we do with numbers.

Cross Multiplication

We shall now learn how to solve a linear equation by the method of cross multiplication.

Consider a linear equation in the form $\frac{ax + b}{cx + d} = \frac{p}{q}$. We can cross multiply it and write it as $\frac{ax + b}{cx + d} \rightleftarrows \frac{p}{q}$.

We get $q(ax + b) = p(cx + d)$ where $q \neq 0$ and p and q are constants. Now we have a linear equation with a variable x. We shall transpose the terms containing the variable x on one side and then solve the equation by the usual method.

Alert!

The method of cross multiplication is applicable to the form $\frac{ax + b}{cx + d} = \frac{p}{q}$. If we have an equation such as $\frac{ax}{c} + \frac{bx}{d} = \frac{p}{q}$, we have to first convert the left hand side to one term by finding the LCM.

There are some examples that illustrate the method of cross multiplication.

Example 1: Solve $\frac{2 + x}{3 + x} = \frac{5}{6}$.

$\frac{2 + x}{3 + x} \times \frac{5}{6}$

(cross multiplying the terms to get a linear equation)

$6(2 + x) = 5(3 + x)$

$12 + 6x = 15 + 5x$ (transposing 5x to the RHS and 12 to the LHS)

$\therefore 6x - 5x = 15 - 12$

$x = 3$

Example 2: Solve $\frac{2 + x}{x - 8} = \frac{3}{5}$.

$\frac{2 + x}{x - 8} \times \frac{3}{5}$ (cross multiplying the terms to get a linear equation)

$5(2 + x) = 3(x - 8)$

$10 + 5x = 3x - 24$ (transposing 3x to the LHS and 10 to the RHS)

$\therefore 5x - 3x = -24 - 10$

$2x = -34$

$x = \frac{-34}{2} = -17$

Example 3: Solve $\frac{6x - 5}{2x} = \frac{7}{9}$.

$\frac{6x - 5}{2x} \times \frac{7}{9}$ (cross multiplying the terms to get a linear equation)

$9(6x - 5) = 7(2x)$

$54x - 45 = 14x$ (transposing 14x to the LHS and (−45) to the RHS)

$\therefore 54x - 14x = 45$

$40x = 45$

$x = \frac{45}{40} = \frac{9}{8}$

$x = \frac{9}{8}$

Example 4: Solve $\frac{y+6}{4} + \frac{y-3}{5} = \frac{5y-4}{8}$.

Method 1:

We find the LCM of the LHS and then use the method of cross multiplication.

Find the LCM of the LHS which is 20.

$$\text{LHS} = \frac{5(y+6) + 4(y-3)}{20}$$

$$= \frac{5y + 30 + 4y - 12}{20}$$

$$= \frac{9y + 18}{20}$$ (using this in the LHS, we get)

$$\frac{9y+18}{20} \times \frac{5y-4}{8}$$ (cross multiplying the terms to get a linear equation)

$8(9y + 18) = 20(5y - 4)$

$72y + 144 = 100y - 80$ (transposing 72y to the RHS and -80 to the LHS)

$\therefore 144 + 80 = 100y - 72y$

$224 = 28y$

$y = \frac{224}{28} = 8$

Method 2:

We find the LCM of the whole equation and then use the method of transposition.

$$\frac{y+6}{4} + \frac{y-3}{5} = \frac{5y-4}{8}$$

Find the LCM of 4, 5 and 8, which is 40.

$$\therefore \frac{y+6}{4} \times \frac{10}{10} = \frac{(y+6)10}{4 \times 10} = \frac{(y+6)10}{40}$$

$$\frac{y-3}{5} \times \frac{8}{8} = \frac{(y-3)8}{5 \times 8} = \frac{(y-3)8}{40}$$

$$\frac{5y-4}{8} \times \frac{5}{5} = \frac{(5y-4)5}{8 \times 5} = \frac{(5y-4)5}{40}$$

$$\frac{(y+6)10}{40} + \frac{(y-3)8}{40} = \frac{(5y-4)5}{40}$$

Multiplying both sides by 40, we get

$(y + 6)10 + (y - 3)8 = (5y - 4)5$

$10y + 60 + 8y - 24 = 25y - 20$

$18y + 36 = 25y - 20$ (transposing 18y to the RHS and (-20) to the LHS)

$36 + 20 = 25y - 18y$

$56 = 7y$

$\frac{56}{7} = y$ or $y = 8$

Example 5: Solve $\frac{3(x-5)}{4} - 4x = 3 - \frac{(x-3)}{2}$.

The equation can be written as

$$\frac{3(x-5)}{4} - \frac{4x}{1} = \frac{3}{1} - \frac{(x-3)}{2}.$$

Method 1:

We find the LCM of the LHS and RHS separately. Thus,

$$\frac{3(x-5) - 4(4x)}{4} = \frac{3 \times 2 - (x-3)}{2}$$

$$\frac{3x - 15 - 16x}{4} = \frac{6 - x + 3}{2}$$

$$\frac{-15 - 13x}{4} \times \frac{9 - x}{2}$$ (cross multiplying the terms)

$2(-15 - 13x) = 4(9 - x)$

$-30 - 26x = 36 - 4x$ (transposing $-26x$ to the RHS and 36 to the LHS)

$\therefore -30 - 36 = 26x - 4x$

$-66 = 22x$

$\frac{-66}{22} = x$

or $x = -3$

Method 2:

We can also solve the equation by finding the LCM of the whole equation.

$$\frac{3(x-5)}{4} - \frac{4x}{1} = 3 - \frac{(x-3)}{2}$$

The LCM of 2 and 4 is 4.

$$\frac{3(x-5)}{4} - \frac{4x}{4} \times 4 = \frac{3}{4} \times 4 - \frac{2(x-3)}{4}$$

$3(x-5) - 16x = 12 - 2(x-3)$

$3x - 15 - 16x = 12 - 2x + 6$

$-13x - 15 = 18 - 2x$

$-13x + 2x = 18 + 15$

$-11x = 33$

$x = \frac{33}{-11} = -3$

Alert!

1. If the LCM of the LHS and RHS are considered separately, then the single terms obtained on either side are cross multiplied.
2. If the LCM of the whole equation is considered, then the LCM can be neglected in further calculations.

Practice Exercise 7.2

Solve the following equations.

1.a. $\frac{2x+3}{x+3} = \frac{3}{2}$ b. $\frac{x+1}{1-x} = \frac{2}{3}$

2.a. $\frac{3x+5}{3x+4} = 5$ b. $\frac{x}{1-x} = \frac{7}{5}$

3.a. $x + 6 = 2x - 4$ b. $3x - 7 = 2x + 1$

4.a. $5x - (3x - 1) = x - 4$ b. $\frac{2x - (7 - 5x)}{9x - (3 + 4x)} = \frac{7}{6}$

5.a. $5x - \frac{1}{3}(x + 1) = 6\left(x + \frac{1}{30}\right)$ b. $\frac{15(2 - y) - 5(y + 6)}{1 - 3y} = 10$

6.a. $\frac{5x+2}{4} = \frac{4x+1}{3}$ b. $\frac{6x-1}{4x+4} = \frac{1}{2}$

7.a. $\frac{0.5x+4}{1.2x+8} = \frac{5}{3}$ b. $\frac{0.3+0.7x}{x} = 0.85$

8.a. $\frac{x}{2} + \frac{x}{4} + \frac{x}{8} = 14$ b. $\frac{x-5}{2} - \frac{x-3}{5} = \frac{1}{2}$

9.a. $\frac{4x+1}{3} + \frac{2x-1}{2} - \frac{3x-7}{5} = 6$ b. $x + 7 - \frac{8x}{3} = \frac{17}{6} - \frac{5x}{8}$

10.a. $\frac{2}{6x-19} = \frac{3}{2x-11}$ b. $\frac{2(3x-1) - (2x+1)}{7x-2} = \frac{1}{2}$

Applications of Linear Equations

A number of everyday problems can be solved using equations. To solve a word problem, it is first translated into an equation with the unknown amount represented by an alphabet.

We have learnt how to solve word problems with the help of linear equations having one variable. The equation is then solved using the following steps.

Step 1 Read the problem carefully and note down the given values and what is required to be found out.

Step 2 Represent the unknown value that is to be found out by any letter of the English alphabet such as x, y, z, m, n or p.

Step 3 Translate the statements in the problem into mathematical statements in the form of equations.

Step 4 Solve the equation by any of the methods learnt earlier.

Step 5 Check whether the solution obtained satisfies the given conditions.

Let us apply the method of solving word problems in linear equations and solve the following examples.

Example 1: The sum of two numbers is 135 and they are in the ratio 4:5. Find the numbers.

Let one number be x. The other number will, therefore, be 135 − x since the sum of the two numbers is 135.

The numbers are in the ratio 4:5, so we can write the equation as $\frac{x}{135-x} = \frac{4}{5}$.

Cross multiply to solve the equation.

$5x = 4(135 - x)$

$5x = 540 - 4x$

$5x + 4x = 540$

$9x = 540$

$x = \frac{540}{9} = 60$

Hence, the two numbers are 60 and 75.

Check:

Substituting the values of the two numbers in the equation, we get

$60 + 75 = 135$ and

$\frac{60}{75} = \frac{4}{5}$

Thus, both the conditions given in the problem are satisfied.

Example 2: The sum of three consecutive multiples of 9 is 324. Find the three multiples.

Let the first multiple be x.

The second consecutive multiple will be (x + 9) and the third will be (x + 9) + 9.

According to the problem, the sum of the three consecutive multiples of 9 is 324, hence

$x + (x + 9) + (x + 9) + 9 = 324$

$3x + 27 = 324$

$3x = 324 - 27$

$3x = 297$

$x = \frac{297}{3} = 99.$

Substituting the values of x, we get the three numbers.

The three consecutive multiples of 9 are 99, 108 and 117.

Check:

$99 + 108 + 117 = 324$

Example 3: The denominator of a fraction is 4 more than the numerator. If 1 is added to the numerator and 2 is added to the denominator, the value of the fraction becomes $\frac{4}{5}$. Find the original fraction.

Let the numerator be x, then the denominator will be x + 4. According to the given problem, the original fraction is $\frac{x}{x + 4}$.

If 1 is added to the numerator, it becomes x + 1.

If 2 is added to the denominator, it becomes x + 4 + 2 = x + 6 and the value of the fraction becomes $\frac{4}{5}$.

Thus,

$$\frac{x + 1}{x + 6} = \frac{4}{5}$$

When we cross multiply, we get

$5(x + 1) = 4(x + 6)$

or $5x + 5 = 4x + 24$

$5x - 4x = 24 - 5$

$x = 19$

Substituting the value of x, we get the original fraction: $\frac{x}{x + 4} = \frac{19}{23}$

The original fraction is $\frac{19}{23}$.

Check:

$$\frac{19 + 1}{23 + 2} = \frac{20}{25} = \frac{4}{5}$$

Example 4: The angles of a triangle are in the ratio 1:5:3. Find their measures. What type of triangle is this?

Let the three angles be x, 5x and 3x since they are in the ratio 1:5:3. We know that the sum of the angles of a triangle is 180°, hence

$x + 5x + 3x = 180$

$9x = 180$

$x = 20°$

Hence, the measures of the angles of the triangle are 20°, 100° and 60°.

Since one angle is more than 90°, it is an obtuse-angled triangle.

The measures of the angles of the triangle are 20°, 100° and 60°. It is an obtuse-angled triangle.

Check:

$20° + 100° + 60° = 180°$

Example 5: The length of a rectangle exceeds its breadth by 7 cm. If the perimeter of the rectangle is 90 cm, find the area of the rectangle.

Let the breadth of the rectangle be x cm. The length of the rectangle will be (x + 7)cm.

Perimeter of a rectangle = 2(l + b)

According to the problem, the perimeter is 90 cm. Thus,

$2(x + 7 + x) = 90$

$2(2x + 7) = 90$

$4x + 14 = 90$

$4x = 90 - 14 = 76$

$\therefore x = \frac{76}{4} = 19$ cm

Thus, the breadth of the rectangle is 19 cm. The length will be 19 + 7 = 26 cm.

Area of the rectangle = (l × b)

$19 \times 26 = 494$ cm^2.

The area of the rectangle is 494 cm^2.

Check:

Breadth = 19 cm

Length = 26 cm

Perimeter = 2(l + b)

= 2(26 + 19)

= 2(45)

= 90 cm.

Example 6: Divide 4,500 into two parts such that 5% of the first part is equal to 10% of the second part.

Let one part be x, then the second part will be (4,500 − x).

According to the problem, 5% of x is equal to 10% of (4,500 − x)

5% of x = 10% of (4,500 − x)

$\frac{5}{100} \times x = \frac{10}{100} \times (4{,}500 - x)$

$5x \times 100 = 10(4500 - x) \times 100$ (by cross multiplying)

Divide both sides by 100, to get,

$5x = 10(4{,}500 - x)$

$5x = 45000 - 10x$

$5x + 10x = 45{,}000$

$15x = 45{,}000$

$x = \frac{45{,}000}{15} = 3{,}000$

One number is 3,000 and the other is 1,500.

The two numbers are 3,000 and 1,500.

Check:

$\frac{5}{100} \times 3000 = \frac{10}{100} \times 1500$

$150 = 150$

Example 7: Radhika's mother is four times as old as Radhika. After 5 years, her mother will be three times as old as she will be then. Find their present ages.

Let Radhika's present age be x years. Her mother's age is 4x years.

After 5 years, Radhika will be x + 5 years old.

Her mother's age after five years will be 4x + 5.

It is given that Radhika's mother will be three times as old as Radhika then. Hence,

$4x + 5 = 3(x + 5)$

$4x + 5 = 3x + 15$

$4x - 3x = 15 - 5$

$x = 10$

Hence, Radhika's present age is 10 years and her mother is $4 \times 10 = 40$ years.

Radhika is 10 years old and her mother is 40 years old.

Check:

5 years hence, Radhika will be $10 + 5 = 15$ years.

Her mother then will be $40 + 5 = 45$ years.

It is given that Radhika's mother will be three times Radhika's age then
$45 = 15 \times 3$.

Example 8: Two trains start from the same place at the same time but in opposite directions. Their speeds are 80 km/hr and 90 km/hr, respectively. After how long will they be 850 km apart?

Let the two trains be 850 km apart after x hours.

The first train's speed is 80 km/hr, so in x hours it will travel $80 \times x$ km. The second train's speed is 90 km/hr, so in x hours it will travel $90 \times x$ km.

After x hours they are 850 km apart. So,

$80x + 90x = 850$

$170x = 850$

$x = \frac{850}{170} = 5$ hours.

The trains will be 850 km apart in 5 hours.

Check: Distance = Speed × Time

Thus,

$$\begin{array}{r} 80 \times 5 = 400 \\ 90 \times 5 = \underline{450} \\ 850 \end{array}$$

Alert!

1. When trains or cars are moving in the opposite direction, their speeds are added. When they move in the same direction, their speeds are subtracted.
2. When trains or cars are moving in the opposite direction, the distance between them increases, hence the distances are added. When they are moving in the same direction, the distance between them decreases, hence the speeds are subtracted.

Example 9: A group of students were registered in a sports academy. One-fourth opted for basketball, one-third for football, two-fifth opted for cricket and 10 opted for volleyball. How many students in all were registered in the academy?

Let the number of students registered be x. Based on the problem, we can frame the equation as:

$$\frac{x}{4} + \frac{x}{3} + \frac{2x}{5} + \frac{10}{1} = x$$

The LCM of 4, 3 and 5 is 60. Hence,

$$\frac{15x + 20x + 24x + 60}{60} = \frac{59x + 600}{60} = \frac{x}{1}$$

or $59x + 600 = 60x$

$600 = x$

A total of 600 students were registered in the sports academy.

Check:

$\frac{600}{4} = 150$ registered for basketball.

$\frac{600}{3} = 200$ registered for football.

$\frac{2}{5} \times 600 = 240$ registered for cricket.

$\frac{10}{600}$ registered for volleyball.

Practice Exercise 7.3

1.a. Twenty-four is divided into two parts such that seven times the first part added to five times the second part is equal to 146. Find each part.

b. The difference of two numbers is 72 and the quotient obtained by dividing one by the other is 3. Find the numbers.

2.a. Three numbers are in the ratio 4:5:6. If the sum of the largest and the smallest number equals the sum of the third plus 55, find the numbers.

b. The weights of five cartons of books that are to be dispatched to schools A, B, C, D and E are in the ratio 5:6:7:8:9, respectively. If the total weight of the books is 700 kg, find the weight of each carton.

3.a. The denominator of a rational number is greater than the numerator by 6. If the numerator is decreased by 2 and the denominator is increased by 4, the new rational number obtained is $\frac{1}{5}$. Find the original number.

b. The numerator of a rational number is less than its denominator by 3. If the numerator becomes three times and the denominator is increased by 20, the new number becomes $\frac{1}{8}$. Find the original number.

4.a. The sum of the digits of a two-digit number is 15. If the number formed by reversing the digits is less than the original number by 27, find the original number.

b. The sum of the digits of a two-digit number is 13. If 9 is added to the number, the digits are reversed. Find the original number.

5.a. The ratio of Pratibha's age to Aradhana's age is 5:6. After twelve years, the ratio of their ages will be 9:10. Find their present ages.

b. Amar is thirteen years older than Supriya. Thirty-five years ago, Amar was twice Supriya's age. Find their present ages.

6.a. Two cars start from the same place but in opposite directions. Their speeds are 60 km/hr and 70 km/hr, respectively. After how long will they be 520 km apart?

b. The distance between two stations A and B is 425 km. Two trains start simultaneously from these stations on parallel tracks and are set to cross each other. The speed of one train is 5 km/hr greater than that of the other. If the distance between the two trains after 3 hours of starting is 20 km, find the speed of each train.

7.a. The perimeter of a rectangle is 52 cm. If its width is 2 cm more than one-third of its length, find the length and breadth of the rectangle.

b. The perimeter of a rectangular plot of land is 80 m. If the length of the plot is decreased by 2 m and its breadth is increased by 2 m, the area is increased by 36 m^2. Find the length and breadth of the plot of land.

8.a. A sum of ₹90,000 is to be divided between three business partners, A, B and C, in the ratio 5:6:7. How much money will each partner get?

b. Bhairav collected coins in his piggy bank to buy a gift for his mother. He had ₹320 in the denomination of ₹1 coins and ₹5 coins. If there are 200 coins in all in the piggy bank, find the number of coins of each type.

9.a. Two angles of a triangle are in the ratio 4:5. If the sum of these angles is equal to the third angle, find the angles of the triangle.

b. Mr Gupta distributed a certain amount of money amongst his family members. He gave half the amount to his wife, one-third to his son and the remaining to his daughter. If the daughter received ₹25,000, how much money in total did Mr Gupta distribute to his family? What were the shares of his wife and son?

10.a. The total weight of four boxes is 113 kg. The weight of Box P is 3.5 kg more than Box Q and the weight of Box R is 3.5 kg less than that of Box Q. The weight of Box S is twice the weight of Box R. Find the weight of each box.

b. The sum of two numbers is 500. If 12% of one number is equal to 15% of the other number, find the numbers.

Highlights

- A statement of equality involving one variable and whose degree (or power or exponent) is 1 is called a linear or simple equation.

- The value of the variable that satisfies a linear equation is known as the solution of the linear equation.

- The value of an equation does not change if we:
  - add any number or variable on both sides of the equation.
  - subtract any number or variable from both sides of the equation.
  - multiply both sides of the equation by the same number or variable.
  - divide both sides of the equation with the same number or variable.

- Transposing a term means taking a term from one side of the equation to the other.

- On transposition, the operation of the term changes, that is, addition becomes subtraction, subtraction becomes addition, multiplication becomes division and division becomes multiplication.

- If $\dfrac{ax + b}{cx + d} = \dfrac{p}{q}$, then $q(ax + b) = p(cx + d)$.

  This is called cross multiplication. It is a very useful operation in solving equations.

- The following steps are useful in solving word problems.
  - Read the question carefully.
  - Denote the unknown quantity by a letter of the alphabet.
  - Write the statement as a mathematical statement in the form of a linear equation.
  - Solve the linear equation.

How many triangles are there in the figure below?

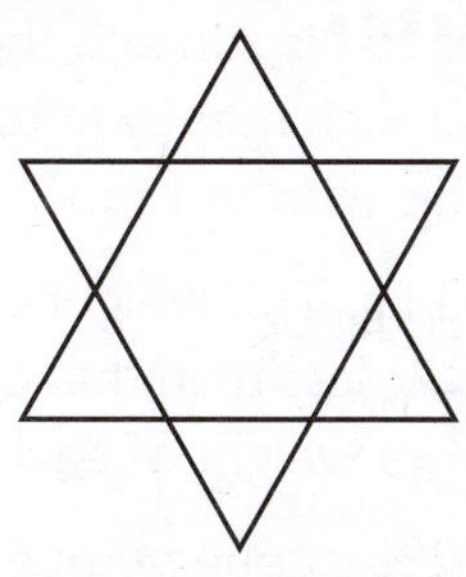

Answer for Brainteaser on page 134

Maths Lab Activity

Simplifying Equations

Aim: To understand linear equations and how to solve them.

Material required: a pen

Method: Complete the following tables using the rules.

1. Rule $a = x - 51$

x	7	220	15	176	320	31	51
a							

2. Rule $2a = x^2 + 4x + 1$

x	21	9	3	36	73	28	4
a							

3. Rule $a + 2a = x^3 - 3x^2 + 6x + 3$

x	3	1	77	16	22	50	5
a							

4. Rule $b + c = 2b + 3c + c^2$

b	3	7	8	2	1	15	29
c							

Higher Order Thinking Skills

HOTS

1. Solve the equation and find the value of x.

$$\frac{(3x + 8)}{(4x + 5)} = \frac{(6x + 1)}{(8x + 7)}$$

2. Find the value of p in the following equation.

$$\frac{2}{3}(4p - 1) - \left[4p - \frac{1-3p}{2}\right] = \frac{p - 7}{2}$$

3. Two adjacent angles of a parallelogram are $(3x - 4)^\circ$ and $(3x + 16)^\circ$. Find the value of x and thus find the measure of each angle of the parallelogram.

Rewind

1. Solve the following equations.

   a. $x + \frac{3}{4} = 5\frac{3}{4}$ b. $\frac{p}{2} + \frac{p}{4} + \frac{p}{8} = 21$ c. $\frac{2m}{3} - 15 = -9.$

2. Solve the following equations.

   a. $\frac{7x - 6}{3} = \frac{3x + 1}{2}$ b. $\frac{y}{y + 15} = \frac{4}{9}$ c. $\frac{10a - 6}{16a + 3} = \frac{-1}{11}.$

3. The angles of a triangle are in the ratio of 1:3:5. Find their measures.

4. Solve the following equations.

   a. $\frac{5}{3p + 5} = \frac{1}{p - 1}$ b. $\frac{(2m + 3) - (m - 5)}{(6m - 1) - (4m + 1)} = \frac{2}{3}$

   c. $\frac{5(2y - 1) + 3(4y + 3)}{4y - 1} = 5$

5. The difference of two numbers is 72 and the quotient obtained by dividing one number by the other is 3. Find the numbers.

6. Solve the following equations.

   a. $5x - 7 = 2x + 8$ b. $\frac{x - 5}{2} - \frac{x - 3}{5} = \frac{1}{2}$

   c. $\frac{5m - 4}{6} = (4m + 1) - \left(\frac{3m + 10}{2}\right)$

7. Solve the following equations.

   a. $\frac{2}{3}(4z - 1) - \left(2z - \frac{1 + z}{3}\right) = \frac{1}{3}z + \frac{4}{3}$ b. $\frac{2t + 1}{3t - 1} = \frac{3}{2}$

   c. $s(2s + 3) - 2s(s - 5) = 6$

8. Two-third of a number is twenty less than the original number. Find the number.

9. Three numbers are in the ratio 4:5:6. If the sum of the largest and the smallest number equals the sum of the third that is 55, find the numbers.

10. If ten is added to four times a certain number, the sum is four less than five times the number. Find the number.

11. The sum of the digits of a two-digit number is 12. If the new number formed by reversing the digits is greater than the original number by 54, find the original number. Verify your answer.

Rewind

12. The denominator of a rational number is greater than its numerator by 7. If the numerator is increased by 17 and the denominator decreased by 6, the new number becomes 2. Find the original number.

13. The height of a triangle is $\frac{5}{3}$rd the length of its corresponding base. If the height is increased by 4 cm and the base is decreased by 2 cm, the area of the triangle remains the same. Find the base, height and area of the triangle.

14. Two angles of a triangle are in the ratio 3:5. If the third angle is twice the larger angle of the ratio given, find the angles of the triangle.

15. Divide ₹6,300 into two parts such that 10% of one part is equal to 25% of the other part.

16. Find three consecutive odd numbers whose sum is 333.

17. The length of a rectangle is three times its breadth. If the perimeter of the rectangle is 248 cm, find the dimensions of the rectangle.

18. The distance between two stations A and B is 230 km. Two cars start simultaneously from A and B in the opposite directions and the distance between them after three hours is 20 km. If the speed of one car is less than that of the other by 10 km/hr, find the speed of each car.

19. The ratio of the ten's digit to the unit's digit of a two-digit number is 2:3. If 27 is added to the number, the digits interchange their places. Find the number.

20. Mr Mehta buys postage stamps in denominations of ₹1, ₹5 and ₹10 in the ratio 2:5:3. He pays ₹741 to the cashier. Find the number of postage stamps of each kind that Mr Mehta has bought.

Answer for Brainteaser from page 131

There are 8 triangles (2 big triangles and 6 small triangles) in the figure.

Test Yourself

Unit II

1. Add the sum of $5a^2 + 6b^2$ and $9c^2 - 16a^2 - 2b^2$ to $16c^2 - 4a^2 + b^2$.

2. Subtract the sum of $x^2 + y^2 + 2xy$ and $x^2 + y^2 - 2xy$ from the sum of $5x^2 + 10y^2 + 20xy$ and $-3x^2 + 7y^2 - 20xy$.

3. Find the product of $(a + b + c)$ and $(-a + b - c)$ and add it to the product of $(2a + b - c)$ and $(a - 2b + c)$.

4. What should be subtracted from $4x^3 + 8x^2 + 7$ to make it exactly divisible by $2x^2 + x - 1$?

5. Find the quotient and remainder on dividing $a^5 + 10$ by $a^2 - 3$.

6. Find the square of $(3x + 4)$ using the identity $(a + b)^2 = a^2 + 2ab + b^2$.

7. Find the square of $(4x - 3y)$ using the identity $(a - b)^2 = a^2 - 2ab + b^2$.

8. Find the products of the following using suitable identities.

   a. $(2x + 3)(2x - 3)$ b. $(7x - 5)(7x + 5)$ c. $(a + 2b)(a - 2b)$

   d. $\left(\frac{6}{7}x + 5\right)\left(\frac{6}{7}x - 5\right)$ e. $\left(4a + \frac{1}{4a}\right)\left(4a - \frac{1}{4a}\right)$

9. Evaluate the following using suitable identities.

   a. $(58)^2$ b. $(72)^2$ c. $(99)^2$ d. $(101)^2$ e. $(308)^2$

10. If $a + 2b = 9$ and $ab = 7$, find the value of $a^2 + 4b^2$.

11. Factorise the following.

    a. $24p^2q^3 - 36pq^2$ b. $42a^3 - 49a^5$

    c. $20a^4b^3 - 10a^2b^3 + 5ab$ d. $65p^2q^3 - 39p^2q^2 + 13p^3q^2$

    e. $64a^2b^2 + 32ab^2 + 16a^2b$

12. Factorise the following.

    a. $3p^2 + 3pq + 2p + 2q$ b. $2m^2 + 3n + mn + 6m$

    c. $6x^2 + 3xy - yz - 2xz$ d. $3a(2 - b) - 4c(2 - b)$

    e. $12m(n+p) - 6(n + p)$

13. Factorise the following.

a. $36x^2 + 60x + 25$
b. $121m^2 - 22m + 1$
c. $16a^2b^2 - 49c^2d^2$
d. $64p^2 - x^2 - y^2 + 2xy$
e. $100m^2 - 20m + 1 - 100$

14. Factorise the following.

a. $a^2 - 8ab - 48b^2$
b. $3b^2 - 12b - 63$
c. $8c^2 - 22cd + 15d^2$
d. $d^2 - 6d - 40$
e. $e^2 + 5e - 14$

15. Solve the following equations.

a. $14x - 7 = 21$
b. $\frac{x}{2} + \frac{x}{4} + \frac{x}{8} = 56$
c. $6x - 8.2 = 3.8$
d. $9x + 18 = 0$
e. $1\frac{1}{2} + 8x = 3\frac{1}{2}$

16. Solve the following equations.

a. $\frac{3x - 5}{2x + 15} = \frac{8}{9}$
b. $\frac{2}{6y - 19} = \frac{3}{2y - 11}$
c. $\frac{(2m + 3) - (m - 5)}{(6m - 1) - (4m + 1)} = \frac{2}{3}$
d. $\frac{0.7p + 0.5}{3.5p + 4.5} = \frac{2}{5}$
e. $\frac{2(2a + 1) - (3a - 2)}{(3a + 1) - (a - 7)} = \frac{1}{2}$

17. The sum of the two digits of a two-digit number is 8. If 36 is subtracted from the number, its digits are reversed. Find the number.

18. The denominator of a fraction is 5 more than the numerator. If 2 is added to both the numerator and denominator, the fraction becomes $\frac{3}{8}$. Find the original fraction.

19. Rekha is four times as old as her brother Raman. After 10 years she will be twice as old as her brother. Find their present ages.

20. The distance between two stations, A and B is 455 km. Two trains start simultaneously from these stations on parallel tracks towards each other. The speed of one is greater than the other by 5 km/hr. If the distance between the two trains after 3 hours is 20 km, find the speed of each train. Verify your answer.

Application of Percentage

CHAPTER 8

In the previous classes we have learnt about the concept of percentage. The word percentage comes from percentum which means per hundred. Expressing quantities in percentages makes it easy to compare them, by having a common denominator (i.e., 100). Percentage is deonted by the symbol %. Marks on a report card, annual rate of interest in a bank and profit and loss figures are generally expressed as a percentage.

We shall study the following applications of percentage.

Profit and loss	Discount	Sales tax or Value-added tax (VAT)
Simple interest	Compound interest	

Profit and Loss

The basic formulae regarding profit and loss are as follows:

1. If selling price (SP) > cost price (CP), then,

   Profit = SP − CP.

   $$\text{Profit } \% = \frac{\text{Profit} \times 100}{\text{CP}}$$

2. If CP > SP, then

   Loss = CP − SP.

   $$\text{Loss } \% = \frac{\text{Loss} \times 100}{\text{CP}}$$

3. To find SP when CP and profit % or loss % are given.

   $$\text{SP} = \left(\frac{100 + \text{Profit } \%}{100}\right) \times \text{CP} \qquad \text{(in case of profit)}$$

   $$\text{SP} = \left(\frac{100 - \text{Loss } \%}{100}\right) \times \text{CP} \qquad \text{(in case of loss)}$$

4. To find CP when SP and profit % or loss % are given.

   $$\text{CP} = \frac{100 \times \text{SP}}{100 + \text{Profit } \%}$$

   $$\text{CP} = \frac{100 \times \text{SP}}{100 - \text{Loss } \%}$$

Overhead Expenses

Expenses that are paid on repairs, transportation, maintenance, cartage, salary of employees, etc., are called overhead expenses and are added to the cost price of the goods.

The actual cost price includes the overhead expenses.

Alert!

1. Profit or loss per cent is always calculated on the cost price.
2. Overhead expenses are included or added to the cost price and profit or loss is calculated on this actual cost price.
3. Profit is also called gain.

Let us understand the concept of profit and loss with the help of a few examples.

Example 1: Ishita bought a cooking range for ₹5,000 and sold it for ₹6,500. Find the profit per cent.

CP = ₹5,000 SP = ₹6,500

SP > CP

Profit = SP − CP

Profit = 6,500 − 5,000

Profit = ₹1,500

$$\text{Profit } \% = \frac{\text{Profit}}{\text{CP}} \times 100$$

$$= \frac{1500}{5000} \times 100$$

Profit % = 30%

Ishita made a profit of 30%.

Example 2: Bhairvi bought a book for ₹250 and later sold it for ₹100 as a second-hand book. Find her loss per cent.

CP = ₹250 SP = ₹100

CP > SP

Loss = CP − SP

Loss = 250 − 100 = ₹150

$$\text{Loss } \% = \frac{\text{Loss}}{\text{CP}} \times 100$$

$$= \frac{150}{250} \times 100$$

Loss % = 60%

Bhairvi made a loss of 60%.

Example 3: Mr Malwani bought an air conditioner for ₹20,000, and a voltage stabiliser for ₹2,000 and sent it to a customer's home paying a cartage of ₹500. The customer paid Mr Malwani ₹25,000. Calculate Mr Malwani's profit or loss per cent.

CP of Mr Malwani = 20,000 + 2,000 + 500

= ₹22,500

SP of Mr Malwani = ₹25,000 (The money that the customer paid)

Here, SP > CP so Mr Malwani has made a profit.

Profit = SP − CP = 25,000 − 22,500 = 2,500

$$\text{Profit } \% = \frac{\text{Profit}}{\text{CP}} \times 100$$

$$= \frac{2,500}{22,500} \times 100 = \frac{100}{9}\%$$

$$\text{Profit } \% = 11\frac{1}{9}\%$$

Mr Malwani made a profit of $11\frac{1}{9}\%$.

Example 4: Rishi bought a computer for ₹25,500 and sold it at a gain of 5%. Find his selling price.

CP = ₹25,500   Gain % = 5%

We know that

$$SP = \left(\frac{100 + \text{Gain }\%}{100}\right) \times CP$$

$$= \frac{100 + 5}{100} \times 25{,}500$$

$$= \frac{105}{100} \times 25{,}500$$

The selling price is ₹26,775.

Example 5: On selling a mobile for ₹1,216, Mohan loses 5%. Find the cost price.

SP = ₹1,216   Loss % = 5%

We know that

$$CP = \frac{100 \times SP}{100 - \text{Loss}\%}$$

$$= \frac{100 \times 1216}{95} = ₹1{,}520$$

CP = ₹1,520

The cost price is ₹1,520.

Example 6: By selling a garment for ₹460, a shopkeeper incurs a loss of 8%. At what price should he sell the garment to get a profit of 5%?

Here, the problem is divided into two parts. We are given the SP and the loss %, from where we can calculate the CP. If the CP is known and the profit % is given, we can find the SP.

SP = ₹460

Loss % = 8%

$$CP = \frac{100 \times SP}{100 - \text{Loss }\%}$$

$$= \frac{100 \times 460}{92} = ₹500$$

CP of the garment is ₹500

For a profit of 5%, the shopkeeper has to sell it at the following SP.

$$SP = \left(\frac{100 + \text{Profit }\%}{100}\right) \times CP$$

$$= \frac{100 + 5}{100} \times 500$$

$$= \frac{105}{100} \times 500 = 525$$

SP = ₹525

The shopkeeper should sell the garment at a price of ₹525.

Example 7: Suhas sold two paintings for ₹99,000 each. On one he incurred a loss of 10% and on the other he gained by 10%. Find his actual gain or loss per cent on the transaction.

Loss or gain is always on the CP, so in each case we need to find the CP.

Let the two paintings be Painting A and Painting B

Painting A

SP = ₹99,000 Loss% = 10%

$$CP = \frac{100}{100 - \text{Loss }\%} \times SP = \frac{100 \times 99{,}000}{90}$$

CP = ₹1,10,000

Painting B

SP = ₹99,000 Gain% = 10%

$$CP = \frac{100}{100 + \text{Gain}\%} \times SP$$

$$= \frac{100}{110} \times 99{,}000$$

CP = ₹90,000

Total CP = ₹1,10,000 + ₹90,000

= ₹2,00,000

Total SP = ₹99,000 + ₹99,000

= ₹1,98,000

CP > SP

Loss = ₹2,00,000 − ₹1,98,000 = 2,000

$$\text{Loss }\% = \frac{2{,}000}{2{,}00{,}000} \times 100$$

Loss % = 1%

Suhas made a loss of 1% on the transaction.

Example 8: Mr Aggarwal bought 6 dozen notebooks for ₹1,080. On opening the packet he found that 18 notebooks were damaged. At what price should he sell the remaining notebooks to make a profit of 10%?

6 dozen notebooks is equal to 72 notebooks.

72 notebooks were bought for ₹1,080

$\therefore$ 1 notebook costs $\frac{1080}{72}$ = ₹15

18 notebooks are damaged, so the number of undamaged notebooks is = 72 − 18 = 54 notebooks

Profit is calculated on the CP.

Mr Aggarwal has to earn a 10% profit

Profit = CP × Profit %

$\therefore$ $1080 \times \frac{10}{100}$ = ₹108

SP = CP + Profit = 1080 + 108

= ₹1,188

Hence, he has to sell the remaining 54 notebooks for ₹1,188.

$\therefore$ each notebook needs to be sold at a price of $= \frac{1,188}{54}$

$= ₹22$

Each notebook has to be sold for ₹22.

Example 9: If the cost price of a packet of 25 greeting cards is equal to the selling price of 20 greeting cards, find the gain or loss per cent.

Let the CP of each card be ₹x.

The CP of 20 cards = ₹20x

SP of 20 cards = CP of 25 cards

= 25x

CP of 20 cards = ₹20x

SP of 20 cards = CP of 25 cards = ₹25x

SP > CP, hence there is a profit

Profit = SP − CP = ₹25x − ₹20x

= ₹5x

$\text{Profit\%} = \frac{\text{Profit}}{\text{CP}} \times 100 = \frac{5x}{20x} \times 100$

Profit% = 25%

There is a gain of 25%.

Example 10: Sohail bought a plot of land for ₹96,000. He sold $\frac{2}{5}$ of it at a loss of 6%. At what profit per cent should he sell the remaining part to get a profit of 10% on the whole.

Total CP for the plot of land = ₹96,000

$\frac{2}{5}$ of ₹96,000 = ₹38,400

$\frac{3}{5}$ of ₹96,000 = ₹57,600

CP of $\frac{2}{5}$ of land = ₹38,400

Sohail incurred a loss of 6% on the sale of $\frac{2}{5}$ of the plot. SP for $\frac{2}{5}$ of the plot:

$\text{SP} = \frac{100 - \text{Loss\%}}{100} \times \text{CP}$

$= \frac{100 - 6}{100} \times 38,400 = \frac{94 \times 38,400}{100} = ₹36,096$

10% of the profit on the whole means,

$\frac{10}{100} \times 96,000 = 9,600$

But he incurs a loss of ₹38,400 − ₹36,096

= ₹2,304 on $\frac{2}{5}$th of the plot.

So to get a profit of 10% on the whole transaction, he should get a profit of ₹9,600 + ₹2,304 = ₹11,904

CP of the remaining $\frac{3}{5}$th of the land is ₹57,600.

He needs to make a profit of ₹11,904.

$$\therefore \quad \text{Profit\%} = \frac{11,904}{57,600} \times 100$$

$$= \frac{62}{3}\%$$

$$\text{Profit\%} = 20\frac{2}{3}\%$$

Sohail should sell the remaining plot of land at a profit of $20\frac{2}{3}$%.

Practice Exercise 8.1

1.a. Reema bought a book for ₹600 and sold it for ₹750. Find her profit or loss per cent.

b. Ritu purchased a television trolley for ₹3,600 and later sold it to her friend Neetu for ₹3,000. Find Ritu's gain or loss per cent.

2.a. Suhani purchased a mobile phone for ₹4,500 and sold it at a profit of 5%. Find the amount of money she received on the deal.

b. Karan bought a thermos flask for ₹970 and sold it at a loss of 10%. Find his selling price.

3.a. Lily sold a tea set for ₹4,914 at a profit of 5% to her friend, Chetna. At what price did Lily purchase the tea set?

b. Bhairav sold his bicycle for ₹4,600 at a loss of 8%. Find his loss.

4. a. Manpreet bought an old computer for ₹18,500 and spent ₹1,500 on its repairs. He then sold it to his friend Taranjit for ₹23,000. Did Manpreet incur a loss or profit and how much? Give your answer in per cent.

b. Rahul bought a second-hand car for ₹1,90,000 and spent ₹3,200 on its insurance and ₹10,500 on repairs. He then sold it for ₹2,50,000. Find his gain or loss per cent.

5.a. A television dealer sold a model of television for ₹24,840 at a loss of 8% and another model of television for the same price at a gain of 8%. Find his total gain or loss per cent.

b. Madhav bought two pairs of jeans for ₹960 each. He sold one of them at a loss of 4% and the other at a gain of 8%. Find Madhav's gain or loss per cent on the whole transaction.

6.a. At a gift shop a teddy bear was sold for ₹1,104 and the shopkeeper lost 8% on this deal. At what price should he have sold the teddy bear to earn a profit of 10%?

b. By selling a rocking chair for ₹2,700, a furniture dealer will incur a loss of 10%. If he wants to make a profit of 15%, for how much should he sell the rocking chair?

7. a. A fruit seller bought oranges at the rate of ₹45 per dozen and sold them at the rate of ₹45 per 10. Find his gain or loss per cent.

b. The cost price of a pack of 12 candles is equal to the selling price of 15 candles. Find the loss per cent.

8.a. Monica bought a table for ₹25,000 and spent some amount to get it polished. She sold the table for ₹36,000 earning a profit of 25%. How much did she spend on getting the table polished?

b. Anupam bought a motorbike for ₹25,650. He spent some money on overhauling and painting it. He then sold it for ₹33,300 at a profit of 11%. How much money did he spend on overhauling and painting the motorbike?

9.a. Ganga bought a set of glasses for ₹620 and sold them for ₹713. Jamuna bought a set of glasses for ₹345 and sold them for ₹372.60. Who made more profit? Give the answer as profit percent.

b. Vibha sold a watch to Nandini at a gain of 12%. Nandini sold it to Neeta at a loss of 5%. If Neeta paid ₹1,330 for it, how much did Vibha pay for the watch?

10.a. By selling 125 books, a shopkeeper gains an amount equal to the selling price of 5 books. Find his profit per cent.

b. By selling 12 dozen pens, Rahul lost an amount equal to the selling price of 6 pens. Find his loss per cent.

Discount

An article that is to be sold has a price on it which is known as its marked price (MP). When stores offer a discount during sales such as Diwali sale, winter sale or monsoon sale, the articles are sold at a price that is less than the marked price. This reduced price is a certain percentage of the marked price and is known as the discount. To find the discount per cent we use the following formula.

$$\text{Discount } \% = \frac{\text{Discount}}{\text{MP}} \times 100$$

If an article has a MP of ₹500 and is sold at ₹400, then the discount is ₹100.

Thus, $\frac{100}{500} \times 100 = 20\%$

$$\text{MP} = \frac{100 \times \text{SP}}{100 - \text{Discount}\%}$$

Sometimes more than one discount is offered on a particular brand of items. For example, an article has a 20% discount on it. If the article is bought in larger numbers, an additional 5% discount is offered. Such discounts are called successive discounts.

Alert!!

1. Discount is always calculated on the marked price.
2. Selling price = Marked price − Discount

Example 1: The marked price of an air conditioner is ₹25,000. The shopkeeper offers a discount of 10% on its purchase. Find its selling price.

MP = ₹25,000 Discount = 10%

Discount = 10% MP

$= \frac{10}{100} \times 25{,}000 = ₹2{,}500$

Discount = ₹2,500

Now, SP = MP − Discount

= 25,000 − 2,500

= ₹22,500

SP = ₹22,500.

The selling price is ₹22,500.

Example 2: At the annual sale at a supermarket, a silk kurta marked at ₹900 is sold for ₹765. Find the discount per cent.

MP = ₹900 SP = ₹765

Discount = MP − SP

= ₹900 − ₹765

= ₹135

∴ Discount per cent is = $\frac{\text{Discount}}{\text{MP}} \times 100 = \frac{135}{900} \times 100$

= 15%

The discount is 15%.

Example 3: During a Diwali sale, a saree is sold for ₹3,250 after allowing a discount of 35%. Find the marked price.

Method 1 (unitary method)

Let the MP be ₹100

Discount = 35%

∴ SP = MP – Discount = 100 − 35 = ₹65

If SP is ₹65, then MP = ₹100

If SP is ₹3,250, then MP = $\frac{100}{65} \times 3250$

= ₹5,000

Hence, MP = ₹5,000

Method 2 (using the formula)

$$\text{MP} = \frac{100 \times \text{SP}}{100 - \text{Discount\%}}$$

$$= \frac{100 \times 3250}{100 - 35}$$

$$= \frac{100 \times 3250}{65} = ₹5{,}000$$

The marked price is ₹5,000.

Example 4: The marked price of a television set is ₹28,600. After allowing a discount of 25%, the dealer still makes a profit of 10%. Find the cost price of the television set.

MP = ₹28,600

Rate of discount = 25%

Discount = 25% of ₹28,600

$= \frac{25}{100} \times 28{,}600$

$= ₹7{,}150$

SP = MP − Discount

$= ₹28{,}600 - ₹7{,}150$

$= ₹21{,}450$

Now, $CP = \frac{100 \times SP}{100 + \text{Profit \%}} = \frac{100 \times 21{,}450}{100 + 10}$

$= \frac{100 \times 21{,}450}{110} = ₹19{,}500$

The cost price of the television set is ₹19,500.

Example 5: During a summer season sale, all goods in a store were at a discount of 10%. The woollen section had an additional discount of 20%. Tanuja bought woollens worth ₹8,000. How much did she have to pay for them?

MP of woollens is ₹8,000

Tanuja got a discount of 10% on them.

$\frac{10}{100} \times 8{,}000 = ₹800$

So, the SP will be 8,000 − 800 = ₹7,200

But she got an additional discount of 20%.

$\frac{20}{100} \times 7{,}200 = ₹1440$

₹7,200 − ₹1,440 = ₹5,760

Tanuja paid ₹5,760 for the woollens.

Example 6: During a book exhibition, a set of books were sold for ₹9,000 after giving successive discounts of 20% and 10%, respectively. Find the marked price of the set of books.

Let the MP be ₹100

First discount = 20%

$\therefore$ SP = ₹(100 − 20) = ₹80

Second discount = 10% of 80

$= \frac{10}{100} \times 80 = ₹8$

SP after second discount = ₹80 − ₹8 = ₹72

When the SP is ₹72, the MP ₹100

$\therefore$ When the SP is ₹9,000, the MP is $\frac{100}{72} \times 9{,}000 = ₹12{,}500$

The marked price of the set of books is ₹12,500.

Alert!

In successive discounts, the discounts are given *successively*. The first selling point is found and the next discount is given on it.

Sales Tax or Value-Added Tax (VAT)

Sales tax or value-added tax is collected by the state government on the sale of items. This tax is charged by the shopkeepers, which is then paid to the government. Value-added tax is not a profit for the shopkeeper but is recorded in the bill book and then paid to the government.

There are various types of taxes that the government collects in the form of taxes. These include income tax, wealth tax, professional tax, etc., that are collected as direct taxes. The indirect taxes are in the form of excise tax, sales tax, value-added tax (VAT), etc. This tax collected by the government in various forms is used for making roads, dams, bridges and other infrastructure for the citizens of the country. The taxes are also used for providing health, education and other facilities.

Alert!

1. Value-added tax is calculated on the sale price of an item.
2. The range of VAT is different for different kind of items. It is more on luxury items than on items of common use or daily use.

Let us understand how VAT is calculated with the help of a few examples.

Example 1: The price of a refrigerator is marked at ₹15,400. If 15% VAT is charged, find the total amount Priti will have to pay to the shopkeeper to buy the refrigerator.

Since VAT is 15%, Priti will have to pay an additional 15% of ₹15,400 as VAT.

Therefore, the additional amount Priti will have to pay as VAT is

$$\frac{15}{100} \times 15{,}400 = 15 \times 154$$
$$= ₹2{,}310$$

The total amount that Priti has to pay is MP of refrigerator + VAT = ₹15,400 + ₹2,310 = ₹17,710

Priti has to pay ₹17,710 for the refrigerator.

Example 2: Rohini paid 12% VAT on an air conditioner bought for ₹28,000. What was the actual selling price of the air conditioner?

Let the SP be ₹100.

12% VAT is paid on the SP. Hence, the amount paid will be ₹100 + ₹12 = ₹112.

When ₹112 is paid, the SP is ₹100.

∴ when ₹28,000 is paid, the SP will be:

$$\frac{100}{112} \times ₹28{,}000 = ₹25{,}000$$

The actual selling price of the air conditioner was ₹25,000.

Example 3: A chemist bought medicines for ₹60,000 and sold them at a bill amount of ₹66,150 which included 5% VAT. Find his profit or loss per cent.

If the SP is 100, SP and VAT together will be 105 since VAT is 5%. Thus, the bill amount will be ₹105.

When the bill amount is ₹105, the SP is ₹100.

∴ When the bill amount is ₹66,150, the SP will be:

$$\frac{66{,}150 \times 100}{105} = ₹63{,}000$$

Profit = SP − CP

= ₹63,000 − ₹60,000

= ₹3,000

$$\text{Profit\%} = \frac{\text{Profit}}{\text{CP}} \times 100$$

$$= \frac{3{,}000}{63{,}000} \times 100 = 5\%$$

The chemist made a profit of 5%.

Practice Exercise 8.2

1.a. Find the selling price of an article marked at ₹750, if a discount of 20% is offered on it.

b. Rini bought a pair of silver candle stands for ₹4,650 in a discount sale of 7%. What was the marked price of the silver candle stands?

2.a. The price of a raincoat was reduced from ₹960 to ₹720 during a sale. What was the discount per cent offered?

b. A pocket transistor is marked at ₹2,500. The shopkeeper allows a discount of 15% on it. Find the net selling price.

3.a. During the festival season, the price of a washing machine is reduced from ₹14,500 to ₹12,325. Find the percentage of discount offered.

b. Shobhana paid ₹1,260 for a tea set after a discount of 10% was allowed on the marked price during a clearance sale. What was the marked price of the tea set? How much did Shobhana save due to the discount?

4. A book seller marks his goods at a price that is 20% more than the cost price. If he allows a discount of 10%, what will be his gain or loss per cent?

5.a. During the monsoon sale at a leading saree shop, the marked price of a saree is ₹9,575. The shopkeeper allows a discount of 12% on the marked price and still makes a profit of 10%. Find the cost price of the saree.

b. At a poultry shop, all items are marked 30% above the cost price. Due to a bird flu epidemic, the shopkeeper had to sell the goods at a discount of 30%. Find the gain or loss per cent in the transaction.

6.a. The marked price of a dress was ₹650. All goods in the shop were being sold at a 20% discount. Aanya liked the dress but found a small tear in it. The shopkeeper offered a further discount of 10% to her. How much did Aanya pay for the dress?

b. Find the single discount which is equivalent to two successive discounts of 20% and 5%.

7.a. The marked price of a dining table set is ₹20,500. If the VAT charged is 10%, how much does the customer pay?

b. Aparna bought a gold bracelet for ₹37,450 including 7% VAT. Find the selling price of the bracelet.

8.a. Devyani liked a guitar that was priced at ₹12,000. A 10% VAT was to be charged on the bill, but the shopkeeper agreed to give Devyani a discount of 20%. Find the actual amount paid by Devyani for the guitar.

b. Alka bought six T-shirts for ₹650 each and six long skirts for ₹800 each at a shop that was offering a 20% discount during its annual clearance sale. She had to pay a 5% VAT on the bill. How much did Alka pay the shopkeeper? How much discount did she get on her purchase? How much did she pay as VAT?

9. The marked price of a book shelf is 25% more than its cost price. The shopkeeper gives a discount of 10% on it. If the marked price of the book shelf is ₹14,500, find the cost price, selling price and the shopkeeper profit (as a percentage).

10. There was a 20% discount on a laptop. A VAT of 18% was being charged on it. If Dhiren bought the laptop for ₹23,600, what was its marked price?

Simple Interest

When you deposit money in the bank, it earns an interest. Similarly, when you borrow money from the bank, in the form of a loan, you are required to pay an interest on it. Whenever a sum of money is lent or borrowed by someone either from a bank or from an individual, some money is charged for its use. This extra money charged is called the *interest* on the borrowed sum. The original sum of money is called the *principal*. The principal and the interest together is called the *amount*.

Thus A = P + I, where A is the amount, P is the principal and I is the interest. The principal remains the same for the entire period of time it is borrowed for.

Let us recall the formula for simple interest

$SI = \frac{P \times R \times T}{100}$, where

SI is simple interest

P is the principal

R is the rate of interest

T is the time period

There are four variables in the formula, i.e., SI, P, R and T. If any three are known, the fourth variable can be calculated.

$$\text{Thus, } P = \frac{SI \times 100}{R \times T}$$

$$R = \frac{SI \times 100}{P \times T}$$

$$T = \frac{SI \times 100}{R \times P}$$

Let us study simple interest using a few examples.

Example 1: Madhu borrowed ₹5,000 from her friend Deepa for two years at a simple interest of 10% per annum (year). What will be amount of money that Madhu will return to Deepa at the end of the period?

$P = ₹5{,}000$

$T = 2$ years

$R = 10\%$

$$SI = \frac{P \times R \times T}{100}$$

$$= \frac{5{,}000 \times 10 \times 2}{100}$$

$$= ₹1{,}000$$

Amount to be returned to Deepa after two years $= P + SI$

$= ₹5{,}000 + ₹1{,}000$

$= ₹6{,}000$

Madhu will return ₹6,000 to Deepa.

Example 2: Find the rate of simple interest that Arnav had to pay Ambar if he borrowed ₹10,000 for 5 years and repaid ₹12,000 at that end of the time period.

$P = ₹10{,}000$

$A = ₹12{,}000$ (after 5 years)

$T = 5$ years

$SI = A - P = 12{,}000 - 10{,}000$

$= 2{,}000$

Now, $R = \frac{SI \times 100}{P \times 5}$

$$\therefore R = \frac{2{,}000 \times 100}{10{,}000 \times 5} = 4\%$$

The rate of interest will be 4%.

Example 3: Surabhi lent ₹15,000 to Bhairavi at the rate of 6% SI per annum for a certain period of time. Bhairavi paid back an amount of ₹16,500 to Surabhi. For what time period did Bhairavi use the money borrowed from Surabhi?

$P = ₹15{,}000$

$A = ₹16{,}500$

$\therefore SI = ₹16{,}500 - ₹15{,}000$

$= ₹1{,}500$

Rate of interest is 6%

Now, $T = \frac{SI \times 100}{P \times R}$

$$\therefore T = \frac{1{,}500 \times 100}{15{,}000 \times 6} = \frac{10}{6} = \frac{5}{3} \text{ years}$$

$\frac{5}{3}$ years $= 1\frac{2}{3}$ years

The time period Bhairavi borrowed the money for was 1 year 8 months.

Alert!

While calculating simple interest, the principal remains the same each year of the entire time period.

Compound Interest

Most banks and other financial organisations charge compound interest. If we deposit money in the bank or post office for a certain period of time, it is called a fixed deposit (FD) and we get compound interest on it. Compound interest means each year the principal keeps on increasing. When you receive an interest on your FD, it gets added to your original principal. The new principal is, therefore, the original principal plus the interest earned on it. You now earn interest on the new principal. Let us study compound interest using examples and then formulate the formula.

Example 1: Let us assume that Manita has taken ₹5,000 as loan for 2 years at an interest of 5% per annum, compound interest. Now we calculate the interest on the money for 2 years. While calculating compound interest, we find the interest for each year separately by using the formula for simple interest.

Thus, the interest for the first year will be:

$$SI = \frac{P \times T \times R}{100} = \frac{5{,}000 \times 1 \times 5}{100} = ₹250$$

Now, this interest of ₹250 is added to the principal and it becomes the amount. We know that

$$A = P + SI$$

$$A = 5{,}000 + 250 = ₹5{,}250$$

Now, for the second year this amount is taken as the principal and the interest is calculated on it.

$$SI = \frac{P \times T \times R}{100} = \frac{5{,}250 \times 1 \times 5}{100} = ₹262.50$$

Here, ₹262.50 is the interest for the second year.

The total amount will be ₹5,250 + ₹262.50 = ₹5,512.50

This is the compound interest on ₹5,000 for 2 years at a compound interest of 5% pa

Now, let us calculate the simple interest for the same period.

$$SI = \frac{P \times T \times R}{100}$$

$$= \frac{5{,}000 \times 2 \times 5}{100}$$

$$= ₹500$$

Amount = ₹5,000 + ₹500 = ₹5,500

Thus, the compound interest is more than the simple interest for the same principal, time period and rate of interest.

This happens because in compound interest, the interest is calculated on the interest added to the principal for the next year. In compound interest, the principal keeps increasing annually. In compound interest the amount for one year becomes the principal for the next year.

Let us take another example to study the difference between simple interest and compound interest.

Find the difference between simple interest and compound interest on ₹12,000 at 15% per annum for 3 years.
First, let us calculate the simple interest.

P = ₹12,000   T = 3 years   R = 15%

$$SI = \frac{P \times T \times R}{100} = \frac{12,000 \times 3 \times 15}{100}$$

$= ₹5,400$

SI = ₹5,400

Amount = ₹12,000 + ₹5,400 = ₹17,400

Now, let us calculate the compound interest.

To calculate the compound interest, we calculate the interest for every year using the formula for simple interest and change the principal correspondingly.

$$SI = \frac{P \times T \times R}{100} = \frac{12,000 \times 1 \times 15}{100}$$

$= ₹1,800$

This is the interest for the first year.

Let us say I_1 = ₹1,800

Now the amount = ₹12,000 + ₹1800

= ₹13,800

Thus, amount after 1 year is $A_1 = P_1 + I_1$.

This amount after a year is the principal for the second year. Now, let us calculate the interest on this new principal for the second year.

$$SI = \frac{13,800 \times 1 \times 15}{100} = ₹2,070$$

Now, I_2 = ₹2,070 and $A_2 = P_2 + I_2$

thus A_2 = 13,800 + 2,070

= ₹15,870

This amount after the second year becomes the principal for the third year. Now, we shall calculate the interest on this principal.

$$SI = \frac{15,870 \times 1 \times 15}{100}$$

$= ₹2,380.50$

Now, I_3 = ₹2380.50

$A_3 = P_3 + I_3$

A_3 = ₹15,870 + ₹2380.50 = ₹18,250.50

∴ Compound interest after 3 years = ₹18,250.50 − ₹12,000

= ₹6,250.50

Now, let us compare the values of simple interest and compound interest and find their difference.

Simple interest after 3 years = ₹5,400

Compound interest after 3 years = ₹6,250.50

The difference in interest = ₹6,250.50 − ₹5,400

= ₹850.50

This is the difference in interest after 3 years. If the number of years or time period is increased, the difference will be larger.

Alert!

1. After one year, the amount obtained by both simple and compound interest is the same.
2. There is a substantial difference between the amount of simple interest and compound interest earned when the time period increases.

Now we shall find a formula for compound interest so that we can calculate it directly.

In the examples above we have calculated the compound interest for one year at a time, the rate of interest being the same. Every year the principal and the interest amounts change.

Now let us take the principal for the first year as P_1. Then,

$$I_1 = \frac{P_1 \times R \times 1}{100} = \frac{P_1 \times R}{100}$$

$$\text{Now, } A_1 = P_1 + I_1 = P_1 + \frac{P_1 \times R}{100}$$

$$\text{or } A_1 = P_1\left[1 + \frac{R}{100}\right] \quad \text{(since } P_1 \text{ is a common factor)}$$

Now, the amount for the first year is the principal for the second year.

Thus, $A_1 = P_2$

$$\therefore \quad P_2 = P_1\left[1 + \frac{R}{100}\right] \qquad \text{(i)}$$

Now interest for the second year is

$$I_2 = \frac{P_2 \times R \times 1}{100} = \frac{P_2 \times R}{100}$$

$$= P_1\left[1 + \frac{R}{100}\right] \times \frac{R}{100}$$

$$I_2 = \frac{P_1 R}{100}\left[1 + \frac{R}{100}\right] \qquad \text{(ii)}$$

But, $A_2 = P_2 + I_2$

Replacing the values of P_2 and I_2 from equations (i) and (ii), respectively, we get,

$$A_2 = P_1\left[1+\frac{R}{100}\right] + \frac{P_1R}{100}\left[1+\frac{R}{100}\right]$$

$$A_2 = P_1\left[1+\frac{R}{100}\right]\left[1+\frac{R}{100}\right] \qquad \left[P_1\left(1+\frac{R}{100}\right) \text{ is a common factor}\right]$$

$$A_2 = P_1\left[1+\frac{R}{100}\right]^2 \qquad \text{(iii)}$$

Now, A_2 (amount for the second year) becomes the principal for the third year, hence

$A_2 = P_3$

The interest for the third year is,

$$I_3 = \frac{P_3 \times R}{100} = P_3 \times \frac{R}{100}$$

$$= P_1\left[1+\frac{R}{100}\right]^2 \times \frac{R}{100} \qquad \text{[replacing the value of } P_3 \text{ from equation (iii)]}$$

But, $A_3 = P_3 + I_3$

$$= P_1\left[1+\frac{R}{100}\right]^2 + P_1\left[1+\frac{R}{100}\right]^2 \times \frac{R}{100}$$

Thus, $A_3 = P_1\left[1+\frac{R}{100}\right]^2\left[1+\frac{R}{100}\right] \qquad \left[\text{since } P_1\left(1+\frac{R}{100}\right)^2 \text{ is a common factor}\right]$

$$A_3 = P_1\left[1+\frac{R}{100}\right]^3$$

Thus we see that the amount after three years is $P_1\left[1+\frac{R}{100}\right]^3$. We can generalise the formula for 'n' years which will be,

$$A_n = P_1\left[1+\frac{R}{100}\right]^n$$

Where P_1 is the original principal given. Hence, we can write the formula as,

$$A_n = P\left[1+\frac{R}{100}\right]^n$$

In compound interest formula, we find the amount directly and the compound interest (CI) is given by CI = A – P.

Example 1: Calculate the compound interest on ₹5,000 for 2 years at the rate of 8% per annum when the interest is compounded annually.

We shall use the compound interest formula to solve the problem.

We know that CI = A – P

Now, $A = P\left[1 + \frac{R}{100}\right]^n$

We are given P = ₹5,000, R = 8% pa and n = 2 years

Substituting the values in the formula, we have:

$$A = 5{,}000\left[1 + \frac{\overset{2}{\cancel{8}}}{\underset{25}{\cancel{100}}}\right]^2$$

$$A = 5{,}000\left[1 + \frac{2}{25}\right]^2, A = 5{,}000\left[\frac{25 + 2}{25}\right]^2 \text{ and } n = 5{,}000\left[\frac{27}{25}\right]^2.$$

$$A = 5{,}000 \times \frac{27}{25} \times \frac{27}{25}$$

$A = ₹5{,}832$

$CI = A - P = ₹5{,}832 - ₹5{,}000$

$CI = ₹832$

The compound interest is ₹832.

Example 2: Find the difference between the simple interest and compound interest on ₹10,000 at the rate of 5% pa for 2 years.

Here P = ₹10,000, R = 5% pa and T = 2 years

$$SI = \frac{P \times R \times T}{100}$$

$$SI = \frac{10{,}000 \times 5 \times 2}{100}$$

$= ₹1{,}000$

For compound interest, we find the amount first.

$$A = P\left[1 + \frac{R}{100}\right]^n$$

$$A = 10{,}000\left[1 + \frac{5}{100}\right]^2$$

$$= 10{,}000\left[1 + \frac{1}{20}\right]^2$$

$$A = 10{,}000\left[\frac{21}{20}\right]^2$$

$$A = 10{,}000 \times \frac{21}{20} \times \frac{21}{20}$$

$A = ₹11{,}025$

$CI = A - P$

$CI = ₹11{,}025 - ₹10{,}000$

$= ₹1{,}025$

Difference between CI and SI is CI − SI

$= ₹1025 - ₹1000 = ₹25$

The difference is ₹25.

Example 3: The simple interest on a sum of money for 2 years at 6% per annum is ₹900. What will be the compound interest on that sum at the same rate and for the same period?

$$P = \frac{SI \times 100}{R \times T}$$

$$P = \frac{900 \times 100}{6 \times 2} = ₹7{,}500$$

Principal is ₹7,500.

Now calculating the compound interest on this principal at the same rate and for the same time period, we have

$$A = P\left[1 + \frac{R}{100}\right]^n$$

$$A = 7{,}500\left[1 + \frac{6}{100}\right]^2$$

$$A = 7{,}500\left[1 + \frac{3}{50}\right]^2$$

$$A = 7{,}500\left[50 + \frac{3}{50}\right]^2$$

$$A = 7{,}500\left[\frac{53}{50}\right]^2$$

$$A = 7{,}500 \times \frac{53}{50} \times \frac{53}{50} = 3 \times 53 \times 53$$

$A = ₹8{,}427$

$CI = A - P$

$\therefore CI = ₹8{,}427 - ₹7{,}500$

$= ₹927$

The compound interest is ₹927.

Example 4: What sum of money will amount to ₹13,230 in 2 years time at the rate of 5% per annum compounded annually?

We are given A = ₹13,230, R = 5% pa (CT) and Time = 2 years.

Now, $A = P\left[1 + \frac{R}{100}\right]^n$

Substituting the values in the formula,

$$13{,}230 = P\left[1 + \frac{5}{100}\right]^2$$

$$13{,}230 = P\left[1 + \frac{1}{20}\right]^2$$

$$13{,}230 = P\left[\frac{20 + 1}{20}\right]^2 = P\left[\frac{21}{20}\right]^2$$

$$13{,}230 = P\left[\frac{21 \times 21}{20 \times 20}\right]$$

$$\therefore P = \frac{13{,}230 \times 20 \times 20}{21 \times 21}$$

$P = 30 \times 20 \times 20 = ₹12{,}000$

Principal = ₹12,000

The principal is ₹12,000.

Example 5: The difference between the compound interest and the simple interest on a certain sum of money for 2 years at 5% per annum is ₹50. Find the sum.

Here, let P = ₹P, T = 2 year and R = 5% pa

$$SI = \frac{P \times 5 \times 2}{100} = \frac{P}{10}$$

$CI = A - P$

$= P\left[1 + \frac{5}{100}\right]^2 - P$

$= P\left[1 + \frac{1}{20}\right]^2 - P$

$= P\left[\frac{20 + 1}{20}\right]^2 - P$

$= P \times \left(\frac{21}{20}\right)^2 - P$

$= P \times \frac{21}{20} \times \frac{21}{20} - P$

$= P \times \frac{441}{400} - \frac{P}{1} = \frac{441P - 400P}{400}$

$= \frac{41P}{400}$

$CI = \frac{41P}{400} \qquad SI = \frac{P}{10}$

Difference between CI and SI = CI − SI =

$\frac{41P}{400} - \frac{P}{10} = 50$

$= \frac{41P - 40P}{400} = 50$

$= \frac{P}{400} = 50$

P = 400 × 50 = ₹20,000

The principal is ₹20,000.

Example 6: In what time will ₹10,000 amount to ₹12,100 at the rate of 10% pa?

Here, A = ₹12,100, P = ₹10,000 and R = 10%.

We have to find n.

$A = P\left[1 + \frac{R}{100}\right]^n$

$12{,}100 = 10{,}000\left[1 + \frac{10}{100}\right]^n$

$12{,}100 = 10{,}000\left[\frac{10 + 1}{10}\right]^n$

$12{,}100 = 10{,}000\left[\frac{11}{10}\right]^n$

$\frac{12{,}100}{10{,}00} = \left[\frac{11}{10}\right]^n$

$\frac{121}{100} = \left(\frac{11}{10}\right)^n$

$\frac{11 \times 11}{10 \times 10} = \left(\frac{11}{10}\right)^n$

$\left(\frac{11}{10}\right)^2 = \left(\frac{11}{10}\right)^n$

Since the bases are the same, we can equate the powers.

∴ n = 2 years

The time period is 2 years.

Example 7: At what rate per cent per annum will ₹4,000 amount to ₹4,410 in 2 years when compounded annually?

Here, amount = ₹4,410, P = ₹4,000, T = 2 years.

We have to find the rate per cent (R).

$$A = P\left[1 + \frac{R}{100}\right]^n$$

$$4410 = 4000\left[1 + \frac{R}{100}\right]^n$$

$$\frac{4410}{4000} = \left[\frac{100 + R}{100}\right]^n$$

$$\frac{441}{400} = \left[\frac{100 + R}{100}\right]^n$$

$$\frac{21 \times 21}{20 \times 20} = \left[\frac{100 + R}{100}\right]^n$$

$$\left(\frac{21}{20}\right)^2 = \left(\frac{100 + R}{100}\right)^2$$

$$\frac{21}{20} = \frac{100 + R}{100}$$

$$\frac{21}{20} \times 100 = 100 + R$$

$$105 = 100 + R$$

$$\therefore \quad R = 105 - 100 = 5$$

The rate of interest is 5% per annum.

Practice Exercise 8.3

1. Find the amount and compound interest in each of the following cases.

a. P = ₹32,000	R = 5 % pa	T = 2 years
b. P = ₹18,000	R = 4 % pa	T = 2 years
c. P = ₹15,000	R = 10 % pa	T = 3 years

2. Find the difference between the compound interest and simple interest for each of the following cases.

a. P = ₹625	R = 4 % pa	T = 2 years
b. P = ₹3,000	R = 10 % pa	T = 3 years
c. P = ₹2,500	R = 6 % pa	T = 2 years

3.a. What sum of money amounts to ₹13,230 in 2 years time at the rate of 5% per annum compounded annually?

b. What sum of money will amount to ₹10,648 in 2 years time at the rate of 10% per annum compounded annually?

c. What sum of money amounts to ₹86,515 in 3 years time at the rate of 10% per annum compounded annually?

4. Find the time in which ₹2,000 will amount to ₹2,205 at 5% per annum compound interest?

5. At what rate per cent per annum will ₹62,500 amount to ₹72,900 in two years compounded annually?

6. The difference between the compound interest and the simple interest on a certain sum for 2 years at the rate of 5% per annum is ₹25. Find the sum.
7. Radha borrowed a certain sum of money for 3 years at the rate of 5% per annum compounded annually. Rohini borrowed the same sum of money, for the same time and at the same rate of interest at simple interest. The difference in interest for the two is ₹183. Find the sum borrowed by them.
8. Find the rate of interest per annum that will yield ₹800 as simple interest on ₹8,000 in 2 years. Find out how much ₹10,000 will amount to in 2 years at the same rate of interest, compounded annually.
9. In how much time will ₹5,000 amount to ₹5,600 with simple interest at the rate of 6% per annum? With the same time period and rate, find the compound interest on the same principal.
10. The compound interest on a certain sum of money for 2 years at the rate of 5% per annum is ₹410. Find the sum. Find the rate of interest which will fetch the same interest in 2 years time if the sum of money is given on simple interest.

Now, we shall learn a few variations in the formula of compound interest. We shall also study the applications of the compound interest formula in finding increase or decrease of population, and to find the appreciation or depreciation of the value of an item in a period of time with the help of following examples.

When the interest is compounded annually but rates are different for different years.

Let principal be ₹P, time is 2 years and rate of interest be R% pa and S% pa, then, the amount after two years will be,

$$A = P \times \left(1 + \frac{R}{100}\right) \times \left(1 + \frac{S}{100}\right)$$

If it is R % for 2 years and S% for 1 year, then the formula will be,

$$A = P \times \left(1 + \frac{R}{100}\right)^2 \times \left(1 + \frac{S}{100}\right)^1$$

When the interest is compounded half yearly.

The interest rate mentioned by banks and other financial institutions are on a per annum basis. So, when the interest is compounded half yearly, the rate is halved and the time period is doubled.

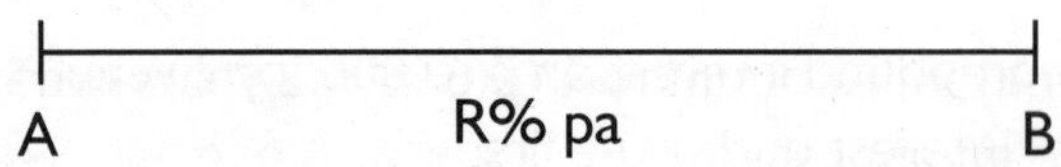

Let us assume that AB represents one year. Now, the rate of interest is R% pa for 1 year. But, if the interest is paid half yearly, then the year is divided into two part.

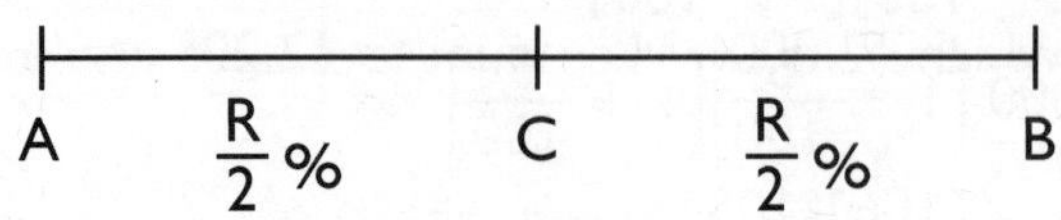

Hence, in one year, the interest is paid twice. Hence, the time period is doubled and the rate is halved.

$$\text{So, } A = P\left[1 + \frac{R}{100}\right]^n$$

$$A = P\left[1 + \frac{R}{2 \times 100}\right]^{2n}$$

Alert!

When the interest is compounded half yearly, the rate of interest (R) is divided by 2 and the time period (T) is multiplied by 2.

When the interest is compounded quarterly.

Here, the interest is paid quarterly. If AB represents a year, then in one year the interest will be paid four times as shown in the figure below.

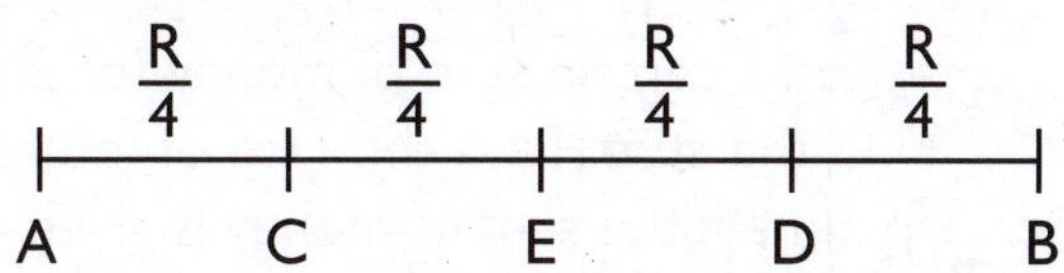

Here, in one year, the interest is paid *four times*, so the time is multiplied by four.

Hence $A = P\left[1+ \frac{R}{100}\right]^n$ becomes $A = P\left[1 + \frac{R}{4 \times 100}\right]^{4n}$

Alert!

When interest is compounded quarterly, the rate of interest (R) is divided by 4 and the time period (T) is multiplied by 4.

When the interest is compounded annually with time as a fraction of a year.

When the time is a fraction of a year, then we find the compound interest for the whole year by the compound interest formula and for the fraction of the year, the interest is calculated by the simple interest formula. The two interests are then added. We can also use the CI formula directly if the rate of interest is exactly divisible by the fraction of the year.

Application of the compound interest formula for finding the increase or decrease of population.

In case of increase or appreciation of a value, we use the same formula, but for decrease or depreciation, the formula becomes,

$$A = P\left[1 - \frac{R}{100}\right]^n$$

Example 1: Find the compound interest on ₹10,000 for 2 years compounded annually when the rate of interest during the first year is 6% per annum and for the next year is 5% per annum.

$$A = P\left[1 + \frac{R}{100}\right]\left[1 + \frac{S}{100}\right]$$

$$A = 10{,}000\left[1 + \frac{6}{100}\right]\left[1 + \frac{5}{100}\right]$$

$$A = 10{,}000\left[\frac{106}{100}\right]\left[\frac{105}{100}\right]$$

$A = ₹11,130$

$CI = A - P = ₹11,130 - ₹10,000$

$\therefore CI = ₹1,130.$

The compound interest is ₹1,130.

Example 2: Find the compound interest on ₹6,40,00 for 2 years at 10% per annum when compounded half yearly.

Here P = ₹6,4,000, Rate = 10% pa and T = 2 years.

Since the interest is compounded half yearly,

$$\text{Rate \%} = \frac{10}{2} = 5\%$$

$$\text{Time} = 2 \times 2 = 4$$

$$\therefore A = P\left[1 + \frac{R}{2 \times 100}\right]^{2n}$$

$$= 6{,}40{,}00\left[1 + \frac{5}{100}\right]^{4}$$

$$= 6{,}40{,}00\left[\frac{21}{20}\right]^{4}$$

$$= 6{,}40{,}00 \times \frac{21}{20} \times \frac{21}{20} \times \frac{21}{20} \times \frac{21}{20}$$

$$= 4 \times 21 \times 21 \times 21 \times 21$$

$$= ₹7{,}77{,}924$$

$$CI = A - P$$

$$CI = ₹7{,}77{,}924 - ₹6{,}40{,}000$$

$$= ₹1{,}37{,}924$$

The compound interest is ₹1,37,924.

Example 3: Find the compound interest on ₹10,00,000 for 9 months at a rate of 12% per annum compounded quarterly.

Given that P = ₹10 00,000, R = 12% pa, and T = 9 months.

Since the interest is compounded quarterly,

$$\text{Rate\%} = \frac{12}{4} = 3\%$$

Time = 9 months

There will be 3 quarters in 9 months

$$\therefore A = P\left[1 + \frac{R}{100}\right]^{n}$$

$$= 10{,}00{,}000\left[1 + \frac{3}{100}\right]^{3}$$

$$= 10{,}00{,}000\left[\frac{103}{100}\right]^{3}$$

$$= 10{,}00{,}000 \times \frac{103}{100} \times \frac{103}{100} \times \frac{103}{100}$$

$$= ₹10{,}92{,}727$$

$$\therefore \quad CI = ₹10{,}92{,}727 - ₹10{,}00{,}000$$

$$= ₹92{,}727$$

The compound interest is ₹92,727.

Example 4: Find the compound interest on ₹5,000 for $2\frac{1}{2}$ years at a rate of 6% per annum compounded annually.

Given that P = ₹5,000, R = 6% pa and T = $2\frac{1}{2}$ years

For 2 years we use the CI formula and for $\frac{1}{2}$ year the SI formula and then add the two interests.

$$A = P\left[1 + \frac{R}{100}\right]^n$$

$$A = 5,000\left[1 + \frac{6}{100}\right]^2$$

$$= 5,000\left[\frac{53}{50}\right]^2$$

$$A = 5,000 \times \frac{53}{50} \times \frac{53}{50} = 2 \times 53 \times 53$$

A = ₹5,618

∴ CI = ₹5,618 − ₹5,000 = ₹618

For the half year we calculate the SI

$$SI = \frac{P \times R \times T}{100}$$

$$= \frac{5000 \times 6 \times 1}{100 \times 2} = ₹150$$

∴ Compound interest after $2\frac{1}{2}$ years is ₹618 + ₹150 = ₹768.

The compound interest is ₹768.

Example 5: The population of a town increased at the rate of 10% per annum. If in the year 2002, it was 5,40,00,000, what did it become in the year 2005?

Population in 2002 is P.

Population in 2005 is A.

$$\therefore \quad A = P\left[1 + \frac{R}{100}\right]^n$$

$$A = 5,40,00,000\left[1 + \frac{10}{100}\right]^3$$

$$A = 5,40,00,000\left[\frac{10 + 1}{10}\right]^3$$

$$A = 5,40,00,000\left[\frac{11}{10}\right]^3$$

$$A = 5,40,00,000 \times \frac{11}{10} \times \frac{11}{10} \times \frac{11}{10}$$

$$A = 54,000 \times 11 \times 11 \times 11$$

A = 7, 18,74,000

The population of the town in 2005 became 7,18,74,000.

Practice Exercise 8.4

1. Find the compound interest on a sum of ₹9,000 for 2 years when the rate of interest for the first year is 8% per annum and for the second year is 10% per annum.
2. Dhiren invests a sum of ₹5,00,000 in a bank for 2 years, which gives him a successive interest of 5% per annum and 6% per annum, respectively. Find the amount that Dhiren will receive after two years.

3. Find the compound interest on ₹1,5625 for $1\frac{1}{2}$ years at 8% per annum, interest being payable half yearly.
4. Shobha takes a loan for ₹10,000 for a year at 10% per annum, interest being payable half yearly. Find the amount of money she has to return after a year.
5. Find the compound interest on ₹6,25,0000 for a year at 8% per annum, interest being payable quarterly.
6. Leena invested ₹15,625 for a short time period of 9 months in a finance company, which paid an interest of 16% per annum, interest being compounded quarterly. Find the amount of money she will receive after 9 months.
7. Find the compound interest on ₹20,000 for $2\frac{1}{2}$ years at a rate of 20% per annum compounded annually.
8. Rohit decides to put a sum of ₹80,000 in a bank for $2\frac{1}{5}$ years at a rate of 5% per annum compounded annually. Find the interest he will receive on the money invested.
9. The population of a village is recorded as increasing at the rate of 10% per annum. If the present population is 15,000, what will it be in 3 years time?
10. Nidhi bought a car for ₹4,00,000 in 2008. She now wants to sell it. If the rate of depreciation is 18% per annum, how much will the sale of her car fetch her?

Higher Order Thinking Skills

HOTS

1. Amit buys a plot of land for ₹96,000. He sells $\frac{2}{5}$ of it at a loss of 6%. At what gain per cent should be sell the remaining part of the plot to gain 10% on the whole transaction?
2. A manufacturer offers a 20% rebate on the marked price of a product. The retailer offers another 30% rebate on the reduced price. The two reductions are equivalent to a single reduction of

   a. 42%? b. 44%? c. 46%? d. 50%?
3. The difference between the compound interest and simple interest on a sum of ₹15,000 for 2 years is ₹96. What is the rate of interest per annum?
4. The population of a village is 30,000. If the birth rate is 6.5% and the death rate is 4.5%, what will be the population after 2 years?
5. Find the compound interest on ₹16,000 after 6 months at the rate of 12%, pa compounded quarterly.

Highlights

- When the selling price is more than the cost price, there is a profit or gain and when the cost price is more than the selling price, there is a loss.
- Profit or loss is always calculated on the cost price.
- Overhead expenses, such as transportation, packaging, maintenance and repair, are added to the cost price, which is then called the actual cost price.
- Discount given on articles is always calculated on the marked price.
- If two or more discounts are allowed one after the other, then such discounts are known as successive discounts.
- Sales tax or value-added tax (VAT) is added to the bill amount. VAT is calculated on the selling price.
- VAT is calculated on the selling price but is not a part of the selling price. It cannot be included to calculate profit or loss.
- In case of simple interest, the principal remains the same each year.
- In case of compound interest, the amount for one year becomes the principal for the next year.
- If interest is compounded half yearly, the time period doubles and the rate becomes half. If interest is compounded quarterly, the time period becomes four times as much and the rate becomes a quarter.
- To find the rate of increase or decrease in population or the appreciation or depreciation of the value of an item, the compound interest formula is applied.

  $$A = P\left[1 \pm \frac{R}{100}\right]^n$$

  (+) for increase or appreciation.

  (−) for decrease or depreciation.

At a pizza place, a man ordered a medium pizza.

The waiter at the restaurant asked him, "Would you like your pizza to be cut into 6 or 8 pieces?"

The man replied, "Cut it into 6 pieces. I don't think I am hungry enough to eat 8 pieces."

Maths Lab Activity

Fractions

Aim: To divide each figure into the correct fractions.

Material required: scale, coloured pencils

Method: Use coloured pencils to divide each of the following shapes into the correct fraction as indicated.

$\frac{1}{2}$

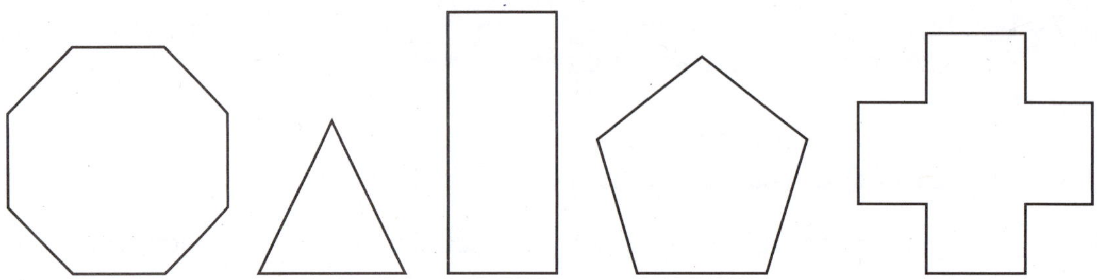

$\frac{1}{3}$

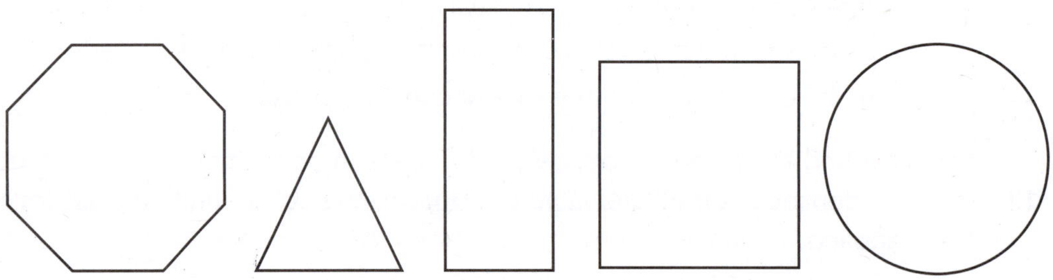

$\frac{1}{4}$

Rewind

1. Pens were bought for ₹60 per dozen and sold at ₹6 per piece. Find the gain or loss per cent.
2. Madhav bought an old car for ₹1,75,000. He spent ₹10,000 on its repairs and ₹6,500 on painting it. Madhav then sold it for ₹2,52,000. Find his total loss or gain per cent.
3. On selling a rocking chair for ₹987, Mr Dhar loses 6%. For how much did he purchase it?
4. Find the rate of discount being given on a book that has a selling price of ₹546 after deducting a discount of ₹104 on its marked price.
5. A dealer purchased a table for ₹1,080. After allowing a discount of 25% on its marked price, he gains 25%. Find the marked price of the table.
6. A washing machine is sold for ₹11,475 after giving successive discounts of 15% and 10%, respectively. Find the marked price of the washing machine.
7. There is a discount of 10% on a dinner set. If the rate of VAT is 12% and the customer paid ₹8,064 for the set, what was its marked price?
8. Find the difference between the simple interest and compound interest on ₹10,000 for 2 years at the rate of 5% per annum.
9. In how many years will ₹8,800 amount to ₹10,648 at 10% per annum, compounded annually?
10. Meeta borrowed ₹45,000 from her office for 9 months at the rate of 16% per annum, compounded quarterly. How much does she have to pay back at the end of the term?
11. Darshan and Tarang both lent ₹10,000 each to their friends for $1\frac{1}{2}$ years. Darshan charged a compound interest of 14%, compounded annually, while Tarang charged a 10% compound interest, compounded half yearly. Who received more money at the end of $1\frac{1}{2}$ years and by how much?
12. The population of a town is 2,50,000 people. If the rate of growth is 10% per annum, find the population after $2\frac{1}{2}$ years.
13. Abhinav borrowed ₹8,000 for 2 years from a friend at the rate of 9% per annum for the first year and 10% per annum for the second year. What is the total amount he has to repay after two years, at compound interest?
14. A sum of money amounts to ₹10,240 in 2 years at $6\frac{2}{3}\%$ per annum compounded annually. Find the sum.
15. The compound interest on ₹30,000 at 7% per annum for a certain time is ₹4,347. Find the time.
16. By selling 50 packets of sweets, a shopkeeper gains the selling price of 10 packets of sweets. Find the gain per cent.
17. Anuradha bought two handbags for ₹750 each from an exhibition. She sold them to her friends, making a profit of 4% on one bag and a loss of 4% on the other. Find her loss or gain per cent on the whole transaction.
18. Rohini bought toffees at 3 for ₹5 and sold them at 5 for ₹12. She gained ₹143 in all. How many toffees did she buy?
19. By selling a photo frame for ₹504, Nandu gains 12%. For how much should he sell it to gain 18%?
20. Vijaya bought a washing machine for ₹11,000 and sold it at a bill amount of ₹13,068, which included 8% VAT. Find her profit or loss per cent.

CHAPTER 9

Direct and Inverse Variation

Variation is derived from the word variable, which mean a quantity that is varying or changing. In algebra, we have variables that are unknown quantities. We find their value by solving the equation. Similarly, in day-to-day life, we observe many things that are always changing such as the price of commodities, the speed of cars, the number of plants in a garden and so on.

The term variation in mathematics means a change in one quantity due to a change in another *related* quantity. Let us study each one in detail with examples to understand the concept.

There are two types of changes or variations:

1. Direct variation
2. Inverse variation

Direct Variation

Direct variation means a change in one quantity due to change in another related quantity such that:

a. *increase* in one quantity brings about an *increase* in the other related quantity.

b. *decrease* in one quantity brings about a *decrease* in the other related quantity.

Hence, an increase or decrease in one quantity with a corresponding increase or decrease in another quantity such that their ratio remains constant is called direct variation.

Example 1: Let us consider the example of the area of a circle.

$$A = \pi r^2 \quad \text{(where A = area and r = radius)}$$

If we *increase* the radius of the circle, the area of the circle will *increase*.

If we *decrease* the radius of the circle, the area of the circle will *decrease*.

Here, area is related to or depends on its radius.

Example 2: Suppose the cost of sugar is ₹40/kg. If we buy 5 kg of sugar, the cost will be ₹200.

If we reduce the consumption to 3 kg, the cost will reduce to ₹120.

The cost of sugar depends on the amount consumed.

If we buy more, we pay more; if we buy less, we pay less.

Example 3: A car travels 45 km on 3 litres of petrol and 150 km on 10 litres of petrol.

As the distance increases, the consumption of petrol increases. As the distance decreases, the consumption of petrol decreases.

Alert!

With respect to direct variation, the following is true:

1. Increase in one quantity produces an increase in the other quantity.
2. Decrease in one quantity produces a decrease in the other quantity.

We can also show direct variation in the form of a ratio.

The quantities x and y vary directly according to the data given below:

x	5	15	20	100	150
y	15	45	60	300	450

Now, the ratio in each of the following remains the same.

$$\frac{x}{y} = \frac{\cancel{5}^{1}}{\cancel{15}_{3}} = \frac{\cancel{15}^{1}}{\cancel{45}_{3}} = \frac{\cancel{20}^{1}}{\cancel{30}_{3}} = \frac{\cancel{100}^{1}}{\cancel{300}_{3}} = \frac{\cancel{150}^{1}}{\cancel{450}_{3}}$$

The value, $\frac{1}{3}$, is called the constant of variation.

Example 1: If 15 books cost ₹750, what is the cost of 20 books?

Number of books		Cost
15	⟶	750
20	⟶	x

If the number of books increases, the cost will also increase.

We can write it as $\frac{15}{20} = \frac{750}{x}$

$$\frac{15}{20} = \frac{750}{x}$$

By cross multiplying we get:

$$15x = 20 \times 750$$

$$x = \frac{20 \times 750}{15} = ₹1{,}000$$

The cost of 20 books is ₹1,000.

Example 2: A class of 25 students collected ₹800 for an excursion. What will be the collection of a class having 40 students?

Number of students		Collection
25	⟶	800
40	⟶	x

This is a case of direct variation. If the number of students increases, the class collection also increases.

$$\frac{25}{40} = \frac{800}{x}$$

By cross multiplying we get:

$$25x = 40 \times 800$$

$$x = \frac{40 \times 800}{25} = 1{,}280$$

The collection will be ₹1,280.

Practice Exercise 9.1

1. If 9 litres of petrol cost ₹531, find the cost of 16 litres of petrol.
2. Kamla is a senior citizen. She pays a fare of ₹630 to travel by AC III tier class by train for a distance of 420 km. How much fare will she pay if she travels a distance of 860 km?

3. If 8 kg of mangoes cost ₹168, how many mangoes can Ravi buy for ₹651?
4. A carpenter makes 21 tables in 6 days. In how many days will he make 105 tables?
5. Ganga earns ₹805 per week. In how many days will she earn ₹1,840?
6. Rudraksh bought 18 toy cars for ₹630. How many toy cars can he buy for ₹455?
7. The cost of 16 school bags is ₹672. Find the cost of 25 such bags.
8. If 146 copies of a book can be packed in 12 cartons of the same size, how many cartons will be required for 219 copies?
9. If 300 trees are planted in 12 rows, how many trees can be planted in 30 rows?
10. Deepak drives his car at a constant speed of 45 km/hr. How far will he reach in 220 minutes?

Inverse Variation

Inverse variation means a change in one quantity due to a change in another related quantity such that:

a. an *increase* in one quantity brings about a *decrease* in the other quantity.

b. a *decrease* in one quantity brings about an *increase* in the other quantity.

Thus, when two quantities vary inversely, an increase in one quantity leads to the decrease in the other quantity and vice versa, in inverse ratio.

Example 1: Let us consider the example of the speed of a car and the distance covered. If we travel at a speed of 60 km/hr by car, we can cover a distance of 360 km in 6 hours. If we travel the same distance at 40 km/hr, we cover the distance in 9 hours.

Hence, the greater the speed, the lesser is the time taken to reach the destination.

Increase in speed ⟶ decrease in time

Decrease in speed ⟶ increase in time

Example 2: Radhika had a birthday party. Her mother baked a big cake. She thought that each of her 8 friends would get a big piece of the cake. But 14 friends turned up for the party so the size of the cake pieces was reduced.

As the number of people *increased,* the size of each cake piece *decreased.*

Example 3: A hostel with 100 students had enough food to last them for 30 days. However, 50 new students arrived. For how long will the food last now?

As the number of students *increases,* the food will last for a fewer number of days.

Alert!

In inverse variation as one quantity increases, the other related quantity decreases. As one quantity decreases the other related quantity increases.

Now we shall study inverse variation with the help of ratio.

The quantities x and y vary inversely as given in the data below.

x	2	4	5	60	3
y	30	15	12	1	20

Now $x \times y = 2 \times 30 = 60$

or $x \times y = 4 \times 15 = 60$

or $x \times y = 5 \times 12 = 60$

or $x \times y = 60 \times 1 = 60$

or $x \times y = 3 \times 20 = 60$

For inverse proportion, the product $x \times y$ should be a constant as:

$$x = \frac{1}{y} \quad \text{or} \quad y = \frac{1}{x}$$

x is the inverse of y or y is the inverse of x.

Hence, when we multiply x and y, we should get a constant value.

Thus, $x \times y =$ constant.

Example 1: If 15 men can paint a building in 24 days, how long will 9 men take to paint the same building?

Men		Days
15	⟶	24
9	⟶	x

If the number of men decreases, the number of days to paint the building will increase.

Thus, $\frac{15}{9} = \frac{x}{24}$ or $15 \times 24 = 9x$

$9x = 15 \times 24$

$x = \frac{15 \times 24}{9} = 40$ days

It will take them 40 days.

Alert!

Direct variation: If one quantity increases, the other also increases.

$$\downarrow \begin{matrix} x_1 & y_1 \\ x_2 & y_2 \end{matrix} \downarrow \qquad \frac{x_1}{x_2} = \frac{y_1}{y_2}$$

Inverse variation: If one quantity increases, the other decreases.

$$\downarrow \begin{matrix} x_1 & y_1 \\ x_2 & y_2 \end{matrix} \uparrow \qquad \frac{x_1}{x_2} = \frac{y_2}{y_1}$$

For inverse variation, the product xy should be a constant.

Example 2: If 35 women can reap a field in 8 days, in how many days can 20 women reap the same field?

Women	Days
↓ 35	8 ↑
20	x

$\frac{35}{20} = \frac{x}{8}$ or $35 \times 8 = 20 \times x$

$20x = 35 \times 8$

$x = \frac{35 \times 8}{20} = 14$ days

20 women can reap the field in 14 days.

Practice Exercise 9.2

1. If 45 men can do a piece of work in 13 days, how many men will complete the work in 9 days?
2. If 16 cows can graze a field in 30 days, how many cows can graze the same field in 24 days?
3. Mahima drives at the rate of 60 km/hr and covers the distance from A to B in 4 hours. Punita drives at 80 km/hr. How long will she take to cover the same distance?
4. In a hostel for 300 students, there was provision of food for 50 days. Now, 200 additional students join the hotel. Find the number of days the food will last.
5. Lalita had enough money to buy 13 boxes of sweets for ₹200 each. The price has increased by 30%. How many boxes of sweets can she buy now?
6. Nidhi wanted to buy return gifts for her son's birthday party. She had enough money to buy 24 toys costing ₹250 each. If the price of the toys has increased by 20%, how many toys can she buy now?
7. Rohini had enough money to buy 36 blankets for an orphanage at ₹500 each. The shopkeeper agreed to give a discount of 10%. How many extra blankets can Rohini buy?
8. Swastika can type 35 words per minute and she completes typing a document in 18 minutes. If the typing has to be completed in 15 minutes, what should be her typing speed?
9. At a construction site, a group of 17 men could complete a task in 56 days. Some men left due to ill health and the work extended to 63 days more. How many men took ill and left the construction site?
10. 17 men can complete painting a school building in 120 days. If the work has to be completed in 102 days, how many more men are required?

Highlights

- Two quantities x and y are said to be in direct variation if an increase in one quantity leads to an increase in the other quantity and vice versa such that $\frac{x}{y} = k$, where k is a constant called the constant of variation.
- In case of direct variation, if x_1 and x_2 have corresponding values, y_1 ,and y_2, then,

$$\frac{x_1}{x_2} = \frac{y_1}{y_2} \quad \text{or} \quad \frac{x_1}{y_1} = \frac{x_2}{y_2}$$

- Two quantities x and y are said to be in inverse variation if an increase in one quantity leads to a decrease in the other quantity and vice versa, such that $x \times y = k$, where k is known as the constant of variation.
- In case of inverse variation, if x_1 and x_2 have corresponding values y_1 and y_2, then

$x_1 \times y_1 = x_2 \times y_2$ or

$$\frac{x_1}{x_2} = \frac{y_2}{y_1}$$

- In direct variation, the ratios of the two quantities are equal.
- In inverse variation, the products of the two quantities are equal.

Higher Order Thinking Skills

HOTS

1. If 5 oxen and 9 cows can graze a field in 19 days, then in how many days will 3 oxen and 6 cows graze the same field?

2. The cost of 16 packets of washing powder, each weighing 900 gm is ₹128. What will be the cost of 27 packets, if each packet weighs 1 kg?

3. If 6 typists work 5 hours a day, they can type the manuscript of a book in 16 days. How many days will 4 typists take to do the same job, if each works 6 hours a day?

Where do mathematicians to go shopping?

Answer for Brainteaser on page 172

Maths Lab Activity

Direct and Inverse Variation

Aim: To reinforce the concepts of direct and inverse variation using examples.

Material required: a pen

Method:

Part A: Direct variation

Visit the stationery shop in school and find the cost of one dozen pencils, one dozen pens and one dozen notebooks.

Make a table showing the cost of:

1. one article
2. three articles
3. six articles
4. two dozen articles
5. five dozen articles

Part B: Inverse variation

Solve the following problems and fill in the blanks.

1. 24 miles in 6 hours = __________ miles in 8 hours
2. 200 chocolates in 7 boxes = __________ chocolates in 3 boxes
3. 12 pages in 4 day = __________ pages in 4 days
4. 7 litres petrol for 80 miles = __________ litres petrol for 4 miles
5. 60 calls in 12 hours = __________ calls in 4 hours
6. 60 miles in 15 hours = __________ miles in 8 hours
7. 12 books for ₹140 = __________ books for 200
8. 20 metres in 4 sec = __________ metres in 5 sec
9. 36 pages in 6 days = __________ pages in 5 days
10. 8 seats in 2 rows = __________ seats in 3 rows

Answer for Brainteaser from page 171

At the deci-mall!

Time and Work Time and Distance

CHAPTER 10

We shall solve the problems of time and work using the 'unitary method' learnt in the previous class. We will also develop different formulae for time, speed and distance using the unitary method. In this chapter, we shall understand and solve problems related to:

1. Time and work
2. Time and distance

Time and Work

The time required to complete a specific amount of work is directly proportional to the amount of work. If there is more work it means that more time will be required and if there is less work then less time will be required. If it takes 10 days to arrange 500 books on a shelf in a library, then to arrange 1,000 books, it would take 20 days. If a certain amount of work can be completed in 5 days, then in one day $\frac{1}{5}$th of the work will be done.

We can thus generalise a few basic rules to solve problems related to time and work.

1. If A can do a piece of work in 'n' days, then the work done by A in 1 day is $\frac{1}{n}$.
2. If A can do $\frac{1}{n}$ of the work in 1 day, he can complete the work in 'n' days.
3. If A can do a piece of work in 'n' days and B can do the same piece of work in 'm' days, then A and B together in one day can complete $\left(\frac{1}{n} + \frac{1}{m}\right)$ of the whole work.

Let us understand these concepts with the help of a few examples.

Example 1: Ashima can complete a piece of work in 10 days and Vandana can complete the same work in 15 days. If they work together, in how many days will the work be completed?

Ashima can complete a piece of work in 10 days.

$\therefore$ In 1 day Ashima can do $\frac{1}{10}$ of the work.

Vandana can complete a piece of work in 15 days.

$\therefore$ In 1 day Vandana can do $\frac{1}{15}$ of the work.

Working together in 1 day they can complete $\frac{1}{10} + \frac{1}{15}$ of the work.

$$= \frac{3+2}{30} = \frac{5}{30} = \frac{1}{6} \text{ of the work.}$$

In 1 day they can complete $\frac{1}{6}$ of the work, therefore, they will complete the entire work in 6 days.

Example 2: Mridula and Sangeeta can embroider a saree in 15 days. Mridula alone can embroider the saree in 20 days. If Sangeeta has to embroider the saree alone, how many days will she take to complete it?

Mridula and Sangeeta can embroider a saree in 15 days.

$\therefore$ In 1 day they can embroider $\frac{1}{15}$ of the saree.

Mridula can embroider the saree in 20 days.

$\therefore$ In 1 day Mridula can embroider $\frac{1}{20}$ of the saree.

Now, Sangeeta alone can embroider how much of the saree in one day?

$\frac{1}{15} - \frac{1}{20} = \frac{4-3}{60} = \frac{1}{60}$

In 1 day, Sangeeta can embroider $\frac{1}{60}$ of the saree.

Hence, she can embroider the whole saree alone in 60 days.

Example 3: Mukul and Nakul can paint their house in 10 days. Nakul and Pakul can paint the house in 15 days. Pakul and Mukul can paint their house in 20 days. In how many days can Mukul paint the house?

Mukul and Nakul can paint the house in 10 days.

In 1 day Mukul and Nakul can paint $\frac{1}{10}$ of the house.

Nakul and Pakul can paint the house in 15 days.

$\therefore$ In 1 day Nakul and Pakul can paint $\frac{1}{15}$ of the house.

Pakul and Mukul can paint the house in 20 days.

$\therefore$ In 1 day Pakul and Mukul can paint $\frac{1}{20}$ of the house.

Together Mukul, Nakul and Pakul can paint the house in how many days.

Mukul and Nakul $= \frac{1}{10}$

Nakul and Pakul $= \frac{1}{15}$

Pakul and Mukul $= \frac{1}{20}$

By adding we get,

$$2(\text{Mukul and Nakul and Pakul}) = \frac{1}{10} + \frac{1}{15} + \frac{1}{20}$$

$$= \frac{6+4+3}{60} = \frac{13}{60}$$

$\therefore$ In 1 day Mukul, Nakul and Pakul can paint:

$= \frac{13}{60} \times \frac{1}{2}$ of the house

$= \frac{13}{120}$

In 1 day Mukul can paint how much of the house?

$\frac{13}{120} - \frac{1}{15} = \frac{13-8}{120} = \frac{5}{120}$

$\therefore$ Mukul can paint the whole house in $\frac{120}{5}$ days $= 24$ days

Example 4: Ravi and Rishi can mow a lawn in 12 hours. Ravi can mow $\frac{1}{3}$ of the lawn in 6 hours. How long will Rishi take to mow the whole lawn on his own?

Ravi can mow $\frac{1}{3}$ of the lawn in 6 hours

$\therefore$ He can mow the entire lawn in 18 hours.

Ravi and Rishi together can mow the lawn in 12 hours, so in 1 hour they can mow $\frac{1}{12}$ of the lawn.

Ravi can mow the entire lawn in 18 hours.

$\therefore$ In 1 hour he can mow $\frac{1}{18}$ of the lawn.

In 1 hour Rishi can mow

$\left(\frac{1}{12} - \frac{1}{18}\right)$ of the lawn

$= \frac{3-2}{36} = \frac{1}{36}$ of the lawn.

Hence, Rishi can complete mowing the lawn in 36 hours working on his own.

Example 5: Vansh can complete a certain amount of work in 25 days and Veer can complete it in 20 days. They worked together for 5 days but then Vansh fell sick. In how many days will Veer be able to complete the remaining work all by himself?

Vansh completes the work in 25 days.

$\therefore$ In 1 day, he completes $\frac{1}{25}$ of the work.

Veer completes the work in 20 days.

$\therefore$ In 1 day, he completes $\frac{1}{20}$ of the work.

Vansh and Veer together in 1 day complete $\left(\frac{1}{20} + \frac{1}{25}\right)$ of the work.

$\frac{1}{20} + \frac{1}{25} = \frac{5+4}{100} = \frac{9}{100}$

They worked together for 5 days, so they completed $\frac{9}{100} \times 5$ of the work

$= \frac{9}{20}$ of the work.

Now the work remaining is $1 - \frac{9}{20}$

i.e., $1 - \frac{9}{20} = \frac{20-9}{20} = \frac{11}{20}$

$\frac{11}{20}$ of the work has to be completed by Veer.

$\frac{1}{20}$ of the work is done by Veer in 1 day

$\therefore$ $\frac{11}{20}$ of the work is done by Veer

in $\frac{11}{20} \times 20$ days

$= 11$ days

Veer will complete the work in 11 days.

Water tanks have two types of pipes:

1. Inlet pipes, which fill the tank.
2. Outlet pipes, which empty the tank.

If a pipe fills a tank in 'm' hours, then in 1 hour it will fill $\frac{1}{m}$ of the tank.

If a pipe empties a tank in 'n' hours, then in 1 hour it will empty $\frac{1}{n}$ of the tank.

If a tank or a water cistern has more than 1 pipe or 1 tap, we can find how much water can be filled by them together.

Alert!

Filling a tank or cistern is the addition of water so the '+' sign is to be used.

Emptying a tank or cistern is the subtraction of water so the '−' sign is to be used.

Example 1: A pipe can fill a tank in 4 hours and another pipe can fill it in 8 hours. If both the pipes are opened together, how long will it take to fill the tank?

The first pipe fills the tank in 4 hours, so in 1 hour it will fill $\frac{1}{4}$ of the tank.

The second pipe can fill the tank in 8 hours.

So, in 1 hour it will fill $\frac{1}{8}$ of the tank.

When both are opened together, in 1 hour they can fill $\left(\frac{1}{4} + \frac{1}{8}\right)$ of the tank.

$\frac{1}{4} + \frac{1}{8} = \frac{2+1}{8} = \frac{3}{8}$ of the tank.

So, the entire tank will be filled in $\frac{8}{3}$ hours $= 2\frac{2}{3}$ hour $=$ 2 hours 40 mins

The entire tank will be filled in 2 hours 40 minutes.

Example 2: An inlet pipe fills a tank in 4 hours and an outlet pipe empties it in 6 hours. If both are opened together, in how many hours will the tank be filled?

The inlet pipe fills the tank in 4 hours.

$\therefore$ In 1 hour it fills $\frac{1}{4}$ of the tank.

The outlet pipe empties the tank in 6 hours.

$\therefore$ In 1 hour it empties $\frac{1}{6}$ of the tank.

When both the pipes are opened, in 1 hour $\left(\frac{1}{4} - \frac{1}{6}\right)$ of the tank will be filled.

i.e., $\frac{1}{4} - \frac{1}{6} = \frac{6-4}{24} = \frac{2}{24} = \frac{1}{12}$

In 1 hour, $\frac{1}{12}$ of the tank will be filled.

$\therefore$ The entire tank will be filled in 12 hours.

Example 3: Tap 'A' can fill a tank in 6 hours. Tap 'B' can fill the tank in 5 hours. Both the taps are opened together. After two hours, Tap B is closed. How long will Tap A take to fill the remaining tank?

In 1 hour, Tap A fills $\frac{1}{6}$ of the tank.

In 1 hour, Tap B fills $\frac{1}{5}$ of the tank.

Together, in 1 hour they fill $\frac{1}{6} + \frac{1}{5}$ of the tank

or $\frac{1}{6} + \frac{1}{5} = \frac{5+6}{30} = \frac{11}{30}$ of the tank is filled.

In 2 hours, $\frac{11}{30} \times 2$ of the tank is filled.

Part of the tank left to be filled is $1 - \frac{11}{15} = \frac{15-11}{15} = \frac{4}{15}$.

Tap A can fill the tank in 6 hours so it will take $\left(\frac{4}{15} \times 6\right)$ hours to fill the tank.

$\frac{4}{15} \times 6 = \frac{8}{5}$ hours = 1 hour 36 minutes.

Tap A will take 1 hour 36 minutes to fill the tank.

Practice Exercise 10.1

1. Appu can complete a task in 9 days and Misha can do it in 18 days. How long will they take to complete the task, if both work together?
2. Rohit and Mohit can complete a task in 6 days, while Rohit alone can complete it in 9 days. How much time will Mohit take to complete it alone?
3. Anita, Mamta and Sunita can together finish a task in 8 days. Anita working alone will take 24 days, while Mamta working alone will take 16 days. How many days will Sunita take if she has to work alone?
4. A and B can complete a task in 12 days; B and C in 15 days and C and A in 20 days. How much time will A take to finish the task if he/she is working alone?
5. Arun and Varun can finish a task in 6 hours and 4 hours, respectively. Arun started the work alone and worked for 2 hours. He was then joined by Varun. Find the total time taken to complete the task.
6. Sapna can type a manuscript in 8 days, while Barkha can do so in 10 days. They started to type together but Sapna had to leave after 2 days. How many days will Barkha take to complete the remaining work?
7. A tap fills a tank in 6 hours. Another tap fills it in 8 hours. The outlet pipe empties it in 12 hours. If all the three taps are opened together, how long will it take to fill the tank?
8. Three taps, A, B and C, can fill up an empty tank in 6 hours, 8 hours and 12 hours, respectively. After two hours, taps A and B are closed. How much time will Tap C take to fill the remaining part of the tank?
9. Taps A, B and C can fill a tank in 6 hours, 8 hours and 12 hours, respectively. Tap D can empty out the tank in 4 hours. The four taps, A, B, C and D, are allowed to run for 4 hours, after which Tap D is closed. How long will it take for the 3 taps to fill the remaining tank?
10. A tap can fill a tank in 6 hours. The outlet tap was left open one day and it took 9 hours to fill the tank. If the inlet tap is closed and the outlet tap opened, how long will it take for the tank to become empty?

Time and Distance

If we are moving in a car, we cover a particular distance in a certain time. So, the distance travelled depends on the time. Thus, distance and time are related quantities. The distance moved in a particular time gives us speed.

We mention the speed of car, a train, an aeroplane in our general conversation. What does speed mean? It is the distance travelled in a particular time.

Hence, we have the formula:

$$\text{Speed} = \frac{\text{Distance}}{\text{Time}}$$

Thus, if we travel a distance of 120 km in 2 hours by car, we can say that the average speed of the car is $\frac{120 \text{ km}}{2 \text{ hours}} = 60$ km/hr.

Thus, Speed $= \frac{\text{Distance}}{\text{Time}}$ or $S = \frac{D}{T}$

or Distance = Speed × Time or $D = S \times T$

or Time $= \frac{\text{Distance}}{\text{Speed}}$ or $T = \frac{D}{S}$

Speed is measured in km per hour or m per second. To solve problems on speed, distance and time, we should know the conversion of one unit into other.

Let us learn how to convert km/hr into m/second, or vice versa.

1 hour = 60 minutes = 60 × 60 seconds

∴ 1 hour = 3,600 seconds

1 km = 1000 m

$$1 \text{ km/hr} = \frac{1000 \text{ m}}{3600 \text{ seconds}} = \frac{5}{18} \text{ m/sec}$$

$$1 \text{m/sec} = \frac{\frac{1}{1000} \text{ km}}{\frac{1}{3600} \text{ sec}} = \frac{3600}{1000} = \frac{18}{5} \text{ km/hr}$$

To convert km/hr to m/sec we multiply by $\frac{5}{18}$.

To convert m/sec to km/hr we multiply by $\frac{18}{5}$.

Alert!

Remember that distance (D), speed (S), and time (T) are in alphabetical order. So D = S × T. Now if S is to be found, make T the denominator and if T is to be found make S the denominator of D, respectively.

$$\frac{D}{T} = S \qquad \frac{D}{S} = T$$

We shall understand the concept of the three related quantities—speed, distance and time—with the help of examples.

Example 1: Express 72 km/hr in m/sec.

$S = 72$ km/hr

To convert it into m/sec, we multiply by $\frac{5}{18}$.

Thus, $72 \times \frac{5}{18} = 20$ m/sec.

Example 2: Convert 30 m/sec to km/hr.

Speed = 30 m/sec

To convert it into km/hr, we multiply by $\frac{18}{5}$.

Thus, 30 m/sec $= 30 \times \frac{18}{5} = 108$ km/hr.

Alert!

Memory aid:

1. km/hr → m/sec.

   From a larger unit to a smaller unit, we multiply by $\frac{5}{18}$ (the numerator is smaller).

2. m/sec → km/hr

   From a smaller unit to a larger unit, we multiply by $\frac{18}{5}$ (the numerator is larger).

Example 3: A bus travels at a speed of 50 km/hr. How far will it travel in $3\frac{1}{2}$ hours?

Here, $S = 50$ km/hr; $T = 3\frac{1}{2}$ hours.

$D = S \times T$

$= 50$ km/hr $\times 3\frac{1}{2}$ hours

$= 50 \times \frac{7}{2} = 175$ km

The bus will cover a distance of 175 km.

Example 4: A train 400 m long is travelling at a speed of 45 km/hr. How long will it take to cross a bridge 500 m long?

The total length for the train to travel is its own length plus the length of the bridge.

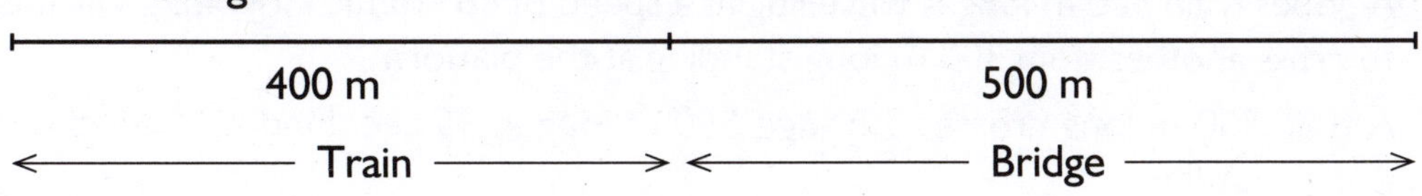

The total distance for the train to cover is 400 m + 500 m = 900 m.

$$T = \frac{D}{S} = \frac{900 \text{ m}}{45 \text{ km/hr}}$$

Since the distance is in metres, we convert speed in m/sec. To convert km/hr into m/sec, we multiply by $\frac{5}{18}$.

$$\text{Thus, } T = \frac{900 \text{ m}}{45 \times \frac{5}{18} \text{ m/sec}} = \frac{900 \times 18}{45 \times 5}$$

$= 72$ sec

$= 1$ min 12 seconds

The time taken is 1 minute 12 seconds.

Example 5: A car leaves Allahabad at 7:00 am for Varanasi, which is 120 km away, and reaches at 9:30 am. Find the speed of the car.

Here, D = 120 km, T = $2\frac{1}{2}$ hours.

$$\therefore \quad S = \frac{D}{T} = \frac{120 \text{ km}}{2\frac{1}{2} \text{ hours}}$$

$$= \frac{120}{5} \times 2 \text{ km/hr} = 48 \text{ km/hr}$$

The speed of the car is 48 km/hr.

Practice Exercise 10.2

1.a. A train is travelling at the rate of 120 km/hr. Express the speed in m/sec.

b. A car is travelling at the rate of 54 km/hr. Express the speed in m/sec.

2.a. A boy is jogging at the rate of 10 m/min. Express the speed in km/hr.

b. Convert 30 m/sec into km/hr.

3. A car travels a distance of 540 km in 6 hours. Find the speed of the car in km/hr and m/sec.
4. Bhairav cycles to his school at a distance of 12 km from home in 48 minutes. Find his speed in km/hr and also in m/sec.
5. Badal was standing at the railway crossing when a train crossed him at a speed of 90 km/hr in 5 sec. Find the length of the train.
6. A train travelling at a speed of 54 km/hr crosses a platform in 42 seconds. Find the length of the platform, if the length of the train is 360 m.
7. A train 350 m long is travelling at a speed of 108 km/hr. How long will it take to cross a tunnel 550 m long?
8. A goods train 500 m long is travelling at a speed of 48 km/hr. How long will it take to cross another train 300 m long standing at the platform?
9. A train 350 m long crosses a bridge 550 m long in 45 sec. Find the speed of the train in km/hr.
10. A bus leaves Disneyland Station at 9:00 am. It is travelling at a speed of 54 km/hr. At what time will it reach Noddyland, which is 432 km away?

Highlights

- If a person completes some work in 'n' number of days, then he does $\frac{1}{n}$ of the work in 1 day.
- If a person does $\frac{1}{n}$ of some work in a day, he will complete the work in 'n' days.
- If two persons can do some work in m and n days, respectively, then working together they will do $\left(\frac{1}{m} + \frac{1}{n}\right)$ of the work in 1 day.
- If a tap fills a tank in 't' hours, then it will fill $\frac{1}{t}$ of the tank in 1 hour.
- If a tap empties a tank in 's' hours, then it will empty $\frac{1}{s}$ of the tank in 1 hour.
- If a tap fills a tank in 't' hours and another tap empties it in 's' hours, then if they are opened together, in one hour $\left(\frac{1}{t} - \frac{1}{s}\right)$ of the tank will be filled.
- Distance = Speed × Time
- Speed = $\frac{\text{Distance}}{\text{Time}}$, Time = $\frac{\text{Distance}}{\text{Speed}}$
- Speed is expressed in km/hr or m/sec.
- When a train crosses a lamp post, an electric pole, a person, etc., then it travels a distance equal to its length.
- When a train crosses a tunnel, a bridge, a platform, etc., it travels a distance equal to the length of the train plus the length of the tunnel, bridge or platform.

Higher Order Thinking Skills

HOTS

1. 'A' can do $\frac{1}{4}$ of a work in 10 days; 'B' can do 40% of the work in 15 days and 'C' can do $\frac{1}{3}$ of the work in 13 days. Who will complete the work first?
2. Pipe A can fill a tank three times as fast as Pipe B. If together the two pipes can fill the tank in 36 minutes, then the slower pipe alone can fill the tank in how many minutes?
3. Pushkar leaves his house at 8:10 am on his motorcycle and reaches his office 40 km away at 9:50 am. At what speed was Pushkar riding his motorcycle?

Maths Lab Activity

Speed-o-meter

Objective: To find the speed of a car when time and distance are given.

Material required: graph sheet, notebook and pen for calculations.

Method: Read the graph carefully and find the speed of the points marked using the formula:

$$\text{Speed} = \frac{\text{Distance}}{\text{Time}}$$

Answer the following questions:

1. What is the total distance travelled?
2. At which points is the car stationery?
3. What is the speed of the car from 0 to A?
4. What is the average speed of the car?

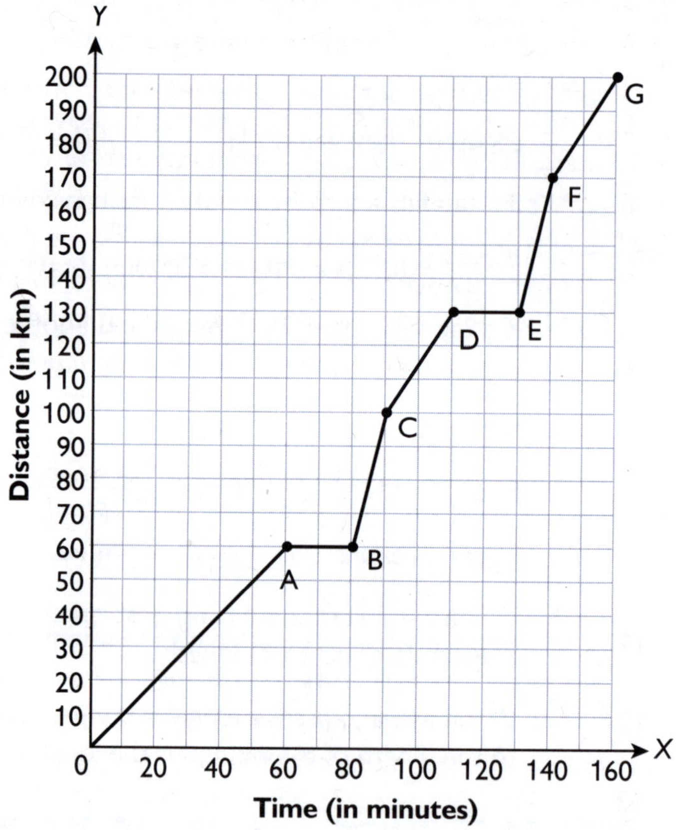

Find out the average speeds of the following.

a. Rajdhani Express from New Delhi to Mumbai.
b. Air India flight from Mumbai to New Delhi.
c. Your school bus.
d. Your cycling speed.
e. Your walking speed.

Now find the distance travelled by each in 3 hours.

Why is the meter stick such a stubborn ruler?

Answer for Brainteaser on page 185

Rewind

CHAPTERS 9–10

1. The taxi fare for 250 km is ₹2,575. What would be the fare for 350 km at the same rate?
2. If 25 books cost ₹1075, what will be the cost of 40 books?
3. A tailor stitches 18 shirts in 4 days. In how many days will he make 27 such shirts?
4. If 20 metres of a uniform wire weigh 15 kg, what will be the length of 48 kg of the same wire?
5. An electric pole 15 m high casts a shadow of 9 m. What would be the length of the shadow of a pole 25 m high under similar conditions?
6. A train running at a speed of 70 km/hr can cover a certain distance in 45 minutes. How long will it take to cover the same distance if its speed is increased by 20 km/hr?
7. Typing at a speed of 33 words per minute, Manish can type a manuscript in 25 minutes. If the work is to be completed in 15 minutes, what should be his typing speed?
8. 65 women can reap a field in 24 days. If the job is to be completed in 20 days, how many more women have to be employed?
9. 1,200 soldiers in a camp had enough rations for 28 days. After 4 days, some soldiers left and thus the rations lasted for 32 more days. How many soldiers left?
10. Raghu walks to school at a speed of 4 km/hr and reaches school in 30 minutes. During examination time he wanted to reach the school in 20 minutes. What should be his speed while walking?
11. Chintoo can do a task in 24 days while Mintoo can do it in 30 days. In how many days can they complete the task if both of them work together?
12. Anuja, Bhawana and Charu can embroider a saree in 8 days, 12 days and 15 days, respectively. How long will they take to embroider the saree if they work together?
13. Abhay, Benoy and Chinmoy can mow a lawn in 15 hours, 12 hours and 20 hours, respectively. They started mowing the lawn together but Chinmoy leaves after 2 hours. In how many hours will the remaining lawn be mowed by Abhay and Benoy?
14. Pipe A can fill an empty tank in 5 hours while Pipe B can empty a full tank in 6 hours. If both are opened at the same time, how long will it take for the empty tank to fill up completely?
15. 6 men can paint a building in 5 days. If 10 men are employed, find the number of days in which the building can be painted?
16. 3 boys or 5 girls can clean the school campus in 8 hours during a cleanliness drive. In how many hours will 2 boys and 2 girls clean the campus?
17. Taps A and B can fill up an empty tank in 15 hours and 12 hours, respectively. Tap C can empty the full tank in 8 hours. If all three taps are turned on simultaneously, in how many hours will the tank fill up completely?
18. A train travelling at a speed of 36 km/hr crosses an electric pole in 30 seconds. Find the length of the train.
19. A train 300 m long is travelling at a speed of 40 km/hr. How long will it take to pass through a tunnel 200 m long?
20. A train 400 m long is travelling at a speed of 72 km/hr. How long will it take to cross a pole?

Test Yourself

Unit III

1. Aruna bought 10 eggs for ₹25 and sold them at ₹25 per dozen. Find her gain or loss per cent.

2. By selling a mobile phone for ₹3,600, Gagan would incur a loss of 10%. For how much should he sell the mobile phone to avoid any loss?

3. A shopkeeper bought a gas stove for ₹2,500. He wants to make a profit of 25% on it after giving a discount of 5% on the marked price. What should the marked price be?

4. The marked price of a shirt is ₹2,200. After allowing a discount of 10%, the shopkeeper still makes a profit of 20%. Find the cost price of the shirt.

5. There is a discount of 15% on a refrigerator marked at ₹15,000. If the rate of VAT is 10%, how much does the customer have to pay for the refrigerator?

6. During a sale, a discount of 20% is offered on a sweater. The rate of VAT is 15%. Pranav paid ₹1,320 for the sweater. What was the marked price of the sweater?

7. Deepak borrowed ₹4,000 from his friend at 10% per annum compound interest for a certain period of time. He paid his friend ₹5,324. For how many years did he borrow the money?

8. Find the rate of interest per annum that will yield ₹1,400 as simple interest on ₹7,000 in 2 years. Find how much ₹7,700 will amount to in 2 years at the same rate of interest, compounded annually.

9. Ishaan bought a car for ₹3,00,000. Its value depreciates at the rate of 10% per annum. Find its value after 3 years.

10. Nabha borrowed ₹1,60,000 as an education loan from a bank for 2 years at 10% per annum, compounded biannually. What amount will she have to pay back after 2 years? What is the interest paid by her?

11. If 15 books cost ₹2025, find the cost of 35 books.

12. If 20 men can dig a trench 15 m deep in a day, how many men will be required to dig a 48 m deep trench?

13. If 45 chickens can consume a certain quantity of bird food in 13 days, how many chickens can consume the same food in 9 days?

14. A train moving at a speed of 120 km/hr can cover a certain distance in 40 minutes. If the speed is increased to 160 km/hr, how long will it take to cover the same distance?

15. Manpreet can complete a task in 12 days and Taranjit can do the same work in 8 days. They work together for 2 days and then Taranjit has to leave. How long will Manpreet take to complete the remaining task?

16. A and B can complete a task in 8 days; B and C can do it in 12 days while C and A can complete it in 15 days. In how many days will A, B, and C finish it if they all work together? In how many days will each of them finish it if they work individually?

17. Express the following as directed:
    a. 25 m/sec in km/hr.
    b. 54 km/hr in m/sec.
    c. 20 m/min in km/hr.

18. A train 500 m long crosses a lamp post in 18 seconds. What is the speed of the train in km/hr?

19. Three taps, A, B and C, can fill a tank in 10 hours, 12 hours and 15 hours, respectively. An outlet pipe can empty the tank in 8 hours. The three taps and the outlet pipe were opened and allowed to run for 5 hours after which the outlet pipe was closed. How long will it take the remaining tank to fill up completely?

20. A train travelling at a speed of 72 km/hr crosses a bridge in 30 seconds. If the length of the train is 250 m, find the length of the bridge.

Answer for Brainteaser from page 182

Because he won't give an inch.

CHAPTER 11

Understanding Shapes

We have studied about different shapes and forms in the previous class. A simple closed curve that consists of only line segments is called a polygon. We have studied the three-sided polygon—triangle. We shall now study four-sided polygons—their different types and properties—in detail. Let us recall the different types of polygons that we are familiar with.

Table 11.1 Polygons

No. of Sides	Name
3	Triangle
4	Quadrilateral
5	Pentagon
6	Hexagon
7	Septagon
8	Octagon
9	Nonagon
10	Decagon

A polygon in which all sides are equal is called a regular polygon.

In an equivalent triangle all three sides are equal, hence it is a regular polygon.

Quadrilaterals

A four-sided polygon is called a *quadrilateral*. It is derived from the word 'quad' meaning four and 'lateral' meaning a line segment.

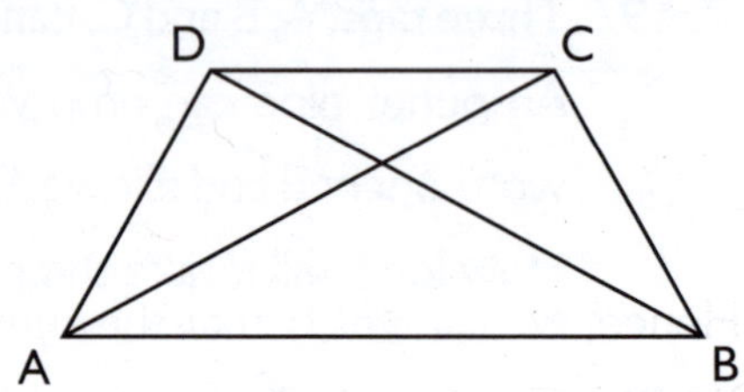

Figure ABCD is a four-sided polygon or a quadrilateral. The four sides are figure AB, BC, CD and DA. The four vertices are A, B, C and D. The four angles are ∠ABC, ∠BCD, ∠CDA and ∠DAB. The two diagonals are AC and BD. The quadrilateral can be denoted in four different cyclic ways ABCD, BCDA, CDAB or DABC.

We start from any one vertex and proceed in a cyclic order.
A diagonal of a quadrilateral divides it into two triangles.

Angle Sum Property of a Quadrilateral

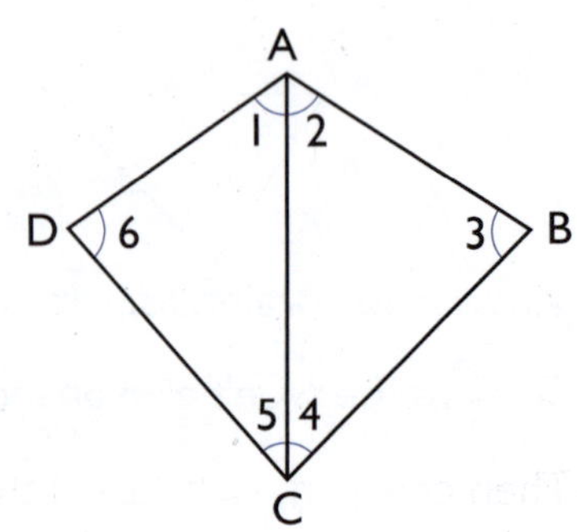

Let ABCD be a quadrilateral. We shall prove that the sum of the angles of a quadrilateral is 360°.

A diagonal of the quadrilateral divides it into two triangles. We know that the sum of the angles of a triangle is 180°.

In the given quadrilateral ABCD, AC is the diagonal. The two triangles formed are ADC and ABC. The angles of $\triangle ADC$ are numbered as $\angle 1$, $\angle 6$, $\angle 5$ and of $\triangle ABC$ are numbered as $\angle 2$, $\angle 3$, $\angle 4$.

$\angle 2 + \angle 3 + \angle 4 = 180°$ (sum of the angles of $\triangle ABC$)

$\angle 1 + \angle 6 + \angle 5 = 180°$ (sum of the angles of $\triangle ADC$)

Adding the two, we get:

$$\angle 2 + \angle 3 + \angle 4 + \angle 1 + \angle 6 + \angle 5 = 180° + 180°$$

$$\text{or } \angle 1 + \angle 2 + \angle 3 + \angle 4 + \angle 5 + \angle 6 = 360°$$

$$\text{Thus, } \angle DAB + \angle ABC + \angle BCD + \angle CDA = 360°$$

$\therefore$ The sum of the angles of a quadrilateral is 360°.

We can verify that the sum of the angles of a quadrilateral is 360° by drawing a few quadrilaterals of different shapes and sizes. Cut out the quadrilaterals along the horizontal and vertical lines drawn as shown in the figures. Put the cut out figures together. The angle at the centre will be 360°.

a.

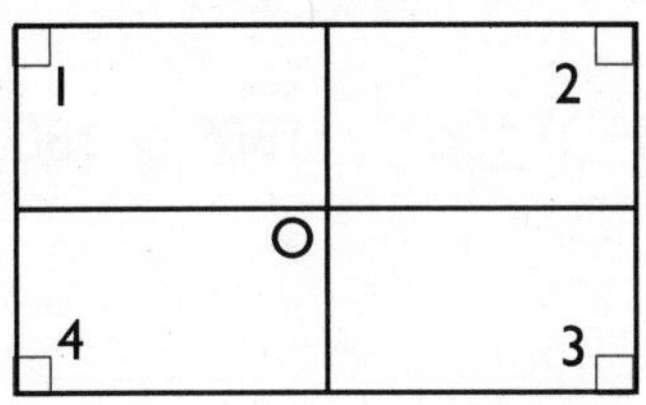

b.

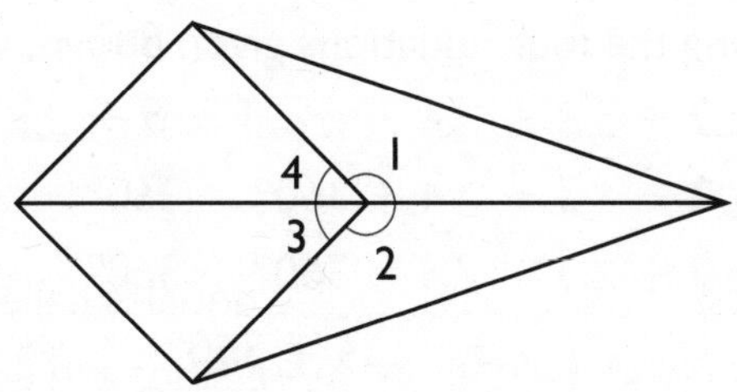

c.

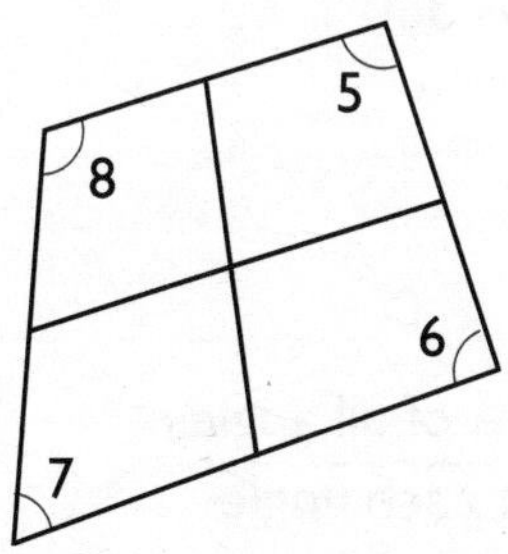

d.

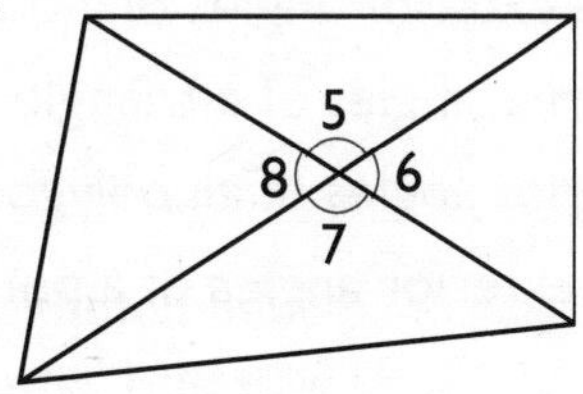

Hence, we can verify that the sum of the angles of a quadrilateral is 360°.

You can also construct a few quadrilaterals at random and measure the angles with a protractor.

e.

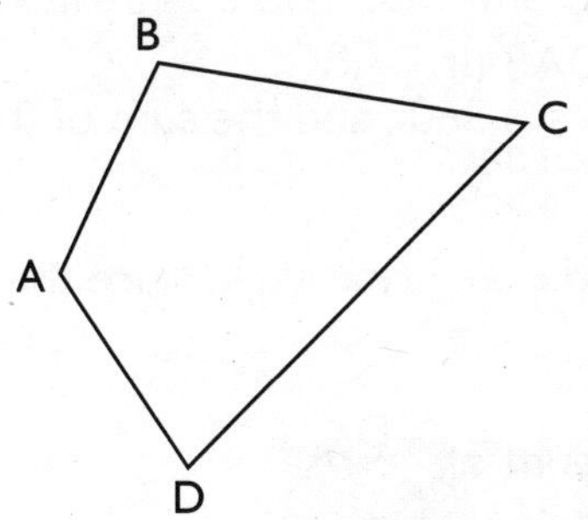

f.

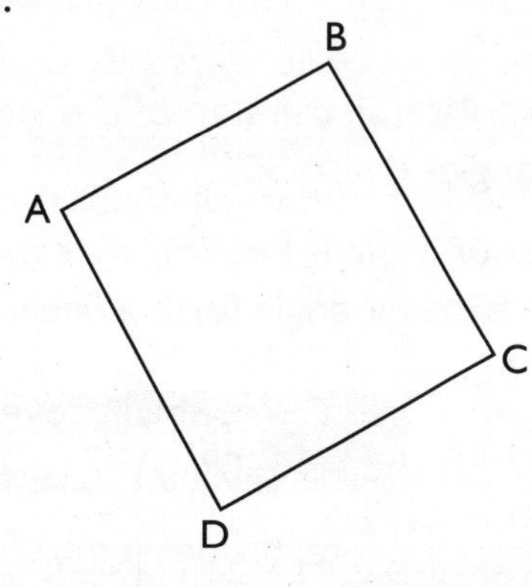

Then check in each case if the sum of $\angle A$, $\angle B$, $\angle C$ and $\angle D$ is equal to 360°.

It is observed that the sum of the angles of a quadrilateral is always 360°.

Sum of the Exterior Angles of a Quadrilateral

Let us draw a quadrilateral PQRS and mark its interior and exterior angles as shown in the figure given here.

Let the interior angles be p, q, r and s at the vertices P, Q, R and S, respectively. Also, let 1, 2, 3 and 4 be the exterior angles at the vertices P, Q, R and S, respectively.

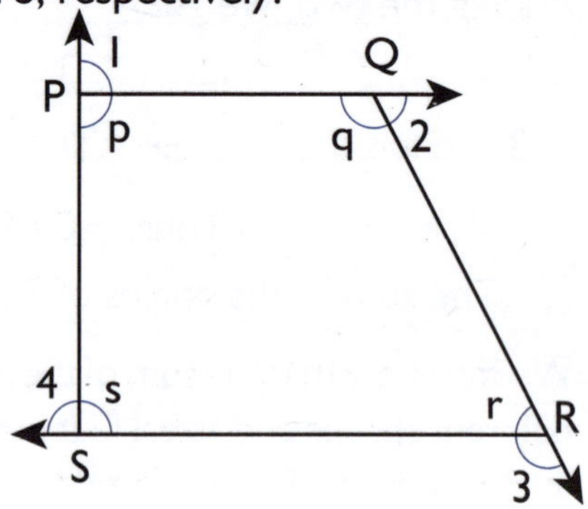

Now, we know that,

$\angle p + \angle q + \angle r + \angle s = 360°$ since the sum of the interior angles of a quadrilateral is 360°.

Now, $\angle 1 + \angle p = 180°$ (linear pair)

$\angle 2 + \angle q = 180°$ (linear pair)

$\angle 3 + \angle r = 180°$ (linear pair)

$\angle 4 + \angle s = 180°$ (linear pair)

On adding the four equations given above, we get,

$\angle 1 + \angle 2 + \angle 3 + \angle 4 + \angle p + \angle q + \angle r + \angle s = 180° + 180° + 180° + 180°$

$\angle 1 + \angle 2 + \angle 3 + \angle 4 + 360° = 360° + 360°$

$\angle 1 + \angle 2 + \angle 3 + \angle 4 = 360° + 360° - 360°$

$\therefore \quad \angle 1 + \angle 2 + \angle 3 + \angle 4 = 360°$

Thus, the sum of the exterior angles of a quadrilateral is always 360°.

The sum of the exterior angles of a triangle is also 360°.

The sum of the exterior angles of all polygons is 360°.

Total measure of all exterior angles of a polygon is 360°.

$$\text{Number of exterior angles} = \frac{\text{Total measure of all angles}}{\text{Measure of each angle}}$$

The number of exterior angles will give the number of sides.

Alert!

1. For a quadrilateral, the sum of the interior angles is 360° and the sum of the exterior angles is also 360°.
2. If the interior angle is known, we can calculate the exterior angle since the interior angle and exterior angle form a linear pair.

Practice Exercise 11.1

1. Draw a quadrilateral. Label it in cyclic order. Draw the diagonals. Name the vertices, the sides, the angles and the diagonals.

2. Find the value of 'x' in the following quadrilaterals.

a.

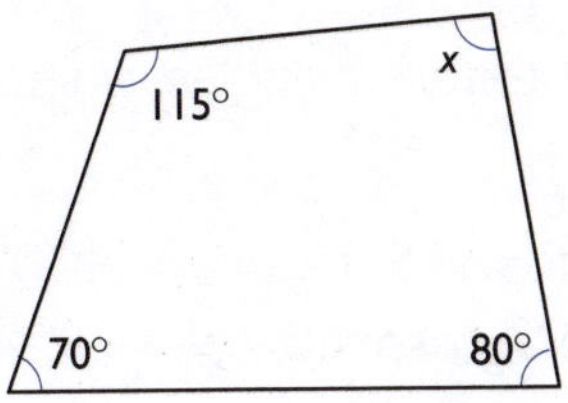

b.

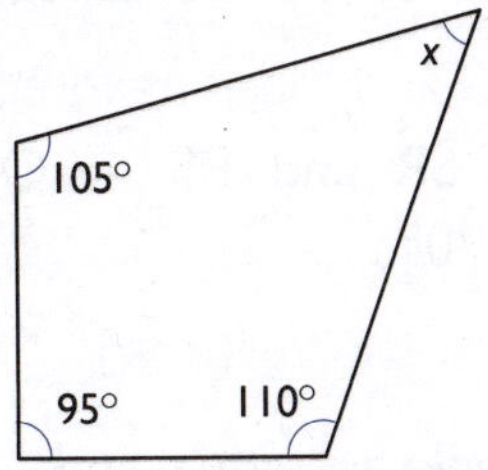

c.

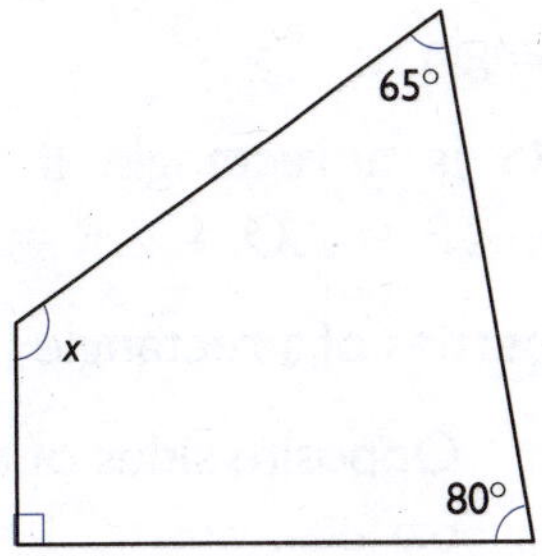

3. Find the value of 'x' in the following polygons.

a.

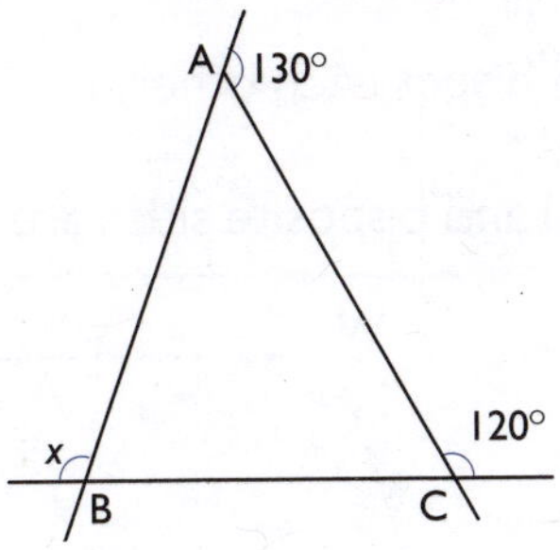

b.

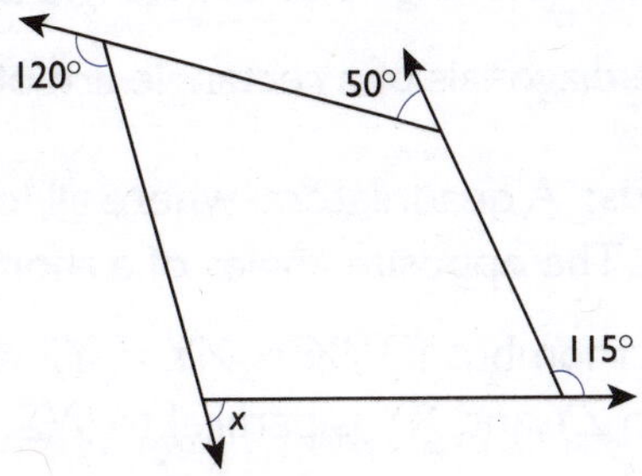

c.

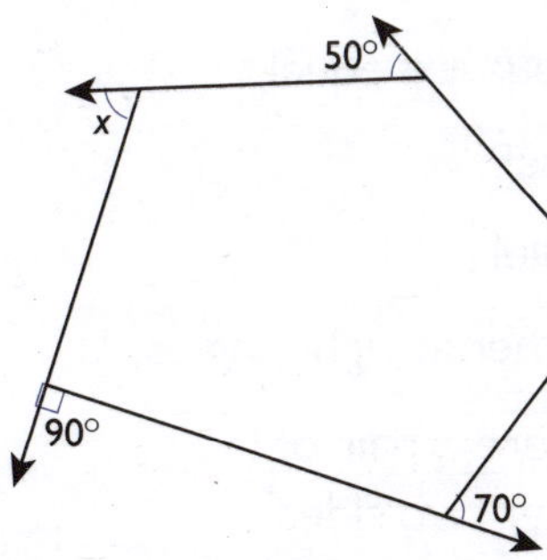

4. Find the number of the sides of a regular polygon where each exterior angle has a measure of 30°.

5. How many sides does a regular polygon have if each of its interior angles is 144°?

Types of Quadrilaterals

1. Square: A quadrilateral with four equal sides and all of whose angles measure 90° is called a square.

ABCD is a square if AB = BC = CD = DA and $\angle A = \angle B = \angle C = \angle D = 90°$.

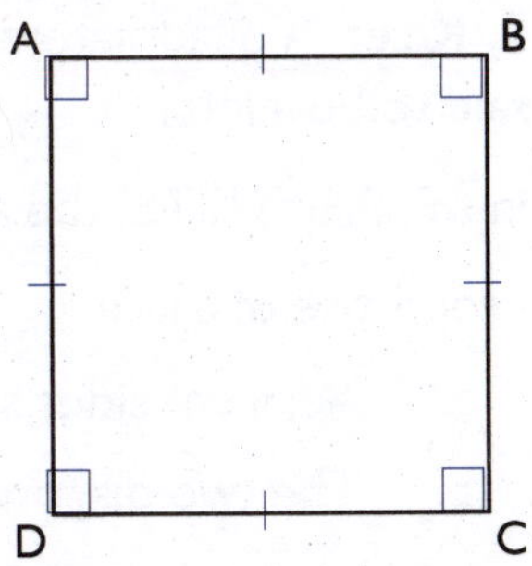

Properties of a square

a. All the four sides of a square are equal.

b. All the four angles of a square are equal and each is 90°.

c. The diagonals of a square are equal and bisect each other at right angles.

d. The angles that a diagonal makes with a side of the square is 45°.

2. Rectangle: A quadrilateral in which opposite sides are equal and each angle measures 90° is called a rectangle.

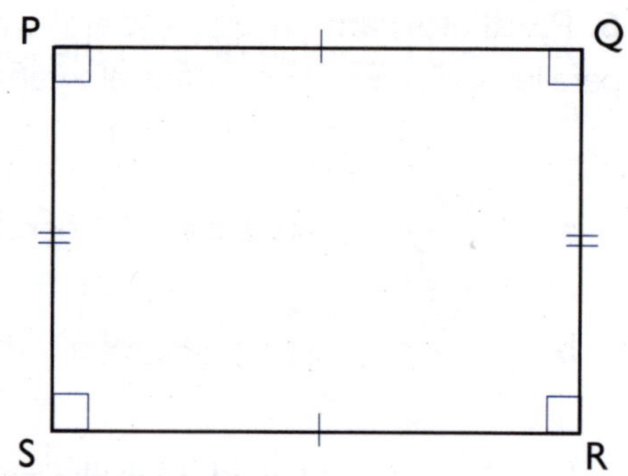

PQRS is a rectangle if PQ = SR and PS = QR. Also, $\angle P = \angle Q = \angle R = \angle S = 90°$.

Properties of a rectangle

a. Opposite sides of a rectangle are equal and parallel.

b. All the four angles of a rectangle are equal and each is 90°.

c. The diagonals of a rectangle are of equal length and bisect each other.

3. Rhombus: A quadrilateral where all four sides are equal and opposite sides are parallel is a rhombus. The opposite angles of a rhombus are equal.

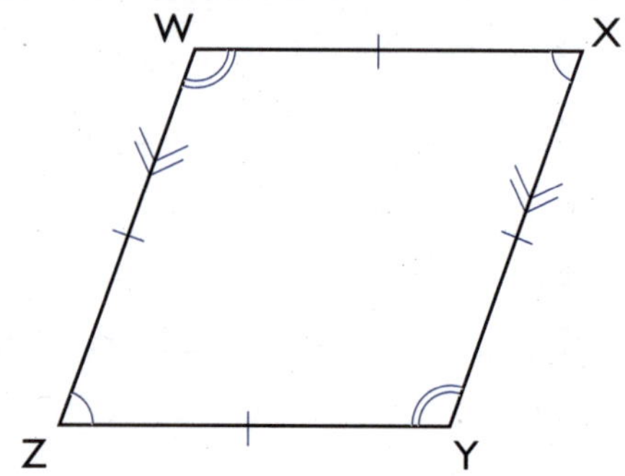

WXYZ is a rhombus if WX = XY = YZ = ZW and WX is parallel to ZY and XY is parallel to WZ.

Properties of a rhombus

a. All the four sides of a rhombus are equal.

b. The opposite angles are equal.

c. The opposite sides are parallel.

d. The diagonals bisect each other at right angles.

4. Trapezium: A quadrilateral where a pair of opposite sides is parallel but the other two sides are non-parallel is called a trapezium.

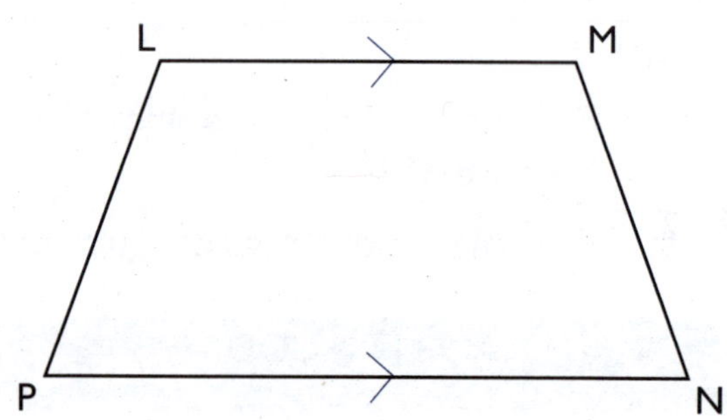

If the non-parallel sides are equal then it is called an isosceles trapezium. LMNP is a trapezium if LM is parallel to PN.

If LP is equal to MN, then it is an isosceles trapezium.

Properties of a trapezium

a. One pair of opposite sides is parallel.

b. If the non-parallel sides are equal, it is an isosceles trapezium.

5. Kite: A quadrilateral where two pairs of adjacent sides are equal is said to be a kite.

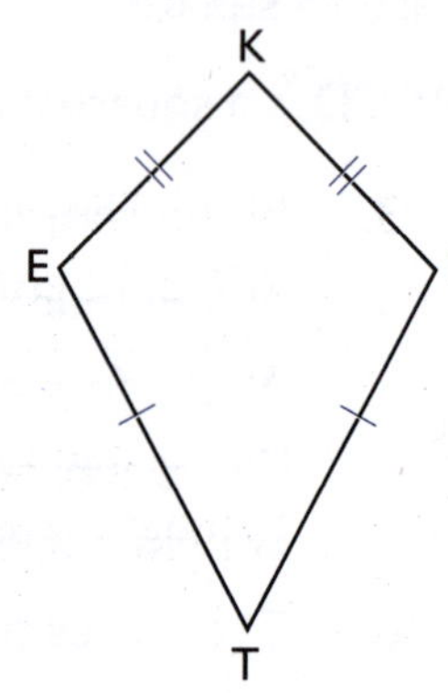

In the figure KITE, the adjacent sides, KE = KI and TE = TI.

Properties of a kite

a. Adjacent sides are equal.

b. The two diagonals are perpendicular to each other.

6. Parallelogram: A quadrilateral where both pairs of opposite sides are parallel is said to be a parallelogram. EFGH is a parallelogram with EF || to HG and EH || to FG.

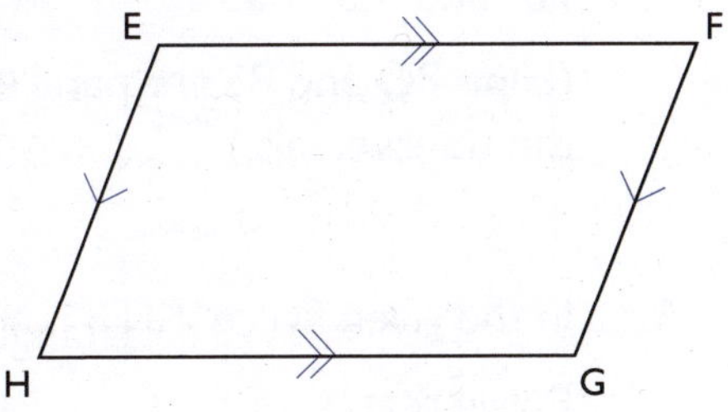

Properties of a parallelogram

a. The opposite sides of a parallelogram are equal.

b. The opposite angles of a parallelogram are equal.

c. The diagonals of a parallelogram bisect each other.

Alert!

1. In a trapezium, the parallel sides need not be of equal length.
2. Every parallelogram is a trapezium, but every trapezium is not a parallelogram.
3. The diagonals of a parallelogram need not be of equal length.
4. Every rhomus is a parallelogram, but every parallelogram is not a rhomus.
5. The diagonals of a rhombus need not be of equal length.
6. Every rectangle is a parallelogram, but every parallelogram is not a rectangle.
7. A parallelogram can symbolically be written as ||ogram.

Practice Exercise 11.2

1. If PQRS is a square, and W, X, Y and Z are the mid points of PQ, QR, RS and SP, respectively, show that WXYZ is a square.

   (Hint: Join W, X, Y and Z and prove that the triangles are congruent by SAS.)

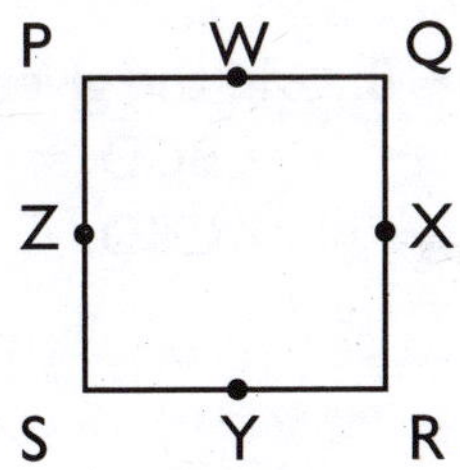

2. If ABCD is a rectangle and AC and BD are the diagonals, show that:

   a. △AOB ≅ △COD

   b. △BOC ≅ △AOD

   (Hint: For a, use the SSS test; for b, use the SAS test.)

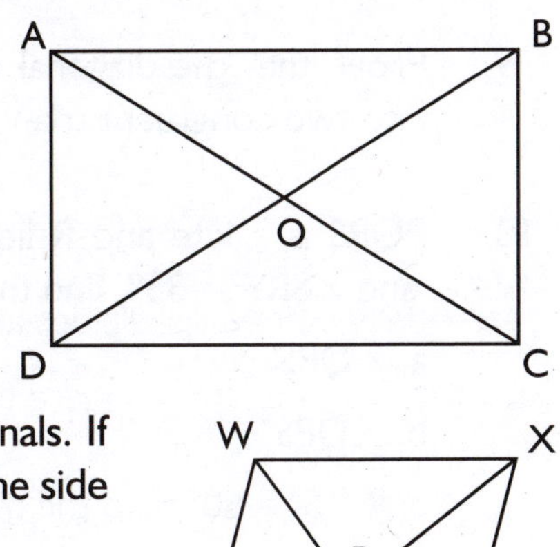

3. In the rhombus WXYZ, WY and XZ are the diagonals. If WY is 12 cm and XZ = 16 cm, find the length of the side of the rhombus.

   (Hint: Use the diagonal property of the rhombus and the Pythagoras theorem.)

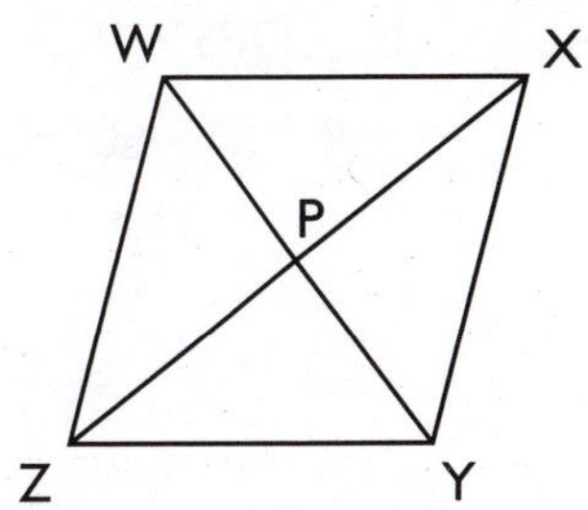

4. If PQRS is a trapezium with PQ || RS, find the measures of the angles P and Q given that $\angle R = 70°$ and $\angle S = 65°$.

(Hint: PQ and RS are parallel and PS and QR are the transversals.)

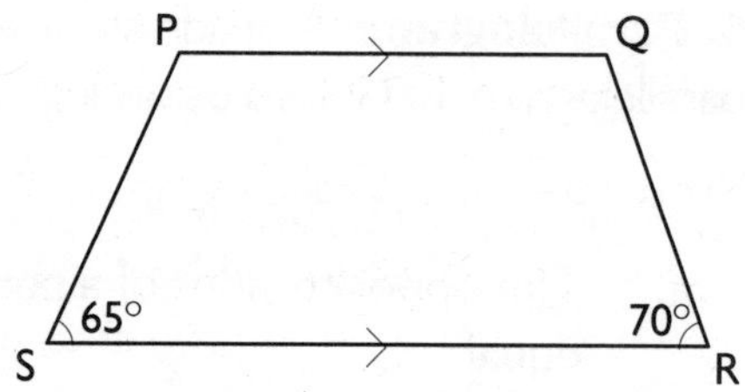

5. In the given figure, KITE is a kite. KT and IE are the diagonals. Prove that

a. $\triangle KES \cong \triangle KIS$

b. $\triangle SET \cong \triangle SIT$

(Hint: The diagonal KT bisects the angles K and T.)

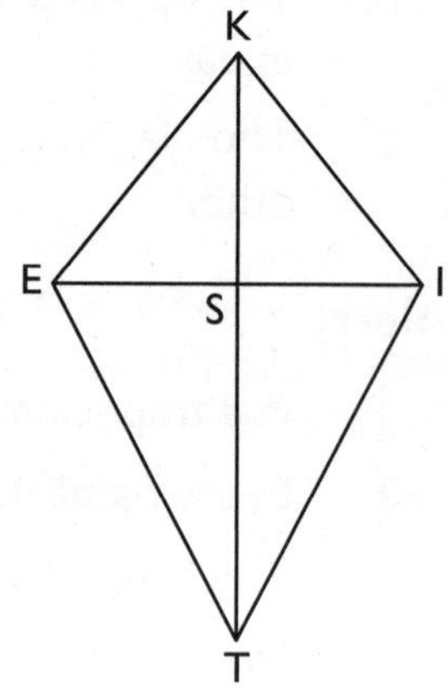

6. ABCD is a parallelogram in which $\angle BAC = 40°$, $\angle DAC = 30°$. Find

a. $\angle ABC$

b. $\angle BCD$.

7. PQRS is a parallelogram and X and Y are the mid points of PQ and RS, respectively. Show that the quadrilateral PXRY is a parallelogram.

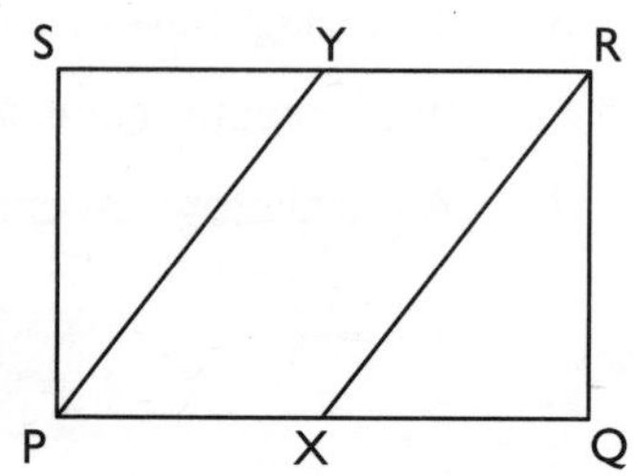

8. In the given figure, ABCD is a parallelogram in which $\angle BCD = 70°$ and $\angle ADB = 60°$. Find $\angle ABD$ and $\angle CBD$.

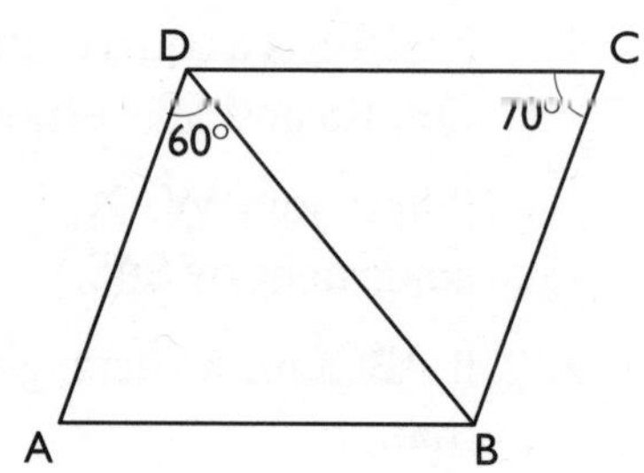

9. Prove that the diagonal of a parallelogram divides it into two congruent triangles.

10. PQRS is a kite and R lies on the line XY. If $\angle QRX = 25°$ and $\angle SRY = 35°$, find the measures of the following

a. $\angle QRS$

b. $\angle QPS$.

c. If $\angle S = 60°$, find the measure of $\angle Q$.

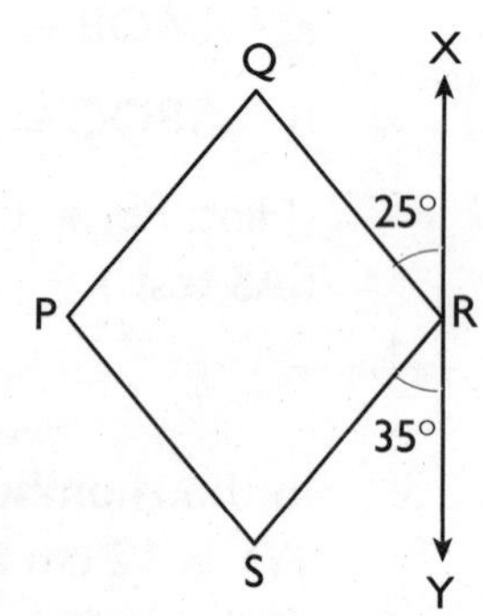

Highlights

- The sum of the interior angles of a quadrilateral is equal to 360°.
- The sum of the exterior angles of a quadrilateral is equal to 360°.
- The sum of the exterior angles of a polygon is equal to 360°.
- Number of exterior angles $= \dfrac{\text{Total measure of all angles}}{\text{Measure of each angle}}$
- Number of exterior angles is equivalent to the number of sides of a regular polygon.
- A quadrilateral that has:
  - exactly *one* pair of opposite sides parallel is called a trapezium.
  - *both* pairs of opposite sides parallel is called a parallelogram.
  - two pairs of adjacent sides equal, but opposite sides unequal is called a kite.
- A parallelogram that has:
  - all sides equal is called a rhombus.
  - all sides equal and each angle is a right angle is called a square.
  - opposite sides equal and each angle is a right angle is called a rectangle.
- A quadrilateral is a parallelogram if its:
  - opposite sides are equal.
  - opposite angles are equal.
  - diagonals bisect each other.
  - one pair of opposite sides are parallel and equal.
- The diagonals of:
  - a rhombus bisect each other at right angles.
  - a rectangle are equal.
  - a square are equal and bisect each other at right angles.
  - a parallelogram bisect each other.

Higher Order Thinking Skills

HOTS

1. If an angle of a parallelogram is two-thirds its adjacent angle, what will be the smallest angle of the parallelogram?

2. In a square ABCD, if AB = (2x + 3) cm and BC = (3x − 5) cm, find the value of x.

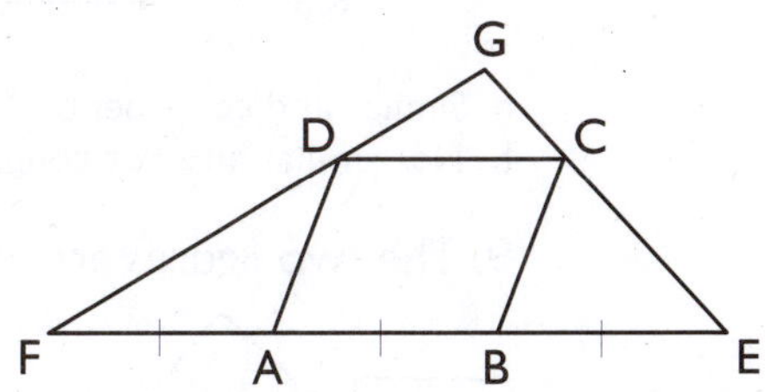

3. ABCD is a rhombus and AB is produced to E and F such that AF = AB = BE. EC and FD are produced to intersect each other at G. Show that ∠EGF = 90°.

Maths Lab Activity

Understanding shapes

Aim: To recognise similar and congruent figures.

Material required: chart paper and sketch pens

Method: Circle the correct options.

Trace each of the following pairs of figures on a chart paper and superimpose them to answer the following questions.

1. The two figures are

a. Not similar but congruent.
b. Not congruent but similar.

2. The two figures are

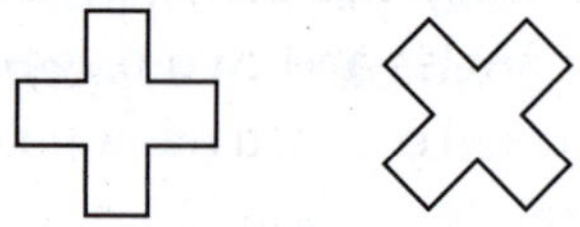

a. Similar.
b. Congruent.

3. The two figures are

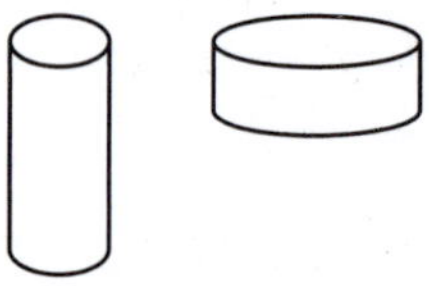

a. Not similar but congruent.
b. Not congruent but similar.

4. The two figures are

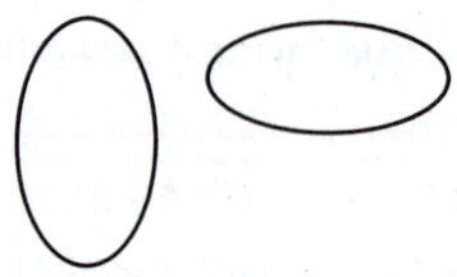

a. Similar.
a. Congruent.

5. The two figures are

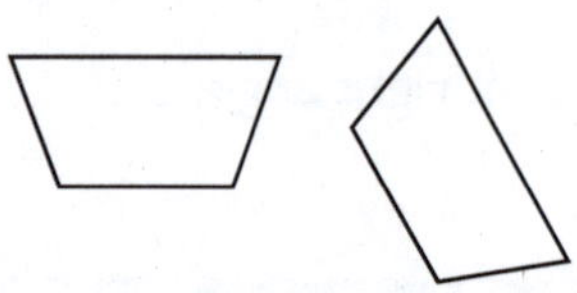

a. Similar and congruent.
b. Not similar and not congruent.

6. The two figures are

a. Not similar but congruent.
b. Not congruent but similar.

7. The two figures are

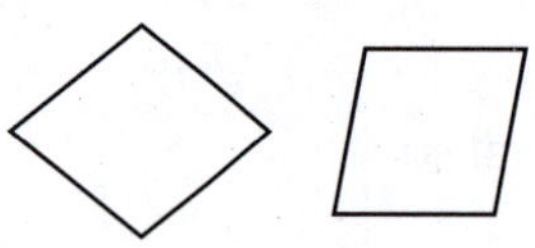

a. Similar and congruent.
b. Not similar and not congruent.

8. The two figures are

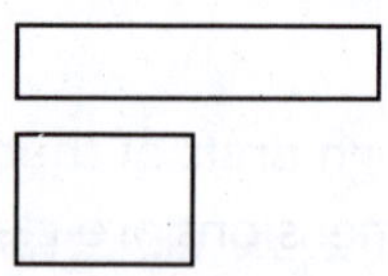

a. Not similar.
a. Not congruent.

9. The two figures are

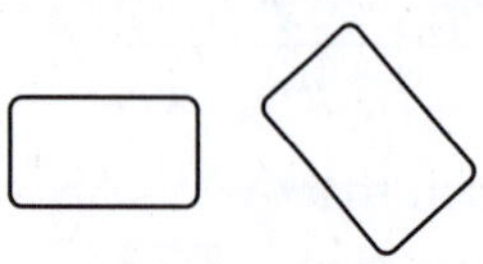

a. Not similar.
b. Not congruent.

10. The two figures are

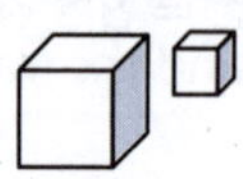

a. Congruent.
b. Similar.

Construction of Quadrilaterals

CHAPTER 12

We have learnt about the construction of triangles. There are certain elements that need to be known to construct a triangle.

The four basic conditions for the construction of a triangle are:

1. When the three sides of a triangle are given.
2. When two sides and the included angle are given.
3. When two angles and the included side are given.
4. When the right angle, hypotenuse and one side is given.

Now, we shall study the construction of a quadrilateral. We know that a quadrilateral has four sides, four angles and two diagonals. Hence, ten elements of a quadrilateral determine its shape and size. To construct a unique quadrilateral, we need to know any five elements of a quadrilateral.

Certain basic conditions are required for the construction of a unique quadrilateral. If four angles and one side of a quadrilateral are given, it is insufficient to construct a quadrilateral.

Let us learn which are the five elements or measurements that are required for the construction of a unique quadrilateral.

These basic and sufficient conditions that are required to construct a unique quadrilateral are:

1. Four sides and a diagonal.
2. Three sides and two diagonals.
3. Four sides and an angle.
4. Three sides and two included angles.
5. Two adjacent sides and three angles.

We shall study each case with examples.

Four Sides and a Diagonal are Known

Construct a quadrilateral ABCD with sides AB = 4.8 cm, BC = 4.5 cm, CD = 3.4 cm, AD = 4.1 cm and diagonal AC = 5.5 cm.

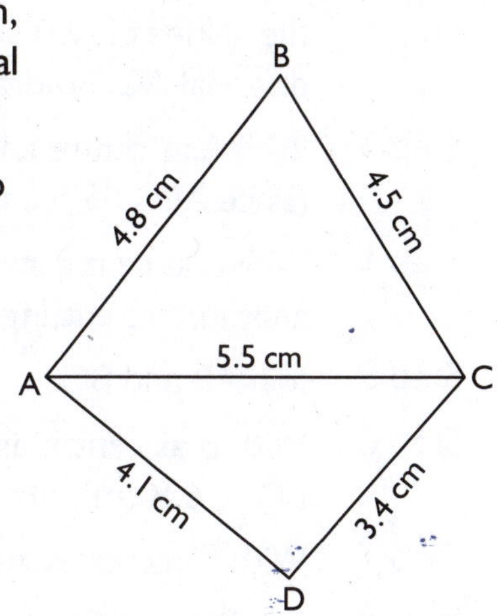

Step 1 Draw a rough draft of the required quadrilateral so that the dimensions are clear.

Step 2 Identify the diagonal. We see that the diagonal divides the quadrilateral into two triangles.

Step 3 Draw a line AC = 5.5 cm. This is the longest side given.

Step 4 With A as centre and radius 4.8 cm (AB = 4.8 cm), draw an arc using a compass.

Step 5 With C as centre and radius 4.5 cm (BC = 4.5 cm), cut the previous arc. Denote the point of intersection as B.

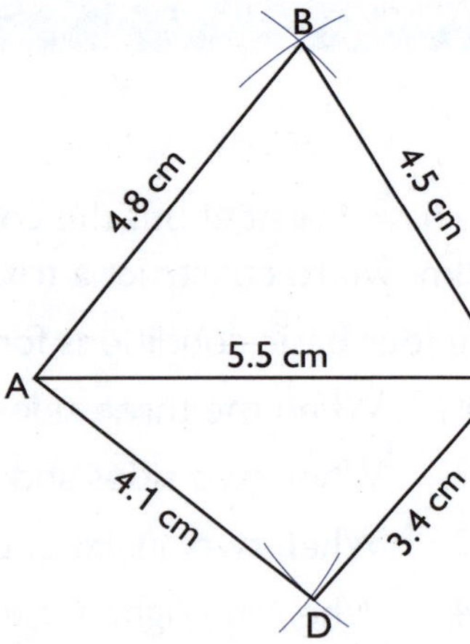

Step 6 Join AB and BC.

Step 7 With A as centre and radius 4.1 cm (AD = 4.1 cm), draw an arc on the other side of the line AC.

Step 8 With C as centre and radius 4.1 cm (as CD = 4.1 cm), cut the previous arc. Denote the point of intersection as C.

Step 9 Join AD and CD.

Thus, ABCD is the required quadrilateral.

Practice Exercise 12.1

1. Construct a quadrilateral PQRS where PQ = 4.2 cm, QR = 6 cm, RS = 5.2 cm, SP = 5 cm and diagonal PR = 8 cm.
2. Construct a quadrilateral ABCD where AB = 5.3 cm, BC = 3.8 cm, CD = DA = 4.5 cm and diagonal BD = 6.0 cm.
3. Construct a quadrilateral WXYZ where WX = 6.5 cm, XY = 5.8 cm, YZ = 6.2 cm, WZ = 7 cm and diagonal WY = 7.8 cm.

Three Sides and Two Diagonals are Known

Construct a quadrilateral ABCD where AB = 5.5 cm, BC = 6.4 cm, CD = 7 cm, AC = 8.6 cm and diagonal BD = 6.8 cm.

Step 1 Draw a rough sketch of the required quadrilateral.

Step 2 Since three sides and two diagonals are given, we first construct the triangle using the values of two sides AB, BC and the diagonal AC. So draw AC = 8.6 cm.

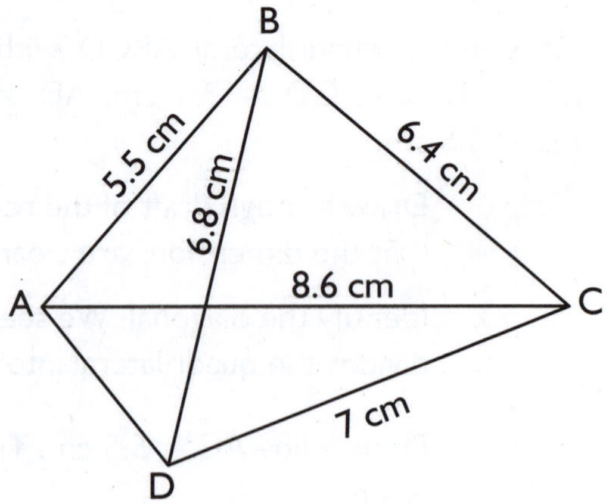

Step 3 With A as centre and radius 5.5 cm (since AC = 5.5 cm), draw an arc.

Step 4 With C as centre and radius 6.4 cm,draw another arc cutting the first of arc at B.

Step 5 Join AB and BC.

Step 6 With B as centre and radius 6.8 cm (as BD = 6.8 cm), draw an arc below AC.

Step 7 With C as centre and radius 7 cm, cut the arc. Name it D.

Step 8 Join BD and CD.

Thus, ABCD is the required quadrilateral.

Practice Exercise 12.2

1. Construct a quadrilateral ABCD where AB = 7.1 cm, BC = 6.4 cm, CD = 5.8 cm, AC = 8.2 cm and diagonal BD = 8 cm.
2. Construct a quadrilateral PQRS where PQ = 5.2 cm, QR = 6 cm, RS = 5.4 cm and PR = QS = 7.2 cm.
3. Construct a quadrilateral LMNP where LM = 5.5 cm, MN = 3.0 cm, NP = 4 cm, LN = 6.5 cm and diagonal MP = 5.2 cm.

Four Sides and an Angle are Known

Construct a quadrilateral ABCD where AB = 6 cm, BC = 7 cm, CD= 4.5 cm, D = 6.5 cm and ∠A = 120°.

Step 1 Draw a rough sketch of the required quadrilateral.

Step 2 Since angle A is given, we must draw line AB = 6 cm first.

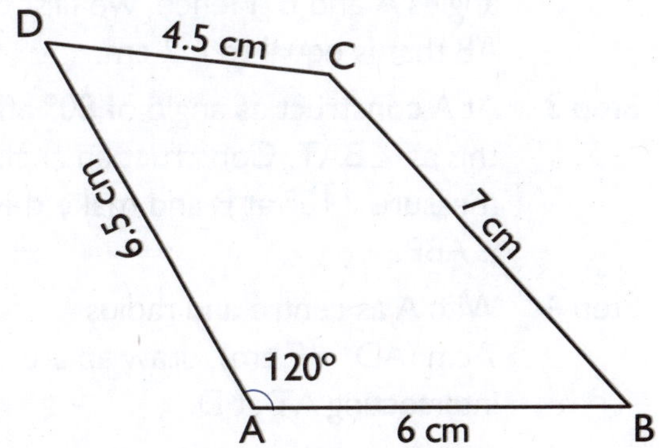

Step 3 At A, construct angle BAT of measure 120°.

Step 4 With A as centre and radius 6.5 cm (AD = 6.5 cm), draw an arc to intersect BT at D.

Step 5 With D as centre and radius 4.5 cm (CD = 4.5 cm), draw an arc perpendicular to A.

Step 6 With B as centre and radius 5 cm (BC = 7 cm), draw an arc to intersect the arc drawn in Step 5 at C.

Step 7 Join BC and DC.

Thus, ABCD is the required quadrilateral.

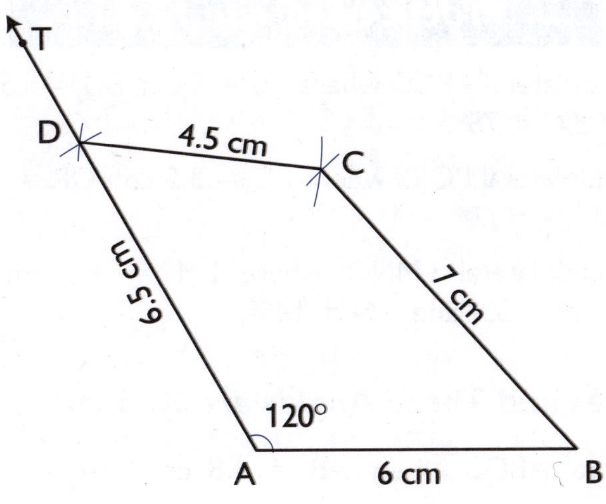

Practice Exercise 12.3

1. Construct a quadrilateral ABCD where AB = 5.5 cm, BC = 6.5 cm, CD = 6.2 cm, AD = 7 cm and $\angle$A = 80°.
2. Construct a quadrilateral WXYZ where WX = 3.5 cm, XY = 3.8 cm, YZ = 4.3 cm, WZ = 5.9 cm and $\angle$X = 90°.
3. Construct a quadrilateral PQRS where PQ = QR = 3.5 cm, PS = RS = 5.5 cm and $\angle$PQR = 110°.

Three Sides and Two Included Angles are Known

Construct a quadrilateral ABCD where AB = 6.2 cm, BC = 5.6 cm, AD = 7 cm, $\angle$A = 80° and $\angle$B = 115°.

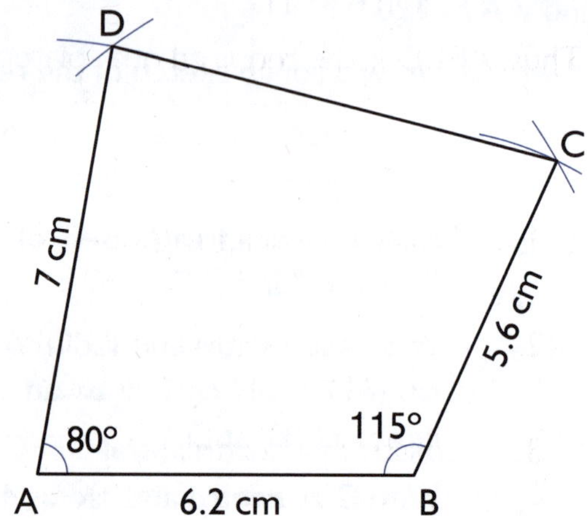

Step 1 Draw a rough sketch of the required quadrilateral.

Step 2 Here, we are given side AB and the angles A and B. Hence, we first draw AB that is equal to 6.2 cm.

Step 3 At A construct as angle of 80° and mark this as $\angle$BAT. Construct an angle of measure 115° at B and make this is $\angle$ABP.

Step 4 With A as centre and radius 7 cm (AD = 7 cm), draw an arc intersecting AT at D.

Step 5 With B as centre and radius 5.6 cm (BC = 5.6 cm), draw an arc intersecting BP at C.

Step 6 Join CD.

Thus, ABCD is the required quadrilateral.

Practice Exercise 12.4

1. Construct a quadrilateral ABCD where AB = 4 cm, BC = 5.5 cm, CD = 4.5 cm, $\angle$B = 120° and $\angle$C = 75°.
2. Construct a quadrilateral PQRS where PQ = 3.5 cm, QR = 5 cm, RS = 4.6 cm, $\angle$Q = 125° and $\angle$R = 60°.
3. Construct a quadrilateral LMNO where LM = 4.2 cm, MN = 3.7 cm, NO = 4.9 cm, $\angle$M = 35° and $\angle$N = 145°.

Two Adjacent Sides and Three Angles are Known

Construct a quadrilateral ABCD where AB = 6.8 cm, $\angle$A = 110°, $\angle$B = 70° and $\angle$C = 100°.

Step 1 Draw a rough sketch of the required quadrilateral.

Step 2 Since side AB is given and the angles A and B are known, we will draw AB first.

Step 3 At A, draw ∠BAD equal to 110°.

Step 4 At B, draw ∠ABX equal to 70°.

Step 5 With B as centre and radius 7 cm (BC = 7 cm), draw an arc intersecting BX at point C.

Step 6 At C, draw ∠BCY equal to 100°, intersecting BP at point D.

Step 7 Join B and D.

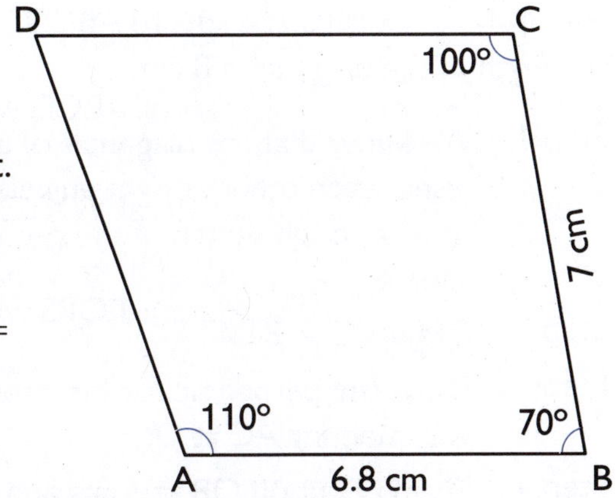

Thus, ABCD is the required quadrilateral.

Practice Exercise 12.5

1. Construct a quadrilateral ABCD where AB = 6.4 cm, BC = 7 cm, ∠A = 90°, ∠B = 110° and ∠C = 60°.
2. Construct a quadrilateral PQRS where PQ = 4.4 cm, QR = 5.5 cm, ∠P = 75°, ∠Q = 110° and ∠R = 100°.
3. Construct a quadrilateral DEFG where DE = 4.5 cm, EF = 3.8 cm, ∠D = 60°, ∠E = 120° and ∠F = 100°.

Construction of Special Quadrilaterals

In special types of quadrilaterals, the construction can be done even when five elements or measurements are not known. We make use of the properties of the specific quadrilateral that is to be constructed.

Example 1: Construct a parallelogram ABCD where AB = 6 cm, BC = 4.5 cm and diagonal AC = 6.8 cm.

Step 1 Draw a rough sketch of the required parallelogram.

Here, only three elements are given—AB, BC and AC. However, we know that the opposite sides of a parallelogram are parallel and equal.

Step 2 Draw AB equal to 6 cm.

Step 3 With B as centre and radius equal to 4.5 cm (BC = 4.5 cm), draw an arc.

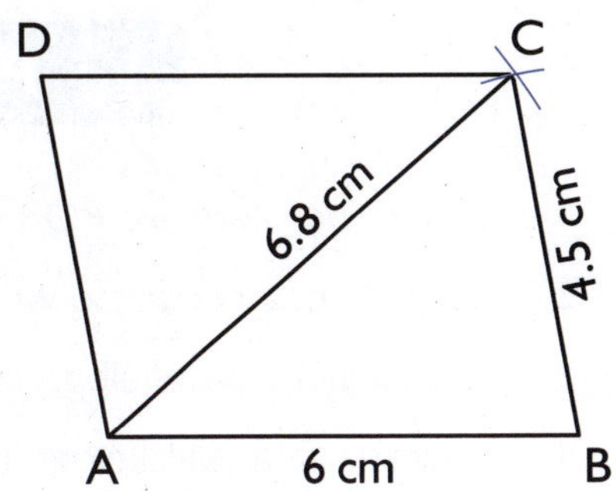

Step 4 With A as centre and radius equal to 6.8 cm (AC = 6.8 cm), draw an arc intersecting the previous arc (constructed Step 2) at point C.

Step 5 Join BC and CD.

Thus, ABCD is the required parallelogram.

Example 2: Construct a square ABCD, where the length of the diagonal is 8 cm.

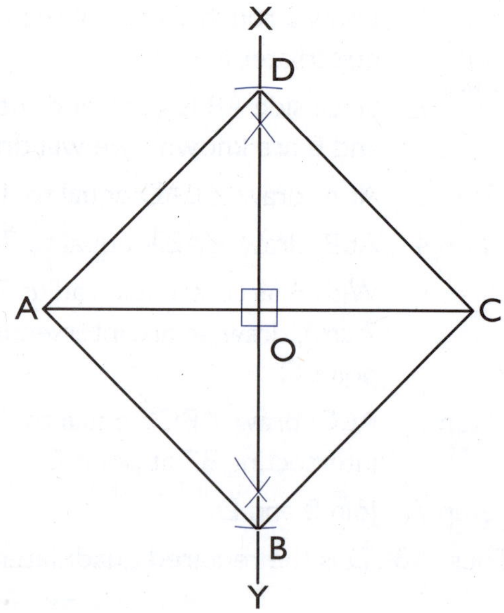

Step 1 We know that the diagonals of a square bisect each other at right angles. We draw a rough sketch of the required square.

Step 2 Draw AC = 8 cm.

Step 3 Draw the perpendicular bisector XY of AC, meeting AC at O.

Step 4 From O cut off OB = 4 cm and OD = 4 cm (half of 8 cm) along OX and OY, respectively.

Step 5 Join AB, BC, CD, DA.

Thus, ABCD is the required square.

Example 3: Construct a rectangle PQRS with side QR = 5 cm and diagonal QS = 6.2 cm.

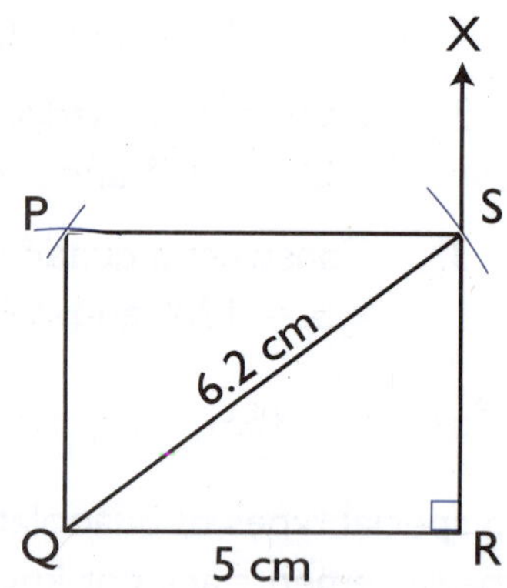

Step 1 Draw a rough sketch of the required rectangle with QR = 5 cm and QS = 6.2 cm.

Step 2 Draw QR equal to 5 cm. At R, construct RX equal to 90°.

Step 3 With centre Q and radius 6.2 cm (QS = 6.2 cm), cut off an intersecting QX at point S.

Step 4 Join QS.

Step 5 With centre S and radius 5 cm (SP = QR = 5 cm), draw an arc.

Step 6 With centre Q and radius equal to RS, cut off the arc drawn in Step 5. Name it P.

Step 7 Join QP and PS.

Thus, PQRS is the required rectangle.

Practice Exercise 12.6

1. Construct a square PQRS with side 6 cm.
2. Construct a rectangle with sides 7 cm and 5.8 cm.
3. Construct a parallelogram with sides 5.2 cm, 4.7 cm and diagonal 7.6 cm.
4. Construct a parallelogram one of whose sides is 5.6 cm and the diagonals are 6.2 cm and 7 cm.
5. Construct a rhombus ABCD with side 4.5 cm and one diagonal 6.4 cm.
6. Construct a trapezium PQRS where PQ || RS, PQ = 7 cm, QR = 5 cm, PS = 6.5 cm and $\angle Q = 60°$.
7. Construct a kite ABCD where AB = AD = 4.5 cm, $\angle A = 60°$ and $\angle B = 130°$.

Highlights

- To construct a unique quadrilateral, we need to know five specific measurements or elements of the quadrilateral.
- We can construct a unique quadrilateral if we are given:
  - four sides and one diagonal.
  - three sides and two diagonals.
  - four sides and one angle.
  - three sides and two included angles.
  - two adjacent sides and three angles.
- A quadrilateral of a specific type can be constructed if less than five elements or measurements are given since we can apply the properties of the quadrilateral to find the relationship between the elements.

Higher Order Thinking Skills

HOTS

1. Construct a parallelogram ABCD in which diagonal AC = 3.8 cm, diagonal BD = 4.6 cm and the angle between AC and BD measures 60°.

2. Construct a rhombus whose side is 7.2 cm and one angle is 60°.

3. Construct a kite whose diagonals measure 8 cm and 12 cm and one of whose sides is 5 cm.

Teacher: "Are you good at maths"?
Student: "Yes and no".
Teacher: "What do you mean by that"?
Student: "Yes, i am 'no' good at maths".

Maths Lab Activity

Comparison of Quadrilaterals

Aim: To study various quadrilaterals and the similarities and differences between them.

Material required: chart paper and sketch pens

Method: Draw the following pairs of figures on the chart paper and make cut outs.

1. Square, rectangle.
2. Square, rhombus.
3. Trapezoid, parallelogram.
4. Rectangle, parallelogram.
5. Rhombus, parallelogram.

Prepare a chart listing the characteristics of each pair.

Answer the following questions.

a. Can a shape fit into more than one category?

b. Which figure is not a parallelogram?

c. What is the difference between a rhombus and parallelogram?

Solid Shapes

As studied in previous classes, plane shapes have two dimensions—length and breadth, while solid shapes have three dimensions—length, breadth and height or depth. Since plane figures have two dimensions, they are known as 2-D figures. Since solids have three dimensions, they are called 3-D figures.

We see many solids around us which are in the shape of cubes, cuboids, spheres, cylinders, cones etc. A few of them have been shown below.

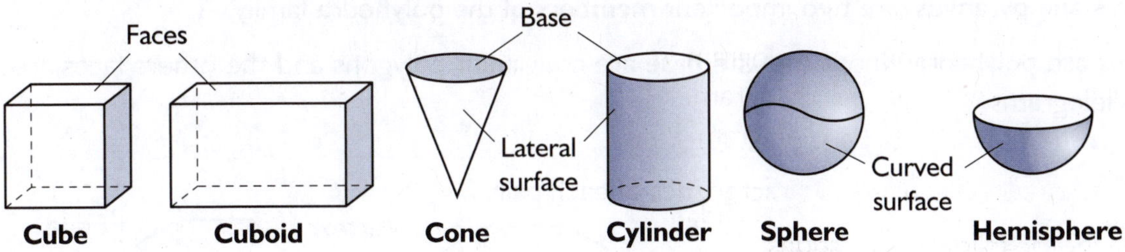

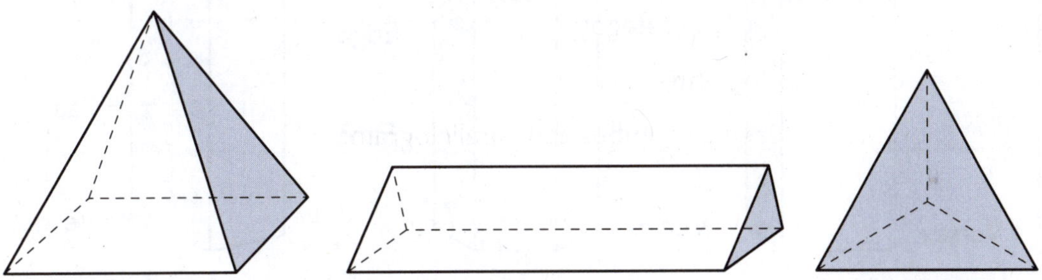

We know that a polygon is a plane figure made of line segments. It is a 2-D figure. Similarly in 3-D shapes, we have a polyhedron, which is made up of plane faces. Hence, a cube, cuboid, pyramid and prism are all polyhedra.

Polygons with equal sides and equal angles are called regular polygons. Similarly, polyhedra with congruent faces are called regular polyhedra. There are five regular polyhedra, tetrahedron, hexahedron, octahedron, dodecahedron and icosahedron each of whose faces, edges and angles are congruent. The regular polyhedra are also called platonic solids.

Platonic solids

Tetrahedron	Hexahedron	Octahedron	Dodecahedron	Icosahedron
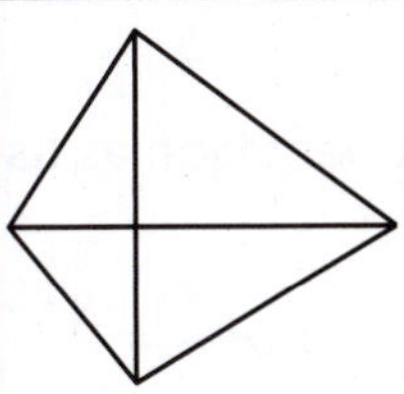	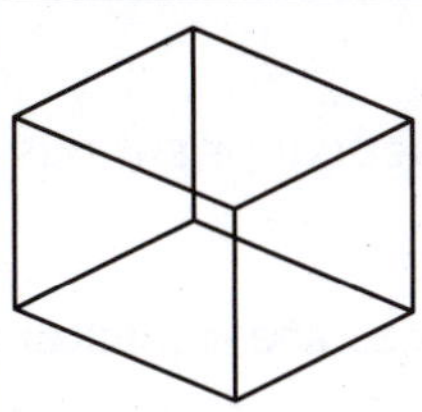	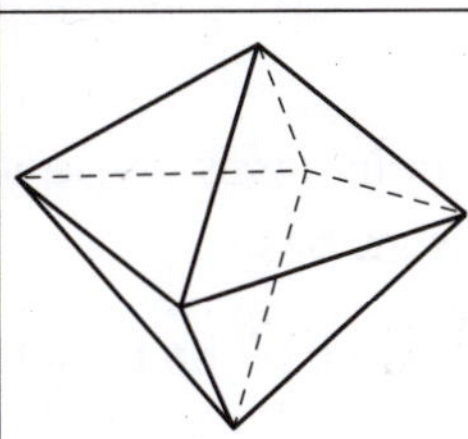	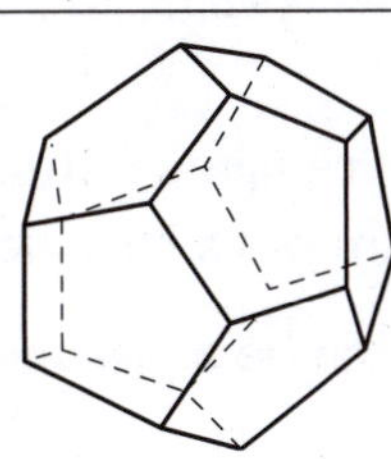	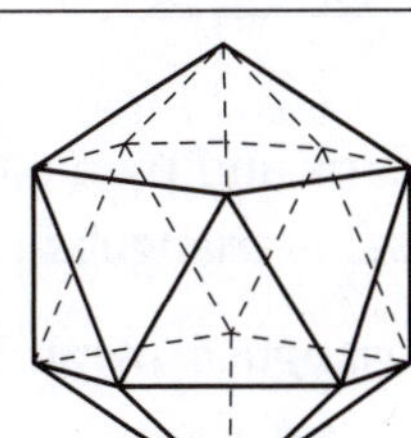

Alert!

Spheres, cones and cylinders are not polyhedra.

Faces, Edges and Vertices of Polyhedra

All polyhedra have plane faces. Two plane faces meet at a line segment known as an edge. The edges meet at a point called a *vertex*. We know that a cuboid has 6 faces, 12 edges and 8 vertices. A cuboid is not a platonic solid as all its faces are not regular polygons.

Prisms and pyramids are two important members of the polyhedra family.

Prisms are polyhedra whose top and base are congruent polygons and the others faces are parallelograms.

Prisms

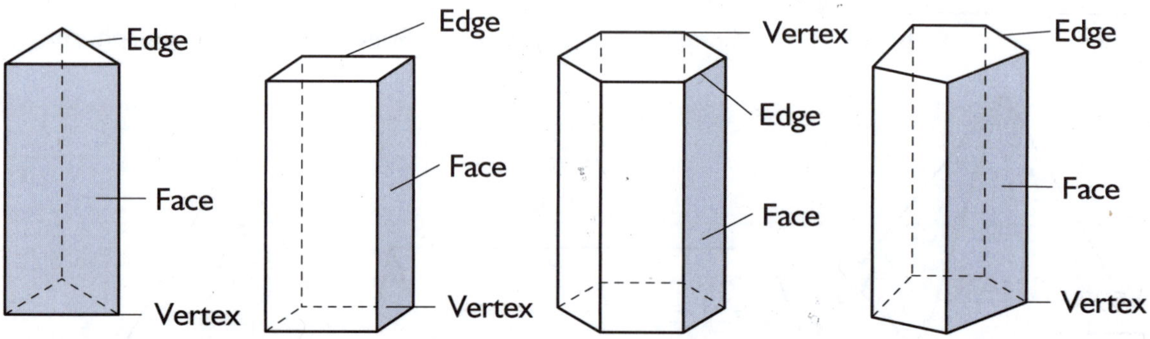

A *pyramid is a* polyhedron with a polygon as its base. All its other faces are triangles that meet at a common vertex. The base of a pyramid can be a polygon with any number of sides. The most common bases are triangles and squares, but the base can also be a pentagon, hexagon and so on.

Pyramids

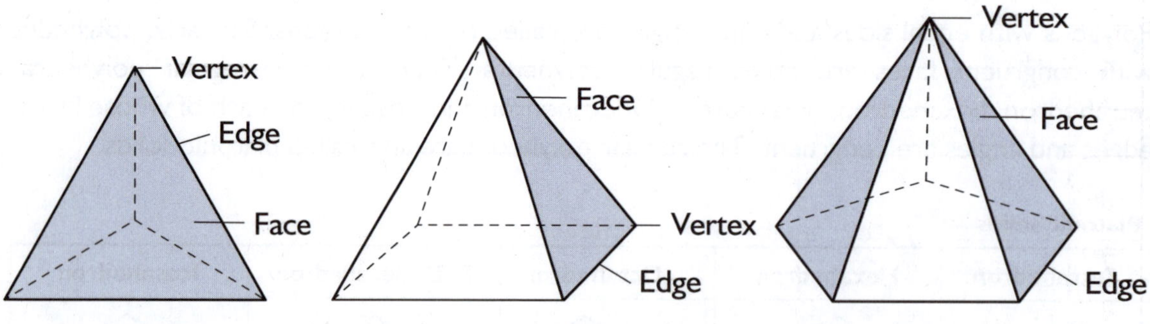

Prisms and pyramids are named after their bases. A pentagonal prism has a pentagon as its base. A triangular prism has a triangle as its base.

A triangular pyramid can be a platonic solid if all its four faces are equilateral triangles.

Euler's Formula

Let us see the relation between the faces, edges and vertices of a polyhedron. Look at the polyhedra shown below and count their faces, edges and vertices.

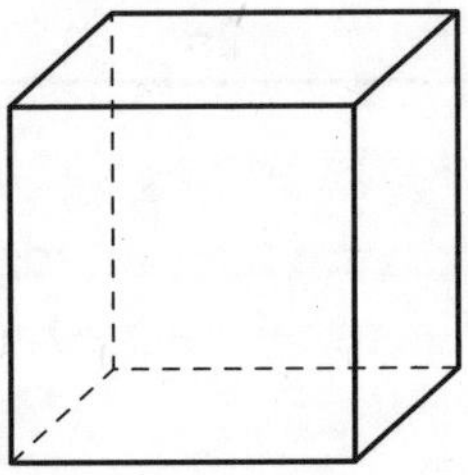

Faces — 6
Edges — 12
Vertices — 8

Faces + vertices
= 6 + 8 = 14
and edges + 2 = 14

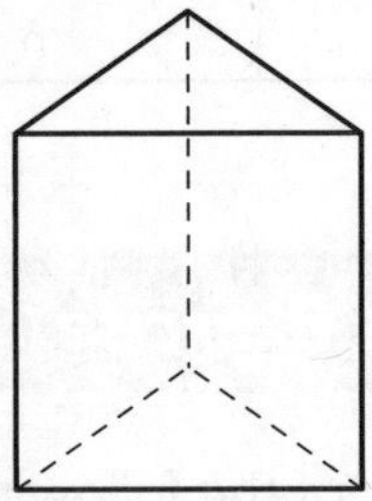

Faces — 5
Edges — 9
Vertices — 6

Faces + vertices
= 5 + 6 = 11
and edges + 2 = 11

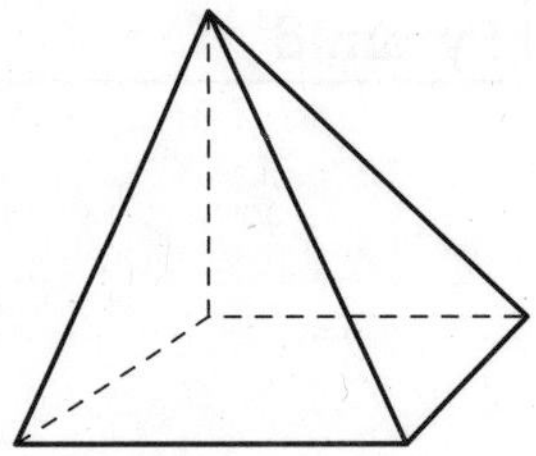

Faces — 5
Edges — 8
Vertices — 5

Faces + vertices
= 5 + 5 = 10
and edges + 2 = 10

In each case we see that, faces + vertices − edges = 2 or faces + vertices = edges + 2

$$F + V - E = 2$$

This is Euler's formula, named after the famous Swiss mathematician, Leonard Euler.

Verification of Euler's Formula

	Solid	Number of Faces (F)	Number of Vertices (V)	Number of Edges (E)	F + V − E = 2
1	Cube	6	8	12	6 + 8 − 12 = 2
2	Cuboid	6	8	12	6 + 8 − 12 = 2
3	Tetrahedron (Triangular Pyramid)	4	4	6	4 + 4 − 6 = 2
4	Right triangular Prism	5	6	9	5 + 6 − 9 = 2
5	Square prism	6	8	12	6 + 8 − 12 = 2
6	Pyramid on a square base	5	5	8	5 + 5 − 8 = 2
7	Pentagonal prism	7	10	15	7 + 10 − 15 = 2
8	Pentagonal pyramid	6	6	10	6 + 6 − 10 = 2
9	Hexagonal prism	8	12	18	8 + 12 − 18 = 2
10	Hexagonal pyramid	7	7	12	7 + 7 − 12 = 2

In general, the number of faces, vertices and edges of prisms and pyramids are given as:

	Faces	Vertices	Edges
Prism	n + 2	2n	3n
Pyramid	n + 1	n + 1	2n

Practice Exercise 13.1

1. Write the number of faces of each of the following solid figures.

   a. Cuboid b. Cube c. Triangular prism
   d. Square pyramid e. Tetrahedron

2. Write down the number of vertices of each of the following figures.

   a. Tetrahedron b. Pentagonal prism c. Hexagonal pyramid
   d. Square prism e. Pentagonal pyramid

3. Write down the number of edges of each of the following figures.

   a. Cuboid b. Right triangular prism c. Pyramid on a square base
   d. Pentagonal pyramid e. Hexagonal prism

4. Fill in the blanks.

   a. The number of edges in a solid that has 4 faces and 4 vertices is ________.
   b. The number of vertices in a solid that has 20 faces and 30 edges is ________.
   c. The number of faces in a solid that has 30 edges and 20 vertices is ________.
   d. The number of vertices in a right prism that has 24 edges is ________.
   e. The number of faces in a right prism that has 16 vertices is ________.

5. a. Draw a cone and a triangular pyramid. Can you identify the similarity between the two?

   b. Draw a cylinder and triangular prism. Can you identify the similarity between the two?

Highlights

- A polyhedron is a solid shape made up of plane faces, for example, a cube, a cuboid, a pyramid and prism.
- The plural of polyhedron is polyhedra.
- All polyhedra have faces, vertices and edges.
- The relation between faces, edges and vertices of polyhedra is given by Euler's Formula, that is, $F + V - E = 2$.

Higher Order Thinking Skills

HOTS

The surface area of a pyramid whose base is a regular polygon is 220 cm^2 and the area of its base is 60 cm^2. Find the number of lateral faces the pyramid has if the area of each lateral face is 20 cm^2.

Complete the following sequence:

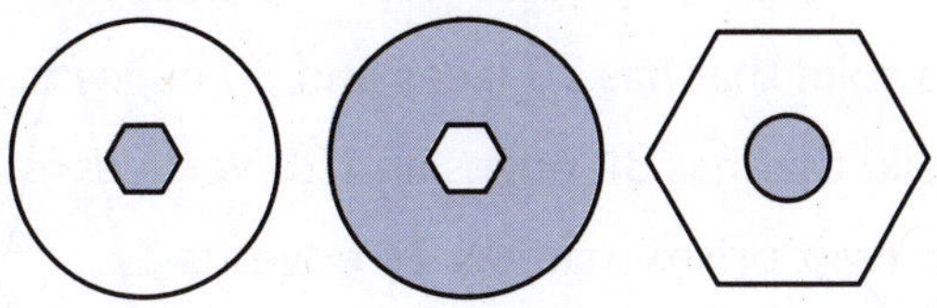

Options:

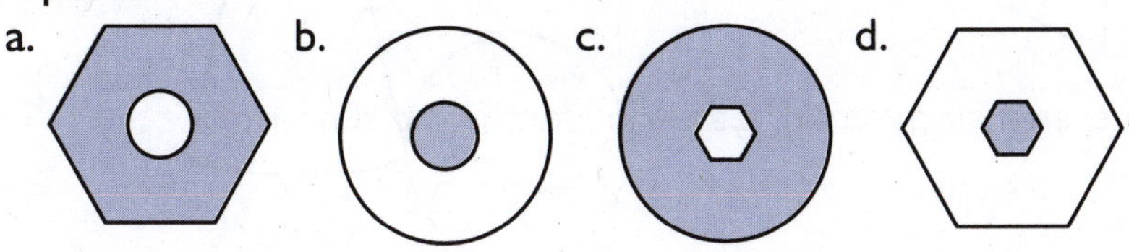

Answer for Brainteaser on page 211

Understanding Solid Shapes

Objective: To visualise and understand 3-D figures.

Material required: chart paper, pencil, ruler and a pair of scissors

Method: Draw the net of 3-D figures on a chart paper. You can draw the diagram of the net of 3-D figures (as given below) on a large scale. Use scissors to cut along the lines. Fold the chart paper to form the solid figures. Now in the figures so formed use different coloured chart paper to decorate your solid shapes with interesting patterns.

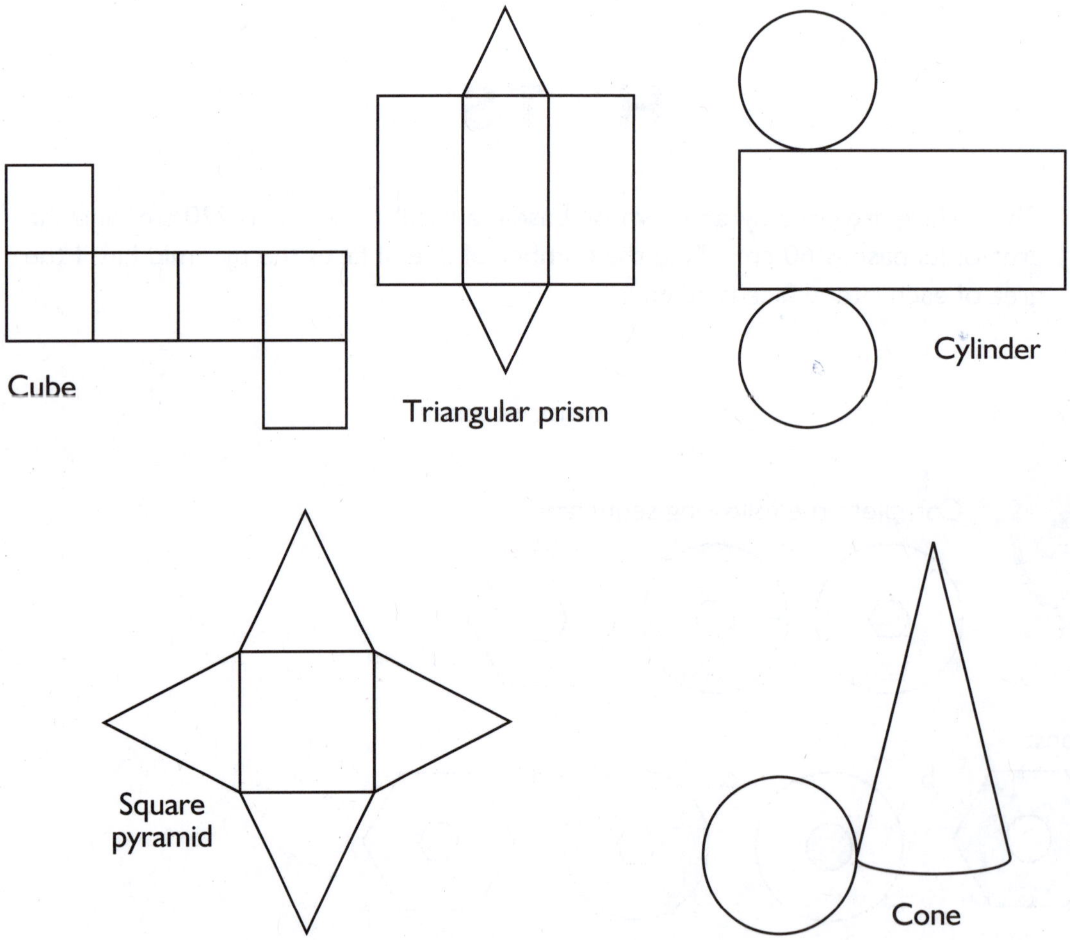

1. Find the value of x in the following figures.

a.

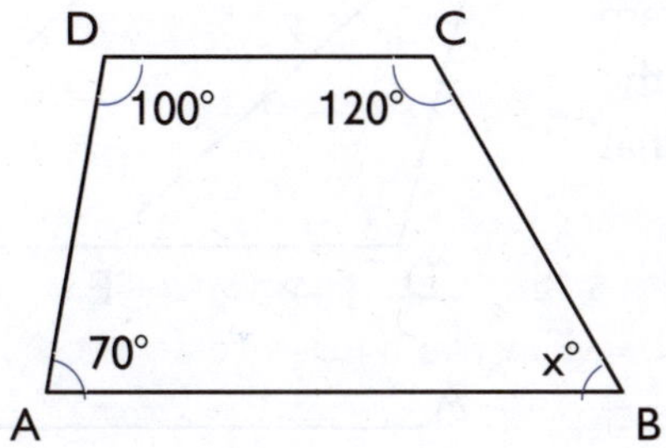

b.

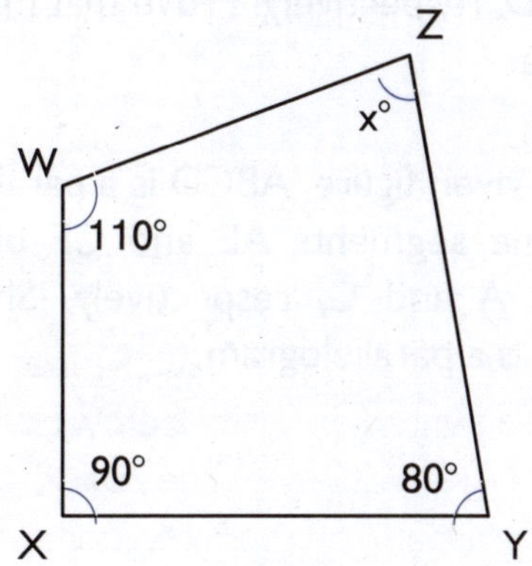

c.

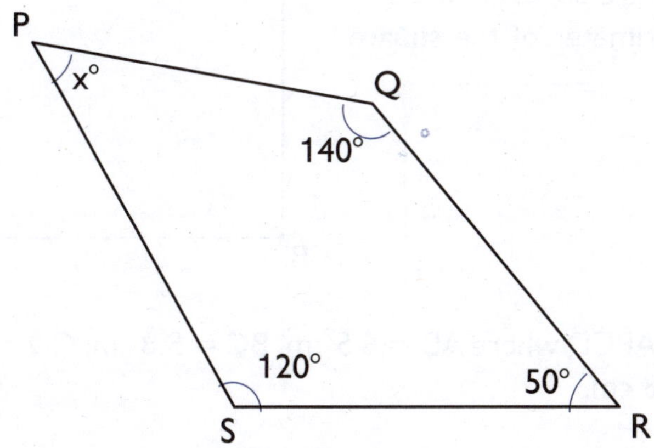

2. The adjacent sides of a parallelogram are in the ratio 3:7 and its perimeter is 100 cm. Find the sides of the parallelogram.

3. In the given figure, the bisectors of $\angle A$ and $\angle B$ meet at a point P. If $\angle C = 60°$ and $\angle D = 100°$, find the measure of $\angle P$.

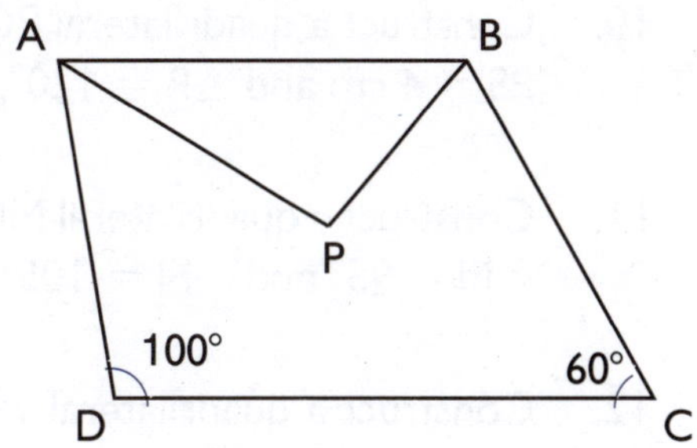

4. In the given figure, ABCD is a trapezium in which AB || CD. Find the measures of $\angle A$ and $\angle B$ given that $\angle C = 75°$ and $\angle D = 60°$.

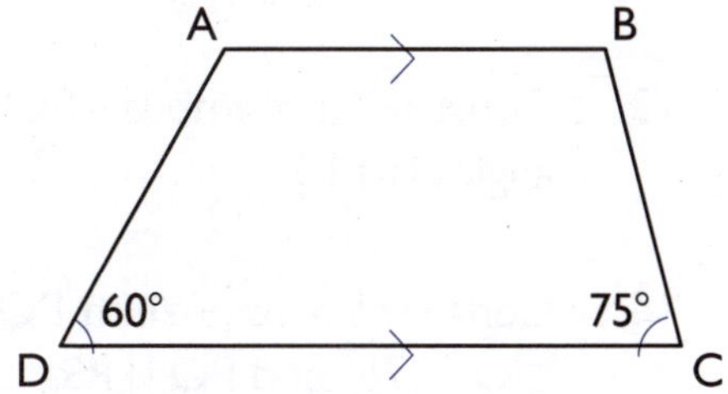

5. Figure ABCD is a square and M, N, O and P are the mid points of AB, BC, CD and AD, respectively. Prove that MNOP is a square.

6. In the given figure, ABCD is a parallelogram and line segments AE and CF bisect the angles A and C, respectively. Show that AECF is a parallelogram.

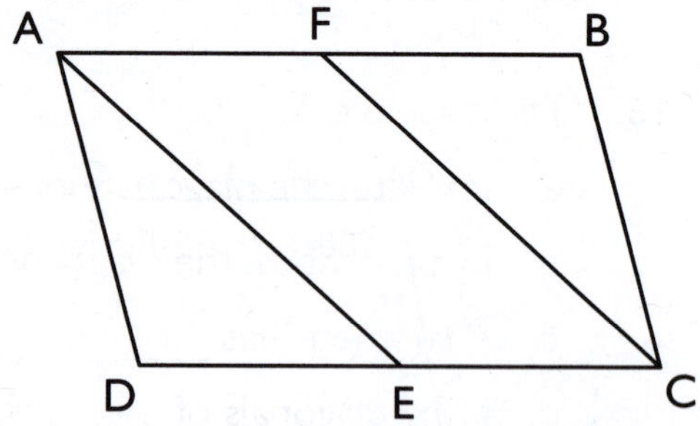

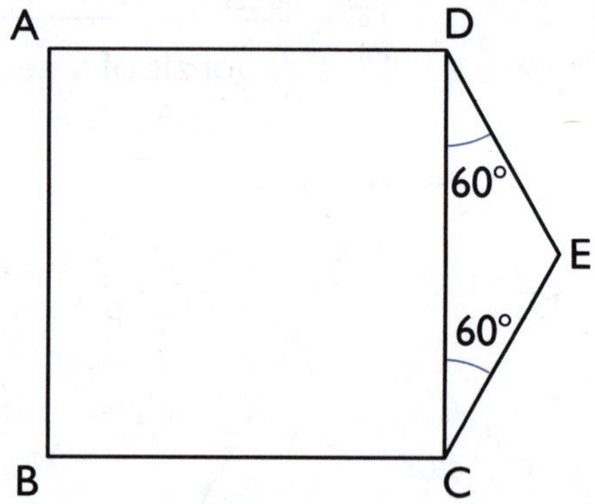

7. ABCD is a square and CDE is a triangle whose angles ∠EDC and ∠ECD are 60° each. If CE = DE = 9 cm, find the perimeter of the square ABCD.

8. Construct a quadrilateral ABCD where AB = 6.5 cm, BC = 5.8 cm, CD = 6.2 cm, AD = 7 cm and BD = 7.8 cm.

9. Construct a quadrilateral EFGH where EF = 5.2 cm, FG = 6 cm, EH = 5.4 cm and EG = FH = 7 cm.

10. Construct a quadrilateral PQRS where PQ = 7.7 cm, QR = 6.8 cm, RS = 5.2 cm, PS = 4 cm and ∠R = 120°.

11. Construct a quadrilateral MNOP where MN = 6.3 cm, NO = 7.2 cm, MP = 7 cm, ∠M = 95° and ∠N = 105°.

12. Construct a quadrilateral WXYZ where WX = 4 cm, XY = 5.2cm, ∠W = 90°, ∠X = 120° and ∠Y = 65°.

13. Construct a rhombus ABCD one of whose sides measures 5 cm and one of whose angles is 110°.

14. Construct a trapezium PQRS in which PQ = 6 cm, QR = 4 cm, RS = 3.2cm, ∠Q = 75° and PQ || RS.

15. Construct a rectangle ABCD with a side 4 cm and a diagonal 5 cm. Find the length of the other side.

16. Fill in the blanks.

    a. In a kite, the diagonals intersect at ___________.

    b. In a rhombus, the diagonal bisect each other at _________.

    c. A rhombus has ___________ pairs of parallel sides.

    d. If the diagonals of a quadrilateral are perpendicular to each other, the quadrilateral is a _______________.

    e. If the diagonals of a quadrilateral bisect and are perpendicular to each other, the quadrilateral is a ____________

    f. The diagonals of a rectangle are _________ and bisect each other.

17. Make two identical pyramids with square bases and equilateral triangles as lateral faces. Join these two pyramids end to end so that the vertices of the squares of the two pyramids coincide. How many edges, vertices and faces are there in the new side?

18. Write down the number of vertices of each of the following figures.

    a. Cuboid b. Square pyramid c. Tetrahedron

    d. Triangular prism e. Pentagonal pyramid

19. Draw a cylinder and a triangular prism. What is the similarity between the two figures? What is the difference?

20. Can Euler's Formula be applied to cylinders, cones and spheres? If not, why? Verify Euler's Formula for the following:

    a. Cube b. Pentagonal prism c. Hexagonal pyramid

Answer for Brainteaser from page 207

a.

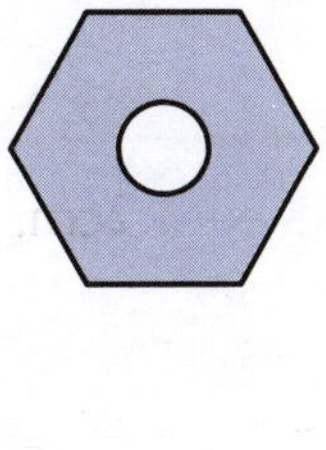

Test Yourself

Unit IV

1. In the quadrilateral PQRS, it is given that:

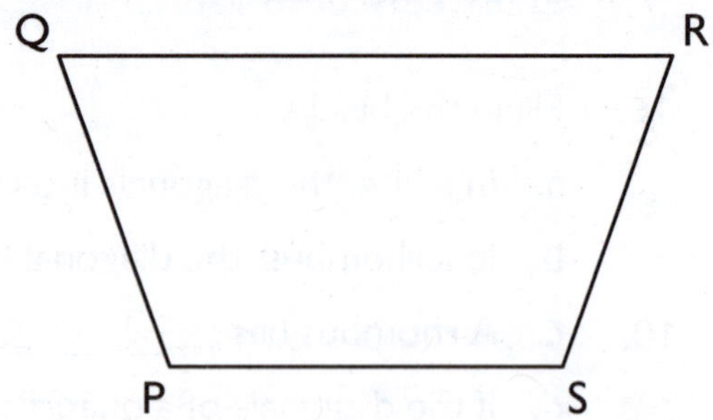

a. $\angle P = \angle S$

b. $\angle Q = \angle R$

c. $\angle P + \angle S = 120^\circ$

d. $\angle R + \angle S = 180^\circ$

e. $\angle P + \angle Q = 180^\circ$

Find $\angle P$, $\angle Q$, $\angle R$ and $\angle S$.

2. In the given parallelogram ABCD, the diagonals AC and BD bisect each other at O. Show that $\triangle AOB \cong \triangle COD$. Which rule of congruency has been applied? Write all the corresponding sides and angles that are equal.

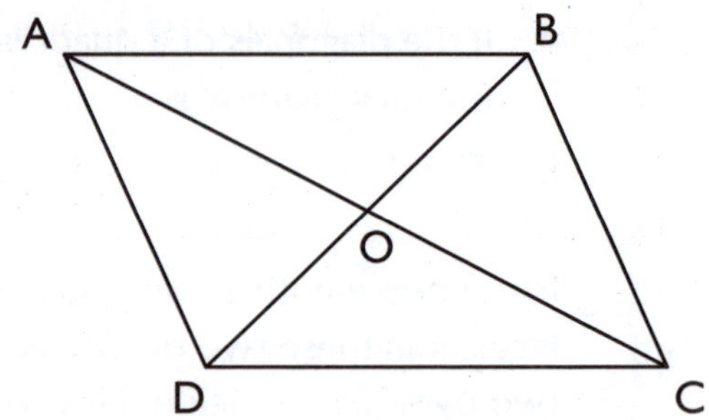

3. The perimeter of a rectangle is 180 cm. If the sides are in the ratio 4:5, find the lengths of the four sides and the two diagonals.

4. ABCD is a parallelogram and AC is the diagonal. BX and DY are perpendiculars from the vertices B and D, respectively, on the diagonal AC as shown in the figure given alongside.

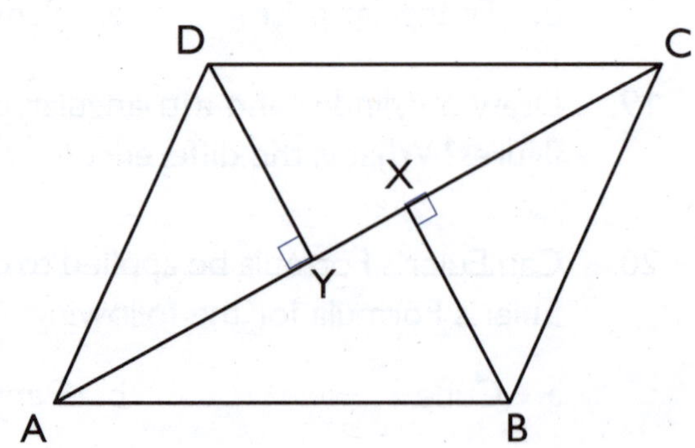

Prove that $\Delta BCX \cong \Delta DAY$ and BX = DY. Write the condition of congruency applied.

5. PQRS is a trapezium in which PS || QR. If $\angle PQR = 60^\circ$ and $\angle QRS = 40^\circ$, find the measure of angles $\angle QPS$ and $\angle RSP$.

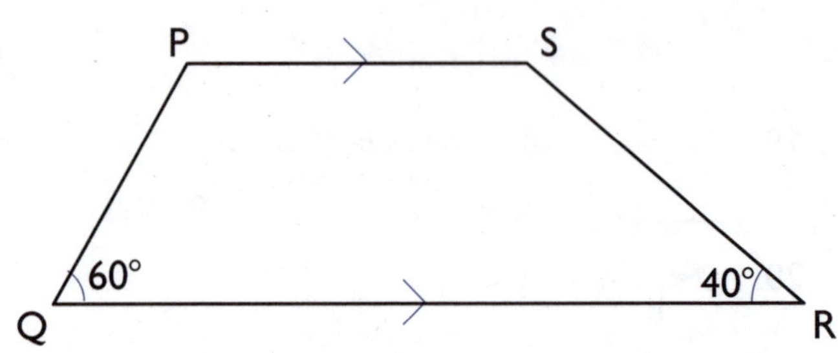

6. Two angles of a quadrilateral are equal and the unequal angles measure 65°and 75°. Find the measure of each of the equal angles.
7. Construct a quadrilateral ABCD in which AB = 4.5 cm, BC = 6 cm, CD = 5.3 cm, DA = 5 cm and diagonal AC = 8.5 cm.
8. Construct a quadrilateral PQRS in which PQ = 4.8 cm and QR = 4.2 cm.
9. Construct a quadrilateral MNOP in which MN = 3.8 cm, NO = 3.5 cm, OP = 4.6 cm, MP = 5.1 cm and $\angle N = 75°$.
10. Construct a quadrilateral WXYZ in which WX = 3.5 cm, XY = 5 cm, YZ = 4.5 cm, $\angle x = 125°$ and $\angle y = 60°$.
11. Construct a quadrilateral ABCD where AB = 5.5 cm, BC = 4.5 cm, $\angle A = 50°$, $\angle B = 110°$ and $\angle D = 75°$.
12. Construct a quadrilateral ABCD in which AB = 4.5 cm, AC = 5 cm, AD = 5.5 cm and $\angle ABC = \angle ACD = 90°$
13. Construct a parallelogram PQRS in which PQ = 5.5 cm, $\angle PQR = 120°$ and CD = 5 cm.
14. Construct a rectangle in which the adjacent sides are 10.5 cm and 8.5 cm.
15. Construct a rhombus in which the sides are 4.5 cm each and one diagonal is 6.5 cm.
16. Construct a rhombus in which the sides are 6 cm each and one of the angles is 70°.
17. Construct a trapezium ABCD in which AB || CD, AB = 8 cm, BC = 6 cm, AD = 7 cm and $\angle B = 70°$.
18. Complete the table by writing the number of faces (F), vertices (V) and edges (E) for each of the solids listed.

Solid	F	V	E
Cube			
Triangular prism			
Square pyramid			
Pentagonal prism			
Hexagonal pyramid			
A pyramid where the base has 'n' sides			

19. Write Euler's Formula and verify it for the following.

    a. Hexagonal prism b. Pentagonal pyramid c. Cuboid

20. Fill in the blanks.

    a. A cuboid is also known as a rectangular ____________.

    b. A triangular pyramid is called ____________.

    c. A kaleidoscope is a type of ____________.

CHAPTER 14

Perimeter and Area

We have learnt about the perimeter and area of different shapes and figures in the previous classes. We know that perimeter is the length of the boundary of a figure while area is the region bounded by the figure. Perimeter has a single unit, such as mm, cm, m or km, and area has square units mm^2, cm^2, m^2, km^2, etc.

We have studied the perimeter and area of a triangle, square, rectangle, parallelogram and circle. Now we shall study the perimeter and area of a trapezium and other quadrilaterals. We shall also study the perimeter and area of polygons.

Let us recall the perimeter and area of the following shapes.

Figure	**Perimeter**	**Area**
Triangle	$P = a + b + c$ where a, b, c are the sides of the triangle	$A = \frac{1}{2}$ base $\times$ height
Parallelogram	$P = 2(a + b)$ where *a*, *b* are the sides of the parallelogram	$A =$ base $\times$ height
Circle	$C = 2\pi r$ where r is the radius of the circle	$A = \pi r^2$

We shall study examples based on the formulae given above.

Example 1: Find the area of a parallelogram whose base is 5.6 m and height or altitude is 2.8 m.

Area of a parallelogram = Base × Height

$= 5.6 \times 2.8$

$= 15.68\ m^2$

The area is $15.68\ m^2$.

Example 2: The area of a triangle is $43.98\ m^2$. If its base is 7.33 m, find its height.

Area of a triangle $= \frac{1}{2} \times$ Base $\times$ Height

Height $= \frac{2 \times \text{Area}}{\text{Base}}$

$= \frac{2 \times 43.98}{7.33} = 12$ m.

The height of the triangle is 12 m.

Example 3: A circular table top is to be polished. If the diameter of the top is 70 cm, find the cost of polishing it at the rate of Rs 250 per m^2.

Area of a circle $= \pi r^2$

$= \frac{22}{\cancel{7}} \times \overset{5}{\cancel{35}} \times 35$ (since d = 70 cm)

$= 110 \times 35$

$= 3{,}850\ cm^2$

$$\text{Cost of polishing the table top} = \frac{385\cancel{0}}{100 \times 1\cancel{00}} \times 25\cancel{0}$$

$$= ₹96.25$$

The cost of polishing the table top is ₹96.25.

Example 4: In a rectangular park with dimensions 21 m by 14 m (as shown in the figure below), two semicircular flower beds as well as two square beds of side 2 m each are laid. Find the remaining area of the park.

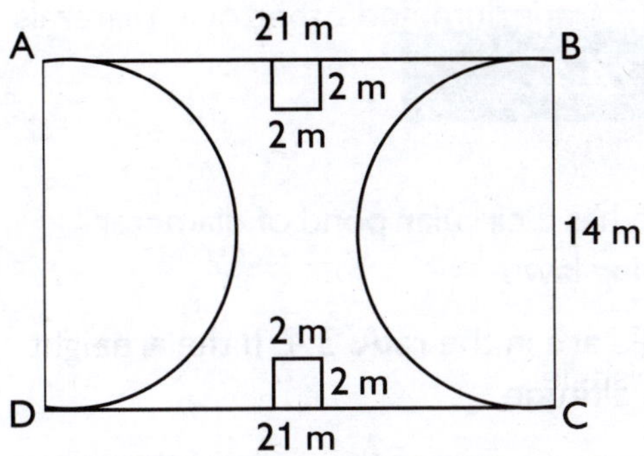

Area of the rectangular park $= \ell \times b$

$= 21 \times 14$

$= 294 \text{ m}^2$

Area of the semicircle $= \frac{1}{2} \times \pi \times r^2$

$= \frac{1}{2} \times \frac{22}{7} \times 7 \times 7$

(Side of rectangle = Diameter of the circle = 14 m $\therefore$ radius = 7 m)

$= 11 \times 7 = 77 \text{ m}^2$

There are 2 semicircular flower beds.

$\therefore$ Area of semicircular flower beds $= 77 \times 2 = 154 \text{ m}^2$

Area of a square $= \text{side}^2$

$= 2 \times 2 = 4 \text{ m}^2$

Area of 2 square beds $= 4 \times 2 = 8 \text{ m}^2$

Total area of flower beds $= 154 \text{ m}^2 + 8 \text{ m}^2$

$= 162 \text{ m}^2$

Area of the remaining park $= 294 \text{ m}^2 - 162 \text{ m}^2$

$= 132 \text{ m}^2$

The area of the rest of the park is 132 m^2.

Example 5: A rectangular floor of sides 15 m by 12 m is to be tiled with right triangular marble pieces of size 60 cm, 80 cm and 100 cm. How many marble pieces will be required to cover the floor?

Area of the floor $= 15 \text{ m} \times 12 \text{ m} = 180 \text{ m}^2$

Area of a triangular marble piece $= \frac{1}{2} \text{ base} \times \text{height}$

$= \frac{1}{2} \times 60 \times 80 \text{ cm}^2$

$= \frac{1}{2} \times \frac{6}{10} \times \frac{8}{10} \text{ m}^2$

(The base and height are 60 cm and 80 cm as the longest side is the hypotenuse of a right triangular piece)

$$\text{Number of marble pieces} = \frac{\text{Area of the floor}}{\text{Area of a marble piece}}$$

$$= \frac{15 \times 12}{\frac{1}{2} \times \frac{6}{10} \times \frac{8}{10}} = \frac{15 \times 12 \times 2 \times 10 \times 10}{6 \times 8}$$

$$= 750$$

750 marble pieces will be required.

Practice Exercise 14.1

1. A rectangular lawn of dimensions 75 m by 50 m has a circular pond of diameter 35 m at the centre. Find the area of the remaining lawn.
2. The base and corresponding altitude of a triangle are in the ratio 3:4. If the area of the triangle is 294 cm^2, find the base and the altitude.
3. A circular plot has a radius of 56 m. A 7 m wide road runs on the inside of the plot around it. Find the area of the road. Also find the cost of paving the road at ₹50 per m^2.
4. The diameter of the wheel of a car is 77 cm. How many revolutions will it make to travel 121 km?
5. The area of a parallelogram is 512 cm^2. Its base is twice its height. Find the dimensions of its base and height.
6. The adjacent sides of a parallelogram are 15 cm and 8 cm. If the distance between the longer sides is 4 cm, find the distance between the shorter sides.
7. Each side of a square park is 80 m. At each corner of the park there is a flower bed in the form of a quadrant of a circle of radius 14 m. Find the area of the remaining part of the park.
8. The difference between the circumference and radius of a circle is 37 cm. Find the area of the circle.
9. The hour and minute hands of a clock are 4.2 cm and 7 cm long, respectively. Find the sum of the distances covered by their tips in 2 days.
10. A brass tray in the shape of a parallelogram was polished at a total cost of ₹2,250 at the rate of ₹20 per 10 cm^2. If the altitude of the parallelogram is 45 cm, find the length of its base.

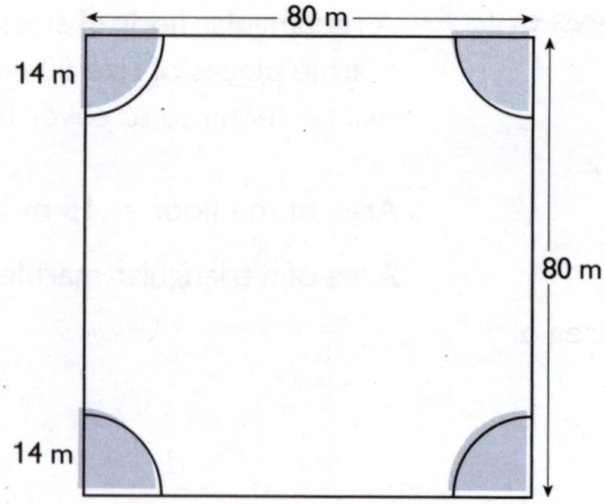

Area of a Trapezium

A trapezium is a quadrilateral with one pair of opposite sides parallel to each other.

We know that a quadrilateral is divided into two triangles by a diagonal. We shall find the area of the trapezium based on this concept and prove that the distance between two parallel lines is constant or fixed.

Let us consider the trapezium ABCD, where AB is parallel to CD. AX = CY = h is the distance between the parallel sides and AC is the diagonal of the trapezium.

Let AB be 'a' units, and DC be 'b' units.

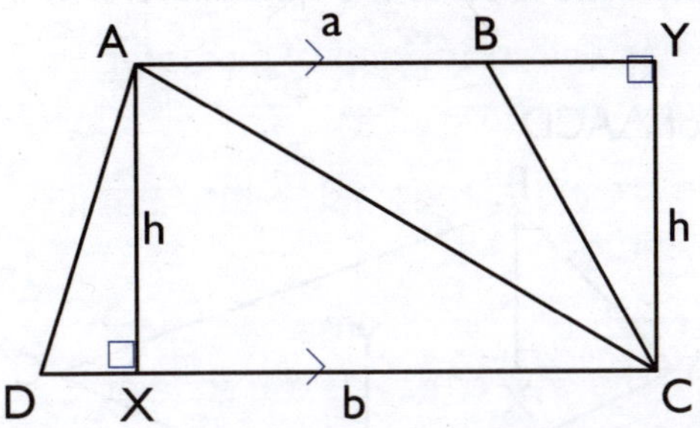

Area of trapezium ABCD = Area of $\triangle ADC$ + Area of $\triangle ABC$

$$= \frac{1}{2} \times DC \times AX + \frac{1}{2} \times AB \times CY$$

$$= \frac{1}{2} \times b \times h + \frac{1}{2} \times a \times h$$

$$= \frac{1}{2} \times h \times (b + a)$$

$$= \frac{1}{2} \times h \times (a + b)$$

$\therefore$ Area of trapezium $= \frac{1}{2} \times$ Height $\times$ (Sum of parallel sides)

Area of a Rhombus

A rhombus is a parallelogram, hence its area can be determined using the formula:

Area of a parallelogram = Base × Height.

We can derive another formula for the area of a rhombus if the lengths of its diagonals are given. Let ABCD be a rhombus and AC, BD be the diagonals. The diagonals of a rhombus bisect each other at right angles.

Area of rhombus ABCD = Area of $\triangle ABC$ + Area of $\triangle ADC$

Area of $\triangle ABC = \frac{1}{2} \times$ Base $\times$ Height

$$= \frac{1}{2} \times AC \times OB$$

$$= \frac{1}{2} \times d_1 \times \frac{d_2}{2}$$

$$= \frac{1}{4} \times d_1 \times d_2$$

Area of $\triangle DBC = \frac{1}{2} \times$ Base $\times$ Height

$$= \frac{1}{2} \times AC \times OD$$

$$= \frac{1}{2} \times d_1 \times \frac{d_2}{2}$$

$$= \frac{1}{4} \times d_1 \times d_2$$

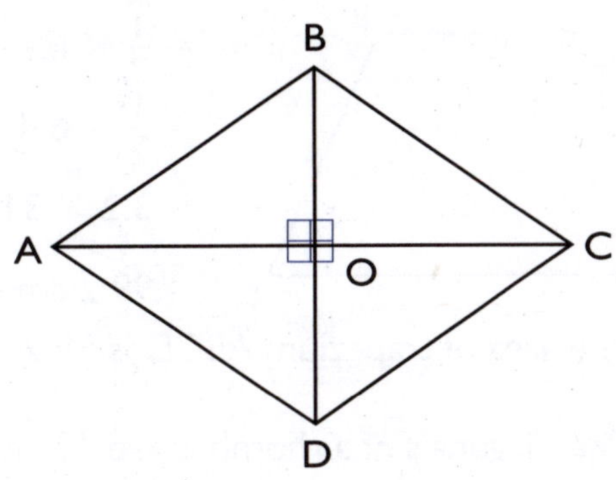

Let AC = d_1 and BD = d_2

Area of rhombus ABCD = Area of $\triangle ABC$ + Area of $\triangle DBC$

$$= \frac{1}{4} \times d_1 \times d_2 + \frac{1}{4} \times d_1 \times d_2$$

$$= \frac{1}{2} \times d_1 \times d_2$$

$$= \frac{1}{2} \times \text{(product of the diagonals)}$$

We can also use this formula to find the area of a square, since a square is also a rhombus.

Area of a Quadrilateral

If ABCD is any quadrilateral with AC as the diagonal, then the area of the quadrilateral will be the sum of the areas of the two triangles.

Area of quadrilateral ABCD = Area of $\triangle ABC$ + Area of $\triangle ACD$

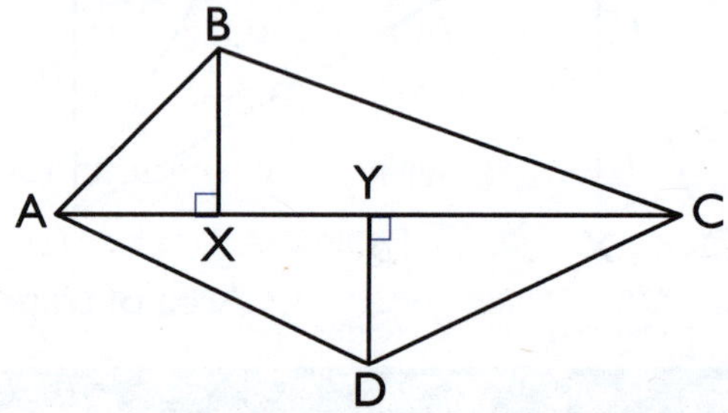

Area of $\triangle ABC = \frac{1}{2} \times \text{Base} \times \text{Height}$

$$= \frac{1}{2} \times AC \times BX$$

Area of $\triangle ACD = \frac{1}{2} \times \text{Base} \times \text{Height}$

$$= \frac{1}{2} \times AC \times DY$$

Area of quadrilateral ABCD $= \frac{1}{2} \times AC \times BX$

$$= \frac{1}{2} \times AC \times DY$$

$$= \frac{1}{2} \times AC \times [BX + DY]$$

$$= \frac{1}{2} \times \text{Diagonal} \times \text{(Sum of the perpendicular distance from the opposite vertices on the diagonal)}$$

Example 1: In the given figure, ABCD is a trapezium with AB || CD. AB = 12.5 cm, CD = 18.5 cm and AY = 6.4 cm, where AY is $\perp$ to CD. Find the area of ABCD.

Area of trapezium ABCD $= \frac{1}{2} \times$ Perpendicular distance $\times$ Sum of || sides

Area of trapezium ABCD $= \frac{1}{2} \times AX \times (AB + CD)$

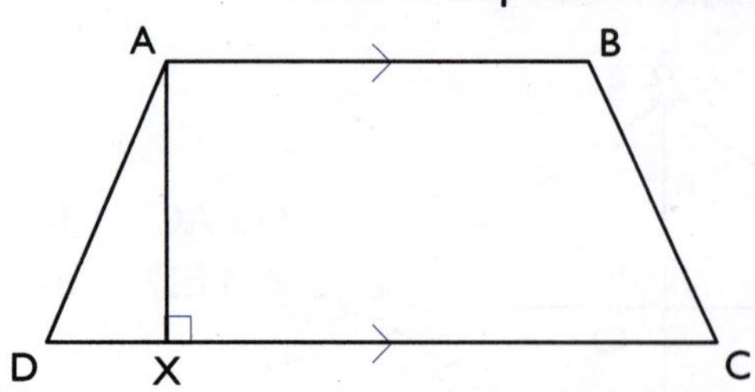

$$= \frac{1}{2} \times 6.4 \times (12.5 + 18.5)$$

$$= \frac{1}{2} \times 6.4 \times (31.0)$$

$$= 3.2 \times 31$$

$$= 99.2 \text{ cm}^2$$

The area of trapezium ABCD is 99.2 cm^2.

Example 2: The diagonals of a rhombus are 12 cm and 16 cm. Find the area and perimeter of the rhombus.

Let AC = d_1 = 12 cm, BD = d_2 = 16 cm

Area of a rhombus $= \frac{1}{2} \times$ Product of diagonals

$= \frac{1}{2} \times d_1 \times d_2$

$= \frac{1}{\not{2}} \times \not{12}^{6} \times 16$

The area of the rhombus is 96 cm^2.

In △AOB, AO = 6 cm, OB = 8 cm. △AOB is a right-angled triangle, so we apply the Pythagoras theorem to find the hypotenuse AB.

$AB^2 = AO^2 + OB^2$

$= 6^2 + 8^2$

$= 36 + 64$

$AB^2 = 100$

∴ AB = 10 cm.

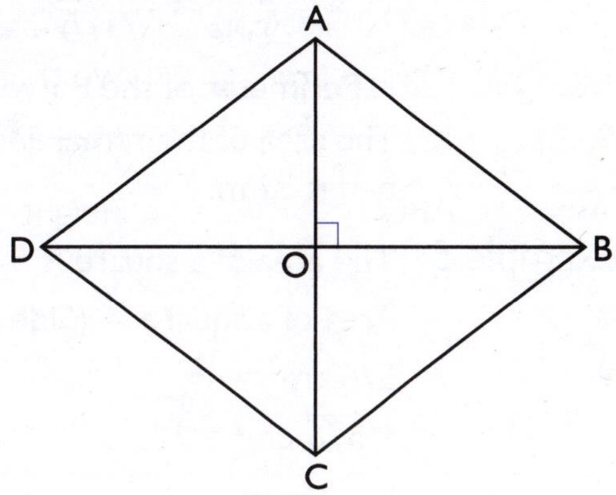

All sides of a rhombus are equal

∴ Perimeter = 4 × AB

= 4 × 10

= 40 cm

Area of the rhombus is 96 cm^2 and perimeter is 40 cm.

Example 3: Find the area of a field in the form of a quadrilateral that has the following dimensions:
BD = 24.8 m, AX = 14.6 m and CY = 12.2 m.

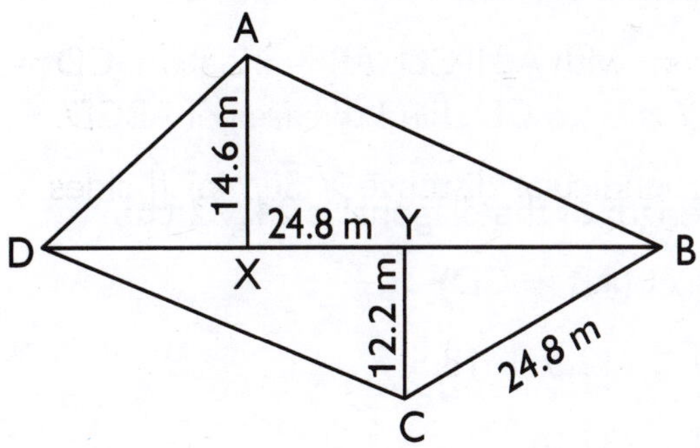

Area of the field $= \frac{1}{2} \times$ Diagonal × (Sum of the perpendiculars on the diagonal)

$= \frac{1}{2} \times BD \times (AX + CY)$

$= \frac{1}{2} \times 24.8 \times (14.6 + 12.2)$

$= \frac{1}{2} \times 24.8 \times 26.8$

$= 12.4 \times 26.8 \text{ m}^2 = 332.32 \text{ m}^2$

$= 332.32 \text{ m}^2$

The area of the field is 332.32 m^2

Example 4: A lawn is in the shape of a trapezium. Its parallel sides measure 36 m and 60 m. The distance between the parallel sides is 16 m. In the centre of the lawn is a square flower bed that has an area of 169 m^2. Find the area of the remaining lawn and the perimeter of the flower bed.

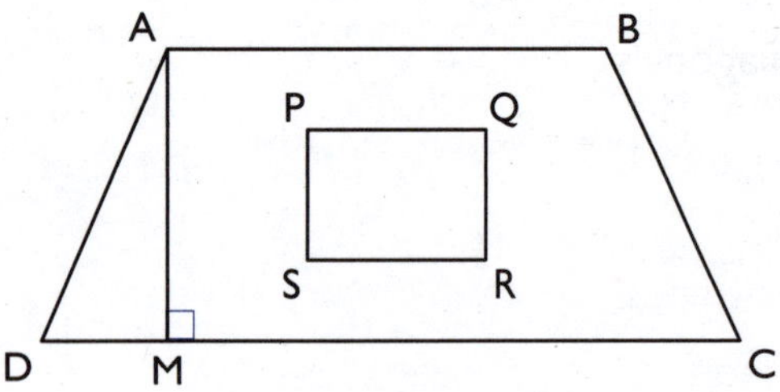

Area of trapezium ABCD $= \frac{1}{2} \times AM \times (AB + CD)$

$= \frac{1}{2} \times 16 \times (36 + 60)$

$= \frac{1}{2} \times 16 \times 96$

$= 8 \times 96$

$= 768 \text{ m}^2$

Area of the square bed $= 169 \text{ m}^2$

Remaining area of the lawn $= 768 - 169 = 599 \text{ m}^2$

Area of the square bed $= 169 \text{ m}^2$

$(\text{Side})^2 = 169$

Side $= \sqrt{169} = 13$

$\therefore$ Perimeter of the flower bed $= 13 \times 4 = 52$ m

The area of the remaining lawn is 599 m^2 and the perimeter of the flower bed is 52 m.

Example 5: The area of a square is 576 cm^2. Find the length of its side and diagonal.

Area of a square $= (\text{Side})^2$

$576 \text{ cm}^2 = l^2$

$\sqrt{576} \text{ cm}^2 = l$

$l = 24$ cm

Length of the square $= 24$ cm

Diagonals of a square are equal and bisect each other at right angles.

Area of square $= \frac{1}{2} \times d \times d$

$576 = \frac{1}{2} \times d^2 \qquad (d_1 = d_2 = d)$

$576 \times 2 \text{ cm}^2 = d^2$

$\sqrt{576 \times 2} = d$

$\sqrt{2} \times 24 = d$

Diagonal $= 24\sqrt{2}$ cm

The length of the side of the square is 24 cm. The length of the diagonal is $24\sqrt{2}$ cm.

Alert!!

1. Side of a square $= \sqrt{\text{Area}}$
2. Diagonal of a square $= \text{Side} \sqrt{2}$

Practice Exercise 14.2

1. The parallel sides of a trapezium are in the ratio 3:5. Its height is 16 cm and area is 768 cm^2. Find the lengths of the parallel sides.
2. The perimeter of a rhombus is 40 cm and the length of one of the diagonals is 16 cm. Find the length of the other diagonal.

3. The area of a square is 625 cm^2. Find the length of its side and diagonal.
4. A floor is made up of 400 rhombus-shaped tiles with diagonals measuring 18 cm and 12 cm as well as 250 trapezium-shaped tiles with parallel sides measuring 10 cm and 12 cm and a height of 8 cm. Find the area of the floor and also the cost of polishing it at ₹300 per m^2.
5. The lengths of the parallel sides of an isosceles trapezium are 6 cm and 14 cm. The length of each non parallel side is 5 cm. Find the area of the trapezium.

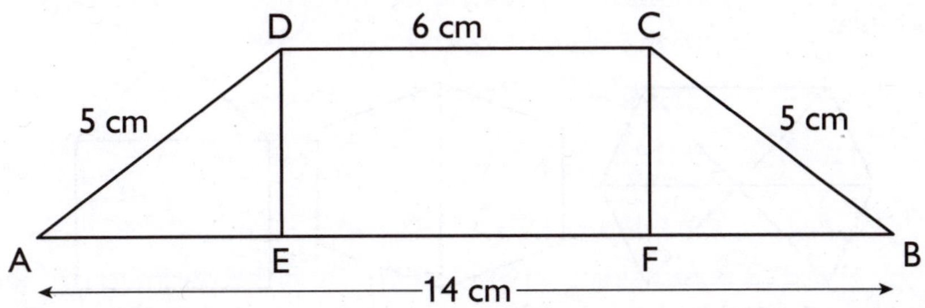

6. A field is in the shape of a quadrilateral. Its diagonal measures 27 m and the perpendicular distances of the other two vertices to the diagonal are 12 m and 10 m. Find the area of the field and the cost of ploughing it at the rate of ₹50 per m^2.
7. A circle with radius 7 cm is drawn inside a rhombus with diagonals 24 cm and 32 cm. Find the area of the shaded region.

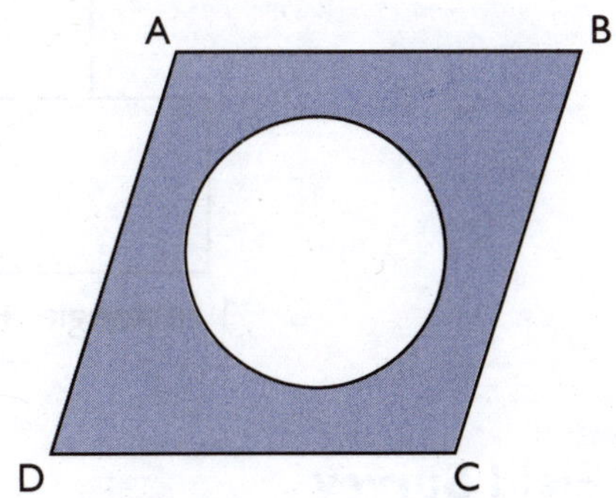

8. The area of a trapezium is 768 cm^2. Its altitude is 16 cm and one of the parallel sides is 10 cm longer than the other. Find the length of the parallel sides.
9. a. Find the altitude of a rhombus with perimeter 48 cm and area 360 cm^2.
   b. The area of a rhombus is 468 cm^2. If its height is 18 cm, find its perimeter.
   c. Find the area of a rhombus that has diagonals 30 cm and 40 cm in length. Also find its perimeter.
10. Find the area of the shaded region where ABCD is a trapezium and two circles of equal radii are drawn within it.

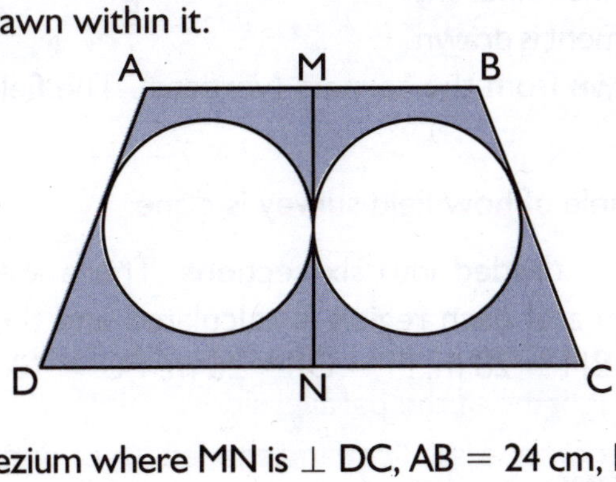

ABCD is the trapezium where MN is $\perp$ DC, AB = 24 cm, DC = 64 cm, MN = 40 cm and the radius of the circles is 14 cm.

Areas of Polygons

We have learnt to find the area of a quadrilateral (four-sided polygon) by dividing it into two triangles. We find the area of the triangles and add them to get the area of the quadrilateral. Similarly we can find the area of any polygon by dividing it into the shapes whose areas we know. We then add the different areas, calculated separately, and get the area of a polygon. The polygon may consist of a triangle, square, rectangle, trapezium, parallelogram, etc. The figures given below have been similarly divided into shapes whose areas we can calculate by appropriate formulae.

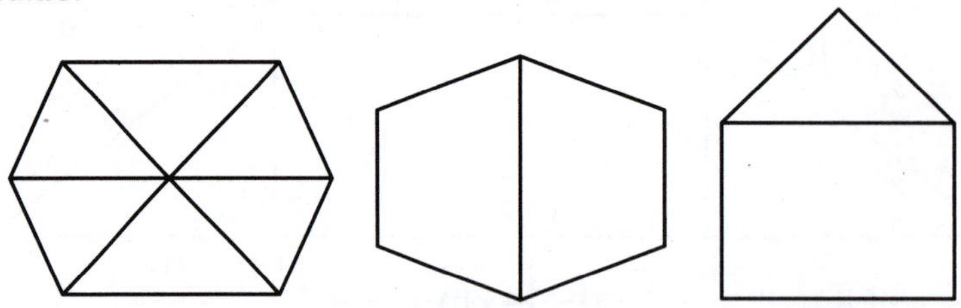

6 triangles | 2 trapeziums | 1 triangle + 1 rectangle

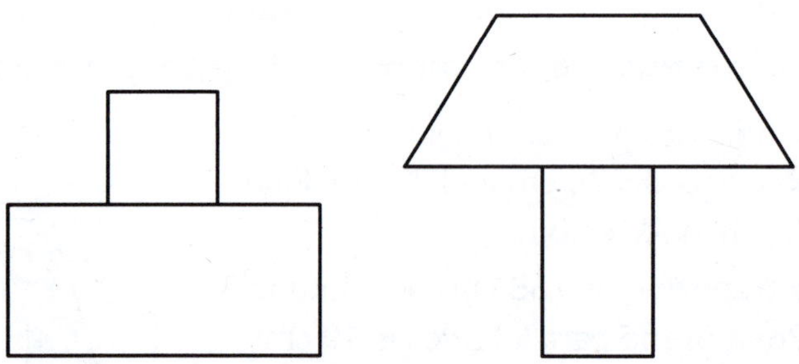

1 rectangle + 1 square | 1 trapezium + 1 rectangle

Field Survey

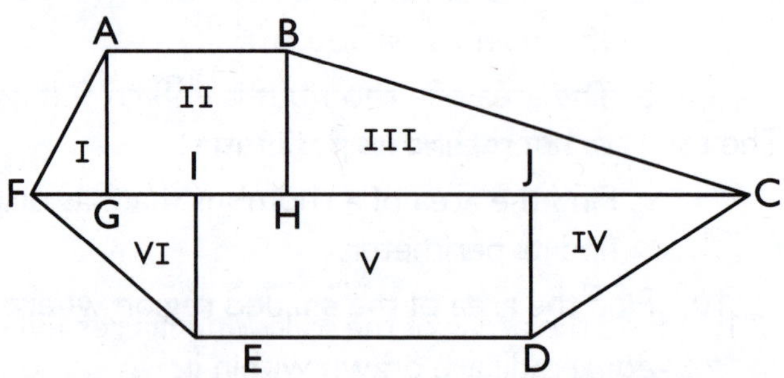

The fields owned by farmers and agriculturists are not always rectangular or square in shape. They may be in the shape of irregular polygons. To find the area of the land, it is divided into different shapes. The longest line segment is drawn and perpendiculars are drawn from the corners (vertices). The field map is drawn on paper using an appropriate scale.

The given figure is an example of how field survey is done.

The plot of land ABCDEF is divided into six sections. There are four triangular and two rectangular regions. The area of each region is calculated and then added to get the total area of the field. Let AG = BH = 28 m, EI = DJ = 26 m, FG = 10 m, GI = 6 m, IH = 20 m, HJ = 8 m, JC = 15 m.

Now, let us calculate the areas.

a. Area of $\triangle AFG = \frac{1}{2} \times FG \times AG = \frac{1}{2} \times 10 \times 28 = 140\ m^2$

b. Area of rectangle $ABHG = GH \times AG = (GI + IH) \times AG$

$$= (6 + 20) \times 28$$
$$= 26 \times 28 = 728\ m^2$$

c. Area of $\triangle BHC = \frac{1}{2} \times CH \times BH = (HJ + JC) \times BH$

$$= \frac{1}{2}(8 + 15) \times 28$$
$$= \frac{1}{\cancel{2}} \times 23 \times \overset{14}{\cancel{28}} = 322\ m^2$$

d. Area of $\triangle JCD = \frac{1}{2} \times JC \times JD$

$$= \frac{1}{\cancel{2}} \times 15 \times \overset{13}{\cancel{26}}$$
$$= 15 \times 13 = 195\ m^2$$

e. Area of rectangle $DEIJ = IJ \times JD = (IH + HJ) \times JD$

$$= (20 + 8) \times 26$$
$$= 28 \times 26 = 728\ m^2$$

f. Area of $\triangle FIE = \frac{1}{2} \times FI \times IE$

$$= \frac{1}{2}(FG + GI) \times IE$$
$$= \frac{1}{2}(10 + 6) \times 26$$
$$= \frac{1}{\cancel{2}} \times \overset{8}{\cancel{16}} \times 26$$
$$= 208\ m^2$$

The area of the plot of land = Areas a + b + c + d + e + f

$$= 140\ m^2 + 728\ m^2 + 322\ m^2 + 195\ m^2 + 728\ m^2 + 208\ m^2$$
$$= 2{,}321\ m^2$$

The total area of the plot is 2,321 m^2

Practice Exercise 14.3

1. Find the areas of the following figures (all measurements are in cm).

a.

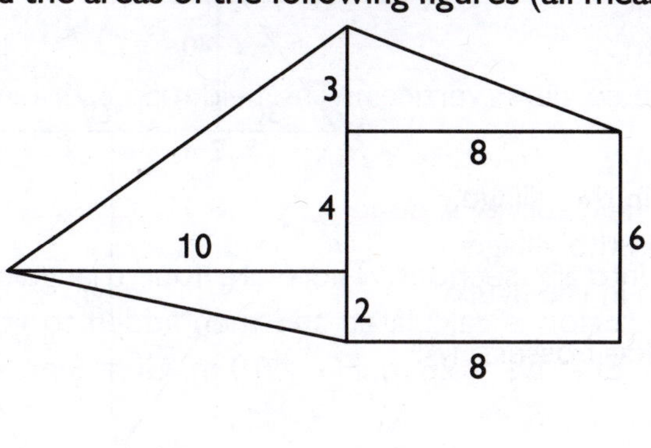

b.

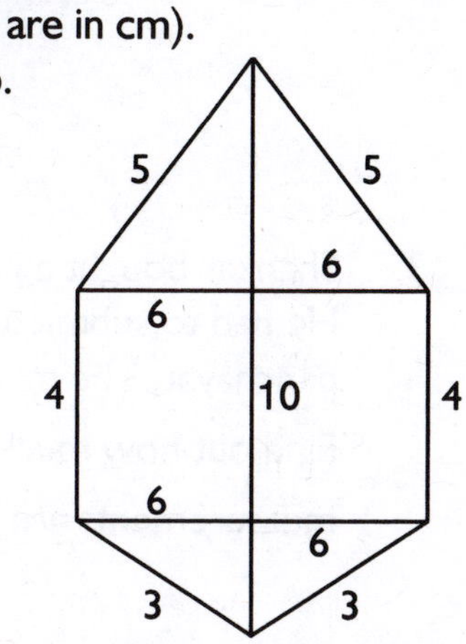

c.

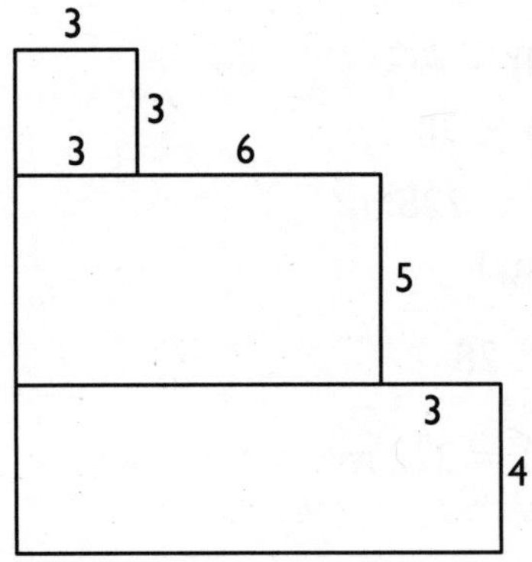

2. Find the areas of the following figures. (All measurements are in cm.)

a.

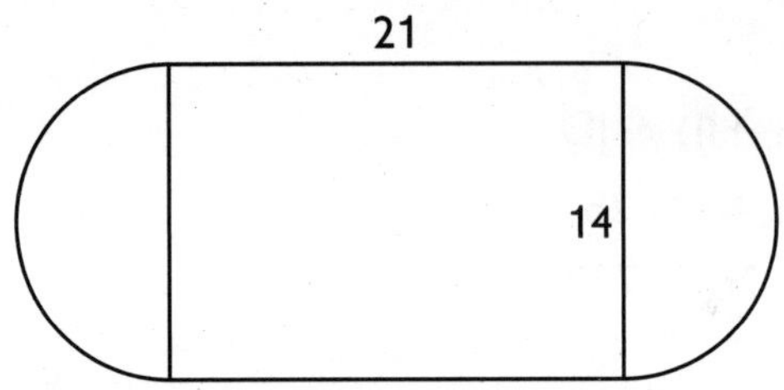

b.

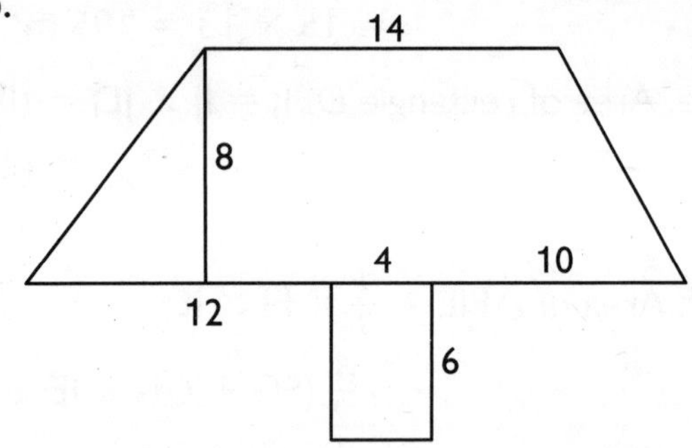

c.

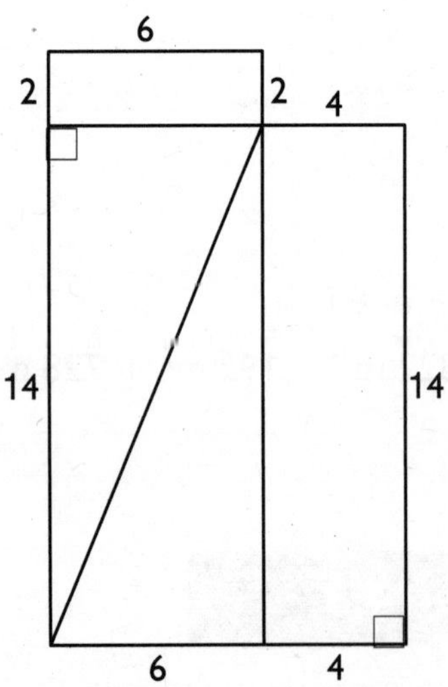

3. Shankar bought a plot of land in the village. He had to submit a field map in the village panchayat. The map is as given in the figure. Find out how much land Shankar possess. (All measurements are in m).

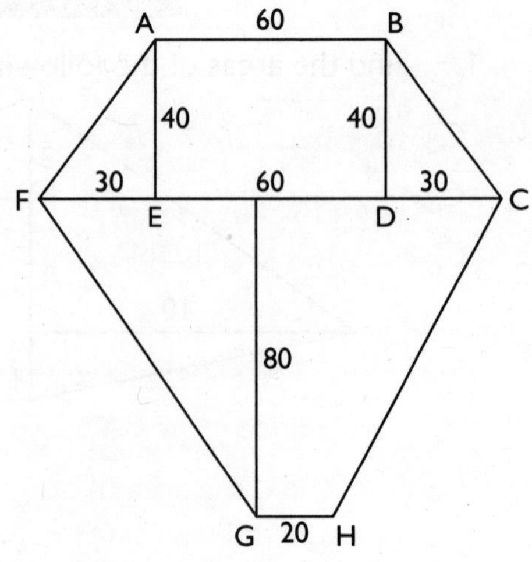

4. Ramu and Shyam are neighbours in the village. Each owns a plot of land. Each thinks his plot of land is bigger. Please help them calculate who has the bigger plot of land and by how much.

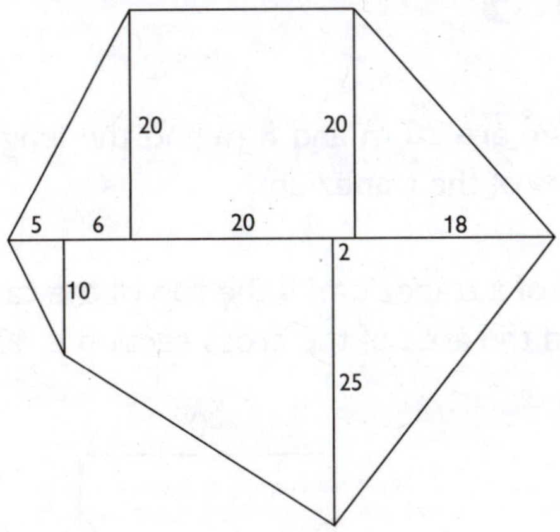

Ramu's plot

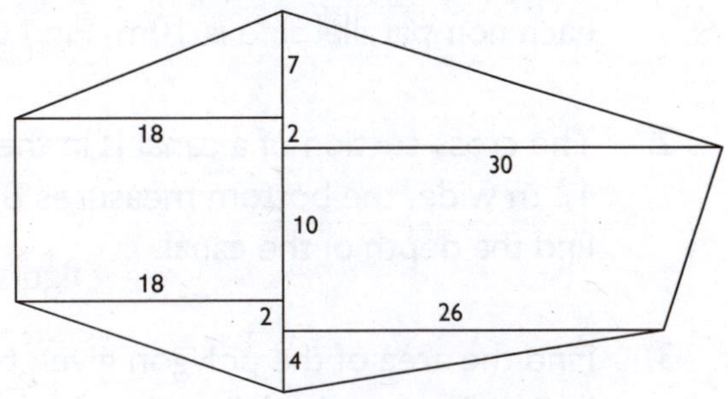

Shyam's plot

5. Beera owns an apple orchard. His plot of land is four different shapes joined together. Identify the shapes and find the total amount of land that Beera owns. (All measurements are in m).

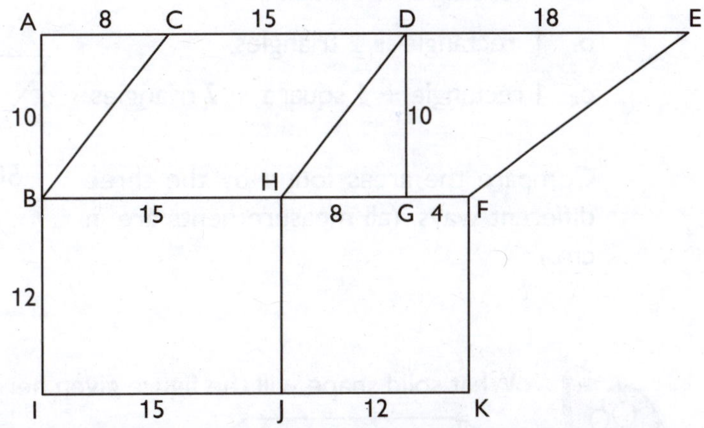

Highlights

- Area of a triangle $= \frac{1}{2} \times$ Base $\times$ Height
- Area of a parallelogram $=$ Base $\times$ Height
- Area of a circle $= \pi r^2$
- Circumference of a circle $= 2\pi r$
- Diameter of a circle $= 2r$, where r is the radius of the circle
- Area of a trapezium $= \frac{1}{2} \times$ Sum of parallel sides $\times$ Height.
- Area of a rhombus $= \frac{1}{2} \times d_1 \times d_2$, where d_1 and d_2 are the lengths of the diagonals
- Area of any quadrilateral $= \frac{1}{2} \times$ Diagonal $\times$ (Sum of the perpendicular distance from the other vertices on the diagonal)
- To find the area of polygons, we divide them into shapes whose area we can calculate using formulae.

Higher Order Thinking Skills

HOTS

1. The parallel sides of an isosceles trapezium are 20 m and 8 m and the length of each non-parallel side is 10m. Find the area of the trapezium.

2. The cross-section of a canal is in the form of a trapezium. If the top of the canal is 12 m wide, the bottom measures 8 m and the area of the cross-section is 40 m^2, find the depth of the canal.

3. Find the area of the polygon given below by dividing it in the following three ways:

   a. 1 rectangle + 1 trapezium

   b. 1 rectangle + 2 triangles

   c. 1 rectangle + 1 square + 2 triangles

   Compare the areas found by the three different ways. (all measurements are in cm.)

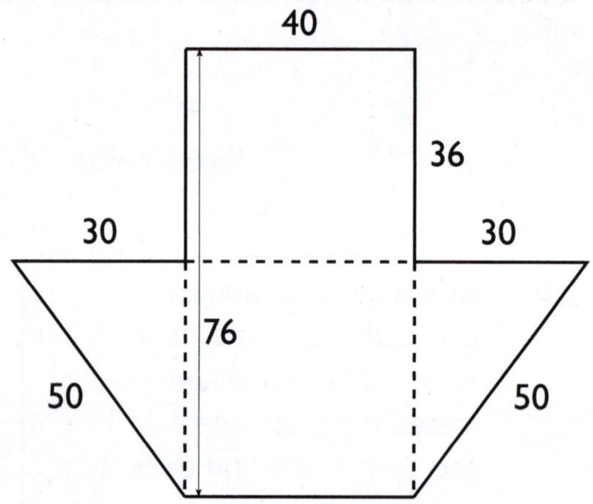

What solid shape will the figure given here form when it is folded?

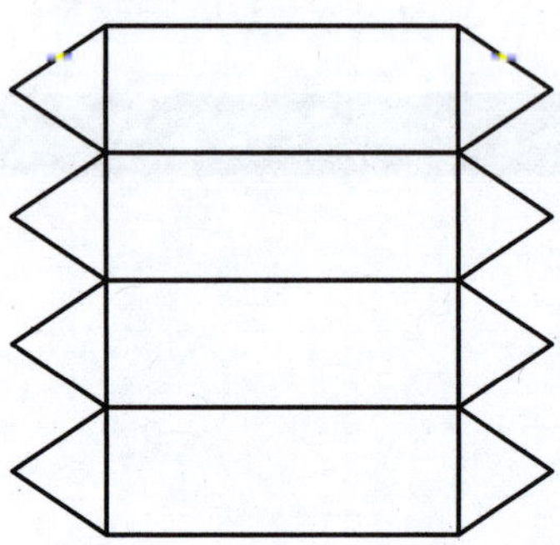

a.

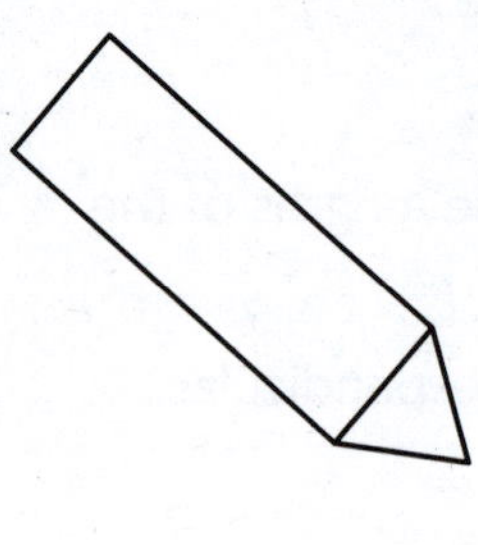

b.

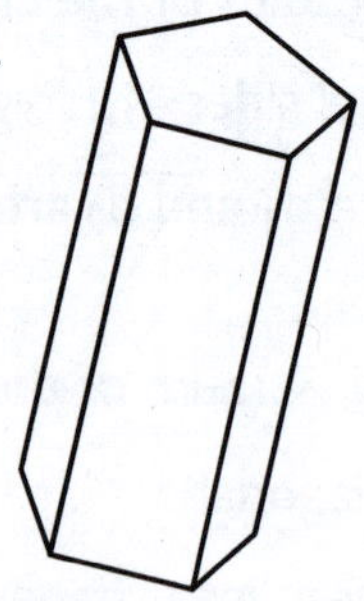

c.

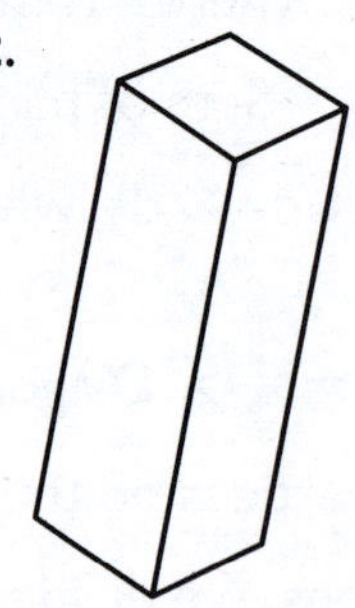

d.

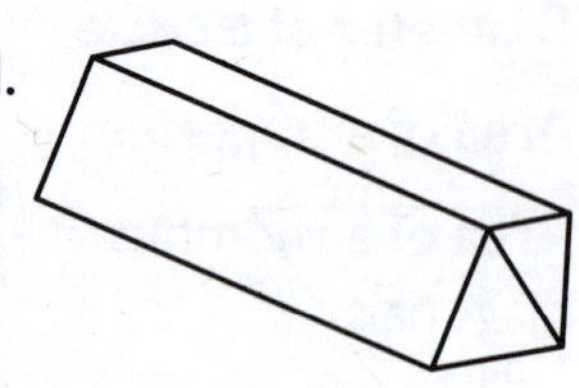

Answer for Brainteaser on page 227

Pythagorean Theorem

Aim: To determine the length of a third side of the right triangle when the measure of the other two sides is known.

Material required: a pen, chart paper, scissors, scale

Method: Draw each of the following figures on a chart paper using the dimensions provided. All measurements are in centimeters. Use a scale to measure and find the length of the unknown side. Then find the value of each unknown side using the Pythagorean formula.

1.

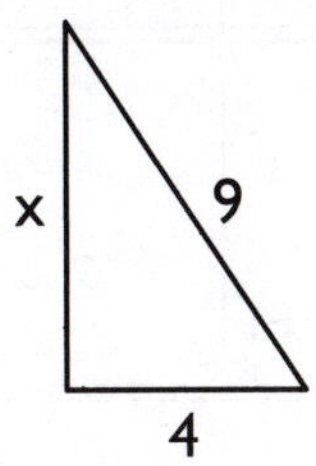

2.

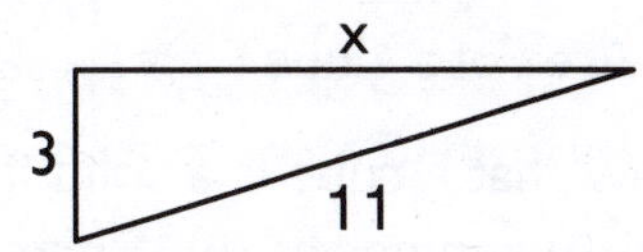

3.

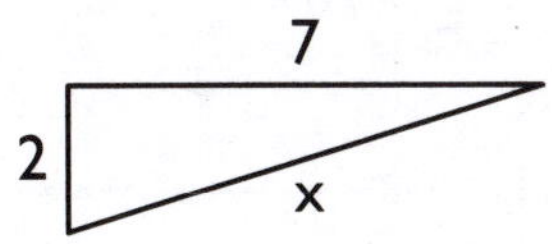

4.

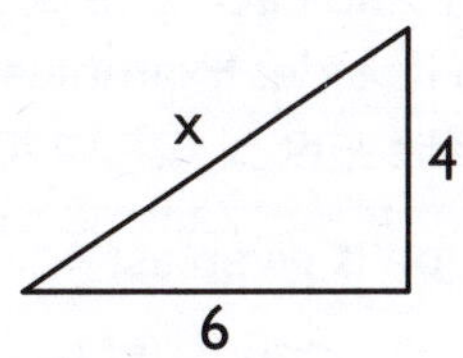

5.

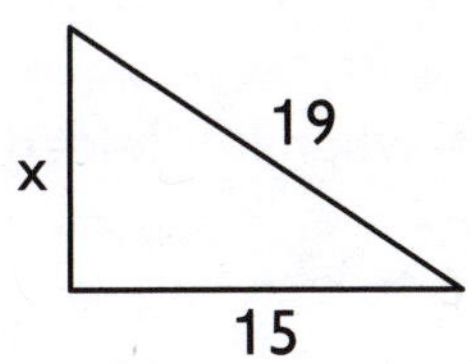

6.

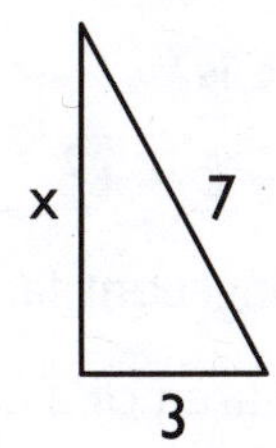

7.

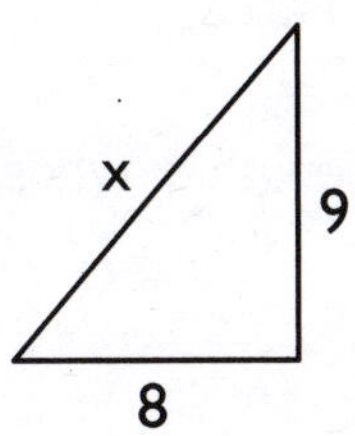

8.

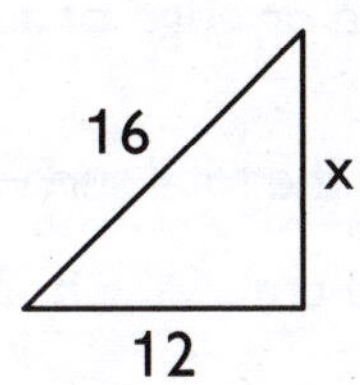

9.

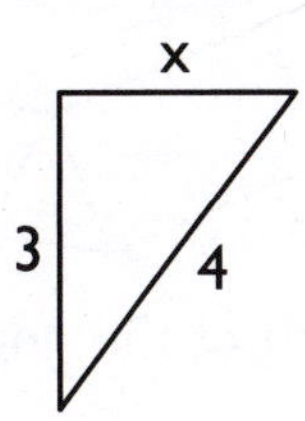

10

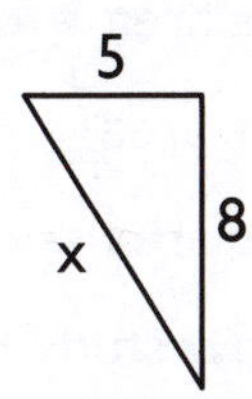

Answer for Brainteaser from page 226

Shape c

CHAPTER 15

Volume and Surface Area

Shapes, such as triangles, circles, squares, rectangles, parallelograms, trapezuims, rhombi, quadrilaterals and polygons, lie in one plane. They have only two dimensions—length and breadth. Solid shapes however, do not lie in one plane. They have three dimensions—length, breadth and height. Let us study the area and volume of 3-D figures or solid shapes. We shall study in detail the following solid shapes:

1. Cubes 2. Cuboids 3. Cylinders

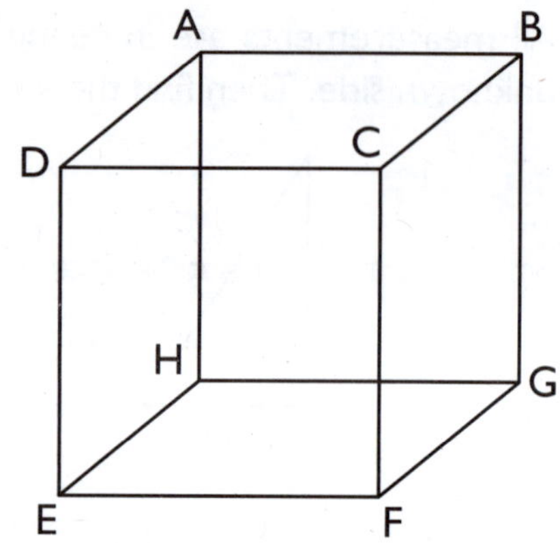

Cube

Surface Area of a Cube

We know that a cube is a solid figure that has length (ℓ), breadth (b) and height (h). Since it has three dimensions, ℓ, b and h, it is a 3-D figure. A cube has 6 faces, 12 edges and 8 vertices. The six faces of a cube are congruent and hence $\ell = b = h$ and each face is a square and each edge of a cube is called its side. Examples of a cube are: ice cubes, sugar cubes, a dice, etc.

The net of a cube is given as:

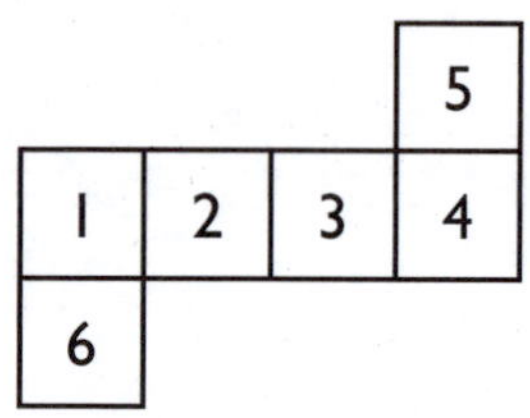

Area of a square = Side $\times$ Side

If the length of a square is ℓ

Area of a square $= \ell \times \ell = \ell^2$

Since a cube has six congruent faces, the total surface area is $6 \times \ell^2$

Thus, the total surface area of a cube $= 6\ell^2$

If we know the side or edge of a cube, we can find its total surface area.

Example 1: Find the total surface area of the following cubes the length of whose edges are:

a. 10 cm b. 20 cm c. 30 cm

We know that the surface area of a cube $= 6\ell^2$

a. Surface area $= 6 \times \ell^2 = 6 \times 10 \times 10 = 600$ cm^2

b. Surface area $= 6\ell^2 = 6 \times 20 \times 20 = 2{,}400$ cm^2

c. Surface area $= 6 \times \ell^2 = 6 \times 30 \times 30 = 5{,}400$ cm^2

Let us now study the relationship between the length of the edge of a cube and its surface area.

Let us take the cubes studied is Example 1.

	Length of edge	Surface area
Cube A	10 cm	600 cm^2
Cube B	20 cm	2,400 cm^2
Cube C	30 cm	5,400 cm^2

We see that:

$$\frac{\text{Edge of cube A}}{\text{Edge of cube C}} = \frac{\text{Surface area of A}}{\text{Surface area of C}}$$

$$\frac{10}{30} = \frac{600}{5400}$$

$$\frac{1}{3} = \frac{1}{9}$$

If the edge of the cube is increased three times or trebled, the surface area increases nine times.

If the edge of the cube is increase five times, the surface area increases 25 times.

Hence, we can generalise and say that if the edge of a cube is increased 'n' times, its surface area will increase n^2 times

If we know the surface area of a cube, we can find its side or edge.

Example 2: The surface area of a cube is 2,646 cm^2. Find its side.

We know that the surface area of a cube is $6\ell^2$

So, $6\ell^2 = 2646$

$$\therefore \ell^2 = \frac{2646}{6} = 441 \text{ cm}^2$$

$$\ell^2 = 441 \text{ cm}^2$$

$$\ell = \sqrt{441}$$

$$\ell = 21 \text{ cm}$$

The length of the edge is 21 cm.

Alert!

1. The length, breadth and height of a cube are the same.
2. If the edge of a cube is increased 'n' times, its surface area increases 'n^2' times.

Volume of a Cube

The measure of the space occupied by a solid shape is called its volume. The space occupied by a cube of edge 1 cm is called a cubic centimetre and is written as 1 cm^3. This is the standard unit of volume.

Volume of a cube = Length × Breadth × Height

However, in a cube, $\ell = b = h$

$\therefore$ Volume of a cube $= \ell \times \ell \times \ell$

Volume $= \ell^3$

Example 1: Find the volume of a cube whose edge is 10 cm.

$V = \ell^3 = \ell \times \ell \times \ell$
$V = 10 \times 10 \times 10 = 1{,}000 \text{ cm}^3$
Volume is $1{,}000 \text{ cm}^3$

Example 2: Find the volume of a cube whose edge is 20 cm.

$V = \ell^3 = \ell \times \ell \times \ell$
$V = 20 \times 20 \times 20 = 8{,}000 \text{ cm}^3$
Volume is $8{,}000 \text{ cm}^3$

From these examples we see that if the side of a cube is doubled, its volume is increased eight times.

In general, if the side of a cube is increased n times its volumes increases n^3 times.

Let us compare the units of length, surface area and volume.

Units of Length	Units of Surface Area	Units of Volume
1 cm = 10 mm	$1 \text{ cm}^2 = (10 \times 10) \text{ mm}^2 = 100 \text{ mm}^2$	$1 \text{ cm}^3 = (10 \times 10 \times 10) \text{ mm}^3 = 1000 \text{ mm}^3 = 1 \text{ m}\ell$
1 dm = 10 cm	$1 \text{ dm}^2 = (10 \times 10) \text{ cm}^2 = 100 \text{ cm}^2$	$1 \text{ dm}^3 = (10 \times 10 \times 10) \text{ cm}^3 = 1000 \text{ cm}^3 = 1\ \ell$
1 m = 10 dm	$1 \text{ m}^2 = (10 \times 10) \text{ dm}^2 = 100 \text{ dm}^2$	$1 \text{ m}^3 = (10 \times 10 \times 10) \text{ dm}^3 = 1000\ \ell$
1 m = 100 cm	$1 \text{ m}^2 = (100 \times 100) \text{ cm}^2 = 1000 \text{ cm}^2 =$ 1 hectare	$1 \text{ m}^3 = (100 \times 100 \times 100) \text{ cm}^3 = 10^6 \text{ cm}^3 = 1 \text{ k}\ell$

Example 1: Find the surface area and volume of a cube whose edge is 7 cm.

$$\text{Surface area of the cube} = 6\ \ell^2 = 6 \times 7 \times 7 = 294 \text{ cm}^2$$

$$\text{Volume of the cube} = \ell^3 = 7 \times 7 \times 7 = 343 \text{ cm}^3$$

Example 2: The surface area of a cube is 864 cm^2. Find its volume.

$$\text{Surface area of a cube} = 6\ \ell^2$$
$$864 = 6 \times \ell^2$$
$$\therefore \ell^2 = \frac{864}{6} = 144 \text{ cm}^2$$
$$\therefore \ell = \sqrt{144} = 12 \text{ cm}$$

$$\text{Volume of the cube} = \ell^3 = 12 \times 12 \times 12 = 1{,}728 \text{ cm}^3$$

Example 3: The volume of a cube is 512 m^3. It is to be painted at the rate of ₹10 per m^2. Find the cost of painting the cube.

Volume of the cube $= \ell^3$

$\therefore 512 = \ell^3$

$\therefore \ell = \sqrt[3]{512} = 8$ m

Now, the edge of the cube is 8 m.

Hence, the surface area of the cube $= 6\ell^2$

$= 6 \times 8 \times 8$

$= 6 \times 64$

$= 384\ m^2$

Cost of painting is ₹10 per m^2

Cost of painting 384 m^2 = ₹3,840

The cost of painting the cube is ₹3,840.

Example 4: A brass cube with length 15 cm is melted and made into smaller cubes each with edge 5 cm. How many such small brass cubes can be made?

Volume of the cube $= \ell^3$

Volume of the large cube $= 15 \times 15 \times 15$

Volume of the smaller cube $= 5 \times 5 \times 5$

Number of the smaller cubes $= \dfrac{\text{Volume of the large cube}}{\text{Volume of the smaller cube}}$

$= \dfrac{\overset{3}{\cancel{15}} \times \overset{3}{\cancel{15}} \times \overset{3}{\cancel{15}}}{\cancel{5} \times \cancel{5} \times \cancel{5}}$

$= 27$ cubes

Example 5: The edge of a cubical water tank is 3 m. How many kilolitres of water can it store?

Volume of a cube $= \ell^3$

Volume of the water tank $= \ell \times \ell \times \ell$

$= 3 \times 3 \times 3$

$= 27\ m^3$

We know that 1 m^3 = 1,000 ℓ

$\therefore 27\ m^3 = 27{,}000\ \ell$

1 kilolitre = 1,000 ℓ.

$\therefore 27{,}000\ \ell = 27\ k\ell$

The tank can store 27 $k\ell$ of water.

Practice Exercise 15.1

1. Find the surface area of the following cubes, the length of whose edges are listed below.

   a. 5 cm　　b. 8 cm　　c. 2.5 cm　　d. 11 cm　　e. 3.4 cm

2. Find the volume of a cube whose edge measures:

a. 6 cm b. 9 cm c. 10.5 cm d. 2.2 cm e. 11 cm

3. Find the length of the edge of a cube whose surface area is:

a. 3,750 cm^2 b. 5,400 cm^2 c. 1,944 cm^2 d. 29,400 cm^2 e. 3,174 cm^2

4. Find the length of the edge of a cube whose volume is:

a. 1,331 cm^3 b. 3,375 cm^3 c. 19,683 cm^3 d. 64,000 cm^3 e. 1 ℓ

5. A cubical box with edge 20 cm is filled with smaller cubes of sides 5 cm each. How many of these small cubes can fit into the larger box?

6. A hundred cubical cardboard boxes are required in a jewellery shop. The length of the edge of each box must measure 15 cm. How many cardboard sheets of size 30 cm × 30 cm will be required to make these boxes?

7. A tin sheet of size 45 cm by 30 cm was used to make 25 identical cubical boxes. The edge of each box measured 3 cm. How much of the tin sheet was left?

8. A cubical tank with edge 4 m is filled with water. How many litres of water are there in the tank? If 4 buckets of 15 ℓ each are filled from the water tank, how much water will be left?

9. 25 identical cubical wooden blocks are to be painted on all sides. If the total cost of painting at the rate of ₹12 per cm^2 is ₹1,29,600, find the measure of the edge of one wooden block.

10. The weight of 100 cm^3 of wood is 8 g. What will be the weight in kg of a cubical wooden box of length 80 cm?

Surface Area of a Cuboid

A cuboid is a solid 3-D figure that has length, breadth and height. A cuboid has 6 faces, 12 edges and 8 vertices. The opposite faces of a cuboid are congruent. Each face is rectangular.

In the cuboid given alongside,

Faces ABCD and EFGH are congruent $= \ell \times b$

Faces BCFH and ADEG are congruent $= b \times h$

Faces ABHG and EFCD are congruent $= \ell \times h$

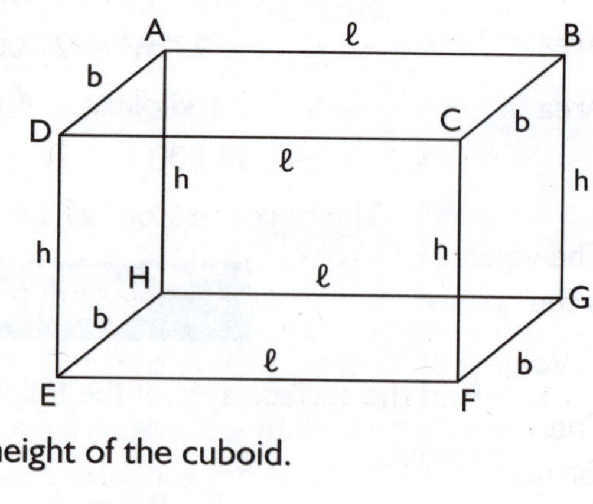

Thus, the sum of the 6 faces of a cuboid is
$2(\ell \times b) + 2(\ell \times h) + 2(b \times h)$

Surface area of a cuboid $= 2\ell b + 2\ell h + 2bh$
$= 2(\ell b + \ell h + bh)$

where ℓ is the length, b is the breadth and h is the height of the cuboid.

The net of a cuboid can be drawn as:

Area of rectangle 1
$= \text{Area of rectangle } 6 = b \times h$

Area of rectangle 2
$= \text{Area of rectangle } 4 = \ell \times h$

Area of rectangle 3
$= \text{Area of rectangle } 5 = b \times \ell$

Sum of rectangles
$(1 + 2 + 3 + 4 + 5 + 6)$
$= 2(\ell b + \ell h + bh)$

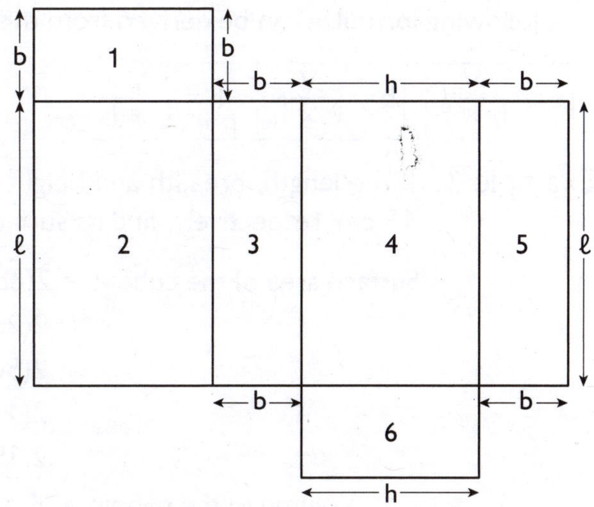

Surface area of a cuboid
$= 2(\ell b + \ell h + bh)$

If the length, breadth and height of a cuboid are, 12 cm, 8 cm and 5 cm, respectively, its surface area will be:

$= 2(12 \times 8 + 12 \times 5 + 8 \times 5)$

$= 2(96 + 60 + 40)$

$= 2 \times 196$

$= 392 \text{ cm}^2$

Surface Area of the Four Walls of a Room

A room can be compared to a cuboid shape since it has walls with dimensions of length, breadth and height. The four walls of a room can have different sizes, but the height remains the same. The two walls facing each other have the same length and height. Hence, if the length and breadth of a room are different, the larger walls will have their area as $\ell \times h$ and the shorter walls will have their area as $b \times h$.

Thus, the area of the four walls of a room are:

$= 2\,\ell h + 2bh$

$= 2h(\ell + b)$

$= 2(\ell + b) \times h$

Area of the four walls = Perimeter of the room × Height of the room

Area of the floor = Area of the ceiling = $\ell \times b$

Volume of a Cuboid

The volume of a cuboid is the space occupied by the solid figure. The capacity of the cuboid is the quantity of matter that it can hold.

Volume of a cuboid $= \ell \times b \times h$ or $V = \ell \times b \times h$.

There are four quantities, length (ℓ), breadth (b), height (h) and volume (v), related by the formula. If any three of the variables are known, the fourth variable can be calculated using the formula $V = \ell \times b \times h$.

The following formulae can be derived from this basic formula:

$\ell = \frac{V}{b \times h}$ $b = \frac{V}{\ell \times h}$ $h = \frac{V}{\ell \times b}$

Example 1: If the length, breadth and height of a cuboid are given as 25 cm, 20 cm and 15 cm, respectively, find its surface area and volume.

$$\begin{aligned}\text{Surface area of the cuboid} &= 2(\ell b + \ell h + bh)\\ &= 2(25 \times 20 + 25 \times 15 + 20 \times 15)\\ &= 2(500 + 375 + 300)\\ &= 2(1175)\\ &= 2{,}350 \text{ cm}^2\end{aligned}$$

$$\begin{aligned}\text{Volume of the cuboid} &= \ell \times b \times h\\ &= 25 \times 20 \times 15\\ &= 7{,}500 \text{ cm}^3\end{aligned}$$

The surface area of the cuboid is 2,350 cm^2 and its volume is 7,500 cm^3.

Example 2: The volume of a cuboid is 550 cm^3. If its length is 11 cm and breadth is 5 cm, find its height and total surface area.

$$h = \frac{V}{11 \times 5} = \frac{550}{11 \times 5} = 10 \text{ cm}$$

$$\begin{aligned}\text{Surface area} &= 2(\ell b + \ell h + bh)\\ &= 2(11 \times 5 + 11 \times 10 + 5 \times 10)\\ &= 2(55 + 110 + 50)\\ &= 2(215)\\ &= 430 \text{ cm}^2\end{aligned}$$

The height of the cuboid is 10 cm and its total surface area is 430 cm^2.

Example 3: The length, breadth and height of a school auditorium are 20 m, 15 m and 10 m, respectively. Find the cost of painting the four walls at the rate of ₹750 per m^2.

$$\begin{aligned}\text{Area of the four walls} &= \text{Perimeter of the room} \times \text{Height}\\ &= 2(\ell + b) \times h\\ &= 2(20 + 15) \times 10\\ &= 2(35) \times 10\\ &= 70 \times 10\\ &= 700 \text{ m}^2\end{aligned}$$

Cost of painting the four walls = 700 × 750 = ₹5,25,000

The cost of painting the school auditorium is ₹5,25,000.

Example 4: A cuboidal water tank with dimensions 8 m × 5 m × 3 m is filled with water. How much water is there in the cuboidal tank? If the water is shifted to a cubical tank of edge 4 m, how much water is shifted to the cubical tank and how much water is left in the cuboidal tank? Give the answer in litres and kilolitres.

Volume of a cuboid = $\ell \times b \times h$

Volume of water in the cuboidal tank is = 8 m × 5 m × 3 m

= 120 m^3

Volume = 120 × 1000 ℓ

= 120000 ℓ

= 120 kℓ (1 kℓ = 1,000 ℓ)

Volume of a cube = ℓ^3

Volume of water shifted to the cubical tank = 4 × 4 × 4

= 64 m^3

= 64,000 ℓ (as 1m^3 = 1,000 ℓ)

= 64 kℓ

Water remaining in the cuboidal tank = 1,20,000 ℓ – 64,000 ℓ

= 56,000 ℓ

= 56 kℓ

The volume of water originally in the cuboidal tank was 120 kℓ. Water left in the tank is 56 kℓ.

Example 5: Four cubes each with 12 cm edge are joined end to end. Find the surface area of the resulting cuboid.

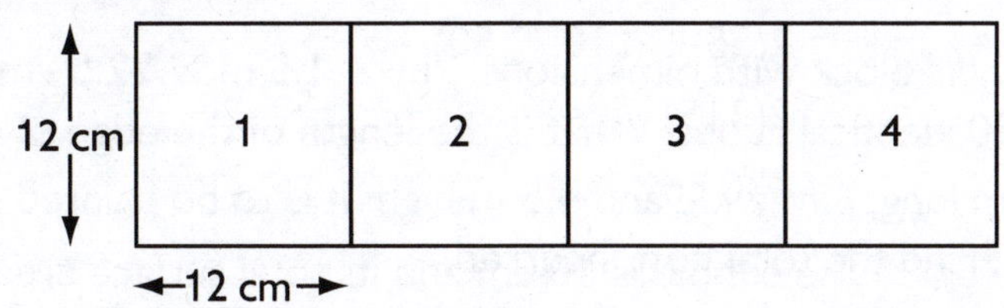

If cubes are joined end to end, the length is increased while the breadth and height remain the same.

length = 4 × 12 = 48 cm, breadth = 12 cm, height = 12 cm

The surface are of the cuboid formed = 2(48 × 12 + 48 × 12 + 12 × 12)

= 2(576 + 576 + 144)

= 2(1296)

= 2,592 cm^2

Practice Exercise 15.2

1. Find the total surface area of the cuboids with the following dimensions.

a. ℓ = 10 cm	b = 8 cm	h = 6 cm
b. ℓ = 1 m	b = 50 cm	h = 25 cm

c. $\ell = 12.5$ cm b = 9.5 cm h = 8 cm
d. $\ell = 8.5$ cm b = 6 cm h = 4.5 cm
e. $\ell = 30$ cm b = 20 cm h = 15 cm

2. Find the volume of the cuboids whose dimensions are as follows:
   a. $\ell = 22$ cm b = 15 cm h = 10 cm
   b. $\ell = 15$ m b = 5 cm h = 8 dm
   c. $\ell = 2$ m b = 75 cm h = 50 dm
   d. $\ell = 10.5$ cm b = 8.5 cm h = 5 cm
   e. $\ell = 12$ cm b = 6 cm h = 3 cm
3. Find the missing dimensions of the cuboids given below:
   a. $V = 4{,}800\ cm^3$ $\ell = x$ b = 15 cm h = 5 cm
   b. $V = 1{,}920\ cm^3$ $\ell = 16$ cm b = x h = 10 cm
   c. $V = 440\ cm^3$ $\ell = 11$ cm b = 5 cm h = x
   d. V = x $\ell = 15$ cm b = 9 cm h = 4 cm
   e. $V = 74{,}088\ cm^3$ $\ell = 63$ cm b = x h = 21 cm
4. Find the number of 6 cm cubes that can be cut out of a piece of wood with dimensions 18 cm × 15 cm × 8 cm.
5. A tank with dimensions 8 m × 5 m × 3 m is filled with water. Find the volume of water in litres and in kilolitres.
6. How many persons can be accommodated in a hall of length 16 m, breadth 12.5 m and height 4.5 m assuming that $3.6\ m^3$ of space is required for each person?
7. A metal cuboidal block with dimensions 2 m × 1.5 m × 22.5 cm is melted and made into 200 identical cubes. What is the length of the edge of each cube?
8. A room is 8 m long, 6 m wide and 4.5 m high. It is to be painted at the rate of ₹550 per m^2. Find the total cost incurred.
9. The dimensions of a rectangular box are in the ratio 5 : 4 : 2. Its total surface area is $7{,}600\ cm^2$. Find the dimensions of the box and also its volume.
10. How many planks of size 2 m × 25 cm × 8 cm can be made from a wooden block of dimensions 5 m × 70 cm × 32 cm, assuming there is no wastage?

Surface Area of a Right Circular Cylinder

Cylindrical shapes are a common feature in everyday life. A gas cylinder, chalk, a pen, pencil and many other articles are cylindrical in shape.

A cylinder has three surfaces—the lateral curved surface and the two circular faces at the top and bottom of the cylinder. The line segment that joins the centre points of the top and bottom faces (or the circular faces) is called the axis of the cylinder.

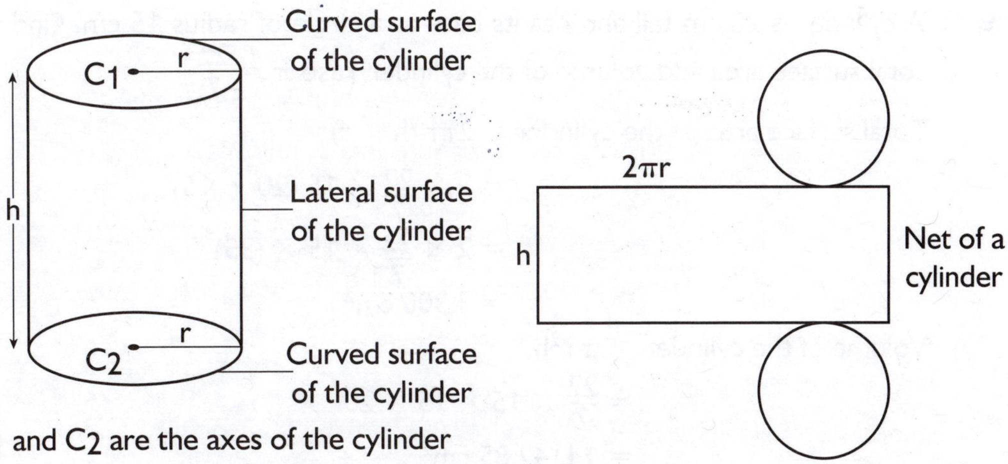

C1 and C2 are the axes of the cylinder

A right circular cylinder has:

1. A top and bottom face (i.e., two circular faces) that are in parallel planes and are congruent.
2. An axis that is perpendicular to the two circular faces.
3. A curved surface that is perpendicular to the circular bases (top and bottom).

Since a cylinder has three faces, the total surface area of the cylinder is the sum of the areas of these three faces—the lateral surface area and the two circular faces.

The lateral surface area of a cylinder is the area of the rectangle shown in the net of the cylinder. The breadth of this rectangle is the height of the cylinder.

The length of this rectangle will be the circumference of the bottom circle which is $2\pi r$, where r is the radius of the circle. Hence, area of the lateral surface $= 2\pi rh$

The area of the circular faces that form the bases are equal, because they are congruent. The area of the circular face is πr^2, where r is the radius.

Area of both the circular faces $= 2\pi r^2$

$\therefore$ The total surface area of a right circular cylinder = The area of the lateral surface + The area of two circular faces (or bases).

$\therefore$ Total surface area of a cylinder $= 2\pi rh + 2\pi r^2$.

$$= 2\pi r\,(h + r)$$

If the cylinder is an open cylinder (for example, a pipe), then the surface area of a cylinder is only the lateral surface area or curved surface area.

Surface area of an open cylinder $= 2\pi rh$

Volume of a Cylinder

The base of a cylinder is a circle. Hence, if we consider the cylinder to be made up of circular discs and we add the area of each disc, then if there are 'h' such disc, the volume of a cylinder $= \pi r^2 \times h$.

Thus, volume of a cylinder = area of the base × height

$$= \pi r^2 \times h$$
$$= \pi r^2 h$$

Example 1: A cylinder is 20 cm tall and has its base as a circle of radius 15 cm. Find the total surface area and volume of the cylinder $\left(\text{use } \pi = \frac{22}{7}\right)$

Total surface area of the cylinder $= 2\pi r\,(h + r)$

$$= 2 \times \frac{22}{7} \times 15\,(20 + 15)$$

$$= 2 \times \frac{22}{\cancel{7}_1} \times 15 \times (\cancel{35}^{5})$$

$$= 3{,}300 \text{ cm}^2$$

Volume of the cylinder $= \pi\, r^2 h$

$$= \frac{22}{7} \times 15 \times 15 \times 20$$

$$= 14142.85 \text{ cm}^2$$

The surface area of the cylinder is 3,300 cm^2 and its volume is 14142.85 cm^2.

Example 2: The height of a cylinder is 15 cm and the curved surface area is 660 cm^2. Find its radius, total surface area and volume.

Curved surface area of the cylinder $= 2\pi rh$

$$660 = 2 \times \frac{22}{7} \times r \times 15$$

$$\therefore r = \frac{660 \times 7}{2 \times 22 \times 15}$$

$$= 7 \text{ cm}$$

Total surface area of the cylinder $= 2\pi r(h + r)$

$$= 2 \times \frac{22}{7} \times 7\,(15 + 7)$$

$$= 2 \times 22 \times 22$$

$$= 968 \text{ cm}^2$$

Volume of the cylinder $= \pi r^2 h$

$$= \frac{22}{7} \times 7 \times 7 \times 15$$

$$= 2{,}310 \text{ cm}^3$$

The radius of the cylinder measures 7 cm. Its surface area is 968 cm^2 and its volume is 2,310 cm^3.

Example 3: A cylindrical tin has a height of 20 cm. The radius of its base is 21 cm. It is open at the top. Find the cost of painting it from outside at ₹5 per cm^2.

Since the tin is open at the top, the surface to be painted is the lateral or curved surface area and the area of the bottom.

The lateral or curved surface area $= 2\pi rh$

$$= 2 \times \frac{22}{7} \times 21 \times 20$$

$$= 6 \times 22 \times 20$$

$$= 132 \times 20$$

$$= 2{,}640 \text{ cm}^2$$

Area of the bottom $= \pi r^2$

$= \frac{22}{7} \times 21 \times 21$

$= 66 \times 21$

$= 1,386 \text{ cm}^2$

Total area to be painted $= 2640 + 1386$

$= 4,026 \text{ cm}^2$

Cost of painting $= 4,026 \times 5$

$=$ ₹20,130

The cost of painting the tin is ₹20,130.

Example 4: A rectangular sheet of paper 88 cm × 15 cm is rolled along its length and a cylinder is formed. Find the volume of the cylinder.

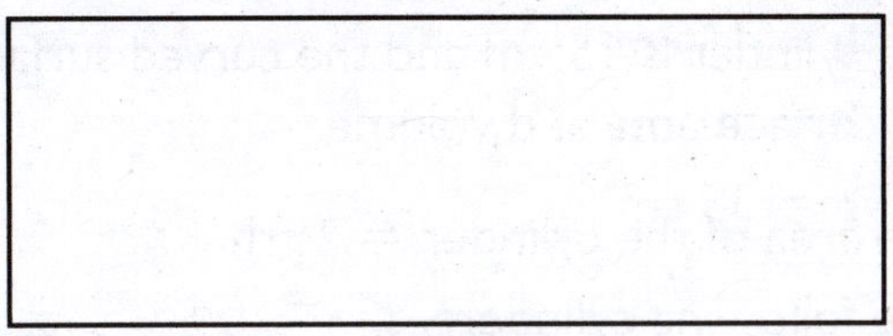

The length of the paper is 88 cm. This will be the circumference of the cylinder.

Circumference $= 2\pi r$

$88 = 2 \times \frac{22}{7} \times r$

$\frac{88 \times 7}{2 \times 22} = r$

$14 \text{ cm} = r$

The height of the cylinder is 15 cm.

Volume of the cylinder $= \pi r^2 h$

$V = \frac{22}{7} \times 14 \times 14 \times 15$

$V = 44 \times 210$

$V = 9,240 \text{ cm}^3$

The volume of the cylinder is $9,240 \text{ cm}^3$.

Example 5: Find the area covered by a roadroller in 50 revolutions if its diameter is 140 cm and its width is 120 cm. Convert the area into m^2.

When a roadroller moves, it covers an area equal to its lateral surface area in revolutions.

Lateral surface area $= 2\pi rh$

$= 2 \times \frac{22}{7} \times 70 \times 120$

$= 2 \times 22 \times 10 \times 120$

$= 44 \times 1200$

$= 52,800 \text{ cm}^2$

The area covered in 1 revolution is 52,800 cm^2.

The area covered in 50 revolutions is $52800 \times 50 = 2{,}64{,}000$ cm^2.

The area covered in m^2 is $= \dfrac{26400}{100 \times 100} \times 100$

$= 26.4$ m^2.

The area covered is 26.4 m^2.

Practice Exercise 15.3

1. Find the total surface area of the following cylinders. $\left(\text{use } \pi = \frac{22}{7}\right)$

   (r = radius; h = height)

   a. r = 7 cm h = 12 cm

   b. r = 14 cm h = 20 cm

   c. r = 3.5 cm h = 15 cm

   d. r = 21 cm h = 40 cm

   e. r = 28 cm h = 35 cm

2. Find the volume of the following cylinders. $\left(\text{use } \pi = \frac{22}{7}\right)$

   (r = radius; h = height)

   a. r = 7 cm h = 10 cm

   b. r = 10.5 cm h = 20 cm

   c. r = 5 cm h = 14 cm

   d. r = 6 cm h = 28 cm

   e. r = 2.5 m h = 3.5 m

3. Find the volume of a right circular cylinder whose curved (lateral) surface area is 2,640 cm^2 and the circumference of the base is 66 cm.
4. Find the depth of a cylindrical water tank whose capacity is 1,848 m^3 and the diameter of whose base is 14 m.
5. A circular pit with diameter 2 m is dug to a depth of 14 m. What is the volume of earth dug out?
6. Find the cost of painting four cylindrical pillars of a school building at ₹25 per square meter if the diameter and height of each pillar are 7 m and 12 m, respectively.
7. The diameter of a roadroller 1m 40 cm long is 80 cm. It takes 500 revolutions to level a playground. Find the cost of levelling the ground at ₹6 per m^2.
8. A metal cylinder with height 10 cm and diameter of base 70 cm is melted to make smaller cylinders of radius 7 cm and height 2 cm. How many small cylinders can be made?
9. Water from a cylindrical water tank of height 16 m and a base with a diameter of 7 m is emptied into a cuboidal tank of dimensions 14 m × 11 m. Find the height of water in the cuboidal tank?
10. Which has a greater volume, a cylinder of height 21 cm and a base of radius 10 cm or a cube with an edge measuring 19 cm? By how much is it greater?

Highlights

- Surface area of a cube is $6\ \ell^2$, where ℓ is the length of the edge.
- Volume of a cube $= \ell^3$, where ℓ is the length of the edge.
- $1\ m\ell = 1\ cm^3$, 1 litre (ℓ) $= 1{,}000\ cm^3$, 1 kilolitre ($k\ell$) $= 1{,}000$ litres $= 1\ m^3$
- Surface area of a cuboid $= 2\ (\ell b + \ell h + bh)$ where ℓ is length, b is breadth and h is height of the cuboid.
- Volume of a cuboid $= \ell \times b \times h$ (where ℓ is length, b is breadth and h is height).
- Surface area of the four walls of a room = Perimeter of room $\times$ height $= 2(\ell + b) \times h$ (where ℓ is length, b is breadth and h is height).
- The line segment that joins the centres of the top and bottom faces of a cylinder is called the axis of the cylinder.
- In a right circular cylinder, the axis is perpendicular to the two circular bases (top and bottom).
- Surface area of a cylinder $= 2\pi(h + r)$ where h is the height of the cylinder and r is the radius of the base.
- Volume of a cylinder $= \pi r^2 h$ (where r is the radius of the base and h is the height of the cylinder).

Higher Order Thinking Skills

HOTS

1. Find the number of coins, each of radius 0.75 cm and thickness 0.2 cm, that should be melted to make a right circular cylinder of height 8 cm and a base of radius 3 cm.

2. A tin sheet is rectangular in shape and measures 48 m $\times$ 36 m. From each of its corners, a square of length 8 m is cutout, so as to make an open box. Find the volume of the open box.

3. Find the volume of a cuboid whose breadth is half of its length and height is double its length.

Maths Lab Activity

Aim: To determine volume and surface area in rectangular solids.

Material required: a pen

Method: To find the volume and surface area using the formulae:

Surface area of a rectangular solid = 2 × (Area of side 1 + Area of side 2 + Area of side 3)

Volume of a rectangular solid = Length × Breadth × Height

1. 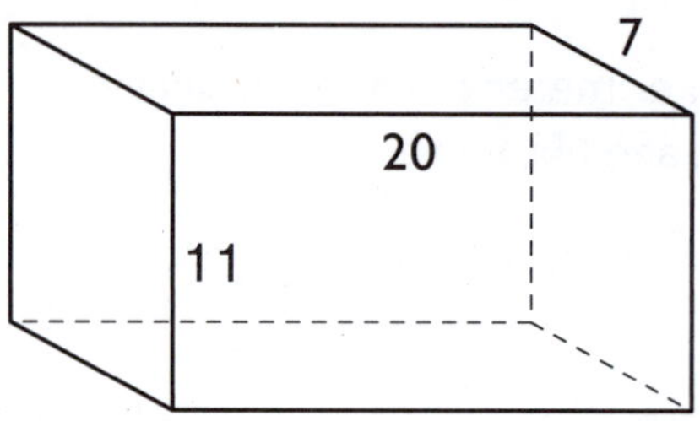

Surface area =
Volume =

2. 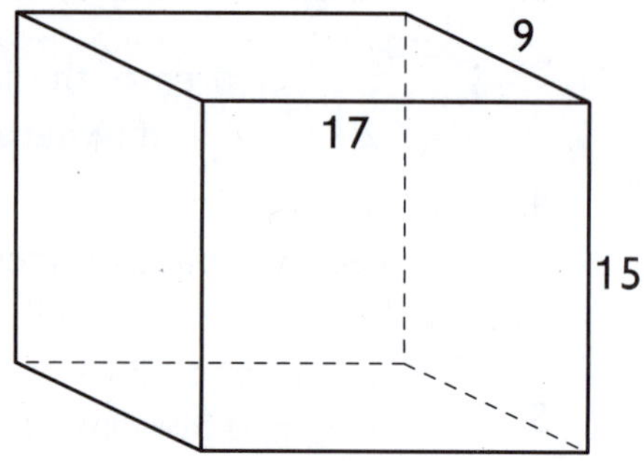

Surface area =
Volume =

3. 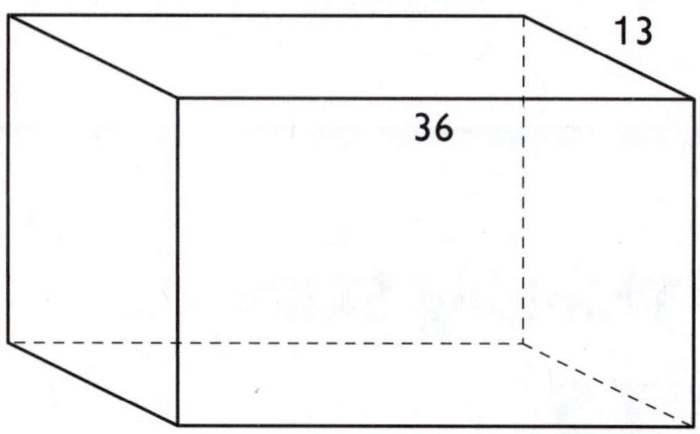

Surface area =
Volume =

4. 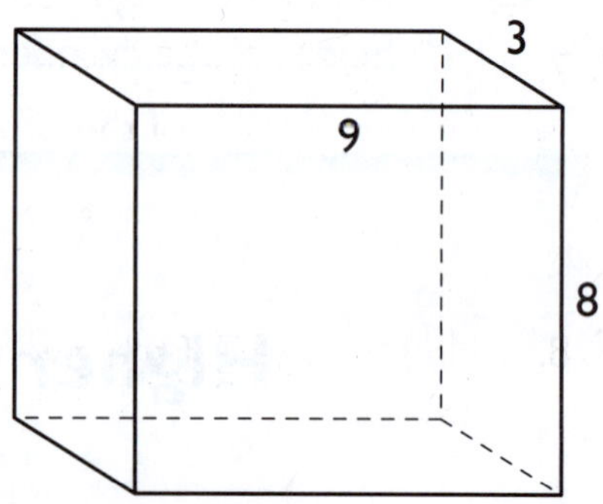

Surface area =
Volume =

Rewind

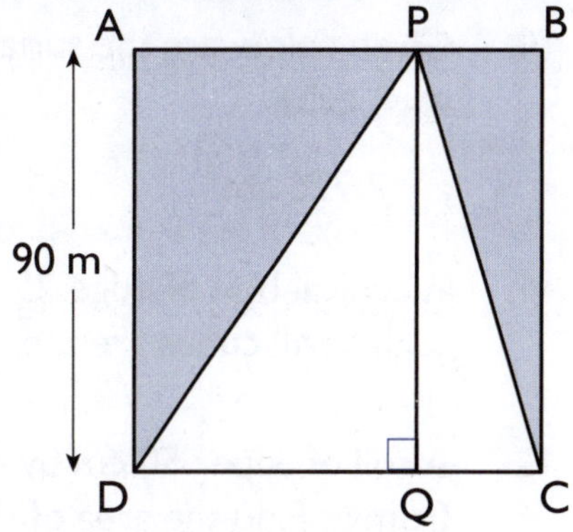

1. ABCD is a square field of side 90 m. If PQ is perpendicular to DC, find the area of $\triangle DPC$. Also find the area of the shaded portion.

2. A wire bent in the shape of a rectangle with sides 14 cm and 8 cm is straightened and bent in the shape of a circle. Find the radius and area of the circle.

3. The area of a trapezium is 78 cm^2. If the two parallel sides are 12 cm and 8 cm, find the height of the trapezium.

4. One of the parallel sides of a trapezium is 8 cm more than the other. If the distance between the parallel sides is 10 cm and the area of the trapezium is 200 cm^2, find the length of each parallel side.

5. Anita walks around a circular track of radius 14 m with a speed of 4 km/hr. If she takes 25 rounds of the track, for how long does she walk?

6. The area of a trapezium with height 14 cm is 504 cm^2. If the parallel sides are in the ratio 5:4, find their lengths.

7. The perimeter of a rhombus is 40 cm and the length of one of the diagonals is 16 cm. Find the length of the other diagonal.

8. Find the area of the given quadrilateral plot of land.

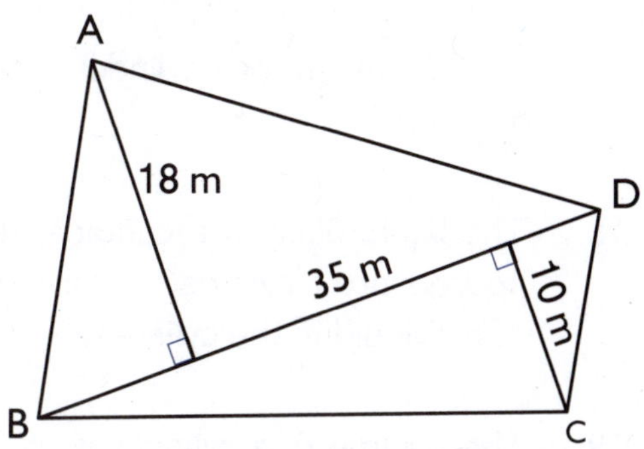

9. Find the area of the field given here. (All measurements are in m)

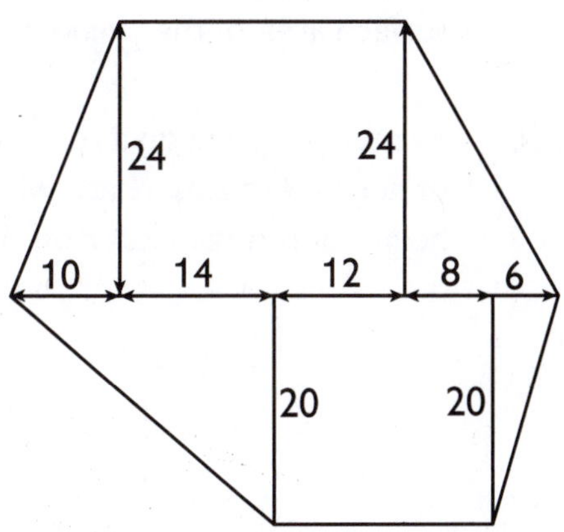

10. Given below are the surface areas of three cubes. Find the measure of the edge of each cube.

    a. 7,776 cm^2 b. 3,750 cm^2 c. 10,584 cm^2

11. A cubical box of edge 25 cm is filled with smaller cubes of edge 5 cm. How many such small cubes are there in the box?

12. A roll of paper 50 cm by 40 cm was cut and 20 cubes with edge 4 cm were made from it. Find the area of the paper left.

13. From a cubic tank filled with water, 225 buckets of capacity 15 litres could be filled. Find the length of the edge of the tank.

14. Find the depth of a tank whose base is a square of edge 8 m and which can hold as much water as another tank whose dimensions are 8m $\times$ 6m $\times$ 5 m.

15. Eight cuboidal metal boxes with dimensions 60 cm $\times$ 30 cm $\times$ 24 cm are to be painted. If the rate of painting is ₹250 per m^2, find the total cost of painting the boxes.

16. The perimeter of the floor of a hall is 250 m. If the height of the hall is 12 m, find the cost of painting the four walls at the rate of ₹30 per square metre.

17. Find the height of a cylinder with base of radius 3.5 cm and curved surface area of 440 cm^2.

18. The liquid filled in a cuboidal tin with dimensions 60 cm $\times$ 15 cm $\times$ 12 cm is poured into a cylinder the area of whose base measures 540 cm^2. Find the height of the liquid in the cylinder.

19. The volume of a cylinder is 69,300 cm^3 and its height is 50 cm. Find the curved surface area of the cylinder.

20. Rainwater falling on a roof measuring 50 m $\times$ 20 m is collected in a cylindrical tank of height 8 m and a base with diameter of 14 m. If the tank is full of water, find the height of the rainwater on the roof.

Data Handling

CHAPTER 16

We know the importance of collection, tabulation and interpretation of data. This branch of mathematics dealing with data is called statistics. It is applied in many fields. Statistics is widely used for tabulating the run rate in cricket matches, the medal tally in any competition or the goals scored in any match. The price index, the comparison of currency of different countries, the weather report with maximum and minimum temperatures or rainfall are examples of how widely data collection is used.

Bar Graphs

Let us recall the basic steps involved in the construction of bar graphs.

In a bar graph,

a. All bars have the same width.

b. The distance between two successive bars is the same throughout.

c. The scale is decided according to the observations in the data.

d. The scale is mentioned on the graph.

e. The x-axis and y-axis clearly show the quantities that are represented on them.

Example 1: Draw a bar graph to represent the marks obtained by Gaurav in a midterm examination. (Maximum marks per subject was 100.)

Subjects	English	Hindi	Maths	Science	Social science
Marks obtained	80	70	95	90	85

Step 1 On the graph paper, draw the horizontal line OX and vertical line OY, representing the x-axis and y-axis, respectively.

Step 2 Along x-axis, write the names of the subjects.

Step 3 On the y-axis, represent the marks.

Step 4 Choose a scale on the y-axis say 1 unit = 1 cm = 10 marks.

Step 5 Construct five bars of equal width and equidistant from each other. The height of the bars will depend on the marks scored.

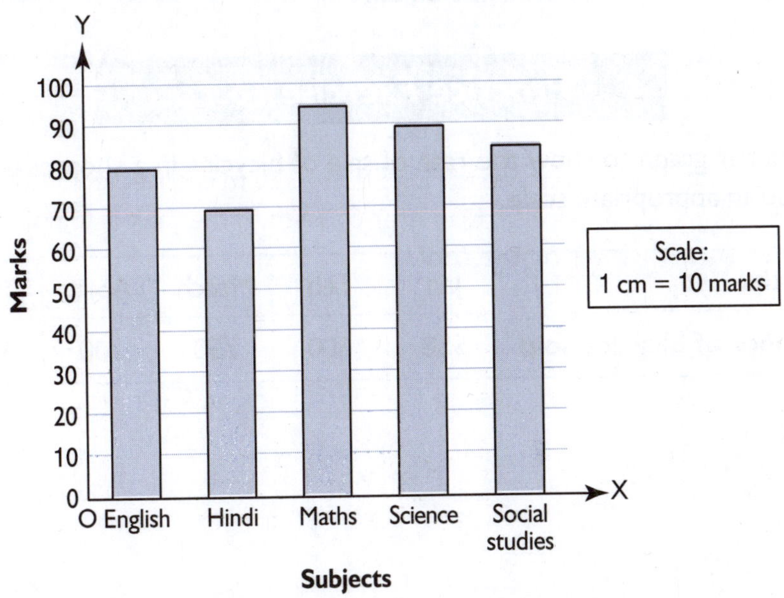

Example 2: In a music school, five different musical instruments are being taught. The given table shows the preference of boys and girls for the respective instruments. Draw a double bar graph to depict the data.

Musical instrument	Drums	Guitar	Piano	Sitar	Tabla
Boys	40	30	10	20	25
Girls	25	20	15	30	10

Step 1 Since there are two values for each instrument, we will draw a double bar graph.

Step 2 Draw the two axes, x-axis and y-axis.

Step 3 On the x-axis we will write the names of the instruments and on the y-axis, the number of students.

Step 4 We shall choose a scale, say 1 unit = 1 cm = 5 students, and write it on the graph.

Step 5 There should be space between two bars representing different instruments.

Step 6 To distinguish between boys and girls, we shall shade the bars differently.

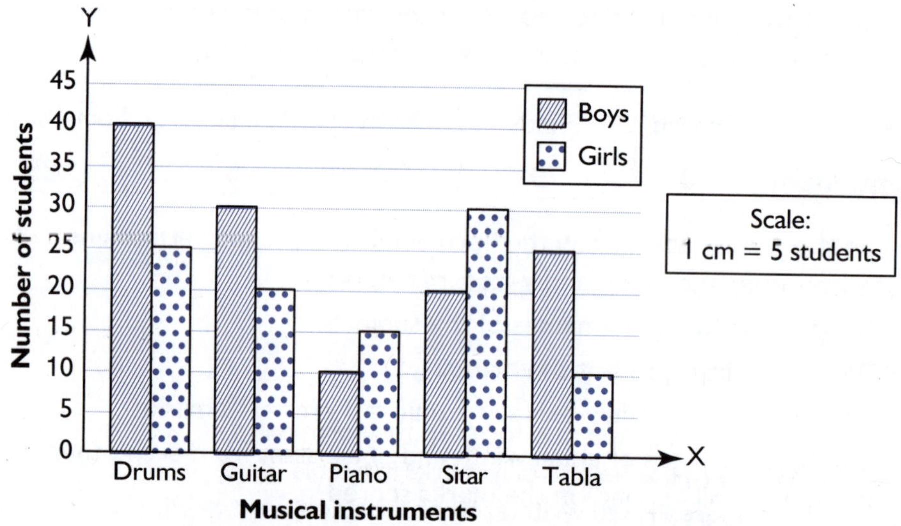

Practice Exercise 16.1

1. Draw a bar graph to show the rate of sale of bicycles in a shop over six months. Choose an appropriate scale.

Months	Jan	Feb	March	April	May	June
Number of bicycles sold	550	600	750	700	800	400

2. Choose an appropriate scale and draw a bar graph to depict the favourite sports of students.

Sports	Badminton	Cricket	Football	Basketball	Tennis
Number of students	25	75	60	40	50

3. Draw a double bar graph to show the *mean* performance of boys and girls in a midterm examination.

Subjects	English	Hindi	Maths	Science	Social science
Boys	60	55	90	95	75
Girls	75	70	80	85	80

4. Draw a double bar graph to show the population of males and females in five villages, A, B, C, D and E. (Population is in thousands.)

Villages	A	B	C	D	E
Females	50	20	30	45	15
Males	55	30	20	40	35

5. Draw a double bar graph to show the maximum and minimum temperatures in five cities during a day.

Cities	M	N	O	P	Q
Max temp	35°C	30°C	25°C	46°C	10°C
Min temp	28°C	20°C	20°C	35°C	8°C

Grouping of Data

When data is collected, it is in the raw form. In this form the data is difficult to analyse. Raw data can be tabulated with the help of tally marks in a table. If the number of observations are large, it becomes cumbersome to write each observation. To convert a large amount of data into a compact form, we organise it in groups. These groups are called class intervals. If there are 50 observations in the raw data, we can make 5 groups of 10 observations each. The group or classes are of the same size. The difference of the upper limit and lower limit of a group is called the class size.

Consider the following data showing the marks of 50 students in a test (out of 50):

23, 19, 18, 14, 36, 42, 48, 11, 17, 40, 38, 46, 33, 29, 31, 9, 17, 25, 32, 41, 46, 42, 33, 8, 17, 30, 41, 45, 18, 16, 2, 27, 33, 35, 45, 12, 9, 27, 28, 40, 32, 36, 40, 36, 21, 16, 5, 12, 45.

Marks	Tally Marks	Frequency
0–10	𝍸	5
10–20	𝍸 𝍸 II	12
20–30	𝍸 III	8
30–40	𝍸 𝍸 II	12
40–50	𝍸 𝍸 III	13

This is a large amount of data. So we form 5 groups of 10 observations each. the 5 groups are 0–10, 10–20, 20–30, 30–40, 40–50. All marks from 0 till 9 will be in the group 0–10. All marks from 10 to 20 will be in the group 10–20. The common observation is placed in the higher class.

The groups, 0–10, 10–20, 20–30, 30–40, 40–50 are the class intervals. The difference between the upper limit of a class interval and the lower limit is the class size. In the class interval 20–30, 30 is the upper class limit and 20 the lower class limit. The midpoint of a class is called its class mark. This is the mean of the class upper limit and the class lower limit.

Example:

Class interval	Upper class limit	Lower class limit	Class size
20–30	30	20	$30 - 20 = 10$

Class mark

$$\frac{20 + 30}{2} = 25$$

Alert!

1. A common observation always belongs to the higher class, i.e., if 10–<u>20</u> and <u>20</u>–30 are the class intervals, then 20 will belong to 20–30.
2. The class size is the same but the class marks are different for all class intervals.
3. The difference between the class marks of successive class intervals will be the same as the class size.

Example:

1. The height of 50 students (in cm) is as given in the table.

90	95	120	140	145	149	92	96	105	110
135	125	115	141	146	121	139	136	142	105
107	96	92	148	136	137	125	129	128	116
140	139	125	116	118	97	108	109	110	96
141	115	129	111	129	140	130	120	112	119

Draw a grouped frequency table using class intervals 90–100, 100–110, 110–120, 120–130, 130–140, 140–150. Find the class marks of the class intervals.

Height (in cm)	Tally marks	Frequency
90–100	𝍸 III	8
100–110	𝍸 III	8
110–120	𝍸 II	7
120–130	𝍸 𝍸	10
130–140	𝍸 II	7
140–150	𝍸 𝍸	10

Class intervals are given in Column 1. The upper class limit and lower class limit for each class interval is known. Hence, the class size is 10.

Class marks are given below for each class interval

a. $\frac{90+100}{2} = 95$ b. $\frac{100+110}{2} = 105$

c. $\frac{110+120}{2} = 115$ d. $\frac{120+130}{2} = 125$

e. $\frac{130+140}{2} = 135$ f. $\frac{140+150}{2} = 145$

Histogram

We have learnt to draw bar graphs and double bar graphs for ungrouped data. When data is represented as grouped frequency distribution, we draw a histogram. A histogram is similar to a bar graph, but there is no space between the bars.

To draw a histogram, we draw the two axes. We choose suitable scales for both the axes. The scale need not be the same on both the axes. The scale is chosen according to the data.

Let us draw a histogram to depict the marks obtained by 50 students in a class. The data is given under the subhead Grouping of Data.

Example 1:

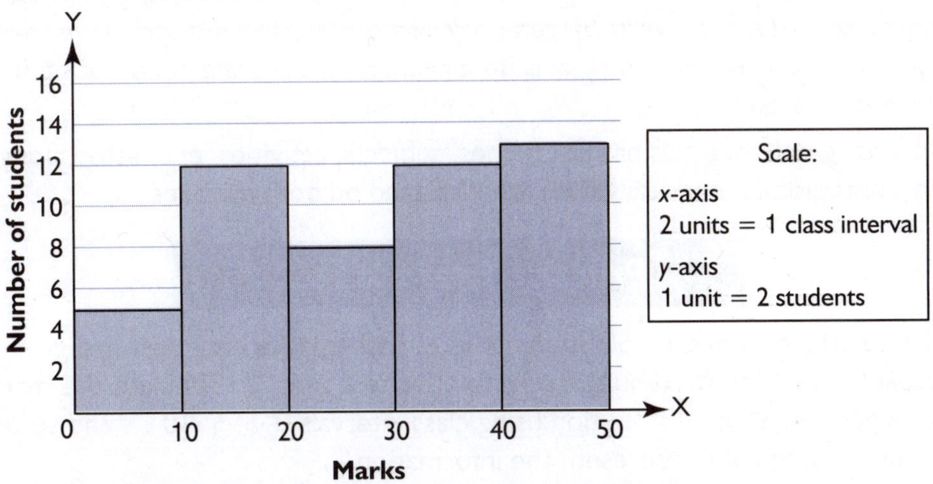

On the x-axis, we plot the class 0–10, 10–20, 20–30, 30–40 and 40–50. On the y-axis, we plot the frequency of marks. Since the frequency varies from 5 to 15, we can take one unit to be 2. We construct rectangles with class intervals as the breadth and the corresponding frequency as the length. We can shade or colour the rectangles.

Example 2:

Study the histogram and answer the questions.

a. What is the highest class interval?

The highest class interval is 45–50.

b. How many students get less than ₹30 as pocket money per day?

$8 + 6 + 10 + 10 + 9 + 8 = 51$

51 students get less then ₹30 as pocket money per day.

c. How many students get ₹40 or more as pocket money? 4 + 2 = 6 students

d. How many students have been surveyed? 8 + 6 + 10 + 10 + 9 + 8 + 7 + 6 + 4 + 2 = 70 students

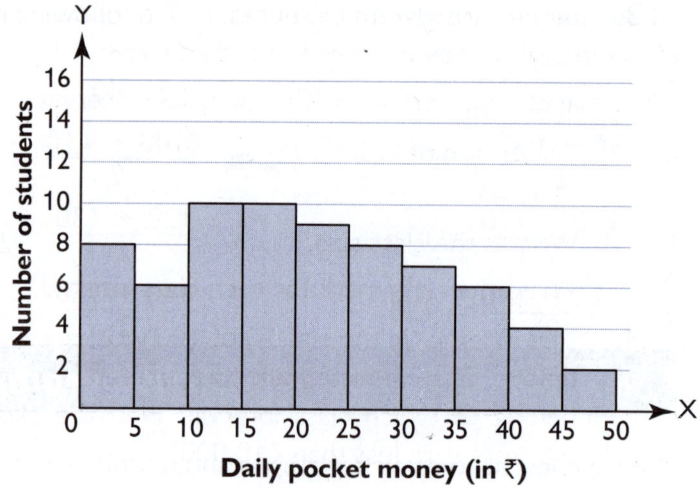

e. What is the class mark of the class interval with frequency 9?

Class interval 20–25, Class mark $\frac{20 + 25}{2} = 22.5$

The class mark is 22.5.

Differences between a Bar Graph and a Histogram

1. In a bar graph, the bars are at a distance from one another (equal width), while in a histogram, the bars (rectangles) touch each other.
2. In a bar graph, we have a scale for the x-axis or y-axis according to whether the bars are horizontal or vertical (generally vertical), but in a histogram we have scales for both the x-axis and the y-axis. In a histogram, the scale need not be the same on both the axes.
3. In a bar graph, one axis has just names, subjects, activities, etc., listed along it, but in a histogram, numerical values are displayed on both the axes.

Practice Exercise 16.2

1. The marks obtained by 50 students in a mathematics class test are given in the table below. The maximum marks for this test was 25. Tabulate the marks in a grouped frequency distribution using class intervals 0–5, 5–10 … and so on. Also draw a histogram to represent the information.

24	20	12	14	17	6	8	10	4	0
11	14	19	22	20	25	15	14	13	9
6	7	9	4	3	11	15	19	18	20
10	0	23	16	15	18	21	25	22	21
2	3	4	17	21	9	19	7	17	18

2. The given data indicates the weights (in grams) of 35 oranges picked from a basket. Draw a grouped frequency table to represent the data. Use class intervals 75–80, 80–85, 85–90, 90–95, 95–100, 100–105, 105–110 for the groups. Also draw a histogram to represent the information.

   106, 107, 108, 76, 82, 109, 107, 115, 92, 95, 83, 87, 117, 95, 103, 116, 76, 92, 86, 77, 84, 88, 93, 108, 78, 84, 86, 93, 99, 101, 105, 85, 83, 88, 94

3. Draw a histogram to represent the following data.

Diameter (in mm)	30–35	35–40	40–45	45–50	50–55
Number of circles	15	17	21	22	25

What is the class size?

Write the class mark for each class interval.

4. The income (in thousands) of 100 workers is given in the grouped frequency table below. Draw a histogram to represent the information. The maximum workers belong to which class interval? Find the class mark of that group. How many workers earn less than ₹10,000?

Income (in ₹)	Number of workers
7,000–8,000	15
8,000–9,000	25
9,000–10,000	30
10,000–11,000	20
11,000–12,000	10

5. Study the histogram and answer the following questions.
   a. What is the size of the class interval?
   b. Which is the class interval with the highest frequency?
   c. What is the class mark of that class interval?
   d. How many students cleared the admission test if the qualifying mark was 30?
   e. What scale was used on the x-axis and y-axis?

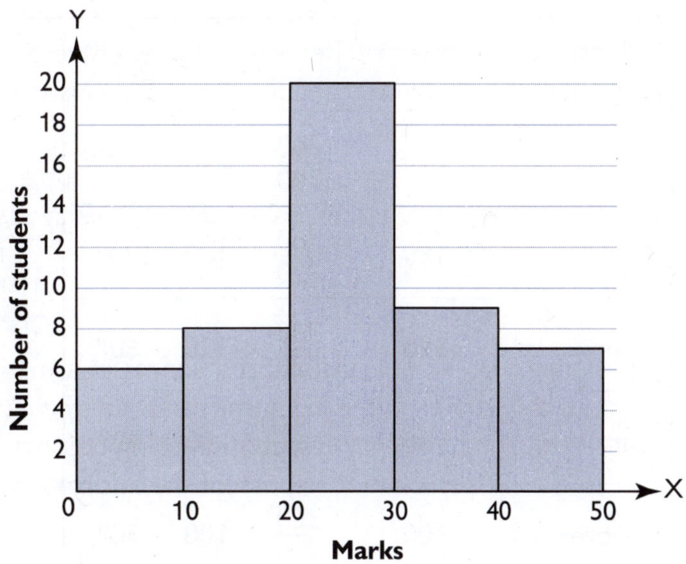

Pie Chart

Another way of representing data is in the form of a pie chart or pie diagram. In a pie chart, we represent different items of data with the help of sectors of a circle. The different parts look like the slices of a pie. Pie charts are very eye-catching and often used by the media and organisations to represent their data.

The angle at the centre of a circle is 360°. The sum or total data is represented by 360°. The different parts are divided into proportional sectors. These sectors are shaded or coloured differently to represent the given data. The sum of the angles of the different sectors at the centre should add up to 360°. Let us study the construction of a pie chart with the help of examples.

Example 1: The data given shows the mode of transport used by students to reach school. Represent the data with the help of a pie chart.

Mode of transport	Bus	Cycle	Train	Car	Scooter
Number of students	240	180	120	80	100

Step 1 Add up the various parts of the data and get the total value.

Step 2 Find the sector angles for each part by the formula $\left(\frac{360}{\text{Total value}} \times \text{Value of part}\right)$

Step 3 Draw a circle of any radius and draw its diameter either horizontally or vertically.

Step 4 Identify the part with the largest value and draw its sector using the diameter as the initial line.

Step 5 Continue with the construction of the sectors representing the other parts.

Step 6 Label each sector and also mark the angles.

Mode of transport	Number of students	Central angle
Bus	240	$\frac{360}{720} \times 240 = 120°$
Cycle	180	$\frac{360}{720} \times 180 = 90°$
Train	120	$\frac{360}{720} \times 120 = 60°$
Car	80	$\frac{360}{720} \times 80 = 40°$
Scooter	100	$\frac{360}{720} \times 100 = 50°$
Total	720	360°

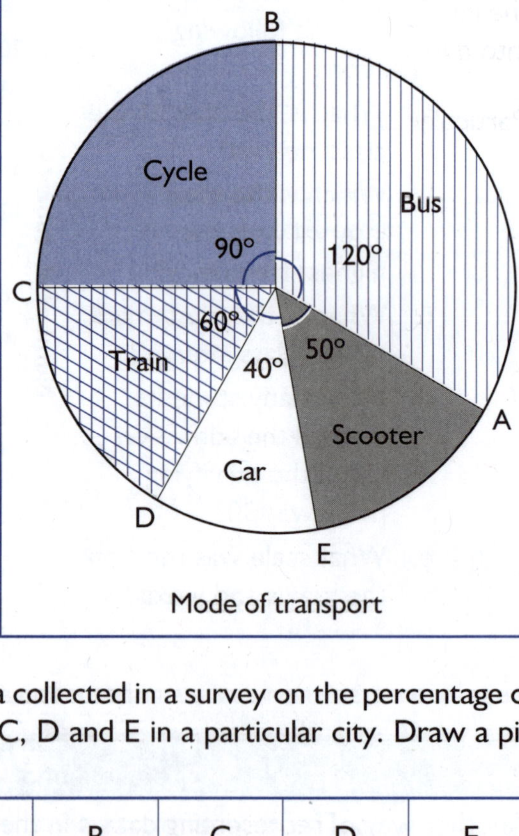

Mode of transport

Example 2: The following table shows the data collected in a survey on the percentage of people reading newspapers A, B, C, D and E in a particular city. Draw a pie chart to represent the data.

Newspaper	A	B	C	D	E
Percentage of readers	15%	20%	10%	25%	30%

We first find the central angle in each case.

Newpapers	Percentage of readers	Central angle
A	15%	$\frac{15}{100} \times 360 = 54°$
B	20%	$\frac{20}{100} \times 360 = 72°$
C	10%	$\frac{10}{100} \times 360 = 36°$
D	25%	$\frac{25}{100} \times 360 = 90°$
E	30%	$\frac{30}{100} \times 360 = 108°$
Total	100%	360°

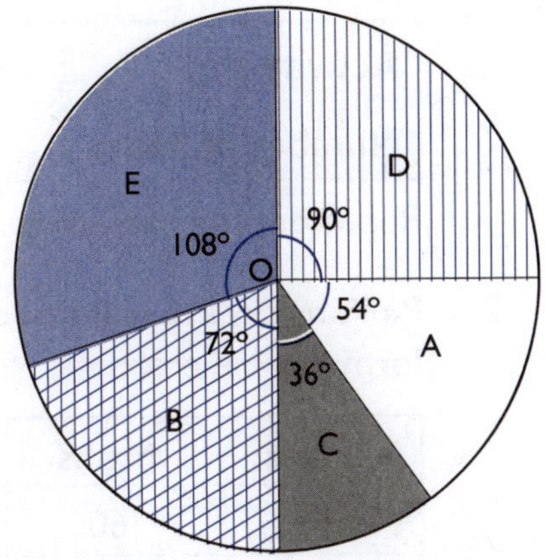

We follow the steps and construct the central angles. The sectors are shaded differently and labelled.

Reading and Interpreting a Pie Chart

We have learnt the method of constructing a pie chart for a given data. Now we will study the interpretation of a pie chart. We convert the central angles that are given in the pie chart into data by the formula:

$$\text{Particular part} = \frac{\text{Central angle} \times \text{Total of all parts}}{360°}.$$

Example: The given pie chart depicts the expenditure of a family under various heads. If the total expenditure of the family is ₹18,000, find out the expenditure in each case. On what does the family spend most of its money?

$$\text{Food} = \frac{13\cancel{0} \times \overset{500}{\cancel{18,000}}}{\cancel{360}} = ₹6,500$$

$$\text{Clothing} = \frac{6\cancel{0} \times \overset{500}{\cancel{18,000}}}{\cancel{360}} = ₹3,000$$

$$\text{Education} = \frac{5\cancel{0} \times \overset{500}{\cancel{18,000}}}{\cancel{360}} = ₹2,500$$

$$\text{Rent} = \frac{3\cancel{0} \times \overset{500}{\cancel{18,000}}}{\cancel{360}} = ₹1,500$$

$$\text{Miscellaneous} = \frac{9\cancel{0} \times \overset{500}{\cancel{18,000}}}{\cancel{360}} = ₹4,500$$

Total expenditure = ₹18,000

The maximum expenditure is on food, which is ₹6,500.

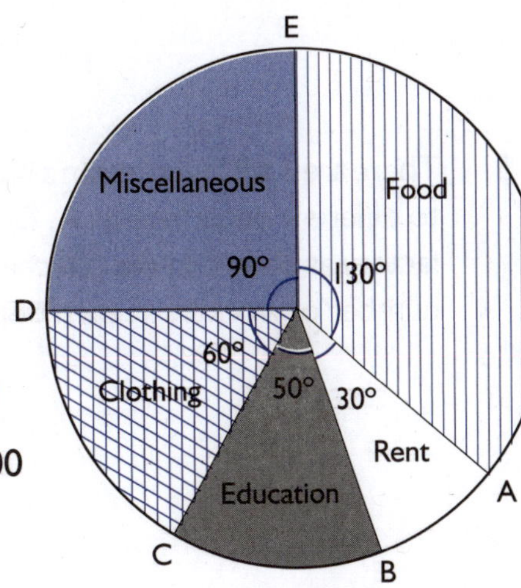

Alert!

For easy calculation, simplify $\frac{\text{Total parts}}{360}$ and then multiply with the given central angles.

Practice Exercise 16.3

1. The number of hours spent by a student on various activities on a school working day are given below.

Activity	School	Commuting	Homework	Playing	Sleeping
Number of hours	6	2	4	4	8

Represent the data using a pie chart.

2. Rini's marks in a unit test are as given in the table below. Represent the data in the form of a pie chart.

Subject	Maths	Science	Social science	English	Hindi
Marks	60	40	30	20	30

3. Rohan had his birthday celebrations at an ice cream parlour. The data as given is of the different flavours of ice cream chosen by his friends. Represent the data on a pie chart and shade the flavours in appropriate colours.

Flavour	Chocolate	Pista	Mango	Strawberry	Grape
Number of friends	6	4	3	3	2

4. In a library, there are 5,400 books in all. The proportion of books on history, geography, physics, chemistry, biology and mathematics available in the library are shown in the pie chart below. Find the exact number of books available for each subject.

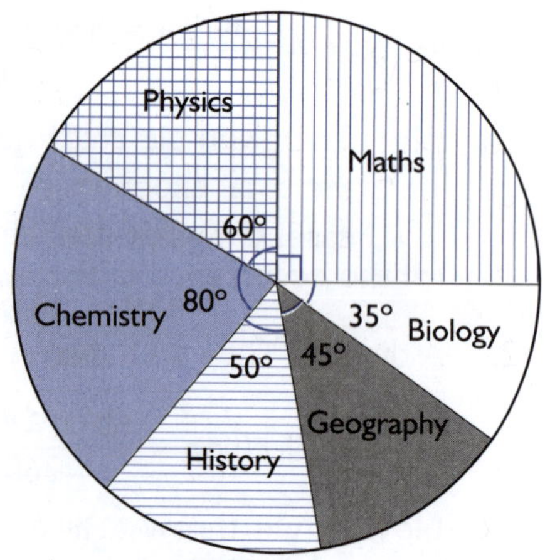

5. There are 1,080 workers in a factory. They belong to different departments A, B, C, D and E of the factory as shown in the pie chart below. Find the number of workers in each department.

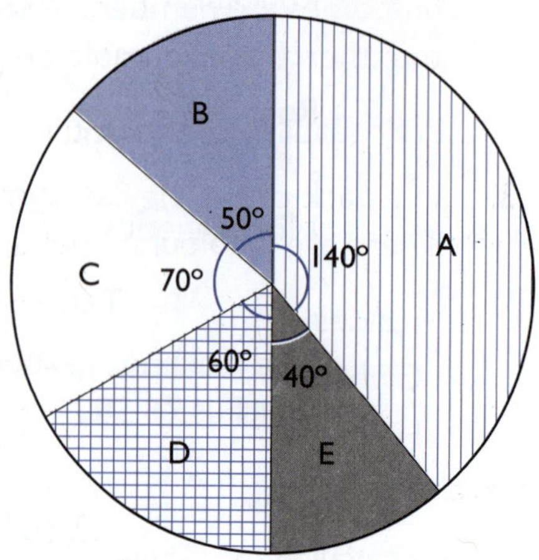

6. The amounts of various agricultural products produced by a state in a year are as given in the table below.

Agricultural product	Wheat	Rice	Maize	Millet	Sugarcane
Production (in thousands of quintals)	1500	900	600	400	200

Draw a pie chart to represent the data. Use different columns to shade the different sectors.

Probability

In our daily conversations we use probability very often. For example, it *may* rain today, India *may* win the cricket match, the price of petrol *may* increase, Rohit *may* top in the Class X examination. These are all examples of things that 'may' happen.

Probability is the measure of the chance of the happening of an event.

Random experiment: An experiment in *which all possible outcomes are known* and the *exact outcome cannot be predicted* in advance is called a random experiment. Let us illustrate it with examples.

1. When we toss a coin, we are performing a random experiment. We know that the possible outcome (result) will either be head or tail. But, we cannot predict whether we will get a head or a tail. The measure of the chance of getting a head or a tail is done by a simple formula

   Probability of occurrence of an event $= \dfrac{\text{Favourable outcomes}}{\text{Total number of outcomes}}$

   In tossing a coin, the total number of outcomes are only two—heads or tails.

   If the *event* is to get a head then the favourable outcome is one and the Probability (of the occurrence of the event) $= \dfrac{1}{2}$

2. A dice is a cube with the numbers 1 to 6 written on its six faces as

   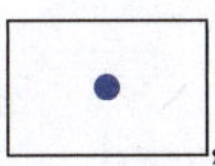, 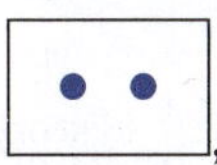, 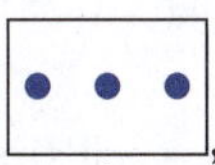, 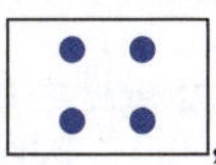, 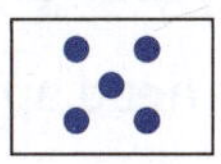 and 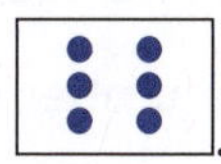.

   Now, if we throw a dice, it is a random experiment. We know that the total outcomes are numbers from 1 to 6. Now if our event is to get a prime number on top, then the favourable outcomes are 2, 3 and 5.

   $\therefore$ Probability of the occurrence of the event $= \dfrac{3}{6} = \dfrac{1}{2}$.

3. In a pack of playing cards, there are 52 cards. There are 4 suits of 13 cards each. There are 2 colours—red and black. The suits are as shown in the table.

Spades	(♠)	(Black)	13 cards
Clubs	(♣)	(Black)	13 cards
Hearts	(♥)	(Red)	13 cards
Diamonds	(♦)	(Red)	13 cards

King, Queen and Jack are the face cards. There are 3 face cards per suit.

Therefore, in 1 deck of cards there are $3 \times 4 = 12$ face cards.

If we perform the random experiment of picking a card from a pack of cards, then the total possible outcomes are 52. If the event is to get a red card, then the favourable outcomes are 26.

Probability of the occurrence of the event $= \frac{\text{Favourable outcomes}}{\text{Total outcomes}} = \frac{26}{52} = \frac{1}{2}$.

The probability of a *sure event* is 1.

If we have to pick out a blue bead from a bag containing 10 blue beads, the event is sure to occur. Hence, the probability is $\frac{10}{10} = 1$.

The probability of an impossible event is 0.

Thus, if we have to pick out a yellow bead from a bag containing 10 blue beads, the event cannot happen. Hence, the probability is $\frac{0}{10} = 0$.

Alert!

Probability cannot be negative or less than 0 and it cannot be greater than 1.

If the probability of the occurrence of an event is 'p', then the probability of its non-occurrence is $1-p$.

Repeated Trials

By trial we mean performing an experiment. Repeated trials means performing the same experiment a number of times under the same conditions.

Example 1: Suppose we toss a coin 100 times and get a head 60 times. Now, if we toss a coin at random, what is the probability of getting a head?

Here the total number of trials = 100

Number of times head appeared = 60

$$\therefore \text{Probability of getting a head} = \frac{\text{Number of times head appeared}}{\text{Total number of trials}} = \frac{60}{100} = \frac{3}{5}$$

Example 2: Suppose we toss a coin 150 times and head is obtained 71 times. Now, if a coin is tossed at random. What is the probability of getting a tail?

Total number of trials = 150

Number of times head appeared = 71

$\therefore$ Number of times tail appeared = 79

$$\text{Probability of getting a tail} = \frac{\text{Number of times tail appeared}}{\text{Total number of trials}} = \frac{79}{150}$$

Example 3: A dice is rolled 65 times and the number 5 appeared 21 times. Now, in a random roll of the dice, what is the probability of getting a 5?

Total number of trials = 65

Number of times 5 appeared = 21

$$\therefore \text{Probability of getting a 5} = \frac{\text{Number of times 5 appeared}}{\text{Total number of trials}}$$
$$= \frac{21}{65}$$

Example 4: Find the number of outcomes when *two* coins are tossed simultaneously. The possible outcomes are head, head (HH), head, tail (HT), tail, head (TH) and tail, tail (TT).

HT and TH will be considered as two different cases since HT means the first coin shows heads, while the second coin shows tails and TH means that the first coin shows tails, and the second coin shows heads.

Hence the total outcomes are 4.

Example 5: Find the number of outcomes when three coins are tossed simultaneously.

The possible outcomes are

H H H
H H T
H T H
H T T
T H H
T H T
T T H
T T T

} 8 possible outcomes

The possibilty of having 3 heads is 1.

The possibility of 2 heads and 1 tail is 3.

The possibility of 1 head and 2 tails is 3.

The possibility of having 3 tails is 1.

Example 6: If two dice are thrown together, find the number of outcomes.

There are 36 possibilities, which are listed below.

1,1	2,1	3,1	4,1	5,1	6,1
1,2	2,2	3,2	4,2	5,2	6,2
1,3	2,3	3,3	4,3	5,3	6,3
1,4	2,4	3,4	4,4	5,4	6,4
1,5	2,5	3,5	4,5	5,5	6,5
1,6	2,6	3,6	4,6	5,6	6,6

Practice Exercise 16.4

1. A dice is rolled. Find the probability of getting:

   a. an odd number b. a prime number c. a number more than 4

2. A pack of 52 cards is shuffled. Find the probability of getting:

   a. a red card b. a black card

   c. a card from the suit of hearts d. a face card

   e. a spades

3. In a bag there are 10 blue pens, 12 green pens, 13 red pens and 15 black pens. Find the probability of getting:

   a. a red pen b. a blue pen c. a black pen

   d. a green pen e. a yellow pen

4. Five boxes are kept closed. One of them contains a silver coin. Radha is asked to choose a box. What is the chance that she will pick the box with the silver coin?

5. Ten cards, from the ace of diamonds to the ten of diamonds are placed face down on the table. Find the probability of getting:

   a. the ace b. the ten c. a card below ten

   d. an even number card e. a prime number card

6. A coin is tossed 200 times and tail is obtained 138 times. Now, if a coin is tossed at random, what is the probability of getting a tail?

7. In 100 rolls of a dice, 6 is obtained 44 times. In a random throw of the dice, what is the probability of getting a 6?

8. A survey of 200 families shows the result given below.

Number of girls in the family	2	1	0
Number of families	32	154	14

   Out of these families, one is chosen at random. What is the probability that the chosen family has 1 girl?

9. A coin and a dice are thrown simultaneously. List the number of possible outcomes.

   [Hint: Number of outcomes for the coin = 2
   Number of outcomes for the dice = 6]

10. Find the total number of possible outcomes when three coins are tossed simultaneously.

If there are 15 cats on a boat and one jumps out, how many would be left? None, they were all copycats!!

Highlights

- Bar graphs and composite bar graphs are a diagrammatic representation of the data by a number of bars of equal width but varying height.
- When the number of observations is large, the data has to be condensed by grouping it in suitable groups or classes.
- A group or class is called the class interval, e.g. 20–30, where 20 is the lower class limit and 30 is the upper class limit.
- By convention, a common observation, such as 20–30, 30–40, where the common observation is 30, always belongs to the higher class. For example, 30 belongs to the class 30–40 and not the class 20–30.
- The difference between the upper class limit and the lower class limit is called the class size. For example, in 20–30, the class size is 30–20 = 10.
- The midpoint of a class is called the class mark. The class mark of the class 20–30 is $\frac{20 + 30}{2} = 25$.
- Histogram is a graph that displays the grouped frequency distribution of data.
- In a histogram, both x-axis and y-axis have a scale which need not be the same.
- Data can be represented by a pie chart or pie diagram.
- In a pie chart, the given numerical data is in the form of sectors of a circle.
- Central angle for a component $= \left(\frac{\text{Value of the component} \times 360}{\text{Total value}}\right)^{\circ}$.
- The total sum of all central angles is 360°.
- Probability is the measure of the chance of an event taking place.
  $\text{P(of an event)} = \frac{\text{Favourable outcomes}}{\text{Total outcomes}}$
- Probability has a value between 0 and 1. Zero is the probability of an impossible event and 1 is the probability of a sure event.
- If the probability of an event taking place is 'p', then the probability of it not taking place is (1 − p).
- An experiment in which all possible outcomes are known and the exact outcome cannot be predicted in advance is called a random experiment.
- Repeated trials are when a random experiment is repeated a number of times under the same conditions.
- Probability of the occurrence of an event
  $= \frac{\text{Number of trials in which the event occurred}}{\text{Total number of trials}}$
- When different outcomes have the same chance of occurrence, they are said to be equally likely events.
- The number of outcomes when 'n' coins are tossed = 2^n.
  The number of outcomes when 'n' dice are thrown = 6^n.

Maths Lab Activity

Aim: To understand the concept of probability.

Material required: a pen

Method: Answer the following questions.

1. What is the probability of getting a 1 on rolling a dice? ________________
2. What is the probability of pulling a king from a pack of cards? ________________
3. What is the probability of pulling a square chocolate from a box containing 10 square chocolates? ________________
4. What is the probability of getting an even number on rolling the dice? ________
5. Answer questions based on the figure

   a. Probability of selecting 'A'

   b. Probability of selecting 'D'

A	B	A	C
C	A	B	A
C	A	A	B
D	D	A	C

Higher Order Thinking Skills

HOTS

1. In a pie chart representing the percentage of students having interest in various activities, the central angle of the sector representing students interested in music is 81°. What is the percentage of students interested in music?

2. In a survey of 200 children, it was found that 82 like milk while 118 dislike it. From these children, one is chosen at random. What is the probability that he or she dislikes milk?

3. The table below shows the monthly income of 100 workers in a factory.

Monthly income (in ₹)	5000–8000	8000–11,000	11,000–14,000	14,000–17,000	17,000–20,000
Number of workers	18	28	30	16	8

Write the class size and class mark of the class interval with the maximum frequency.

Graphs

CHAPTER 17

A point on the number line is either a natural number, whole number, integer or rational number. In this lesson we will learn how to locate a point on a plane. If one was asked to denote a point P on the plane of a notebook, there will be different positions for different students. Some may mark it on the right hand corner of the page, some in the centre of the page, some at the bottom of the page in the left hand corner as shown in the figures.

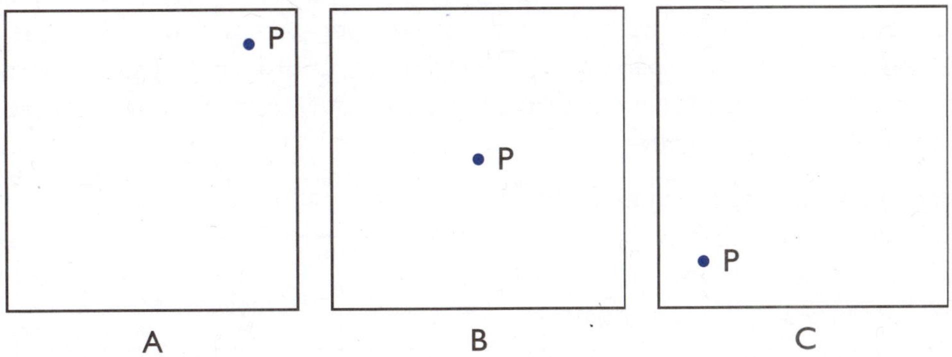

We will learn a new system of representing a point in a plane called the Cartesian system. This is an interesting and useful method to study the identification and location of a point in a plane.

The Cartesian System

The system of locating a point in a plane by vertical and horizontal measurements is called the Cartesian system.

We are all familiar with graph paper, which has horizontal and vertical lines. On this paper, 10 small divisions are marked within a length of 1 cm. Graph papers are useful for representing various data as bar graphs, line graphs, etc.

Take a graph sheet and draw two lines mutually perpendicular to each other as shown in the figure.

The point where the two lines intersect is represented by 'O' and is called the *origin*. The horizontal line is X′OX is called the x-axis. The vertical line is YOY′ and is called the y-axis. The two lines together are called the coordinate axes. The plane of the paper is called the Cartesian plane, which consists of the coordinate axes and the origin marked on it. The coordinate axes divide the plane into four regions, which are called the quadrants. All distances on the right of the origin on the x-axis are positive (just as in the number line). All distances above the origin on the y-axis are positive; all distances below the origin on the y-axis are negative.

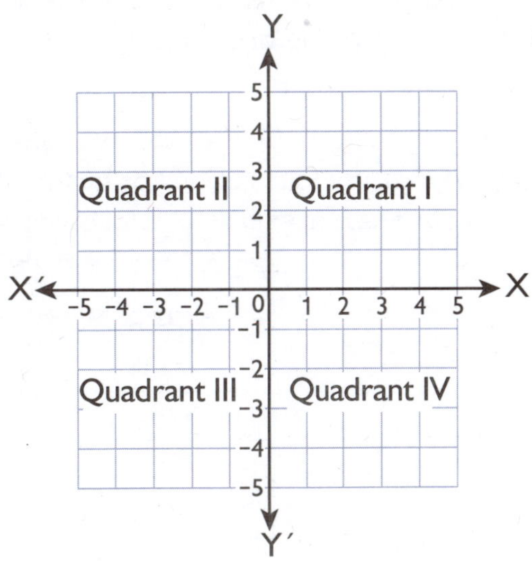

In the given figure we have,

XOX′ as the x-axis

YOY′ as the y-axis.

Together they are called coordinate axes. 'O' is the origin.

There are four quadrants, I, II, III, IV. They are marked in the anticlockwise direction.

Any point in the plane is represented by its horizontal distance and vertical distance measured from 'O'. The two distances are written together as a pair called an ordered pair. They are written as (X, Y). They are called an ordered pair because by convention X is written first and then Y. This ordered pair (X, Y) are called the coordinates. The X coordinate is called abscissa and the Y coordinate is called ordinate. Any point P is represented on the Cartesian plane by its coordinates.

Let us learn how to plot a point on the Cartesian plane. We first draw the horizontal axis or the x-axis, then the vertical axis or the y-axis. The point where the two intersect is named as 'O' or the origin. We choose a suitable scale on both the axes. If a point P (3, 4) is to be plotted on the Cartesian plane, it means that the x coordinate is 3 and the y coordinate is 4. We first move 3 units on the right of the origin on the x-axis and then more 4 units vertically upwards parallel to the y-axis, where we locate the point P (3, 4)

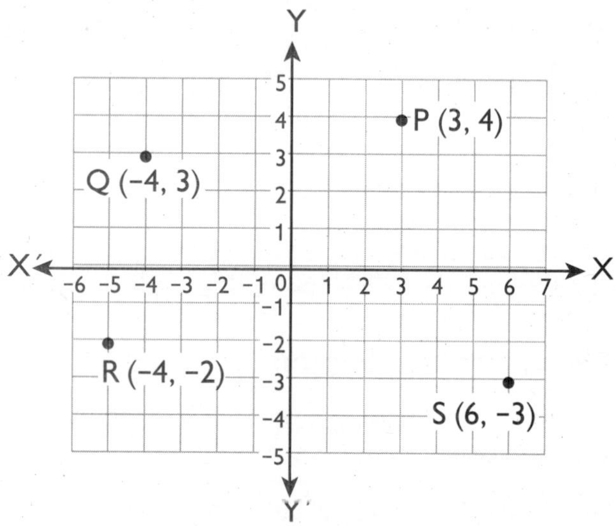

If we have to plot a point Q (−4, 3), we move −4 units to the left of the origin on the x-axis and 3 units vertically upwards (parallel to y-axis).

If we have to plot R (−5, −2), we move −5 units to the left of the origin on the x-axis and −2 units downwards (parallel to the x-axis). If we have to plot S (6, −3), we move 6 units to the right of the origin on the x-axis and then −3 units vertically downwards (parallel to the x-axis).

The four points P, Q, R and S have been shown on the Cartesian plane in the figure. This also shows that the four regions or quadrants in which the Cartesian plane has been divided by the coordinate axes have the following signs of coordinates:

Region	Quadrant	Signs of the coordinates
XOY	I	(+, +)
YOX′	II	(−, +)
X′OY′	III	(−, −)
Y′OX	IV	(+, −)

Hence, if the coordinates of a point are given, we can identify in which quadrant the point will lie.

Example: State the coordinate in which the points with the following coordinates lie.

a. A (−3, 4) b. B (4, 2) c. C (−5, −7) d. D (4, −6)

a. A (−3, 4) lies in Quadrant II as the x coordinate is negative and the y coordinate is positive.

b. B (4, 2) lies in Quadrant I as the x coordinate is positive and the y coordinate is positive.

c. C (−5, −7) lies in Quadrant III as the x coordinate is negative and the y coordinate is also negative.

d. D (+4, −6) lies in Quadrant IV as the x coordinate is positive and the y coordinate is negative.

Special coordinates

The coordinates of the origin 'O' are (0, 0) as it neither moves right or left, nor upwards or downwards.

Any point on the x-axis or XOX′ is (X, 0) because its distance from the origin vertically upwards or downwards is 0.

Any point on the y-axis or YOY′ is (0, Y) because its distance from the origin towards the left or right is 0.

Example : Plot the following points on the Cartesian plane.

P (3, 0), Q (0, 3), R (0, −3) and S (−3, 0)

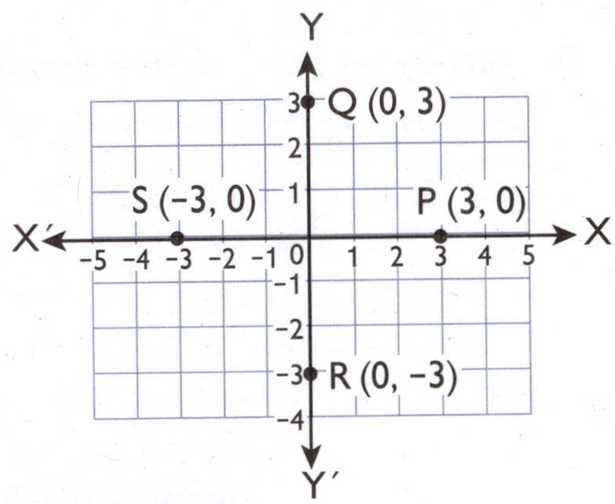

Practice Exercise 17.1

1. State the quadrant in which the points with the following coordinates lie.

a. (3, 4) b. (−3, 4) c. (−3, −4) d. (3, −4) e. (5, −6)

f. (−6, −5) g. (5, 6) h. (−6, 5) i. (7, 10) j. (−7, −10).

2. On which axis will the following points lie?

a. (4, 0) b. (−2, 0) c. (0, 3) d. (−3, 0) e. (0, −4)

f. (6, 0) g. (0, −6) h. (−6, 0) i. (1, 0) j. (−1, 0)

3. Write the coordinates of the points marked A, B, C, D, E, F, G, H, I and J in the graph that follows.

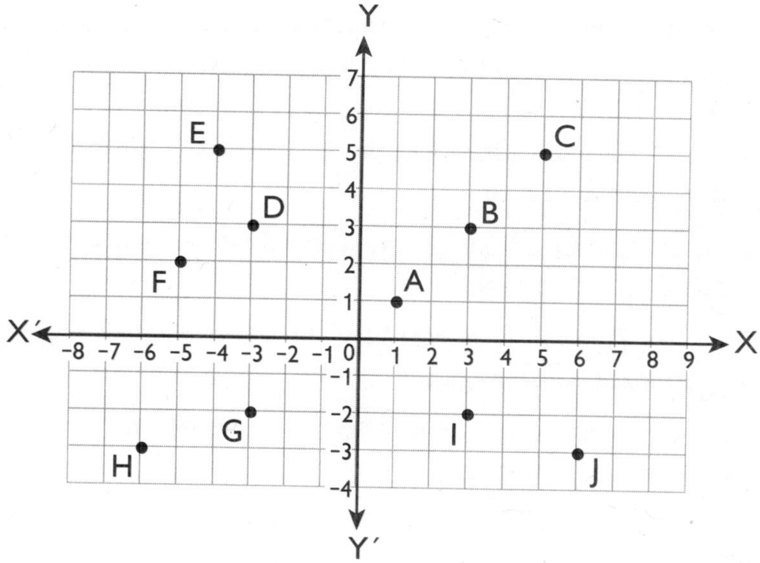

4. Plot the following points on the Cartesian plane (use a graph paper).

a. P(0, 3) b. Q(4, 0) c. O(0, 0) d. R(1, 4) e. M(−3, 0)

f. N(4, 1) g. S(5, 6) h. T(−4, −5) i. W(−3, 6) j. Z(4, −3)

5. Identify the points (letters) that represent the following coordinates.

a. (2, 0) b. (3, −2) c. (4, 2) d. (−5, −2) e. (−5, 0)

f. (−2, 1) g. (−3, 3) h. (−6, 3) i. (7, 4) j. (0, −2)

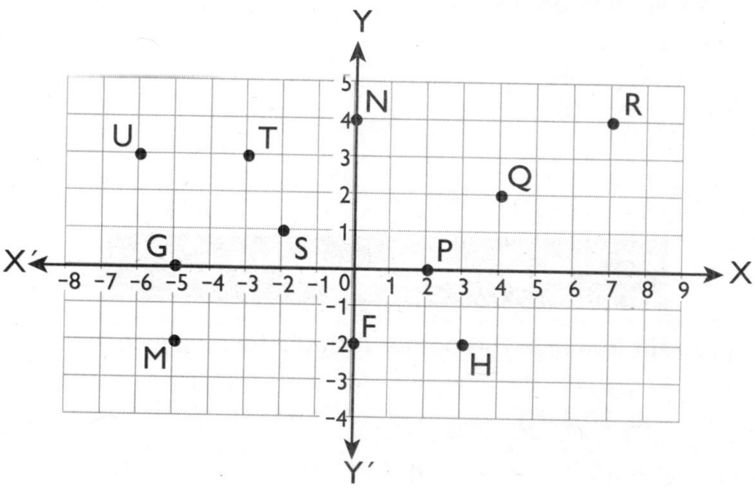

6. a. Plot the following points on a Cartesian plane: A (2, 1), B (2, 3), C (2, −3), D (2, 5) and E (2, 0). Join the points. What do you observe?

b. Plot the following points on a Cartesian plane: P (4, 3), Q (−2, 3), R (0, 3), S (5, 3) and T (−3, 3). Join the points. What do you observe?

c. Plot the following points on a Cartesian plane: M (4, 4), N (2, 3), O (0, 0), P (−3, −3) and Q (−1, −1). Join the points. What do you observe?

7. Plot each of the following points on a graph paper using the same coordinate axes. Join the points. Name the kind of figure formed in each case.

   a. O (0, 0), B (0, 5), C (5, 0)

   b. P (−2, 3), Q (−4, 0), R (−1, 0)

   c. O (0, 0), M (−3, −3), N (3, −3)

8. Plot the following points on a Cartesian plane. Join the points. Identify the figure formed in each case.

   a. A (2, 2), B (2, 4), C (4, 4), D (4, 2)

   b. P (−1, 3), Q (−1, 4), R (−4, 4), S (−4, 3)

   c. L (−1, −2), M (−3, −4), N (4, −3), P (7, −2)

9. Plot the following points on the Cartesian plane and identify and name the figure formed.

   A (20, 40) B (30, 60) C (60, 60) D (80, 40) E (50, 30)

   (Hint: Use an appropriate scale on the coordinate axes.)

10. i. Find the distance of the following points from the x-axis.

    a. (3, 4) b. (−3, 5) c. (7, 8) d. (0, 5) e. (−5, −5)

    ii. Find the distance of the following points from the y-axis.

    a. (3, 5) b. (−2, 6) c. (5, 8) d. (−4, −3) e. (7, −2)

Line Graphs

We have learnt about plotting a point in the Cartesian plane. A point in the Cartesian plane is represented by coordinates (XY). Hence, there are two variables involved, which have a certain relationship between them

Let us study a few cases where two variables are involved:

a. cost of petrol and the litres bought.

b. speed of a car and the distance travelled.

c. the temperature of a patient with time.

d. the perimeter of a square and its side.

In all these cases, we observe that the value of one quantity depends on the value of the other. Both the values are changing and are called variables. Now we name the two variables as independent variable and dependent variables. The cost of petrol is an independent variable; the quantity bought depends on the price of petrol. Hence, litres of petrol bought is the dependent variable. The distance travelled by a car depends on the speed of the car. Speed of the car is an independent variable and the distance travelled is the dependent variable. By convention, the x coordinate or the first coordinate represents the independent variable and the y coordinate represents the dependent variable. Hence, on the Cartesian plane, we plot the independent variable on the x-axis and the dependent variable on the y-axis.

If any relationship is indicated between two variables in a given data and we plot the points, on joining them we get a line graph. We shall understand line graphs using examples.

Example 1: Plot a line graph for the equation $y = 3x$. From the graph find the value of y when:

a. $x = 8$ b. $x = -1$ c. $x = 6$

Here, the value of y depends on the value of x. As 'x' changes, 'y' also changes. We shall make a table for different values of x and the corresponding values of y.

x	0	1	2	3	4	5
$y = 3x$	0	3	6	9	12	15

Now, to plot the points, we take an appropriate scale on the x-axis and y-axis. The scale on the two axes can be different. On the x-axis, we take 1 cm = 10 divisions = 1 unit. On the y-axis, as the values of y are multiples of 3, the appropriate scale will be 1 cm = 10 divisions = 3 units. We plot the points using data from the table, and join the points.

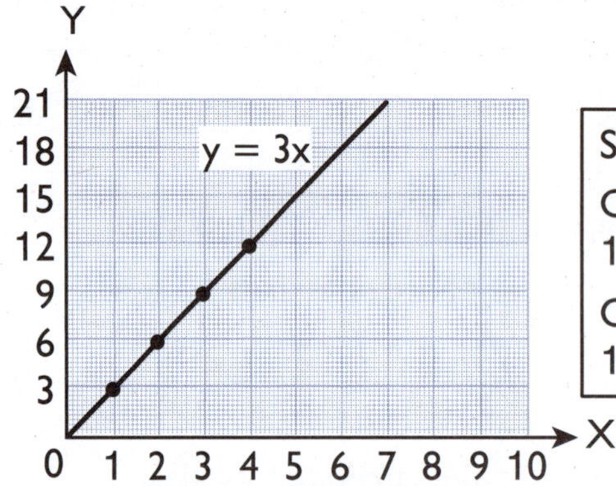

Scale:
On the x-axis,
10 division = 1 unit
On the y-axis,
10 division = 3 units

The line graph represents the relationship between the x variable and the y variable. We can find the corresponding value of variable y if the value of variable x is given using the line graph.

If we have to find the value of y when $x = 8$, we draw a line parallel to the y-axis at $x = 8$. Where it intersects the given line, we read the value of y, which is 24.

Example 2: The following table shows the temperature of a patient over a certain time period. Draw a line graph to represent the given data.

Time	Temperature (in °C)
6 am	36
10 am	38
2 pm	40
6 pm	39
10 pm	37

As time is an independent variable, we will represent it along x-axis and the temperature along the y-axis. Along the x-axis we take 2 cm = 4 hours and on the y-axis we take 1 cm = 1°C.

Now we shall plot the points as given in the table.

The graph is the required 'time–temperature' graph.

The kink on the y-axis indicates that the distance 0–35°C is not completely shown.

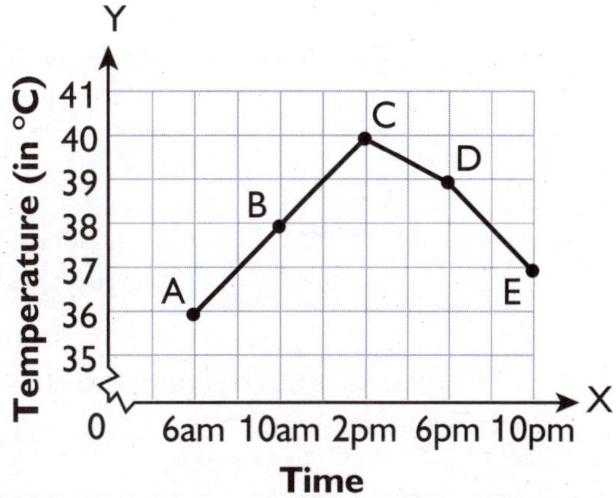

Example 3: The following graph shows the runs scored by a batsman in 10 overs of a cricket match. Read the graph and answer the following questions.

a. In which over did the batsman score the maximum runs?

b. In which over did the batsman score the minimum runs?

c. How many runs did the batsman score in the third over?

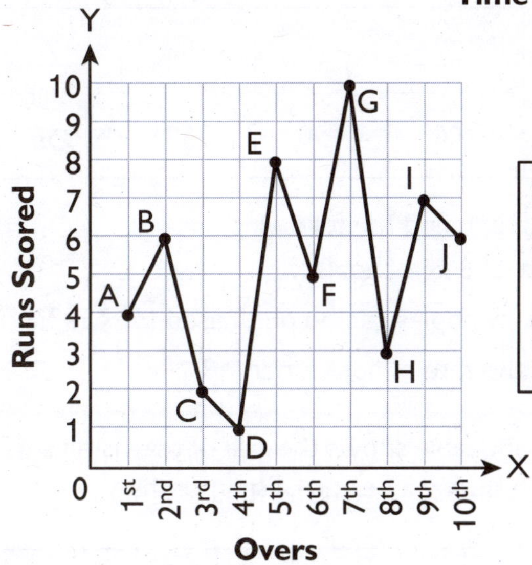

Scale:
x-axis
1 cm = 1 unit
y-axis
1 cm = 1 units

d. In which two overs did he score the same runs?

e. What is the mean run rate of the batsman in 10 overs?

Answers:

a. In the seventh over, the batsman scored the maximum runs, which was 10 runs. The point is marked G

b. In the fourth over, the batsman scored the minimum run, which was 1. The point is marked D

c. The batsman scored 2 runs in the third over.

d. In second over and tenth over he scored the same runs.

e. The mean run rate of the batsman in 10 overs is =

$$\frac{4 + 6 + 2 + 1 + 8 + 5 + 10 + 3 + 7 + 6}{10}$$

$$= \frac{52}{10} = 5.2 \text{ runs.}$$

Practice Exercise 17.2

1. Draw a graph of the function p = 4x. From the graph find the value of p when:

a. x = 3 b. x = 5 c. x = 7

2. A patient is admitted in the hospital and the time-temperature graph is to be plotted. The data is given below. Express the data as a line graph.

Time	6 am	8 am	10 am	12 noon	2 pm	4 pm	6 pm
Temperature in °C	36	38	40	42	41	39	37

3. The following table shows the cost of apples in the supermarket. Draw a line graph to depict the data.

Apples (in kg)	2	3	5	7	9	11	15
Cost (in ₹)	100	150	250	350	450	550	750

From the graph find the following.

a. The cost of 6 kg of apples.

b. How many apples can be purchased for ₹500?

c. What is the rate of apples per kg?

4. The following table shows the sale of television sets in a store. Express the data by a line graph during a period of six months.

Months	March	April	May	June	July	Aug
Number of television sets (in hundreds)	12	10	14	9	11	8

5. The following table shows the interest rate of a given bank on fixed deposits for a period of 6 years. Represent the data by a line graph.

Years	2001	2002	2003	2004	2005	2006
Rate of interest pa	12%	10%	8%	8%	9%	7%

6. Given below is a distance–time graph. Read the graph carefully and answer the following questions.

a. Find the distance covered when time is 3 seconds.

b. Find the distance covered when time is 5 seconds.

c. Find the time in which the body covered 30 m.

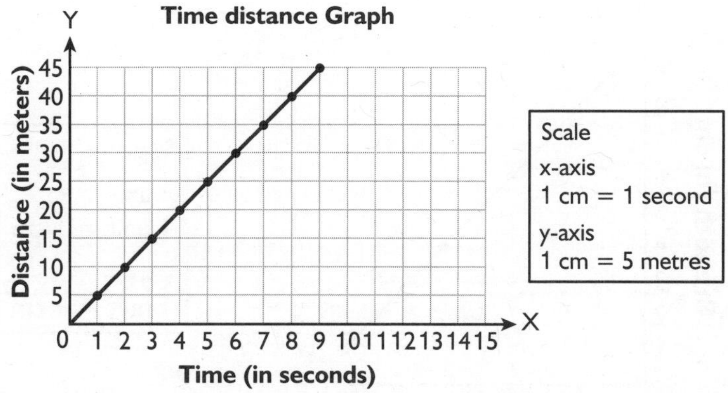

7. The following graph shows the marks obtained by Sangeeta in a midterm examination. Read the graph carefully and answer the questions.

   a. In which subject did Sangeeta score the maximum marks?

   b. In which subject did Sangeeta score the minimum marks?

   c. Find Sangeeta's average marks.

   d. Write the scale used on the y-axis.

   e. In which two subjects did she score the same marks and how much?

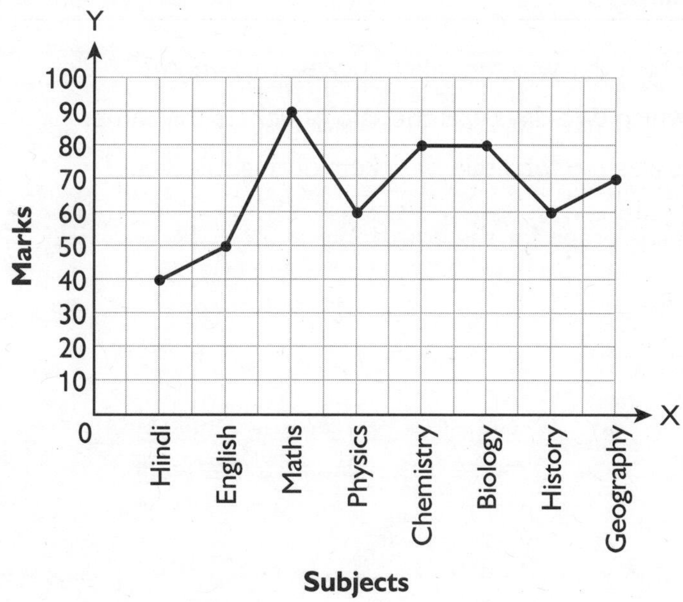

8. The relationship between the length and breadth of a rectangle is indicated in the graph given below. Read the graph and solve the following.

   a. The value of breadth when length is 9 cm.

   b. The value of length when breadth is 6 cm.

   c. The perimeter of the rectangle.

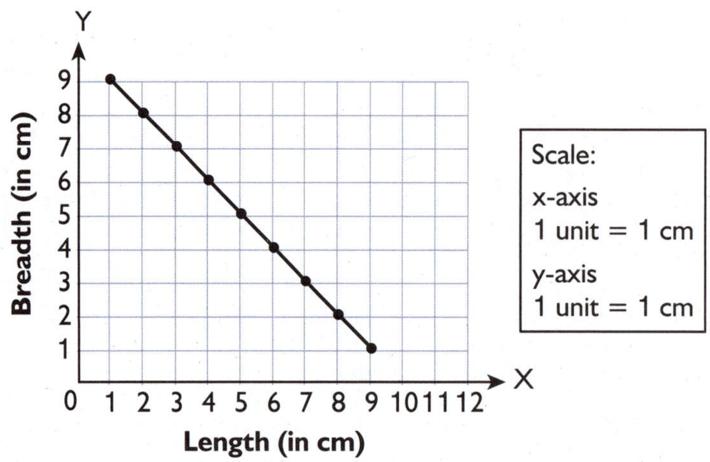

9. In a multiplex theatre, the sale of tickets during the week is given in the following table. Represent the information on a line graph.

Days	Mon	Tue	Wed	Thur	Fri	Sat	Sun
Number of tickets sold	50	200	100	100	350	400	300

a. On which day was the sale of tickets maximum?

b. On which two days was the sale of tickets the same?

c. What was the total sale of tickets during the week?

10. Draw a line graph for the equation $y = 2x + 1$.

Highlights

- The position of a point in a plane is represented on a Cartesian plane.
- The Cartesian system uses two axes that are at right angles to each other. The axes divide the plane into four quadrants.
- The x coordinate of a point is its distance from the y-axis and the y coordinate its distance from the x-axis.
- The coordinates of the origin of the point are 0 (0, 0).
- All the points on the x-axis have 0 as their y coordinates.
- All the points on the y-axis have 0 as their x coordinates.
- A line graph shows the relation between two variables, one of which depends on the other.
- The independent variable is plotted on the x-axis and the dependent variable on the y-axis.
- The two axes in a line graph need not have the same scale.
- The graph of a linear equation is always a straight line.

Higher Order Thinking Skills

HOTS

1. A sum of ₹5,000 is deposited in a bank at the rate of 10% simple interest. Plot a line graph with interest and number of years as variables.
2. In a square, the perimeter is four times the side of a square. Make a table of ordered pairs (X, Y) and plot the line graph where X = length and Y = perimeter.
3. The area of a triangle is 64 cm^2. There are two variables—the base of the triangle and the height of the triangle. Make a table of ordered pairs as (base, height) and plot the line graph. If the area of the triangle remains constant what happens to the height in the following cases:
   a. When the base increases.
   b. When the base decreases.

Plotting Graphs

Aim: To plot pie charts and bar graphs.

Material required: protractor, graph paper, pencil and crayon

Method: Plot the pie chart and line graph and colour appropriately.

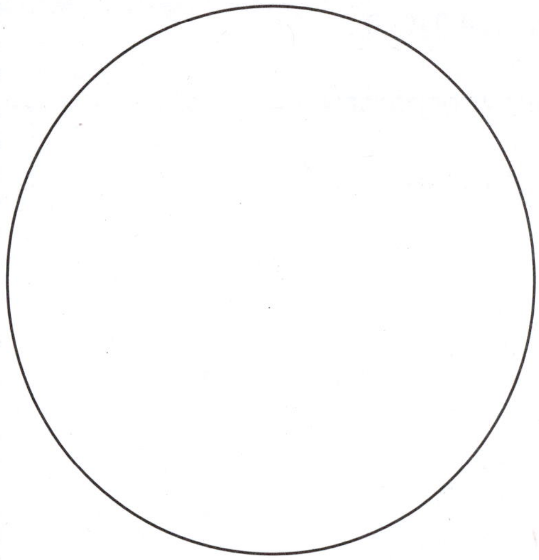

Cake	55%
Pizza	27%
Chips	4%
Cookies	10%
Chocolates	2%
Cold drinks	2%

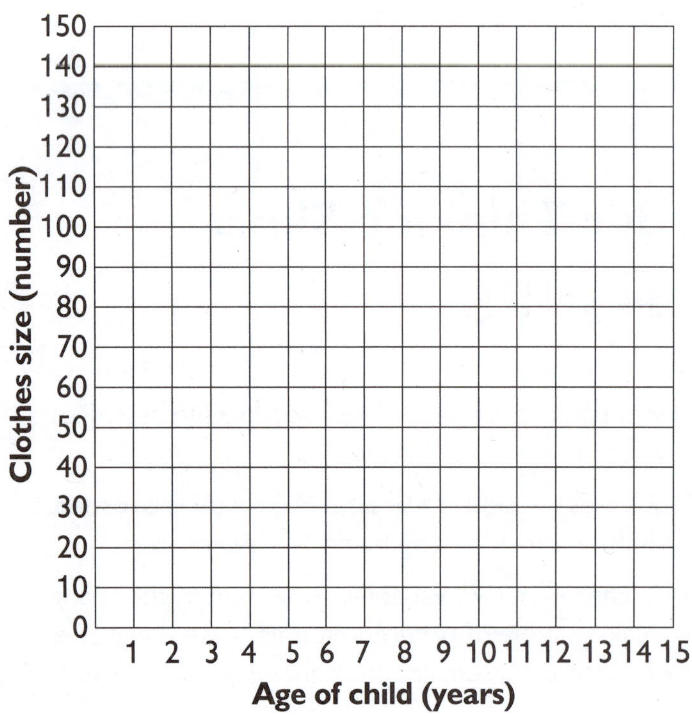

Age of child (years)	Clothes size (number)
1	15
2	20
3	25
5	35
7	50
9	75
12	100

Rewind

CHAPTERS 16–17

1. Draw a bar graph to show the number of primary school students dressed up as various characters for an annual day programme. Use an appropriate scale.

Characters	Fairies	Dwarfs	Beetles	Flowers	Trees
Number of students	55	30	25	60	15

2. Draw a double bar graph to compare the sale of cars during the festival season for two years. Use an appropriate scale.

Months	Aug	Sept	Oct	Nov	Dec
2008	2400	3200	5000	4200	4800
2009	3800	4500	7200	5600	6000

3. The marks obtained by 60 students in English are as given below.

32	36	72	45	51	70	62	68	34	42
51	63	67	33	32	41	54	52	71	65
74	35	43	45	52	58	56	71	66	72
34	36	56	58	73	65	68	38	44	54
59	63	68	71	39	51	43	46	39	31
57	63	62	73	41	32	70	62	52	31

Prepare a grouped frequency distribution table with class intervals as 30−35, 35−40, 40−45 and so on.

Represent the information in the form of a histogram.

4. The following table shows the production of cycles in five consecutive years. Draw a histogram to represent the data

Year	2001	2002	2003	2004	2005
Number of cycles (in thousands)	28	42	30	36	40

5. Study the histogram drawn below and answer the questions.

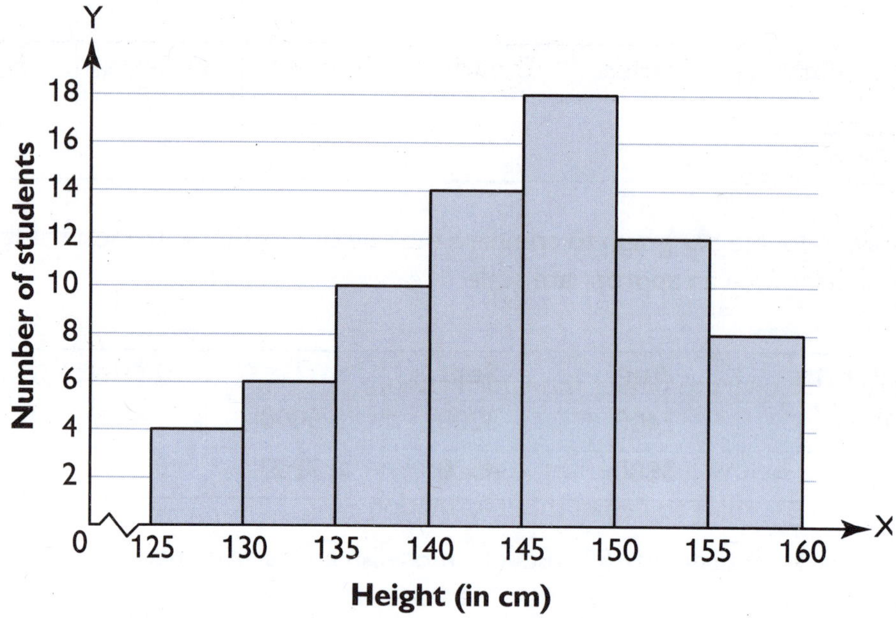

1. What does the histogram depict?
2. What is the class size?
3. How many students are above 145 cm in height?
4. What is the total number of students whose heights are measured?
5. Find the class marks of all the class intervals.

6. The table below shows the number of workers in a factory and their monthly salaries. Represent the information in the form of a pie chart.

Number of workers	Salary per Month
3,000	₹4,000
1,800	₹6,000
1,200	₹8,000
800	₹10,000
400	₹20,000
7,200	₹48,000

7. The following are Shruti marks in an examination.

Subject	Marks
Maths	90
Science	85
Social studies	75
English	65
Hindi	45
Total	360

Draw a pie chart to depict this information.

8. The table below lists the languages spoken by a group of 720 people. Draw a colourful pie chart to depict this information.

Language	Number of People
Hindi	200
Gujarati	100
Bengali	90
Marathi	120
Tamil	130
Telugu	80

9. At a monsoon party at a club, the theme was 'colours of the rainbow'. In all 180 people attended the party dressed in the colours of the rainbow as shown in the pie chart given below. Find the number of people dressed up in the individual colours.

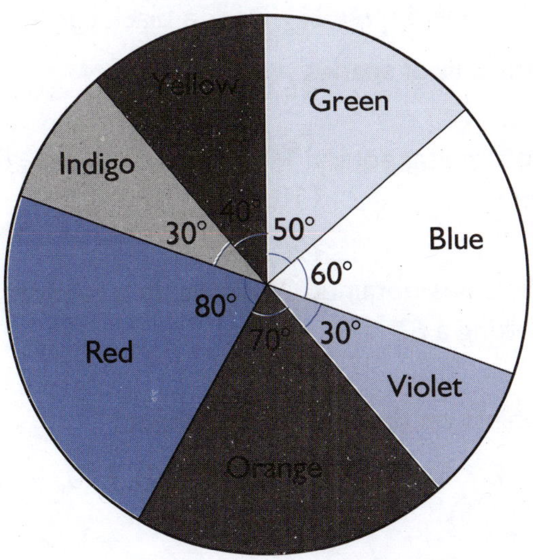

10. The following pie chart represents the number of votes obtained by five students who contested for the position of school captain. The total number of valid votes polled was 540. Answer the following questions.

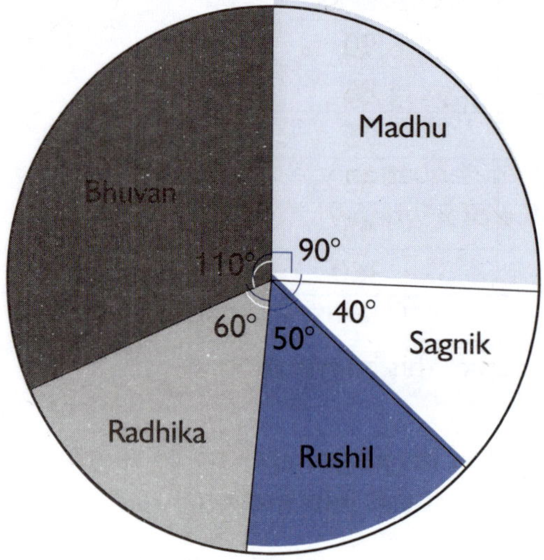

a. Who was elected the school captain?

b. How many votes did each student get?

c. Who got the minimum number of votes?

d. How many votes did Radhika get?

e. If the person getting the second-highest number of votes was appointed vice-captain, who was appointed vice-captain?

11. a. Write an event that is certain to happen.

b. Write an event that is certain not to happen.

12. A pack of 52 cards is shuffled. Find the probability of getting:

a. a red card b. a red queen c. a black card d. an ace

e. any card from the suit of spades.

13. Two dice are rolled simultaneously. How many outcomes are possible? Write all the possible outcomes.

14. In 60 throws of a dice, 6 is obtained 24 times. In a random throw of dice, what is the probability of getting a 6?

15. Plot the following points on the same graph sheet.

A (3, 5), B (5, 3), C (3, −5), D (−3, 5), E (−3, 0), F (0, −3), G (5, 0), H (0, −5), I (5, 2), J (2, 5)

16. The coordinates of the vertices of a quadrilateral are given. Plot them on a graph paper and name the figure.

   a. (0, 0) (4, 0) (4, 4) (0, 4)

   b. (2, 2) (2, −2) (6, −2) (6, 2)

   c. (3, 5) (−3, 5) (−3, 2) (3, 2)

17. Draw a graph for the equation $y = 5x$. From the graph read the value of y when $x = 2$ and the value of x when $y = 20$.

18. Name the quadrants in which the following points lie.

   a. P (−3, 4), b. Q (−3, −4)

   c. R (3, 4), d. S (3, −4)

19. Draw a graph to show the temperature of a city over a week.

Days	Sun	Mon	Tue	Wed	Thur	Fri	Sat
Temperature in °C	25°	28°	31°	29°	24°	27°	35°

20. The following line graph shows the sale in a grocery shop during the week. Read the graph carefully and answer the following questions.

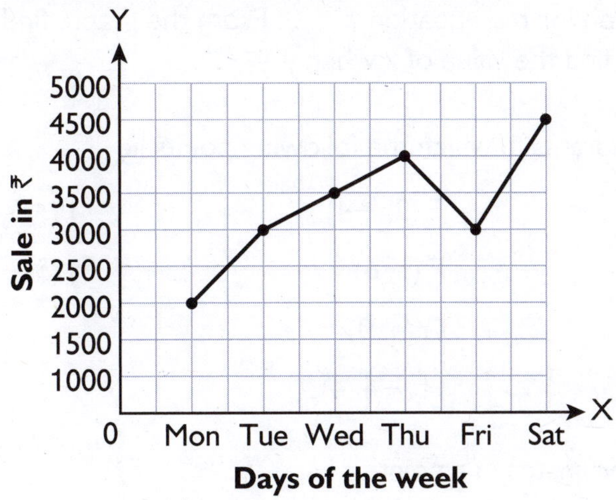

   a. On which day was the sale maximum?

   b. On which day was the sale minimum?

   c. On which day was the shop closed?

   d. What is the total collection of the shopkeeper during the week?

   e. On which two days was the sale the same?

Test Yourself

Unit V

1. Plot the following points on a graph paper and name the figure formed.

   a. A (1, 1), B (3, 1), C (2, 3)

   b. P (7, 2), Q (11, 2), R (7, 5), S (11, 5)

   c. M (4, 3), N (4, 5), O (6, 3), P (6, 5)

   d. V (5, 10), W (3, 8), X (3, 6), Y (7, 6), Z (7, 8)

   e. A (15, 2), B (18, 5), C (18, 8), D (15, 10), E (12, 8), F (12, 5)

2. The following table shows the cost of books.

Books	1	2	5	6	8	9
Cost (in ₹)	100	200	500	600	800	900

   Draw a line graph to depict this information. From the graph find the following.

   a. The cost of 7 books.

   b. The number of books that can be bought for ₹1,000.

   c. Find the ratio of the books to the cost. Is it constant? What type of variation is it?

3. Plot a line graph for the equation $y = \frac{x}{2}$. From the graph, find the value of y when z = 10. Also, find the value of x when y = 4.

4. Write the quadrants in which the following points lie

A (2, 4)	E (2, −4)	I (−5, 0)
B (−2, 4)	F (3, 6)	J (5, −5)
C (−2, −4)	G (4, 0)	
D (4, 2)	H (−4, 4)	

5. Write the coordinates of a point,

   a. lying on the x-axis to the right of the origin at a distance of 4 units.

   b. lying on the x-axis to the left of the origin at a distance of 4 units.

   c. lying on the y-axis at a distance of 4 units above the origin.

d. lying on the y-axis at a distance of 4 units below origin

e. lying in the first quadrant at a distance of 4 units from the x-axis and a distance of 4 units from the y-axis.

6. The following table shows the popular brands of shampoo sold at a shop during the day. Draw a pie chart to depict this information and colour it.

Brands	A	B	C	D	E
Number sold	36	44	32	28	40

7. The following table shows the number of children enrolled in a village school over a period of 5 years.

Academic year	2001–2002	2002–2003	2003–2004	2004–2005	2005–2006
Number of children	150	200	170	180	220

Draw a bar graph to represent the data. Use an appropriate scale.

8. The runs scored by two batsmen in 5 cricket matches are tabulated below. Represent the information using a double bar graph

Match	I	II	III	IV	V
Batsman A	65	40	70	30	95
Batsman B	35	55	60	90	75

Find each batsman's average run rate.

9. The marks scored by 50 students in a class test are listed below. Tabulate the raw data as a grouped frequency distribution with class intervals of 0–5, 5–10, etc.

2	3	7	12	18	17	14	19	21	22
24	14	19	18	4	14	3	21	16	18
22	12	18	17	6	18	20	12	16	18
17	13	11	23	8	17	24	8	7	6
18	11	12	24	10	16	24	14	18	21

Also draw a histogram to represent the data graphically.

10. A few families were surveyed about their monthly expenditure on petrol. Their responses are tabulated in the histogram that follows. Read the histogram carefully and answer the questions that follow.

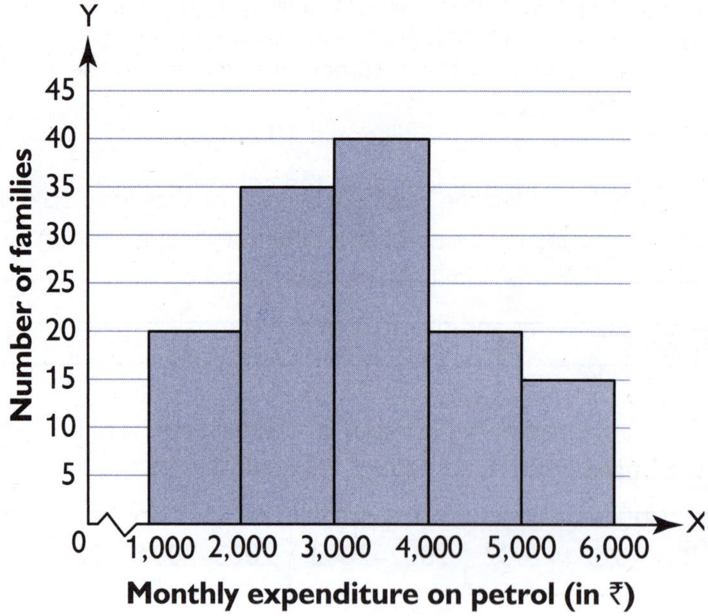

a. How many families spend ₹3000–₹4000 per month on petrol?

b. What is the least expenditure on petrol? How many families spend this amount on petrol monthly?

c. How many families were surveyed?

11. The volume of a cube is 1,728 cm^3. Find the length of its edge and its surface area.

12. A cubical tank with edge 3 m is filled with water. How many litres of water are there in the tank? In a building with 90 flats, how much water can be provided to the residents of each flat?

13. The volume of a cuboid is 8,000 cm^3. Its length and breadth are 25 cm and 20 cm, respectively. Find its height. Also, find the total surface area of the cuboid. If the volume of a cube is the same, find the length of its edge.

14. The dimensions of an aluminium box are 20 cm × 15 cm × 10.5 cm. If 30 such boxes are to be made, find the area of the aluminium sheet required in m^2. Also, if the cost of aluminium sheet is ₹60/m^2, find the total cost of making the boxes.

15. A trench 8 m long 5 m wide and 2 m deep is dug. The soil from this is spread evenly on a patch of ground 16 m long and 4 m wide. What is the height of the soil spread over the patch?

16. The height of a cylinder is 10 cm and its curved surface area is 880 cm^2. Find the radius and total surface area of the cylinder.

17. The ratio between the radius of the base and height of the cylinder is 2:3. If the volume of the cylinder is 12,936 cm^3, find the total surface area of the cylinder.

18. The area of a rhombus with one diagonal 18 cm long is the same as the area of a square of side 18 cm. Find the length of the other diagonal of the rhombus.

19. One parallel side of a trapezium is 10 cm less than the other. If the distance between the parallel sides is 15 cm and the area of the trapezium is 600 cm^2, find the length of each parallel side.

20. Find the area of the given quadrilateral field and the cost of reaping it at the rate of ₹75 per m^2. (All measurements are in m.)

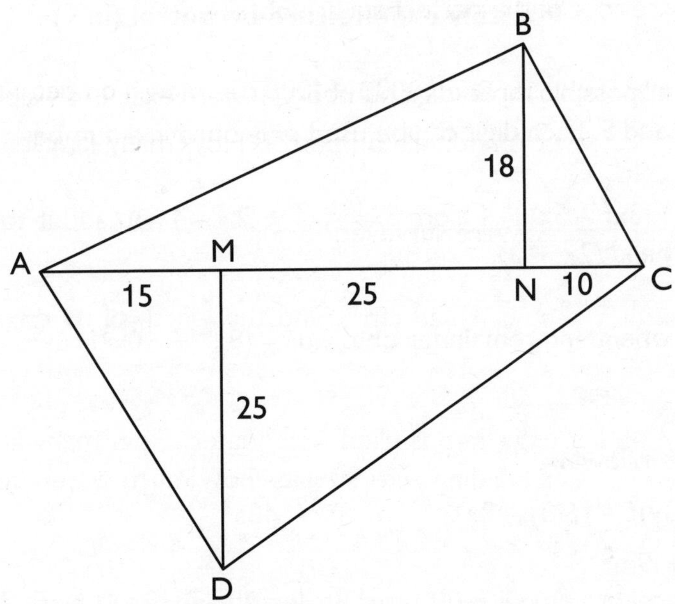

Fun fact

Your total height is about 8 times the height of your head. Try measuring it with the help of a friend.

Model Test Paper

Time: ____________

1. If $x = \frac{(-12)}{13}$ and $y = \frac{+6}{7}$,
   show that $(-x) = x$ and $(-y) = y$.
   Also show that $x + y = y + x$.

2. Find the value of 'm' in the following.
   a. $\left(\frac{1}{2}\right)^5 \times \left(\frac{1}{2}\right)^3 = \left(\frac{1}{2}\right)^{2m}$ b. $\left(\frac{-3}{4}\right)^7 \div \left(\frac{-3}{4}\right)^3 = \left(\frac{-3}{4}\right)^{4m}$
   c. $\left[\left(\frac{1}{9}\right)^3\right]^m = \left(\frac{1}{9}\right)^6 \times \left(\frac{1}{9}\right)^3$

3. Find the least number that must be added to 6,203 to make it a perfect square. Find the square root of the perfect square obtained.

4. Write down all possible three-digit numbers that are exactly divisible by 5 using the digits 0, 3, 4 and 5. Each digit can be used only once in a number.

5. Subtract $x^3 + 3x^2 - 5x + 4$ from $3x^3 - x^2 + 2x - 4$ and add it to the product of $(x^2 - 3x + 7)$ and $(2x + 3)$.

6. Write the quotient and remainder on dividing $(8x^4 + 10x^3 - 5x^2 - 4x + 1)$ by $2x^2 + x - 1$.

7. Factorise the following.
   a. $12(2x - 3y)^2 - 16(3y - 2x)$ b. $3a^5 - 48a^3$
   c. $1 - 6m + 9m^2$

8. Factorise the following.
   a. $y^2 + 7y - 144$ b. $p^2 + 13p + 40$ c. $n^2 - 5n - 24$

9. Solve the following equations.
   a. $3m + \frac{2}{3} = 2m + 1$ b. $\frac{2 + y}{3 + y} = 5$ c. $\frac{3p + 5}{4p + 2} = \frac{3p + 4}{4p + 7}$

10. The altitude of a triangle is five-thirds the length of its corresponding base. If the altitude is increased by 4 cm and the base decreased by 2 cm, the area of the triangle remains the same. Find the base and altitude of the triangle.

11. Manjinder sold a book at a loss of 5%. Had he sold it for ₹104 more, he would have made a profit of 8%. Find the selling price of the book.

12. A grocer purchased 200 kg of rice at ₹25 per kg. He sold 80 kg of it at a profit of 10% and 40 kg at a loss of 4%. At what per cent should he sell the remainder so as to gain 8% on his investment?

13. A dealer marks his goods at 40% above the cost price and allows a discount of 15% on the marked price. Find his profit or loss per cent.

14. At what percentage above the cost price must Randeep mark a painting so as to gain 33%, even after allowing a discount of 5%?

15. Rati deposited a sum of ₹6,40,000 in a bank for 3 years at a rate of $7\frac{1}{2}\%$ per annum (compounded annually). What amount will she receive after 3 years?

16. If the compound interest on a certain sum for 2 years at $12\frac{1}{2}\%$ per annum (compounded annually) is ₹510, find the simple interest on the same sum for the same period and at the same rate of interest.

17. Five men working 9 hours a day can complete a particular work in 16 days. How many days would 8 men take to complete the same work if each person works for 10 hours a day?

18. Three pipes A, B and C can fill an overhead tank in 6 hours, 8 hours and 12 hours, respectively. How long would the three pipes take to fill the empty tank if all the three pipes are operating together.

19. A train 400 m long is travelling at a speed of 72 km/hr. How long will it take to cross an electric pole?

20. Aman lent a sum of money for 2 years at a rate of 20% per annum (compounded annually). Pawan lent the same sum of money for 2 years at a rate of 20% per annum (compounded semi-annually). Pawan earned ₹482 more than Aman. Find the sum of money lent.

21. A quadrilateral has three acute angles each measuring 85°. Find the measure of the fourth angle.

22. Prove that the bisectors of any two adjacent angles of a parallelogram intersect at right angles.

23. Construct a trapezium ABCD in which AB = 6 cm, BC = 4 cm, CD = 3.5 cm, $\angle B = 75°$ and AB || DC.

24. Construct a parallelogram ABCD in which AB = 6.5, AC = 3.5 cm and the altitude AL from A is 2.5 cm.

    Draw the altitude from C and measure it.

25. The area of a trapezium is 540 cm^2 and its height is 18 cm. If one of the parallel sides is longer than the other by 12 cm, find the measure of each parallel side.

26. A square lawn of side 14 m has semicircular flower beds on all the sides. Find the total area of the lawn and the flower beds. Find the cost of fencing the flower beds from the outside and inside at the rate of ₹50 per m^2.

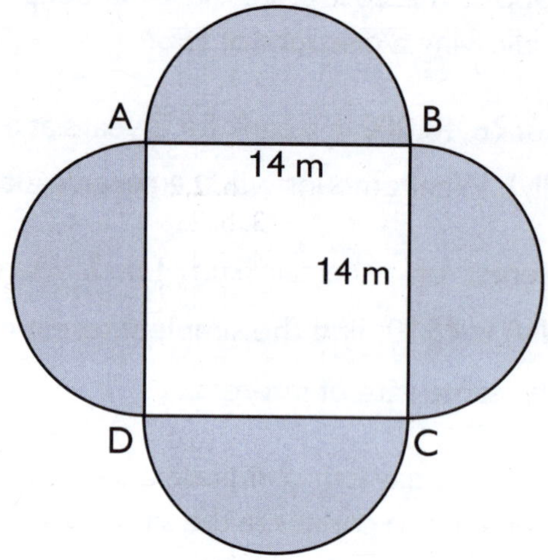

27. A pit 5 m long and 3.5 m wide is dug to a certain depth. If the volume of the soil taken out of it is 14 m^2, what is the depth of the pit?

28. A particular brand of cooking oil is available in two packs— a plastic case with a square base of side 12 cm and height 15 cm and a cylinder with circular base of radius 7 cm and height 12 cm. Which of them has a greater capacity and by how much?

29. The following table gives the number of fruits kept in a hamper. Represent the data using a pie chart.

Fruits	Mangoes	Apples	Oranges	Coconuts	Pomegranates
Number	31	25	18	5	11

30. The weights (in kg) of 40 people are given below.

43	51	47	62	48	40	50	62	53	56
40	48	56	53	50	42	55	52	48	46
45	54	52	50	47	44	54	55	60	63
58	55	60	58	53	44	48	49	53	58

Prepare a group frequency distribution table of equal class size beginning with 40 – 45. Also, draw a histogram on a graph sheet to represent the data.

Answers

Practice Exercise 1.1

1. a. Commutative b. Identity c. Associative
   d. Additive inverse e. Closure
2. To verify a + b = b + a
3. a. $\frac{7}{12}$ b. $\frac{(-4)}{5}$ c. $\frac{2}{3}$ d. $\frac{13}{15}$ e. $\frac{(-6)}{7}$
4. To verify (a + b) + c = a + (b + c)
5. a. $\frac{16}{4} = 4$ b. $\frac{10}{7}$ c. 0 d. $\frac{435}{154}$ e. $\frac{5}{21}$
6. a. (−1) b. $\frac{5}{12}$ c. $\frac{2}{9}$ d. (−1) e. $\frac{(-3)}{10}$
7. Verify that $a - b \neq b - a$
8. a. $\frac{(-21)}{99} \neq \frac{111}{99}$ b. $\frac{5}{36} \neq \frac{37}{36}$ c. $\frac{(-1)}{2} \neq \frac{1}{2}$
9. a. $\frac{1}{6}$ b. $\frac{(-1)}{6}$ c. (−2) d. $\frac{3}{4}$ e. $\frac{1}{5}$
10. a. F b. T c. F d. T e. F
    f. T g. F h. F i. F j. T

Practice Exercise 1.2

1. a. $\frac{15}{56}$ b. $\frac{(-21)}{50}$ c. $\frac{(-27)}{28}$ d. $\frac{85}{6}$ e. $\frac{5}{4}$
2. Commutative property
3. Associative propert 4. Distributive property
6. a. $\frac{3}{2}$ b. $\frac{(-3)}{1}$ c. $\frac{(-11)}{5}$ d. $\frac{(-19)}{4}$
   e. Not defined
7. a. 12 b. $\frac{(-1)}{4}$ c. $\frac{9}{16}$ d. $\frac{(-16)}{75}$ e. $\frac{305}{144}$
9. $\frac{(+13)}{19}$ 10. $\frac{149}{234}$

Practice Exercise 1.3

1. a. $M = \frac{1}{10}$ $N = \frac{3}{10}$ $P = \frac{9}{10}$ $Q = \frac{12}{10}$ $R = \frac{14}{10}$
   b. $A = \frac{(-5)}{7}$ $B = \frac{(-1)}{7}$ $C = \frac{5}{7}$
   c. $X = \frac{(-7)}{4}$ $Y = \frac{5}{4}$ $Z = \frac{9}{4}$
4. $\frac{5}{26}, \frac{5}{27}, \frac{5}{28}, \frac{5}{29}, \frac{6}{31}$
5. $\frac{1}{91}, \frac{1}{90}, \frac{1}{45}, \frac{1}{30}, \frac{2}{45}, \frac{1}{18}, \frac{1}{15}, \frac{7}{90}, \frac{4}{45}$
6. $\frac{1}{8}, \frac{1}{7}, \frac{1}{6}, \frac{1}{5}, \frac{5}{36}, \frac{7}{36}, \frac{2}{9}, \frac{11}{72}, \frac{13}{72}, \frac{5}{24}$
7. $\frac{-1}{2}, \frac{-1}{4}, \frac{-1}{8}$
8. $4\frac{1}{2}, 4\frac{1}{4}, 4\frac{1}{8}$
9. $-2\frac{1}{2}, 2\frac{1}{4}, -2\frac{1}{8}$
10. a. 0, 1, 2, 3, 4, 5, 6, 7, 8, 9
    b. 0, −1, −2, −3, −4, −5, −6, −7, −8, −9, −10

HOTS (Chapter 1)

1 b. 2. $\frac{(-11)}{28}$ 3. ₹18.50

Practice Exercise 2.1

1 a. 12 c. 6,250 d. 462
  f. 1,118 h. 5,613 i. 6,688
  j. 8,866
2. b. 1,521 d. 15,129 g. 1,225
   h. 2,209 i. 12,321
3. b. 256 e. 1,296 f. 7,744 h. 9,216 j. 6,400
4. a. 135 b. 149 c. 175 d. 197 e. 241
   f. 219 g. 441 h. 667 i. 1,109 j. 1,999
5. a. 4 + 5 b. 12 + 13 c. 24 + 25
   d. 40 + 41 e. 180 + 181 f. 144 + 145
   g. 112 + 113 h. 84 + 85 i. 60 + 61
   j. 220 + 221
6. b. 30,40,50 $(50)^2 = (30)^2 + (40)^2$
   c. 9, 40, 41 $(41)^2 = (40)^2 + (9)^2$
   e. 50, 624, 626 $(626)^2 = (50)^2 + (624)^2$
7. a. 3, 4, <u>5</u> b. 10, 24, <u>26</u> c. 16, 63, <u>65</u>
   d. 36, 323, <u>325</u> e. 50, 624, <u>626</u>
8. a. 16 b. 36 c. 64 d. 25 e. 121
9. a. 30^2 b. 55^2 c. 16^2 d. 24^2 e. 80^2
   f. $\frac{101}{100}$ g. 100^2 h. 48^2 i. 11^2 j. 160^2
10. a. 1 + 3 + 5 + 7 + 9 + 11 + 13 + 15
    b. 1 + 3 + 5 + 7 + 9 + 11 + 13 + 15 + 17 + 19 + 21
    c. 1 + 3 + 5 + 7 + 9 + 11 + 13
    d. 1 + 3 + 5 + 7 + 9 + 11 + 13 + 15 + 17 + 19
    e. 1 + 3 + 5 + 7 + 9 + 11 + 13 + 15 + 17 + 19 + 21 + 23

Practice Exercise 2.2

1. a. 21 b. 25 c. 42 d. 56 e. 49
   f. 60 g. 69 h. 75 i. 78 j. 99
2. a. 21, 210 b. 7, 154 c. 3, 147 d. 5, 210 e. 5, 220
3. a. 7, 22 b. 7, 33 c. 2, 63 d. 3, 55 e. 5, 39
4. a. $\frac{18}{21}$ b. $\frac{19}{27}$ c. $\frac{25}{36}$ d. $\frac{65}{80}$ e. $\frac{44}{51}$
5. $\frac{31}{5}$ b. $\frac{53}{11}$ c. $\frac{42}{13}$ d. $\frac{64}{23}$ e. $\frac{77}{12}$
6. a. 2.5 b. 2.7 c. 0.3 d. 0.09 e. 0.11
7. 28 m 8. 77 9. ₹3,108 10. 900

Practice Exercise 2.3

1. a. 59 b. 96 c. 97 d. 101 e. 109
   f. 245 g. 316 h. 333 i. 625 j. 410
2. a. 9, 50 b. 12, 87 c. 11, 79
   d. 9, 111 e. 212, 212
3. a. 38, 79 b. 64, 92 c. 149, 103
   d. 191, 124 e. 103, 212

4. a. 8.6 b. 11.5 c. 15.8 d. 5.12 e. 20.31
5. a. 1.204 b. 0.228 c. 2.074 d. 0.612 e. 9.210
6. a. 9 b. 16 c. 19 d. 30 e. 25
7. 10.23 m 8. 6.8 m 9. 99, 856 10. 75, 55

Practice Exercise 2.4

1. a. $\frac{343}{1331}$ b. $\frac{(-64)}{125}$ c. $\frac{(-216)}{2197}$ d. $\frac{2197}{64}$ e. $\frac{6859}{512}$
2. a. 0.125 b. (−0.000216) c. (−32.768) d. 68.921 e. 15.625
3. a. 5; 2,74,625 b. 9; 7,04,969 c. 3, 4,56,533 d. 0; 7,29,000 e. 8; 32,768 f. 1; 1,32,651 g. 7; 2,50,047 h. 4; 5,92,704 i. 6; 46,656 j. 2; 1,95,112
4. a. 3.375 cm^3 b. 13.824 cm^3 c. 46.656 cm^3 d. 9.663597 cm^3 e. 0.343 cm^3
5. a. F b. F c. F d. F e. F

Practice Exercise 2.5

1. a. (−5) b. (−13) c. 15 d. 30 e. 35 f. 33 g. 42 h. (−39) i. 45 j. (−36)
2. a. $\frac{7}{5}$ b. $\frac{6}{5}$ c. 0.1 d. 0.4 e. (−0.5) f. $\frac{4}{3}$ g. $\frac{10}{9}$ h. 0.7 i. (−0.9) j. 0.11
3. a. 1.6 b. 2.1 c. 3.5 d. 4.2 e. 4.8
4. a. 25; 55 b. 9; 66 c. 7; 112 d. 49; 147 e. 25; 160
5. a. 9; 15 b. 25; 12 c. 4; 16 d. 3; 20 e. 25; 18
6. a. 6 b. 9 c. 11 d. 14 e. 17
8. 2.6 cm 9. 0.5 cm, 27 10. 2.4 cm

HOTS (Chapter 2)

1. 16 m 2. 225, 3025 3. 17 km.

Rewind (Chapters 1–2)

1. $\frac{13}{48}$ 2. $\frac{(-3)}{10}$ 3. ₹$93\frac{1}{8}$ 4. $\frac{125}{8}$
5. $\frac{19}{64}$ 6. x = 3 7. c. 8. $\frac{4}{3}$ 9. $\frac{21}{100}$ m^2
10. a. $\left(\frac{1}{3}\right)^3$ b. $\left(-\frac{1}{3}\right)^5$ c. $\left(-\frac{1}{4}\right)^3$ d. $\left(-\frac{1}{10}\right)^3$ e. $\left(-\frac{3}{5}\right)^5$
11. a. $\frac{1}{27}$ b. $\frac{1}{64}$ c. $\frac{1}{4}$ d. 1 e. 1
12. $5\frac{1}{30}$ m 13. $106\frac{8}{15}$ 14. 4,250 km 15. 140 m
16. $\frac{13}{48}, \frac{7}{24}, \frac{5}{16}$ 17. $\frac{97}{33}$ 18. Distributive property
19. a. > b. = c. > d. < e. <
20. a. 2.76×10^{11} b. 7.6×10^{-11} c. 1.0×10^{-13}

Practice Exercise 3.1

1.

	Base	Exponent
a.	2	7
b.	(−7)	4
c.	$\frac{4}{5}$	6
d.	$\left(-\frac{3}{8}\right)$	5
e.	$\left(-\frac{9}{13}\right)$	2

2. a. $(-3)^5$ b. 9^4 c. $\left(\frac{2}{5}\right)^5$ d. $\left(-\frac{1}{10}\right)^4$ e. $\left(\frac{5}{12}\right)^3$
3. a. $\frac{8}{343}$ b. $\frac{81}{2401}$ c. $\frac{1}{729}$ d. $\frac{16}{14641}$ e. $\left(-\frac{32}{3125}\right)$
4. a. $\left(-\frac{1}{3}\right)^3$ b. $\left(\frac{1}{3}\right)^5$ c. $\left(-\frac{1}{10}\right)^3$ d. $\left(\frac{3}{5}\right)^5$ e. $\left(\frac{2}{5}\right)^6$
5. a. $\frac{1}{5^3}$ b. $\frac{1}{7^2}$ c. $\frac{1}{11^8}$ d. $\frac{1}{13^5}$ e. $\frac{1}{(-12)^2}$ f. 3^7 g. $\left(-\frac{5}{4}\right)^8$ h. $\left(\frac{8}{5}\right)^9$ i. $\left(-\frac{5}{13}\right)^4$ j. $\frac{1}{(-1)^{10}}$
6. a. $\frac{1}{36}$ b. $\frac{1}{64}$ c. $\frac{1}{32}$ d. $\frac{1}{8}$ e. 243 f. $\left(-\frac{1}{10000}\right)$ g. $\frac{1}{1000}$ h. $\frac{121}{81}$ i. (−64) j. $\left(-\frac{8}{7}\right)$
7. a. $\left(\frac{7}{8}\right)^3$ b. $\left(\frac{14}{19}\right)^4$ c. $\left(\frac{17}{11}\right)^{(-3)}$ d. $\left(\frac{1}{8}\right)^6$ e. $\left(\frac{2}{3}\right)^5$ f. $\left(-\frac{5}{7}\right)^3$ g. $\left(\frac{11}{3}\right)^{(-4)}$ h. $\left(\frac{7}{13}\right)^5$ i. $\left(-\frac{4}{3}\right)^{11}$ j. $\left(\frac{1}{8}\right)^4$
8. a. 36 b. 216 c. 1,60,000 d. $\frac{9}{32}$ e. $\frac{1}{15}$
10. a. $\frac{3}{64}$ b. $\frac{3}{32}$ c. $\frac{1}{8}$ d. $\frac{7}{80}$ e. $\frac{1}{56}$ f. $\left(-\frac{9}{32}\right)$ g. $\left(-\frac{1}{108}\right)$ h. $\frac{125}{512}$ i. $\frac{125}{864}$ j. $\frac{16}{9}$

Practice Exercise 3.2

1. a. $\frac{32}{243}$ b. $\frac{8}{125}$ c. $\left(-\frac{3125}{7776}\right)$ d. $\frac{1}{64}$ e. $\frac{4}{81}$
2. $\frac{4}{49}$ b. 36 c. 64 d. $\frac{81}{625}$ e. $\left(-\frac{2}{5}\right)$
3. a. 9^9 b. $(-8)^{11}$ c. $\left(\frac{3}{7}\right)^7$ d. $(7)^{-7}$ e. $\left(-\frac{4}{7}\right)^6$ f. $-7^{(-12)}$ g. $(45)^{(-6)}$ h. $\left(\frac{1}{2}\right)^{(-3)}$ i. $\left(\frac{5}{9}\right)^7$ j. $\left(-\frac{3}{4}\right)^{20}$
4. a. p = 4 b. 4 c. 3 d. 3 e. 8.
5. a. 1 b. 3 c. 1 d. 0 e. 1
6. a. (−3) b. (−1) c. 2 d. 3 e. 1
7. a. $\frac{1}{64}$ b. $\frac{125}{8}$ c. $\frac{35}{18}$ d. $\frac{203}{108}$ e. 1

8. a. 864 b. $\frac{1}{27}$ c. $\frac{1}{64}$ d. 1 e. 1
9. a. $\frac{19}{64}$ b. $\left(-\frac{4}{13}\right)$ c. 90 d. $\frac{1}{625}$ e. $\frac{16}{81}$
10. a. × b. ÷ c. − d. × e. +

Practice Exercise 3.3

1. a. 5.76×10^{11} b. 3.69×10^{13} c. 1.34×10^{10} d. 1.29×10^{12} e. 2.5×10^{14}
2. a. $4.8 \times 10^{(-13)}$ b. $5.0 \times 10^{(-15)}$ c. $2.5 \times 10^{(-16)}$ d. $2.67 \times 10^{(-18)}$ e. $2.61 \times 10^{(-22)}$
3. a. 72,00,000 b. 24,800 c. 92,10,00,000 d. 2,56,900 e. 7,77,70,000
4. a. 0.0000048 b. 0.000037 c. 0.000000672 d. 0.00000000098 e. 0.00000000431
5. 5.64×10^3 kg

HOTS (Chapter 3)

1. $\left(-\frac{288}{3}\right)$ 2. $\frac{60}{7}$
3. The size of the plant cell is more than the size of the bacteria.

Practice Exercise 4.1

1. a. 10 b. 62,64,66,68
2. a. 1 b. 3 c. 2 d. 1 e. 2 f. 0 g. 1 h. 2 i. 0 j. 1
3. a. 5 b. 2 c. 5 d. 2 e. 0 f. 8 g. 7 h. 5 i. 4 j. 4
4. 25, 30, 35, 40, 45, 50, 55, 60, 65
5. a. 3 b. 4 c. 0 d. 4 e. 4 f. 2 g. 2 h. 1 i. 2 j. 3
6. 1, 2, 7
7. a. a = 8, b = 7, c = 4 b. a = 9, b = 2, c = 3 c. a = 4 d. a = 8, b = 5 e. b = 7, c = 6
8. a. a = 1, b = 3, c = 1 b. a = 9, b = 2, c = 3 c. a = 5, b = 2, c = 3 d. a = 2, b = 5, c = 3 e. a = 2
9. a. c = 2, a. a = 5, b = 6, c = 7 e. a = 1, b = 2, c = 3
10. Divisible by 3, 306, 360, 603, 630
    Divisible by 9, 306, 360, 603, 630
    Divisible by 10, 360, 630, 130, 160, 310, 610
    Divisible by 3, 9 and 10, the numbers are 360 and 630

Practice Exercise 4.2

1. a.

6	11	10
13	9	5
8	7	12

b.

5	15	13
19	11	3
9	7	17

c.

5	30	25
40	20	0
15	10	35

2. a.

18	4	5	15
7	13	12	10
11	9	8	14
6	16	17	3

b.

30	2	4	24
8	20	18	14
16	12	10	22
6	26	28	0

c.

3	14	13	0
8	5	6	11
4	9	10	7
15	2	1	12

3. a. 27, 32, 37 b. 46, 56, 66 c. 64, 128, 256 d. 1,024, 4,096, 16,384 e. 49, 64, 81
4. a = 6, b = 12, c = 10 d = 20
5.

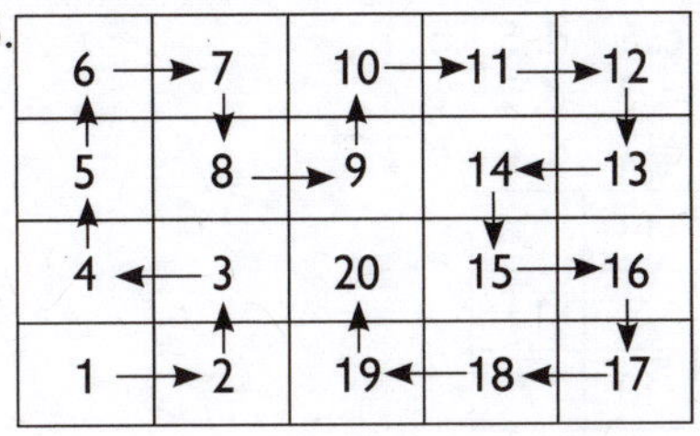

HOTS (Chapter 4)

1. 1+ (2 × 3) − 4 + (56 ÷ 7) + 89
2. a. 21, 25, 29 b. 81, 243, 729 c. 35, 26, 17
3.

6	1	8
7	5	3
2	9	4

Rewind (Chapters 3–4)

1. c 2. 3, 192 3. $\frac{29}{14}$ 4. c 5. $-\frac{12}{14}$
6. a. 12, 93, 48 b. 12, 48 c. none 7. 3, 35

8. $\ell = 154$ m, $b = 77$ m 9. 0.111 10. 1,024, 32
12 a. $x = 1, y = 3, z = 1$ b. $x = 9, y = 2, z = 3$
c. $x = 5, y = 2, z = 3$ 13. 130, 310, 360, 630, 160, 610, 136, 316, 106, 306 14. 27
15. 5, 315 16. 900 17. a. 0 b. 1 c. 6
18. a. 0.512 b. (−1.728) c. $\frac{343}{8}$ 19. 2, 32
20. 2.4 cm

Test Yourself: Unit 1

1. $\frac{(-2)}{3}, \frac{(-5)}{9}, \frac{(-4)}{9}, \frac{(-1)}{3}, \frac{(-2)}{9}, \frac{(-1)}{9}, 0, \frac{1}{9}, \frac{1}{18}, \frac{1}{27}$
2. Associate property
3. a. $\frac{(-3)}{10}$ b. −2 c. $3\frac{1}{2}$
4. Distributive property $\frac{4}{3}, \frac{5}{4}, \frac{3}{2}$ 5. $\frac{43}{280}$
6. a. $\left(\frac{5}{6}\right)^2$ b. $\left(\frac{1}{5}\right)^4$ c. $\left(\frac{(-2)}{5}\right)^3$ d. $\left(\frac{3}{4}\right)^4$ e. $\left(\frac{(-1)}{20}\right)^3$
7. a. x^4 b. x^2 c. x^{15} d. z^2 e. 1
8. a. 5; 180 b. 7; 77 c. 22; 264
9. a. 3; 9 b. 2; 16 c. 3; 35 10. 49
11. a. 7.56 b. 23.2 c. 42.6 12. 2; 12
13. 2.6 cm; 8 times
14. 95, 100, 105, 110, 115, 120, 125
15. a. 1 b. 1 c. 2 d. 1 e. 2
16. a. 5 b. 5 c. 1 d. 4 e. 5
17. a. 8 b. 7 c. 5 d. 5 e. 4
18. a. 3 b. 1 c. 3 d. 2 e. 4
19. a. 4 b. 3 c. 2 d. 6 e. 2
20.

3	14	13	0
8	5	6	11
4	9	10	7
15	2	1	12

Practice Exercise 5.1

1. a. $5xy$ b. $6b$ c. $7x^2$ d. $6mn$ e. 0
2. a. $8mn - 11m^2$ b. $12abc$ c. $10x^2 + 4y^2$ d. $2a^2 + 5b^2$ e. $(-3pq) + 2qr$
3. a. $(-8a^2b)$ b. $14pq$ c. $20p$ d. $(-6abc)$ e. -27 mm
4. a. $3a^2 + 4b^2$ b. $pq + 15qr$ c. $11yz$ d. 32 m -99 mn e. $6a^2b + 5ab^2$
5. a. $6a - 17b - 3c$ b. $14x - 11y - 2z$ c. $(-7ax) + by + 12cz$ d. $6p - 2r$ e. $7x^2 - 17xy + 5y^2$
6. a. $a + b - 3c$ b. $7p - 3q - 8r$ c. $2x^3 - 4x^2 + 7x$ d. $-p^2 - 9q^2 + r^2$ e. $8x^2 - mn - m^2n^2$
7. $14m^2n + 15mn - 2n^2$ 8. $(-27a^2) + 8b^2 + 8c^2$
9. $(-2x^2) + 4y^2 + 24xy$ 10. $2p^2 + 3p + 5$

Practice Exercise 5.2

1. a. $(-42x^3y)$ b. $(-12a^2b^2)$ c. $14x^3y^2$ d. $(-12x^4y^4)$ e. $18xyz^4$
2. a. $8xyz - 12yz^2$ b. $18m^2n - 42m^3$ c. $10a^2b - 15ab^2$ d. $(-6xy^3) - 3x^2y^2$ e. $7a^4 - 7a^3$
3. a. $x^2 + y^2 - 2xy - xz + yz$ b. $a^2b^2 + 2ab^2c + b^2c^2 + bc^2d + abcd$ c. $a^2 + b^2 + 2ac - c^2$ d. $(-3x^4y^2) + 3x^3y + 3x^2$ e. $(-3x^4y^3) + 8x^4y^4 + 2x^3y^4$
4. a. $x^2 - y^2$ b. $a^2 + 5ab + 6b^2$ c. $57x - 8 - 7x^2$ d. $m^2n^2 - mn - 12$ e. $14p^2 + 51\,pq - 54q^2$
5. a. $4x^2 + 6xy + 14x + 9y + 12$ b. $2a^2 - ab + 6ac - 3b^2 - 9bc$ c. $6a^2 - 17ab - 12ac + 12b^2 + 16bc$ d. $2x^2 - 24xy + 7xz + 54y^2 - 63yz$ e. $6a^2 - 37ab + 2ac - 35b^2 - 14bc$
6. a. $2xy - x^2 - y^2 + 1$ b. $a^2 - 2ac - b^2 + c^2$ c. $2m^2 + 5mn - 6m + 2n^2 - 9n + 4$ d. $x^3 - y^3 + x^2y - xy^2 - x^2 - y^2 - 2xy$ e. $m^3 - n^3 - p^3 + mn^2 - m^2n - mp^2 + m^2p + np^2 + n^2p$
7. $6x^2 + 15x - 22$
8. $-(3xy^2 + 8y^2 + 5y + 6xy + 6)$
9. $22m^2 - 16mn - 5n^2 + 1$
10. $ab^2 + b^2 - 34ab - 6b + 2$

Practice Exercise 5.3

1. a. $8xy^2$ b. $(-16m^2n^2)$ c. $-49m^2n$ d. $5x^2y$ e. $9a^3b^2c$
2. a. $8y - 7$ b. $-8m^2 + 2m + 4$ c. $-7y^2 + 6y - 2$ d. $-7x^3 + 6x^2 - 5x + 4$ e. $-4xy + 3y - 5x$
3. a. $a = x - 2$ b. $Q = 5x - \frac{7}{3}, R = \frac{2}{3}$ c. $Q = 2x^2\left(-\frac{5}{2}\right)x + \frac{5}{4}, R = \frac{1}{4}$ d. $Q = x - 1$ e. $Q = 4x^2 + 3x - 2, R = x - 1$
4. a. $Q = 3x^2 - 2x + 9, R = 0$ b. $Q = 3a^2 + 3a + 2, R = 0$ c. $Q = y^2 - 3y + 4, R = 0$ d. $Q = P - 1, R = 0$ e. $Q = 5m + 3, R = m + 1$
6. 3
7. $(-11x - 2)$
8. Not a factor as remainder is $(-6x) + 1$.
9. $9a^2 - 5a + 8$ 10. $2x^2 - 3x + 2$

Practice Exercise 5.4

1.a. $4x^2 + 28x + 49$ b. $25y^2 + 30y + 9$
c. $49 + 28p + 4p^2$ d. $2.25 + 3x + x^2$
e. $\frac{9}{16}a^2 + 3a + 4$

2.a. $x^2 - 14x + 49$ b. $4y^2 - 24y + 36$
c. $m^2 - 16m + 64$ d. $1.44a^2 - 2.4a + 1$
e. $\frac{1}{4}x^2 - 10x + 100$

3.a. $x^2 - 49$ b. $4y^2 - 49$ c. $49x^2 - 36y^2$
d. $16m^2 - 1$ e. $p^2/q^2 - r$

4. a. $4m^2 + 26m + 42$ b. $25a^2 + 50a + 21$
c. $16r^2 + 40r + 9$ d. $\frac{1}{4}p^2 + \frac{11}{2}p + 24$
e. $77 + 36a + 4a^2$

5.a. 10,609 b. 9,216 c. 4,624
d. 9,98,001 e. 42,025

6.a. 8,000 b. 4,000 c. 9,680
d. 2,49,996 e. 9,991

7.a. $25a^2 - 70ab + 49b^2$ b. $25x^2 - 4y^2$
c. $25x^2 + 30x + 9$ d. $4k2 + 20k + 21$
e. $\frac{4}{25}x^2 - \frac{49}{36}y^2$ f. $\frac{25}{4}x^2 - \frac{20}{3}xy + \frac{16}{9}y^2$
g. $\frac{121}{9}x^2 + \frac{286}{57}xy + \frac{169}{361}y^2$
h. $16a^2 - \frac{1}{16}a^2$ i. $z^2 + 13z + 42$
j. $64y^2 + 56y + 12$

8.a. 80 b. 140 c. 400 d. 384 e. 4,800

9. 65 10. 1,320

HOTS (Chapter 5)

1. a. 27 b. 47 2. a. 11,005 b. 2,304 c. 10
3. 1,225

Practice Exercise 6.1

1. a. $8x^2y^2$ b. $6xyz$ c. $4x$
d. $11ab$ e. $5pq$ f. $10mn$
g. $19p$ h. $9xy$ i. (-3)
j. $7s^2$

2. a. $7x$ b. x^2y c. $15mn$
d. $20x^2$ e. $7ab$ f. $9m$
g. $4ab$ h. $7xyz$ i. 5
j. $7abc$

3. a. $6x^2(1 - 3x)$ b. $5xy(1 - y)$
c. $6x^3(4 + 3x)$ d. $10(x^2 + y^2)$
e. $17xy(1 + 3xy)$ f. $(-27a^3)(2a + 1)$
g. $25mn(n + 2m)$ h. $12x^2y(3x - 5y^2z)$
i. $12x^2(2x - 3y)$ j. $3b(2a - 3c)$

4. a. $y^2(y^2 - 4y + 2)$ b. $4xy(3x + 4y - 2xy)$
c. $5(3a^2b^2 + 5ab + 6)$ d. $m^2(m^3 - m^2 + 1)$
e. $30x(x^2 - 2x + 3)$ f. $2xy^2(6x^2 - 7xy + 14y^2)$
g. $7a^2(3 - 2b^2 + 5a^2)$ h. $3x(3x^2 - 2x + 4)$
i. $4x(2x - 18y + 3)$ j. $(-5)(1 + 2p - 4p^2)$

5. a. $(xy + 3)(x + 1)$
b. $(a + c)(b + d)$
c. $(a + b)(a - 2)$ d. $(x - a)(x - b)$
e. $(ab - c^2)(b - 1)$ f. $(x + y)(x - z)$
g. $(a - b)(x + 5)$ h. $6(m + n)$
i. $(7x + 2y)(x + 9)$ j. $(x + 2y)(y + 3)$

Practice Exercise 6.2

1. a. $(2x + 1)^2$ b. $(3y + 2z)^2$
c. $(4p + 5)^2$ d. $(3m + 4)^2$
e. $(2t + 5)^2$ f. $(a + 4)^2$ g. $(b + 7)^2$
h. $(6n + 3)^2$ i. $(1 + 9k)^2$ j. $\left(6x + \frac{1}{2}\right)^2$

2. a. $(x - 3)^2$ b. $(a - 5)^2$ c. $(3p - 2)^2$
d. $(4d - 3)^3$ e. $(1 - m)^2$ f. $(9y - 2)^2$
g. $(11b - 1)^2$ h. $(6 - k)^2$
i. $\left(\frac{1}{2} - 3n\right)^2$ j. $(pq - 1)^2$

3. a. $(2x - y)(2x + y)$ b. $(9 + 5b)(9 - 5b)$
c. $(11p + 7q)(11p - 7q)$
d. $(6ab + 10)(6ab - 10)$
e. $\left(\frac{1}{7}m + \frac{1}{5}n\right)\left(\frac{1}{7}m - \frac{1}{5}n\right)$
f. $(0.7a + 0.6b)(0.7a - 0.6b)$
g. $(2a + 3b + 4c)(2a + 3b - 4c)$
h. $[3 + (a + b)][3 - (a + b)]$
i. $(5x + 4y)(3x - 2y)$
j. $(45a + 5a)(45a - 5a) = 2000a^2$

4. a. $(a + b + 2c)(a + b - 2c)$
b. $(9x + 2y - z)(9x - 2y + z)$
c. $(2m + 3p + 8n)(2m + 3p - 8n)$
d. $(a + b + 11)(a + b - 11)$
e. $(10c + 9)(10c - 11)$
f. $(6y + 7x + 7)(6y + 7x - 7)$
g. $(t + 12s + 12)(t + 12s - 12)$
h. $(5 + a + b)(5 - a - b)$
i. $(3x + y - 2)(3x - y + 2)$
j. $(m + n + 1)(m - n - 1)$

5. a. $m + n$ b. $x - b$ c. $6a - b$
d. $11 - 2x$ e. $x + y + 2z$ f. $15t - 10s$
g. $2q - p - r$ h. $12x + y$ i. $2m + \frac{1}{4}$
j. $5m - 11$

Practice Exercise 6.3

1. a. $(x + 9)(x + 5)$ b. $(x + 6)^2$
c. $(x + 7)(x + 8)$ d. $(x + 15)(x + 4)$

Answers

e. $(x + 8)(x + 5)$ f. $(3x + 4)(x + 2)$
g. $(x + 13)(3x + 9)$ h. $(3x + 2)(x + 4)$
i. $(2x + 5)(x + 4)$ j. $(3x + 2)(x + 3)$

2. a. $(m - 3)(m - 30)$ b. $(m - 2)(m - 7)$
c. $(m - 3)(m - 33)$ d. $(m - 2)(m - 21)$
e. $(m - 9)(m - 13)$ f. $2(m - 3)(m - 8)$
g. $(m - 2)(3m - 4)$ h. $5(m - 2)(m - 7)$
i. $2(m - 7)(m - 5)$ j. $3(m - 2)(m - 3)$
3. a. $(a - 8)(a + 3)$ b. $(a - 15)(a + 2)$
c. $(a - 9)(a + 6)$ d. $(a - 12)(a + 4)$
e. $(a + 25)(a - 6)$ f. $(3a - 2)(2a + 5)$
g. $7(a + 3)(a - 2)$ h. $4(a - 6)(a + 1)$
i. $(2a - 3)(a - 10)$ j. $4(a - 1)(a + 14)$
4. a. $(x + 4)$ b. $(x - 2)$ c. $(y + 1)$
d. $(y - 7)$ e. $(a + 1)$ f. $(a + 4)$
g. $(m + 7)$ h. $(m + 3)$ i. $(a + 4)$
j. $(m + 5)$
5. a. $(x + 5)(x + 1)$ b. $(x - 5)(x + 3)$
c. $(x - 3)(x - 1)$ d. $(x - 13)(x - 5)$
e. $(x - 7)(x + 1)$ f. $(2x + 1)(2x + 3)$
g. $(2x + 3)(2x - 5)$ h. $(2x - 3)(2x - 5)$
i. $(2x - 3)(3x - 5)$ j. $(2x + 5)(x - 1)$

HOTS (Chapter 6)

1. a. $(p - m)(q + n)$ b. $(pq - 1)(q + 1)$
c. $(y + x^2)(y - x)$
2. a. $(a - 2b)$ b. $\left(\frac{2}{3} + 4x\right)$ c. $(2p - 3)$
3. $(2x + y - 3)(2x - y + 3)$

Rewind (Chapters 5–6)

1. $6a - 13b - 3c$ 2. $5x^3 - 11x^2 - 14x + 7$
3. $2x^3 - 4x^2 + 7x - 8$ 4. $-p^2 + pq + q^2 - 2$
5. a. $8x^2 + 14x - 15$ b. $36x^2 + 47xy + 15y^2$
c. $x^3 - xy^2 + 2x^2y - 2y^3$
6. a. $Q = x - 2, R = 0$ b. $Q = 5x - 3, R = 0$
c. $Q = x^2 - x - 1, R = 1$
7. a. $64a^2 + 48ab + 9b^2$ b. $49x^2 + 28xy + 4y^2$
c. $25x^2 + 110x + 121$
9. 61 10. 49
11. a. $12x^2y(3x - 5y^2z)$ b. $(5x - 7)(x - 4)$
c. $3a(3a - 5b)(3 - 4a)$
12. a. $(9 + 7m)(9 - 7m)$ b. $(3ab + 5)(3ab - 5)$
c. $(1 + b - c)(1 - b + c)$
13. a. $(1 + x)^2$ b. $(2x + 5)^2$ c. $\left(x + \frac{1}{2}\right)^2$
14. a. $(x + 3)(x + 9)$ b. $(x + 8)(x + 5)$
c. $(x - 1)(x - 16)$
15. a. $2x - 11$ b. $0.5a + b$ c. $2p - m + n$
16. a. $4m + 5$ b. $2x - 3y$ c. $2a + 1$
17. $x^5 - 15x^3 - 7x^2 + 5x - 2$
18. $Q = m2 - \frac{3}{5}m + \frac{9}{5}, R = \frac{(-57)}{5}m + \frac{66}{5}$
19. a. 1,000 b. 1,000 c 1,000
20. $(2x + 3)$ km/hr, 43 km/hr

Practice Exercise 7.1

1. a. $x = 3$ b. $a = 3$ c. $x = 3$ d. $a = 6$
e. $x = 3$ f. $m = 20$ g. $x = 20$ h. $a = 24$
i. $x = 30$ j. $a = 56$ k. $x = 8$ l. $a = 3$
m. $x = 1$ n. $x = 7.5$ o. $x = 2$ p. $x = 36$
q. $x = (-12)$ r. $x = 7$ s. $x = 8$ t. $x = 8$

Practice Exercise 7.2

1. a. $x = 3$ b. $x = \frac{(-1)}{5}$
2. a. $x = \frac{(-5)}{4}$ b. $x = \frac{7}{12}$
3. a. $x = 10$ b. $x = 8$
4. a. $x = (-5)$ b. $x = 3$
5. a. $x = \frac{(-2)}{5}$ b. $y = 1$
6. a. $x = 2$ b. $x = \frac{3}{4}$
7. a. $x = \frac{-56}{9}$ b. $x = 2$ 8. a. $x = 16$ b. $x = 8$
9. a. $x = \frac{11}{4}$ b. $x = 4$ 10. a. $x = \frac{5}{2}$ b. $x = 4$

Practice Exercise 7.3

1. a. 11, 13 b. 18, 54
2. a. 44, 55, 66 b. 100 kg, 120 kg, 140 kg, 160 kg, 180 kg
3. a. $\frac{5}{11}$ b. $\frac{1}{4}$ 4. a. 96 b. 67
5. a. Pratibha = 15 years, Aradhana = 18 years
b. Supriya = 48 years, Amar = 61 years
6. a. 4 hr b. 65km/hr, 70 km/hr
7. a. length = 18 cm, breadth = 8 cm
b. length = 30, breadth = 10 m
8. a. A = ₹25,000, B = ₹30,000, C = ₹35,000
b. ₹1 coins 170, ₹5 coins 30
9. a. 40°, 50° and 90° b. ₹1,50,000, wife's share = ₹75,000, Soni's share = ₹50,000
10. a. P = 27.5 kg, Q = 24 kg, R = 20.5 kg and S = 41.0 kg
b. $277\frac{7}{9}, 222\frac{2}{9}$

HOTS (Chapter 7)

1. $x = (-1)$ 2. $p = 1$
3. $x = 28°$; 4. Two angles measure 80° and the other two measure 100°

Rewind Chapter 7

1. a. $x = 5$ b. $p = 24$ c. $m = 9$
2. a. $x = 3$ b. $y = 12$ c. $a = \frac{1}{2}$

3. 20°, 60°, 100°
4. a. $p = 5$ b. $m = 28$ c. $m = \frac{(-9)}{2}$
5. 18, 54
6. a. $x = 5$ b. $x = 8$ c. $m = 2$
7. a. $z = \frac{5}{2}$ b. $t = 1$ c. $s = \frac{6}{13}$
8. 60 9. 44, 55, 66 10. 14 11. 39 12. $\frac{15}{22}$
13. base = 12 cm, h = 20 cm 14. 30°, 50°, 100°
15. ₹4,500, ₹1,800 16. 109, 111, 113
17. length = 93 cm, breadth= 31 cm
18. 30 km/hr, 40 km/hr, 19. 69
20. 26 ₹1 stamps, 65 ₹5 stamps and 39 ₹10 stamps,

Test Yourself: Unit II

1. $(-15a^2) + 5b^2 + 25c^2$ 2. $15y^2$
3. $a^2 - b^2 - 2c^2 - 3ab - ac - bc$
4. $(-x + 10)$ 5. $Q = a^3 + 3a$ $R = 10 - 9a$
6. $9x^2 + 24x + 16$ 7. $16x^2 - 24xy + 9y^2$
8. a. $4x^2 - 9$ b. $49x^2 - 25$ c. $a^2 - 4b^2$
   d. $\frac{36}{49}x^2 - 25$ e. $16a^2 - \frac{1}{16a^2}$
9. a. 3,364 b. 5,184 c. 9,801
   d. 10,201 e. 94,864
10. 53 11. a. $12\,pq^2(2pq - 3)$ b. $7a^3(6 - 7a^2)$
   c. $5ab(4a^3b^2 - 2ab^2 + 1)$ d. $13p^2q^2(5q - 3 + p)$
   e. $16ab(4ab + 2b + a)$
12. a. $3(p^2 + q) + p(q + 2)$ b. $(2m + n)(m + 3)$
   c. $(2x + y)(3x - z)$ d. $(3a - 4c)(2 - b)$
   e. $(12m - 6)(n + p)$
13. a. $(6x + 5)^2$ b. $(11m - 1)^2$ c. $(4ab)^2 - (7cd)^2$
   d. $(8p + x - y)(8p - x + y)$
   e. $(10m + 9)(10m - 11)$
14. a. $(a - 12b)(a + 4b)$ b. $3(b + 3)(b - 7)$
   c. $(2c - 3d)(4c - 5d)$ d. $(d + 4)(d - 10)$
   e. $(e + 7)(e - 2)$
15. a. $x = 2$ b. $x = 64$ c. $x = 2$
   d. $x = (-2)$ e. $x = \frac{1}{4}$
16. a. $x = 15$ b. $y = \frac{5}{2}$ c. $m = 28$
   d. $p = \left(-\frac{13}{7}\right)$
17. 62 18. $\frac{1}{6}$
19. Raman = 5 years, Rekha = 20 years
20. 70 km/hr, 75 km/hr

Practice Exercise 8.1

1. a. 25% gain b. $16\frac{2}{3}$ % loss
2. a. ₹4,725 b. ₹873
3. a. ₹4,680 b. ₹400
4. a. ₹3,000 profit, 15% b. 22.73% gain
5. a. 0.64% loss b. 2% gain
6. a. ₹1,320 b. ₹3,450
7. a. 20% gain b. 20% loss
8. a. ₹3,800 b. ₹4,350
9. a. Ganga 15% b. ₹1,250
10. a. $4\frac{1}{6}$ percent b. 4% loss

Practice Exercise 8.2

1. a. ₹600 b. ₹5,000
2. a. 25 % b. ₹2,125
3. a. 15% b. ₹1,400, ₹140
4. a. 8% gain
5. a. ₹7,660 b. 9% loss
6. a. ₹4,68 b. 24%
7. a. ₹22,550 b. ₹35,000
8. a. ₹10,560 b. ₹7,308, ₹1,740, ₹348
9. a. 11,600, ₹13,050, $12\frac{1}{2}$% 10. ₹25,000

Practice Exercise 8.3

1. a. ₹35,280, ₹3,280 b. ₹19,468.80, ₹1468.80
   c. ₹19,965, ₹4,965
2. a. ₹1 b. ₹93 c. ₹9
3. a. ₹12,000 b. ₹8,800 c. ₹65,000
4. 2 years 5. 8% 6. ₹10,000
7. ₹24,000 8. ₹11,025 9. ₹618
10. ₹4,000, $5\frac{1}{8}$%

Practice Exercise 8.4

1. ₹1,692 2. ₹5,56,500 3. ₹1,951
4. ₹11,025 5. ₹515,201 6. ₹17,576
7. ₹11,680 8. ₹9,082 9. 19,965
10. ₹2,68,960

Rewind Chapter 8

1. 20% gain 2. 31.6% gain 3. ₹1,050
4. 16% 5. ₹1,800 6. ₹15,000
7. ₹8,000 8. ₹25 9. 2 years
10. ₹50,618.88 11. Darshan, ₹621.75
12. 3,17,625 13. ₹9,592 14. ₹9,600
15. 2 years 16. 25%
17. Neither loss nor gain
18. 195 19. ₹531 20. 10% profit

HOTS Chapter 8

1. $20\frac{2}{3}$ % 2. 46% 3. 8 %
4. 31,212 5. ₹9,774

Practice Exercise 9.1

1. ₹944 2. ₹1,290 3. 31 kg

Answers

4. 30 5. 16 6. 13
7. ₹1,050 8. 18 9. 750
10. 165 km

Practice Exercise 9.2

1. 65 men 2. 20 cows 3. 3 hr
4. 30 days 5. 10 boxes 6. 20 toys
7. 4 extra blankets 8. 42 words 9. 8, 9
10. 3 more men

HOTS (Chapter 9)

1. $47\frac{1}{2}$ days 2. ₹240 3. 20 days

Practice Exercise 10.1

1. 6 days 2. 18 days 3. 48 days
4. 30 days 5. 3 hrs, 36 mins
6. $5\frac{1}{2}$ days 7. 4 hrs, 48 mins
8. 3 hours 9. 1 hr 20 min 10. 18 hours

Practice Exercise 10.2

1. a. $33\frac{1}{3}$ m/sec b. 15 m/sec
2. a. 0.6 km/hr b. 108 km/hr
3. 90 km/hr, 25 m/sec 4. 15 km/hr, $4\frac{1}{6}$ m/sec
5. 125 m 6. 270 m 7. 30 sec
8. 1 min 9. 72 km/hr 10. 5 pm

HOTS (Chapter 10)

1. B 2. 144 minutes 3. 24 km/hr

Rewind (Chapters 9–10)

1. ₹3,605 2. ₹1,720 3. 6 days
4. 64 m 5. 15 m 6. 35 min
7. 55 words/min 8. 13 more women
9. 300 soldiers left 10. 6 km/hr 11. $13\frac{1}{3}$ days
12. $3\frac{7}{11}$ days 13. 4 hours 14. 30 hours
15. 3 days 16. $7\frac{1}{2}$ hours 17. 40 hours
18. 300 m 19. 12.5 sec 20. 20 sec

Test Yourself: Unit III

1. $16\frac{2}{3}$% loss 2. ₹4,000 3. ₹3,289.47
4. ₹1,650 5. ₹14,025 6. ₹1,434.78
7. 3 years 8. 10% pa, ₹9.317
9. ₹2,18,700 10. ₹1,94,481, ₹34,481
11. ₹4,725 12. 64 men 13. 65 children

14. 30 minutes 15. 7 days
16. $7\frac{3}{11}$ days, A = $18\frac{6}{13}$ days, B = $14\frac{2}{17}$ days
C = 80 days
17. a. 90 km/hr b. 15m/sec c. 1.2 km/hr
18. 100 km/hr 19. $1\frac{1}{2}$ hrs 20. 350 m

Practice Exercise 11.1

2. a. 95° b. 50° c. 125°
3. a. 110° b. 75° c. 70°
4. 12 sides 5. 10 sides

Practice Exercise 11.2

3. 10 cm 4. ∠P = 115°, ∠Q = 110°
6. a. ∠ABC = 110° b. ∠BCD = 70°
8. ∠ABD = 50°, ∠CBD = 60°
10. ∠QRS = 120°, ∠QPS = 120°, ∠Q = 60°

HOTS (Chapter 11)

1. 36° 2. x = 8

Practice Exercise 13.1

1. a. 6 b. 6 c. 5 d. 5 e. 4
2. a. 4 b. 10 c. 7 d. 8 e. 6
3. a. 12 b. 9 c. 8 d. 10 e. 18
4. a. 6 b. 12 c. 12 d. 16 e. 10

HOTS (Chapter 11)

8

Rewind (Chapters 11–13)

1. a. 70° b. 80° c. 50°
2. 15 cm and 35 cm
3. ∠APB = 80° 4. ∠A = 120°, ∠B = 105°
7. 36 cm 16. a. Right angles
b. Right angles c. Two d. Kite e. Rhombus
17. 12 edges, 6 vertices and 8 faces
18. a. 8 b. 5 c. 4 d. 6 e. 6
20. F + V – E = 2

Test Yourself: Unit IV

1. ∠P = ∠S = 60°, ∠Q = ∠R = 120°
2. 40 cm, 50 cm, $10\sqrt{41}$ cm
3. 40 cm, 40 cm, 50 cm, 50 cm, 64.03 cm, 64.03 cm
5. ∠QPS =120°, ∠RSP = 140°
6. 110°
18.

Solid	F	V	E
Cube	6	8	12
Triangular prism	5	6	9
Square pyramid	5	5	8
Pentagonal prism	7	10	15
Hexagonal	7	7	12
A pyramid where base has 'n' sides	n+1	n+1	2n

20. a. solid
b. tetrahedron c. prism

Practice Exercise 14.1

1. 2, 787.5 m^2 2. 21 m, 28 m 3. ₹1,15,500
4. 15,000 revolutions 5. b = 32 cm, h = 16 cm
6. 7.5 cm 7. 5,784 m^2
8. Area = 154 cm^2 9. 22.176 m 10. 25 cm

Practice Exercise 14.2

1. 36 cm, 60 cm 2. 12 cm 3. 25 cm, 35.35 cm
4. 6.52 m^2, ₹1,956 5. 30 cm^2 6. 217 m^2, ₹10,850
7. 230 m^2 8. 43 cm, 53 cm
9. a. 30 cm b. 104 cm c. 100 cm 10. 528 cm^2

Practice Exercise 14.3

1. a. 105 cm^2 b. 84 cm^2 c. 102 cm^2
2. a. 602 cm^2 b. 184 cm^2 c. 152 cm^2
3. 9,200 m^2 4. Ramu's plot is bigger by 656 m^2
5. 664 m^2

HOTS (Chapter 14)

1. 112 m^2 2. 4 m 3. 4,240 cm^2

Practice Exercise 15.1

1. a. 150 cm^2 b. 384 cm^2 c. 37.5 cm^2
d. 726 cm^2 e. 69.36 cm^2
2. a. 216 cm^3 b. 729 cm^3 c. 1,157.625 cm^3
d. 10.648 cm^3 e. 1,331 cm^3
3. a. 25 cm b. 30 cm c. 18 cm d. 70 cm e. 23 cm
4. a. 11 cm b. 15 cm c. 27 cm d. 40 cm e. 10 cm
5. 64 cubes
6. 150 sheets 7. 0 cm^2
8. 64,000 ℓ, 63,940 ℓ
9. 8.48 cm 10. 40.96 kg

Practice Exercise 15.2

1. a. 376 cm^2 b. 17,500 cm^2 c. 589.5 cm^2
d. 232.5 cm^2 e. 2,700 cm^2
2. a. 3,300 cm^3 b. 6,00,000 cm^3 c. 75,00,000 cm^3
d. 446.25 cm^3 e. 216 cm^3
3. a. ℓ = 64 cm b. b = 12 cm c. h = 8 cm
d. 540 cm^3 e. b = 56 cm
4. 10 cubes 5. 1,20,000 ℓ, 120 kilolitres
6. 250 persons 7. 15 cm 8. ₹69,300
9. ℓ = 50 cm, b = 40 cm, h = 20 cm;
V = 40,000 cm^3 10. 28 planks

Practice Exercise 15.3

1. a. 836 cm^2 b. 2,992 cm^2 c. 407 cm^2
d. 8,052 cm^2 e. 11,008 cm^2
2. a. 1,540 cm^3 b. 6,930 cm^3 c. 1,100 cm^3
d. 3,168 cm^3 e. 68.75 cm^3
3. a. 13,880 cm^3 4. 12 m
5. 44 m^3 6. ₹26,500 7. ₹10,560 8. 125 cylinders
9. 4 m 10. Cube, 259 cm^3

HOTS (Chapter 15)

1. 640 coins 2. 5,120 m^3 3. V = ℓ^3

Rewind (Chapters 14–15)

1. Area of $\triangle$DPC = 4,050 m^2, 4,050 m^2
2. r = 7 cm, A = 154 cm^2 3. h = 7.8 cm
4. 16 cm, 24 cm 5. 33 min 6. 40 cm, 32 cm
7. 12 cm 8. 490 m^2 9. 1,612 m^2
10. a. 36 cm b. 25 cm c. 42 cm
11. 125 cubes
12. 80 cm^2 13. 1.5 m 14. 375 cm 15. ₹1,584
16. ₹90,000 17. 20 cm 18. 20 cm 19. 21 cm
20. 1.232 m

Practice Exercise 16.2

3. Class size = 5, Class marks, 32.5, 37.5, 42.5, 47.5, 52.5 4. Maximum workers 9,000 − 10,000 Class mark = 9,500, Less than ₹10,000 = 70
5. a. 10 b. 20 − 30 c. 25 d. 16
e. On X axis, 1 cm = 10 mark on Y axis, 1 cm = 2 students

Practice Exercise 16.3

4. Maths = 1,350, Physics = 900, Chemistry = 1,200, History = 750, Geology = 675, Biology = 525
5. A = 420 workers, B = 150, C = 210, D = 180, E = 120

Answers

Practice Exercise 16.4

1. a. $\frac{1}{2}$ b. $\frac{1}{2}$ c. $\frac{1}{3}$

2. a. $\frac{1}{2}$ b. $\frac{1}{2}$ c. $\frac{1}{4}$ d. $\frac{3}{13}$ e. $\frac{1}{52}$

3. a. $\frac{13}{50}$ b. $\frac{1}{5}$ c. $\frac{3}{10}$ d. $\frac{6}{25}$ e. 0

4. $\frac{1}{5}$ 5. a. $\frac{1}{10}$ b. $\frac{1}{10}$ c. $\frac{9}{10}$ d. $\frac{1}{2}$ e. $\frac{2}{5}$

6. $\frac{69}{100}$ 7. $\frac{11}{25}$ 8. $\frac{77}{100}$

9. (H,1) (H,2) (H,3) (H,4) (H,5) (H,6) (T,1) (T,2) (T,3) (T,4) (T,5) (T,6) 10. 8

HOTS (Chapter 16)

1. 22.5% 2. $\frac{59}{100}$ 3. Class size = 3,000
Class mid-marks = 12,550

Practice Exercise 17.1

1. a. I b. II c. III d. IV e. IV f. III g. I h. II i. I j. III
2. a. x-axis b. x-axis c. y-axis d. x-axis e. y-axis f. x-axis g y-axis h. x-axis i. x-axis j. x-axis
3. A (1, 1), B (3, 3), C (5, 5), D (−3, 3) E (−4, 5) F (−5, 2) G (−3, −2) H (−6, −3) I (3, −2) J (6, −3)
5. a. P b. H c. Q d. M e. G f. S g. T h. U i. R j. F

10 i. a. 4 b. 5 c. 8 d. 5 e. (−5) ii. a. 3 b. (−2) c. 5 d. (−4) e. 7

Practice Exercise 17.2

3. a. ₹300 b. 10 c. ₹50
6. a. 15 m b. 25 m c. 6 sec
7. a. Maths b. Hindi c. 66.25
   d. 1 cm = 10 marks on y-axis
   e. Chemistry and Biology 80 marks, Physics and History 60 marks.
8. a. Breadth = 1 cm, b. Length = 4 cm c. 20 cm
9. a. Saturday b. Wednesday and Thursday c. 1,500

HOTS (Chapter 17)

3. a. Height decreases b. Height increases

Rewind (Chapters 16 – 17)

5. a. The number of students and their heights b. 5 cm c. 38 students d. 72 students e. 127.5, 132.5, 137.5, 142.5, 147.5, 152.5, 157.5
9. Violet = 15, Indigo = 15, Blue = 30, Green = 25, Yellow = 20, Orange = 35, Red = 40 people
10. a. Bhuvan 165 votes
    b. Bhuvan = 165 votes, Madhu = 135 votes, Radhika = 90 votes, Rushil = 75 votes, Sagnik = 60 votes c. Sagnik d. 90 votes e. Madhu
11. a. Sure event b. Impossible event.
12. a. $\frac{1}{2}$ b. $\frac{1}{26}$ c. $\frac{1}{2}$ d. $\frac{1}{13}$ e. $\frac{1}{4}$
13. 36 out comes (1, 1) (1, 2) (1, 3) (1, 4) (1, 5) (1, 6) (2, 1) (2, 2) (2, 3) (2, 4) (2, 5) (2, 6) (3, 1) (3, 2) (3, 3) (3, 4) (3, 5) (3, 6) (4, 1) (4, 2) (4, 3) (4, 4) (4, 5) (4, 6) (5, 1) (5, 2) (5, 3) (5, 4) (5, 5) (5, 6) (6, 1) (6, 2) (6, 3) (6, 4) (6, 5) (6, 6)
14. $\frac{2}{5}$ 18. P = II quadrant, Q = III quadrant R = I quadrant, S = IV quadrant
20. a. Saturday b. Monday c. Sunday d. ₹20,000 e. Tuesday and Friday

Test Yourself: Unit V

4. A, D, F, G - I quadrant, B, H, I - II quadrant c - III quadrant, E, J - IV quadrant
5. a. (4, 0) b. (−4, 0) c. (0, 4) d. (0, −4) e. (4, 4) 8. Batsman A = 60, Batsman B = 63
10. 40 families b. ₹1,000 – ₹2,000, 20 families c. 130 families 11. ℓ = 12 cm, S.A. = 864 cm^2
12. 27l, 300 cubic cm 13. 16 cm 2,440 cm^2, 20 cm 14. 4.005 m^2, ₹240.30 15. 1.25 m
16. r = 14 cm, 2,112 cm^2 17. 64,660 cm^2
18. 36 cm 19. 15 cm, 25 cm 20. ₹80,665

Model Test Paper

2. a. m = 4, b. m = 1 c. m = 3
3. 38, 79
4. 305, 405, 340, 430, 350, 530, 345, 435, 450, 540
5. $4x^3 - 3x^2 + 41$ 6. $Q = 4x^2 + 3x - 2$
   $R = (-2)x - 1$
7. a. $4(2x - 3y)(6x - 9y + 4)$ b. $3a^2(a - 4)(a + 4)$ c. $(1 - 3m)^2$
8. a. $(y + 16)(y - 9)$ b. $(p + 8)(p + 5)$ c. $(n - 8)(n + 8)$
9. a. $m = \frac{1}{3}$ b. $y = \frac{(-13)}{4}$ c. $p = \frac{(-27)}{19}$
10. Base = 12 cm, altitude = 20 cm
11. ₹760 12. ₹2,240 13. 19% profit
14. 40% 15. ₹7,95,070 16 ₹480
17. 9 days 18. 2 hours 40 min 19. 20 sec
20. ₹20,000 21. 105° 25. 24 cm, 36 cm
26. 504 m^2, ₹7,200 27. 0.8 m
28. Plastic can with a square base 312 cm^3.

Assessment of Mathematical Skills				
	Exceptional	**Good**	**Average**	**Needs Improvement**
Notation and Terminology	Uses appropriate mathematical terminology and notation	Uses near correct mathematical terminology and notation	Partial or scattered usage of mathematical terms and notation	Shows incorrect or no understanding of terms and notations of mathematical concepts
Problem Solving/ Strategising	Is able to efficiently analyse a problem and arrive at an efficient solution	Is able to draw on prior knowledge and arrive at an appropriate solution	Shows some evidence of using concepts learnt resulting in only a partially correct solution	Is unable to apply concepts learnt. Faces difficulties in arriving at a solution.
Methodology, Formulation and Steps	Uses clear effective steps and reasonings to demonstrate the solution	Uses appropriate steps to arrive at the solution	Is able to use steps at times but falters at others	Is unable to identify steps and formulae needed for arriving at the solution, and hence arrives at incorrect solutions.
Calculation and Final Result	Is able to calculate and arrive at the final answer with accuracy and precision	Is able to calculate and arrive at the final answer with a fair level of accuracy	Resists advanced computations and tends to perform incomplete or erroneous calculations	Is prone to calculation errors. Limited understanding of units.

Assessment of Mathematical Skills				
	Exceptional	**Good**	**Average**	**Needs Improvement**
Geometry	Has a clear and visual understanding of the relationship between geometrical figures	Has a fairly good understanding of the relationship between various geometrical figures and is able to visualise concepts with minimum assistance	Is able to understand simple geometrical concepts, but falters while visualising concepts or tackling advanced concepts	Has a high level of difficulty in understanding and recalling geometrical concepts and needs assistance at visualising the solution
Mensuration	Has a clear and visual understanding of mensuration concepts and is able to translate real-world problems to math	Has a good understanding of mensuration concepts and is able to visualise and solve problems with minimum errors	Is able to understand simple mensuration concepts but falters while visualising or solving real-world problems.	Has a high level of difficulty in understanding and visualising 3-D-shapes. Needs assistance in attempting a solution
Algebra	Has a clear understanding of algebraic patterns and formulae and is able to formulate approaches to a problem	Has a good understanding of algebraic patterns and formulae and is able to formulate appropriate solution	Is able to solve simple algebraic problems but has trouble identifying complicated patterns	Has a high level of difficulty in identifying and remembering patterns and needs assistance in attempting a solution